YAAAY!

村田雄介

Yusuke Murata

This is Volume 20... It's like a dream. I'll be a dad soon, too. That's also like a dream. I'll work hard so I never have to wake up. Thanks for your support, everyone.

information
note
contact

稲垣理一郎

Riichiro Inagaki

Just for the heck of it, I made an official website for my studio. (*Eyeshield 21* has its own official site, so check out that too!)

***Eyeshield 21*** is the most exciting football manga to hit the scene. A collaborative effort between writer Riichiro Inagaki and artist Yusuke Murata, ***Eyeshield 21*** was originally serialized in Japan's ***Weekly Shonen Jump***. An OAV created for Shueisha's Anime Tour is available in Japan, and the ***Eyeshield 21*** hit animated TV series debuted in spring 2005!

## EYESHIELD 21
Vol. 20: Devils vs. Gods
### The SHONEN JUMP ADVANCED Manga Edition

STORY BY RIICHIRO INAGAKI
ART BY YUSUKE MURATA

English Adaptation & Translation/Craig & Hime Kingsley, HC Language Solutions, Inc.
Touch-up Art & Lettering/James Gaubatz
Cover & Graphic Design/Sean Lee
Editor/Kit Fox

Editor in Chief, Books/Alvin Lu
Editor in Chief, Magazines/Marc Weidenbaum
VP of Publishing Licensing/Rika Inouye
VP of Sales/Gonzalo Ferreyra
Sr. VP of Marketing/Liza Coppola
Publisher/Hyoe Narita

Printed in the U.S.A.

Published by VIZ Media, LLC
P.O. Box 77010
San Francisco, CA 94107

SHONEN JUMP ADVANCED Manga Edition
10 9 8 7 6 5 4 3 2 1
First printing, June 2008

VIZ
MEDIA
www.viz.com

THE WORLD'S MOST
CUTTING-EDGE MANGA
SHONEN JUMP
ADVANCED
www.shonenjump.com

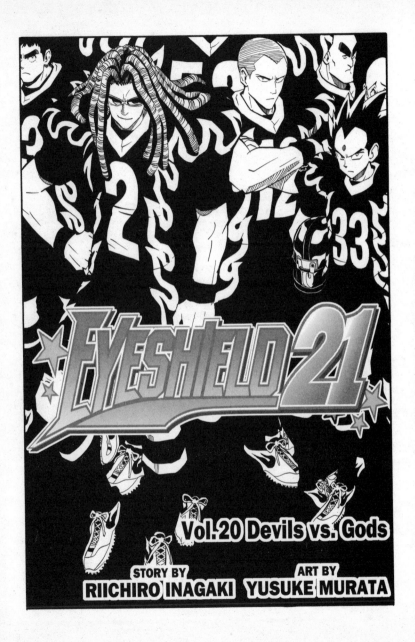

Vol. 20 Devils vs. Gods

STORY BY
RIICHIRO INAGAKI

ART BY
YUSUKE MURATA

# THE PLAYERS

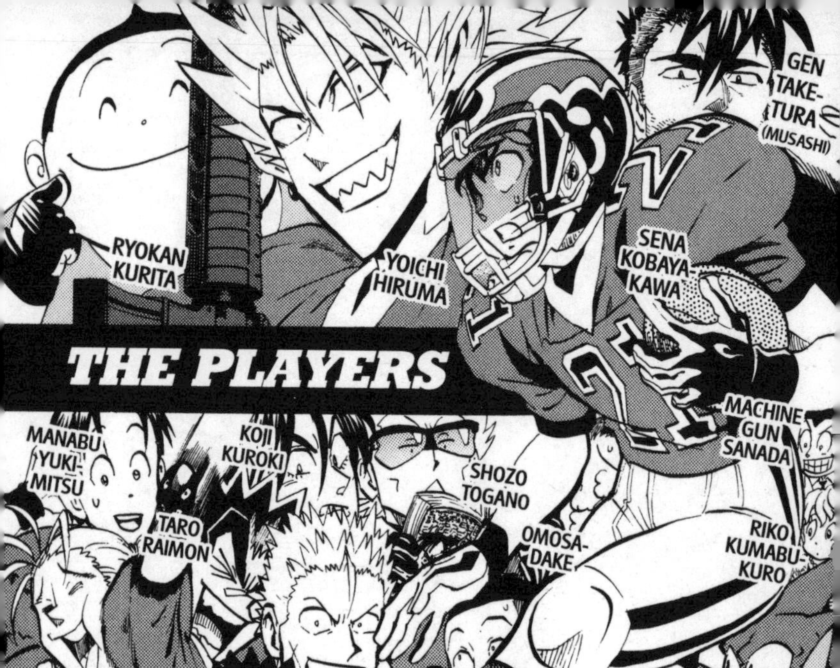
GEN TAKE-TURA (MUSASHI)
SENA KOBAYA-KAWA
YOICHI HIRUMA
RYOKAN KURITA
MACHINE GUN SANADA
RIKO KUMABU-KURO
SHOZO TOGANO
OMOSA-DAKE
KOJI KUROKI
MANABU YUKI-MITSU
TARO RAIMON
TETSUO ISHIMARU
KAZUKI JUMONJI
DAIKICHI KOMUSUBI
NATSU-HIKO TAKI

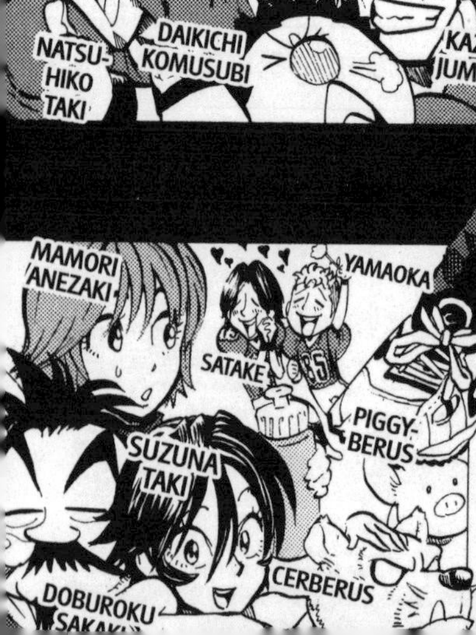
YAMAOKA
MAMORI ANEZAKI
SATAKE
PIGGY-BERUS
SUZUNA TAKI
CERBERUS
DOBUROKU

## *The Story So Far*

Sena Kobayakawa is a shy high school freshman. He joined the school football team to reinvent himself. Sena's exceptional running ability comes to light and he competes under a secret identity, Eyeshield 21.

The goal is the Christmas Bowl! With this lofty ambition before them, Deimon moved into the Fall Tournament. Deimon showed the fruits of their training and made it into the Tokyo Tournament, where they placed third, allowing them to move on to the Kanto Tournament.

Their first opponent will be the Shinryuji Nagas, who have won the tournament for nine years straight and are the strongest team in Kanto...

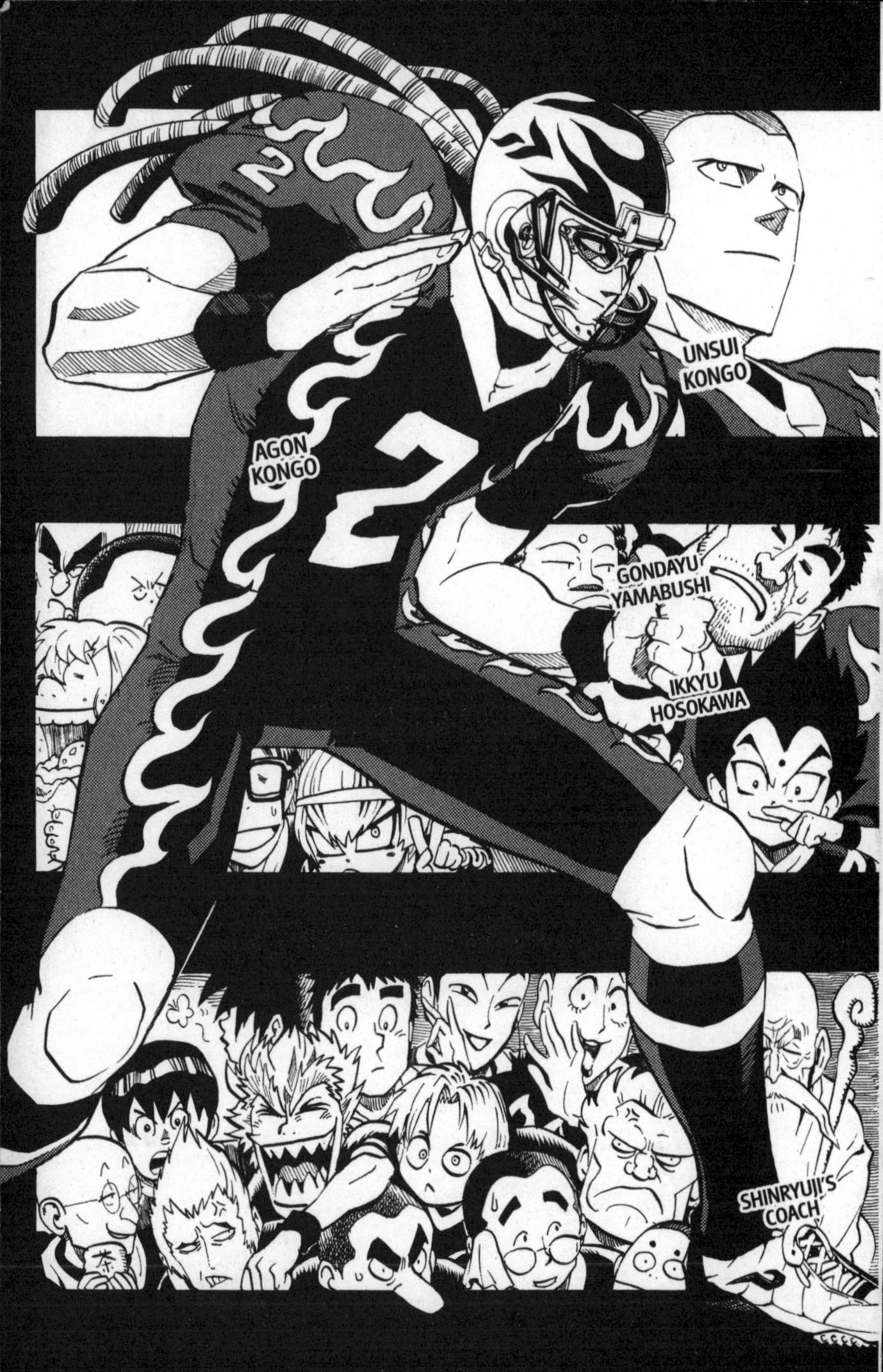
UNSUI KONGO
AGON KONGO
GONDAYU YAMABUSHI
IKKYU HOSOKAWA
SHINRYUJI'S COACH

## Vol. 20:
### Devils vs. Gods

## CONTENTS

# Chapter 170

## Interview 8

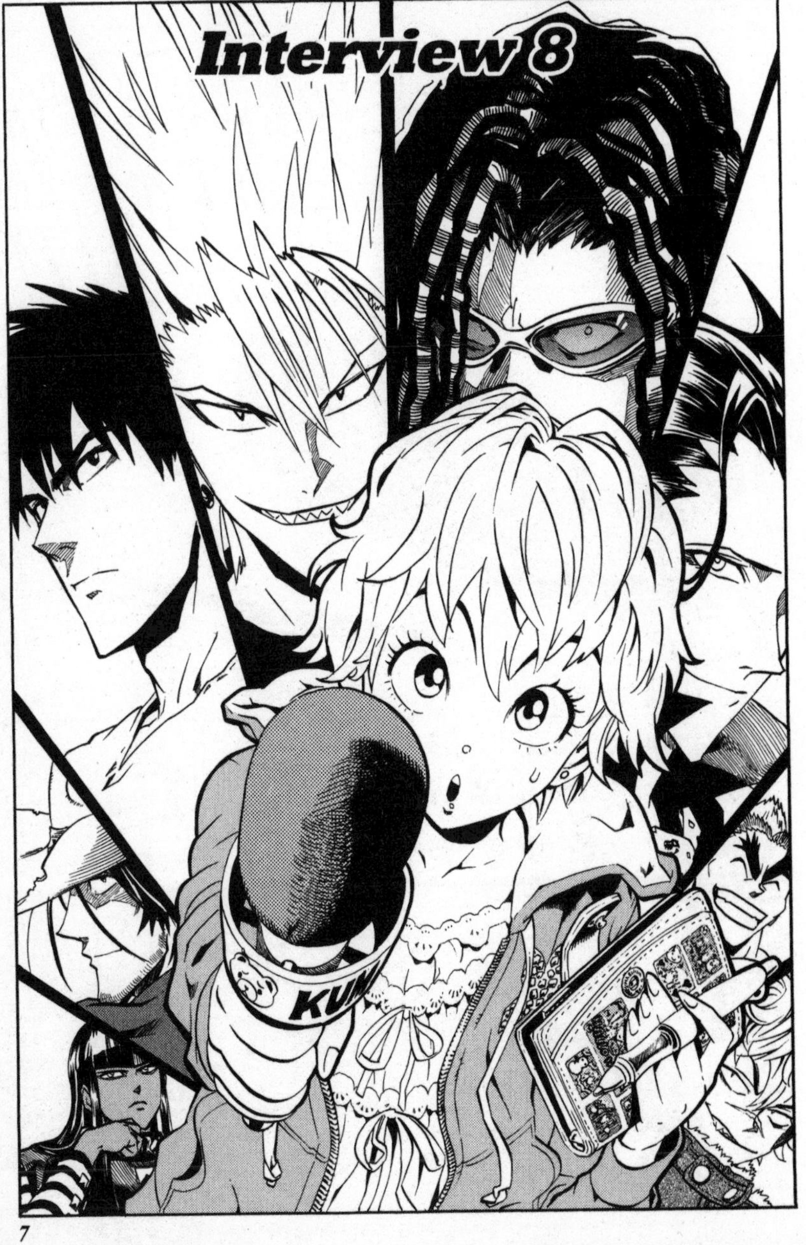

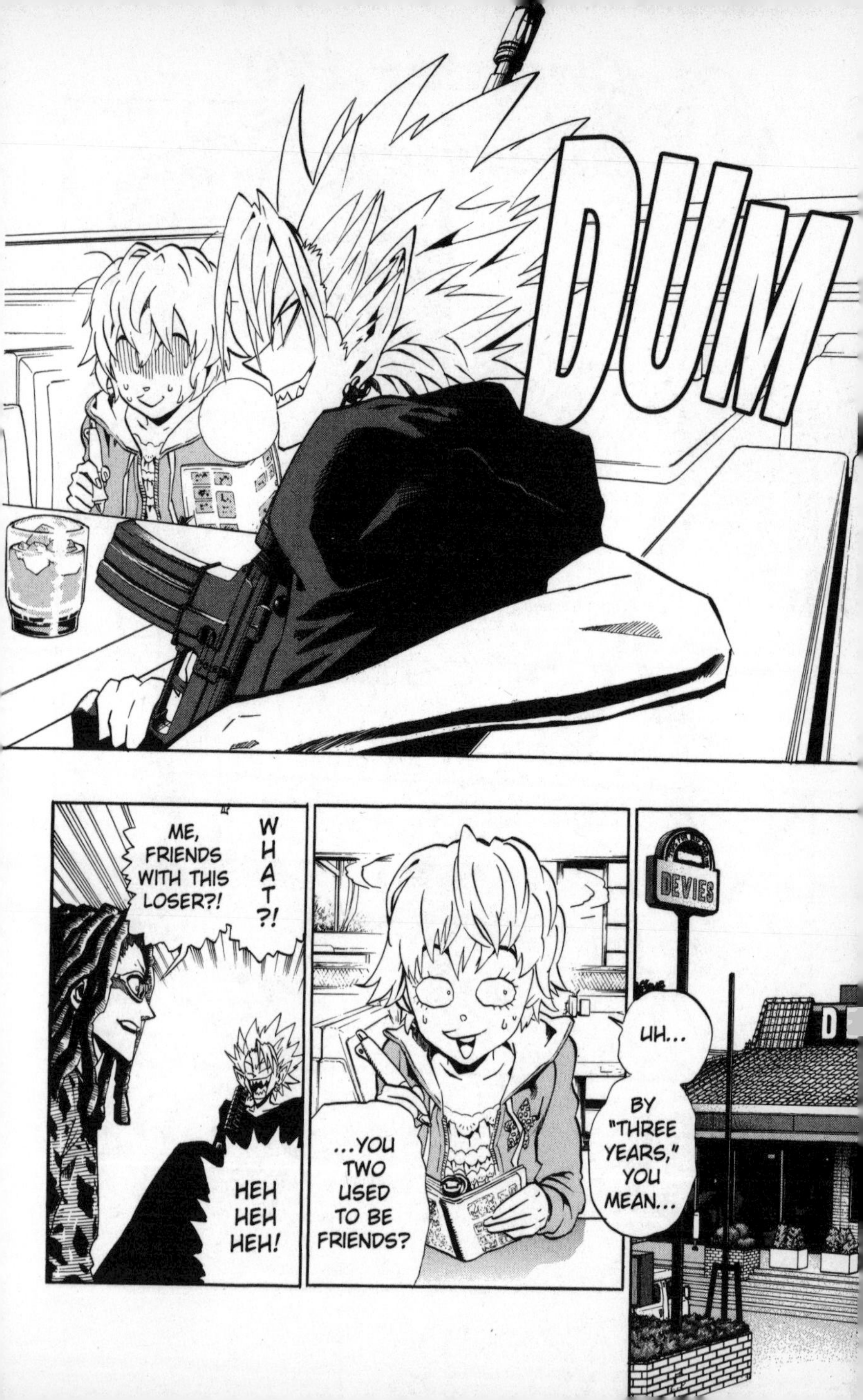
DUM
DEVIES
UH...
BY "THREE YEARS," YOU MEAN...
...YOU TWO USED TO BE FRIENDS?
WHAT?!
ME, FRIENDS WITH THIS LOSER?!
HEH HEH HEH!

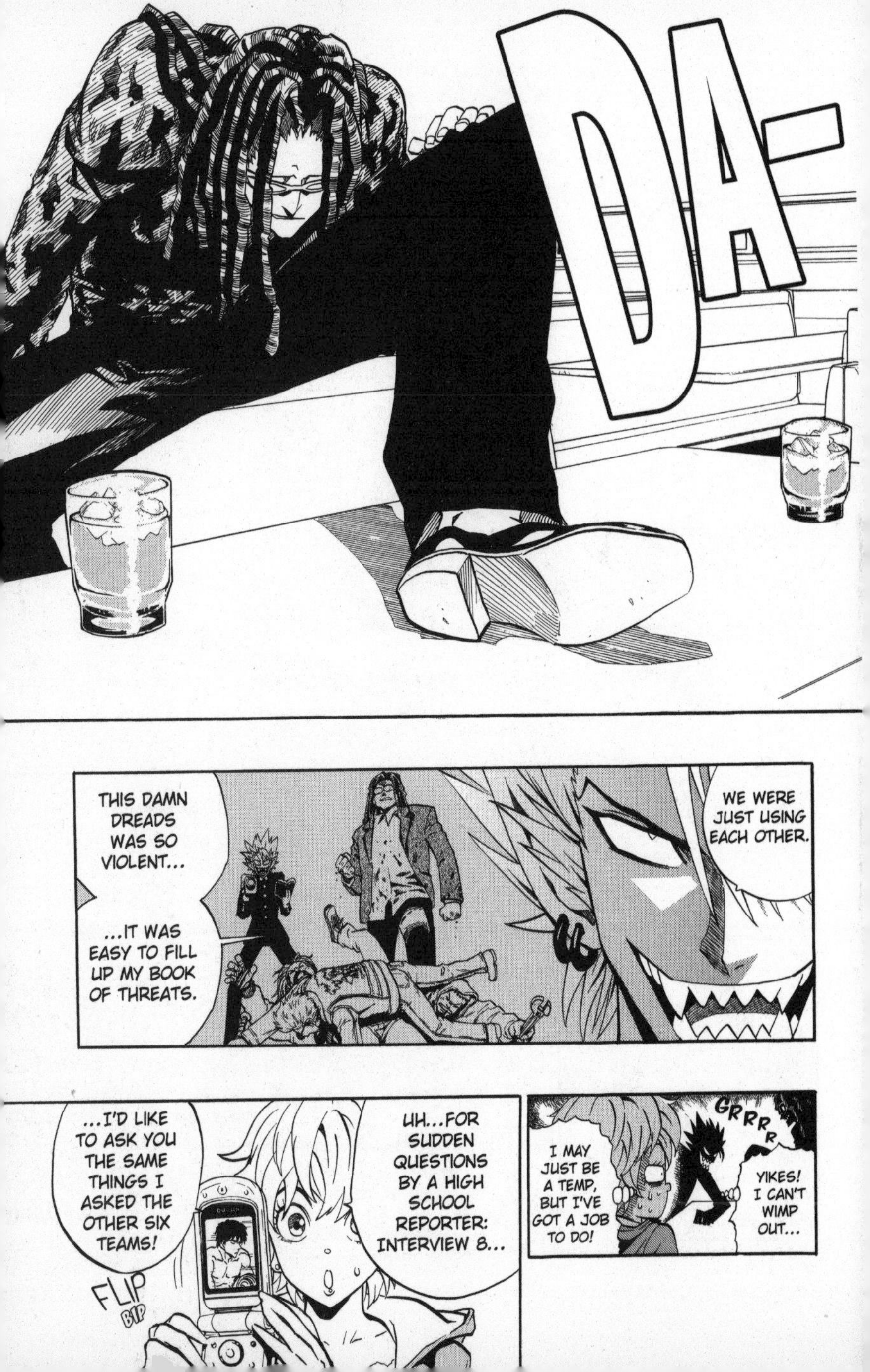
DA-
WE WERE JUST USING EACH OTHER.
THIS DAMN DREADS WAS SO VIOLENT...
...IT WAS EASY TO FILL UP MY BOOK OF THREATS.
GRRRR
YIKES! I CAN'T WIMP OUT...
I MAY JUST BE A TEMP, BUT I'VE GOT A JOB TO DO!
UH...FOR SUDDEN QUESTIONS BY A HIGH SCHOOL REPORTER: INTERVIEW 8...
...I'D LIKE TO ASK YOU THE SAME THINGS I ASKED THE OTHER SIX TEAMS!
FLIP
BIP

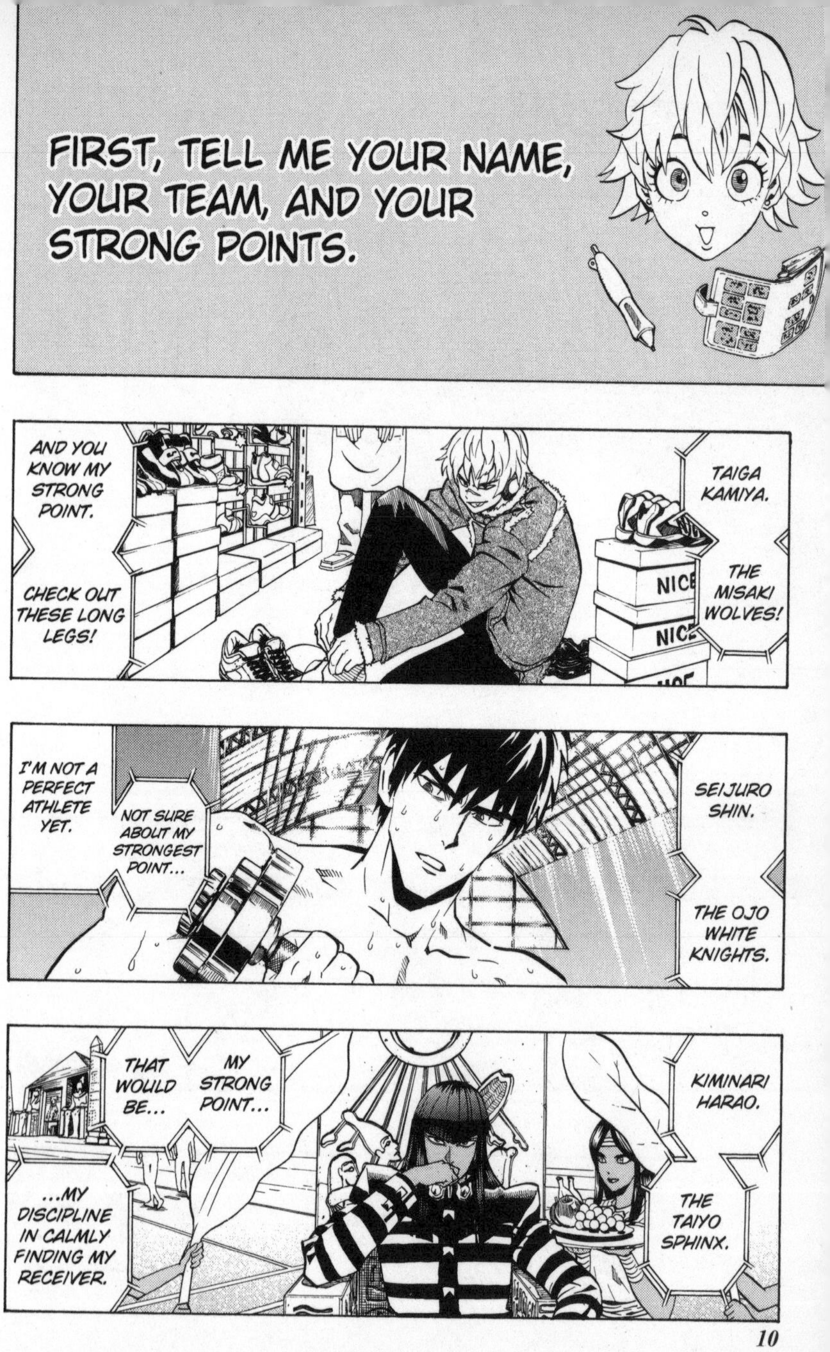
FIRST, TELL ME YOUR NAME, YOUR TEAM, AND YOUR STRONG POINTS.
TAIGA KAMIYA.
THE MISAKI WOLVES!
AND YOU KNOW MY STRONG POINT.
CHECK OUT THESE LONG LEGS!
NICE
NICE
SEIJURO SHIN.
THE OJO WHITE KNIGHTS.
NOT SURE ABOUT MY STRONGEST POINT...
I'M NOT A PERFECT ATHLETE YET.
KIMINARI HARAO.
THE TAIYO SPHINX.
MY STRONG POINT...
THAT WOULD BE...
...MY DISCIPLINE IN CALMLY FINDING MY RECEIVER.

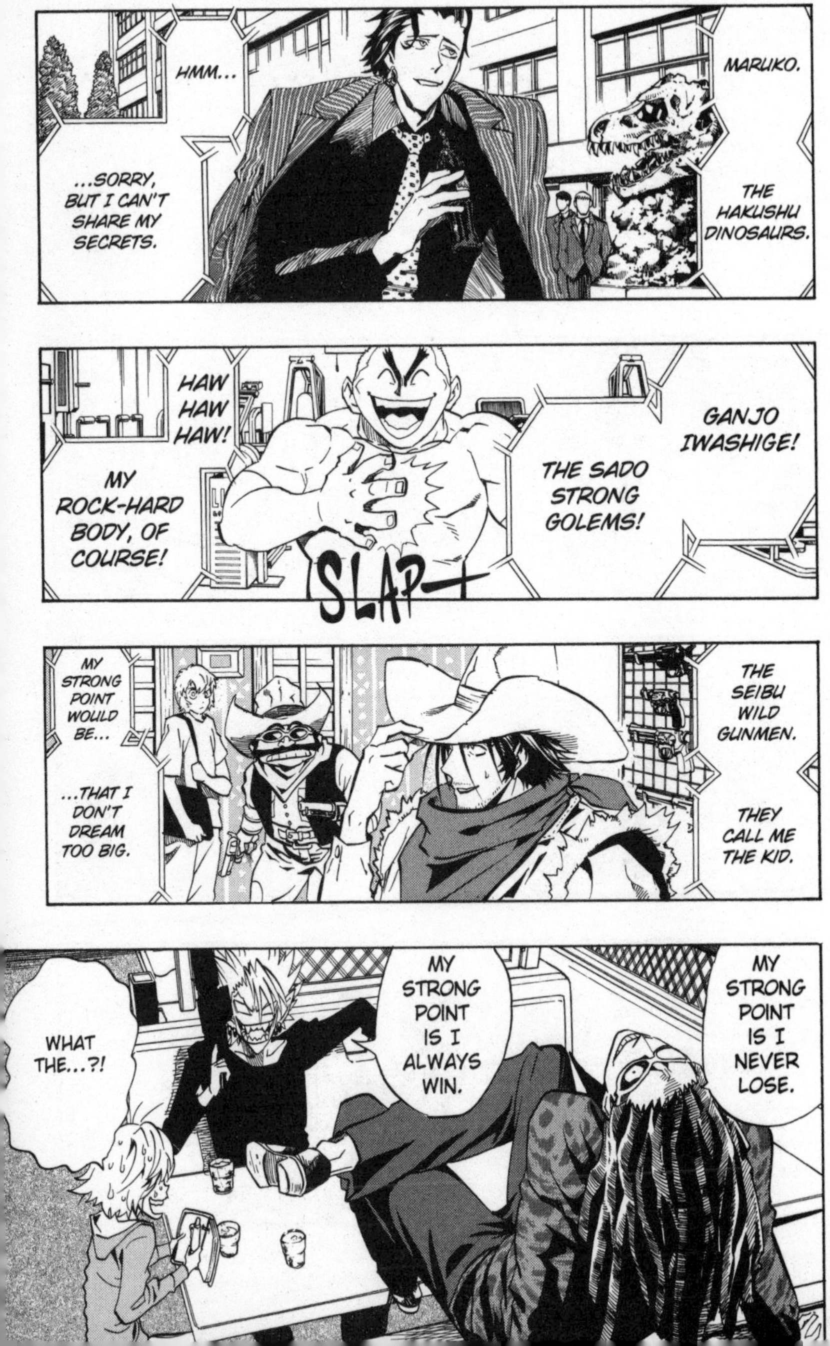
MARUKO.
THE HAKUSHU DINOSAURS.
HMM...
...SORRY, BUT I CAN'T SHARE MY SECRETS.
GANJO IWASHIGE!
THE SADO STRONG GOLEMS!
HAW HAW HAW!
MY ROCK-HARD BODY, OF COURSE!
SLAP
THE SEIBU WILD GUNMEN.
THEY CALL ME THE KID.
MY STRONG POINT WOULD BE...
...THAT I DON'T DREAM TOO BIG.
MY STRONG POINT IS I NEVER LOSE.
MY STRONG POINT IS I ALWAYS WIN.
WHAT THE...?!

## WHO ARE YOU WATCHING OUT FOR IN THE KANTO TOURNAMENT?

ME!
HMM... PROBABLY AGON.
THE NAGAS WON LAST TIME.
IS THAT ANSWER ALL RIGHT? HA HA HA!
BUT I'M STRONGER NOW!
EYESHIELD 21.
SENA KOBAYA-KAWA.
AGON KONGO.
IKKYU HOSO-KAWA.
AGON, SHIN, THE KID...
SO MANY GUYS TO WATCH OUT FOR.
YOU KNOW MY ANSWER!
BANBA!!
SHIN ...
...AND MAYBE SENA.

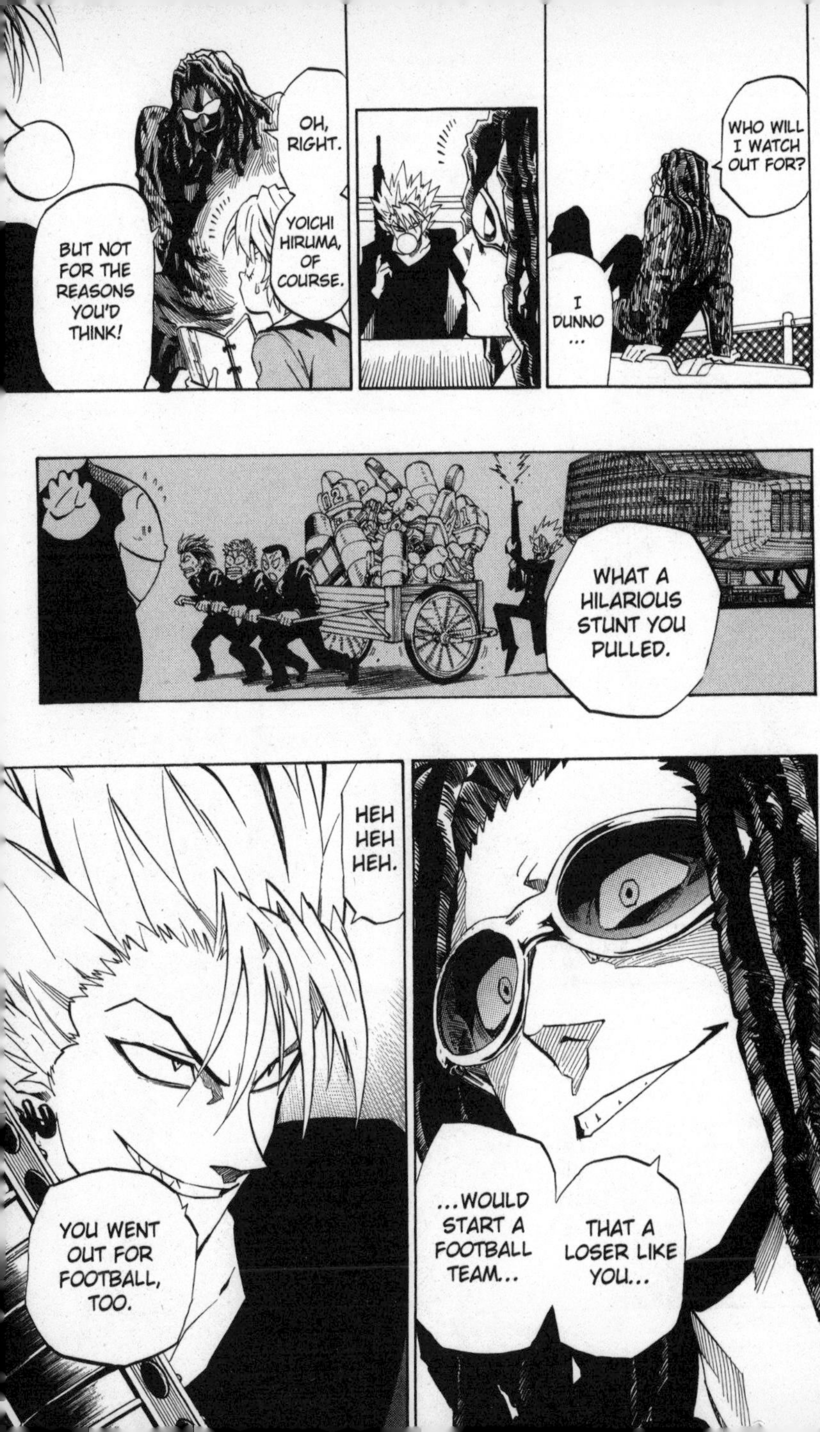
WHO WILL I WATCH OUT FOR?
I DUNNO ...
OH, RIGHT.
YOICHI HIRUMA, OF COURSE.
BUT NOT FOR THE REASONS YOU'D THINK!
WHAT A HILARIOUS STUNT YOU PULLED.
THAT A LOSER LIKE YOU...
...WOULD START A FOOTBALL TEAM...
HEH HEH HEH.
YOU WENT OUT FOR FOOTBALL, TOO.

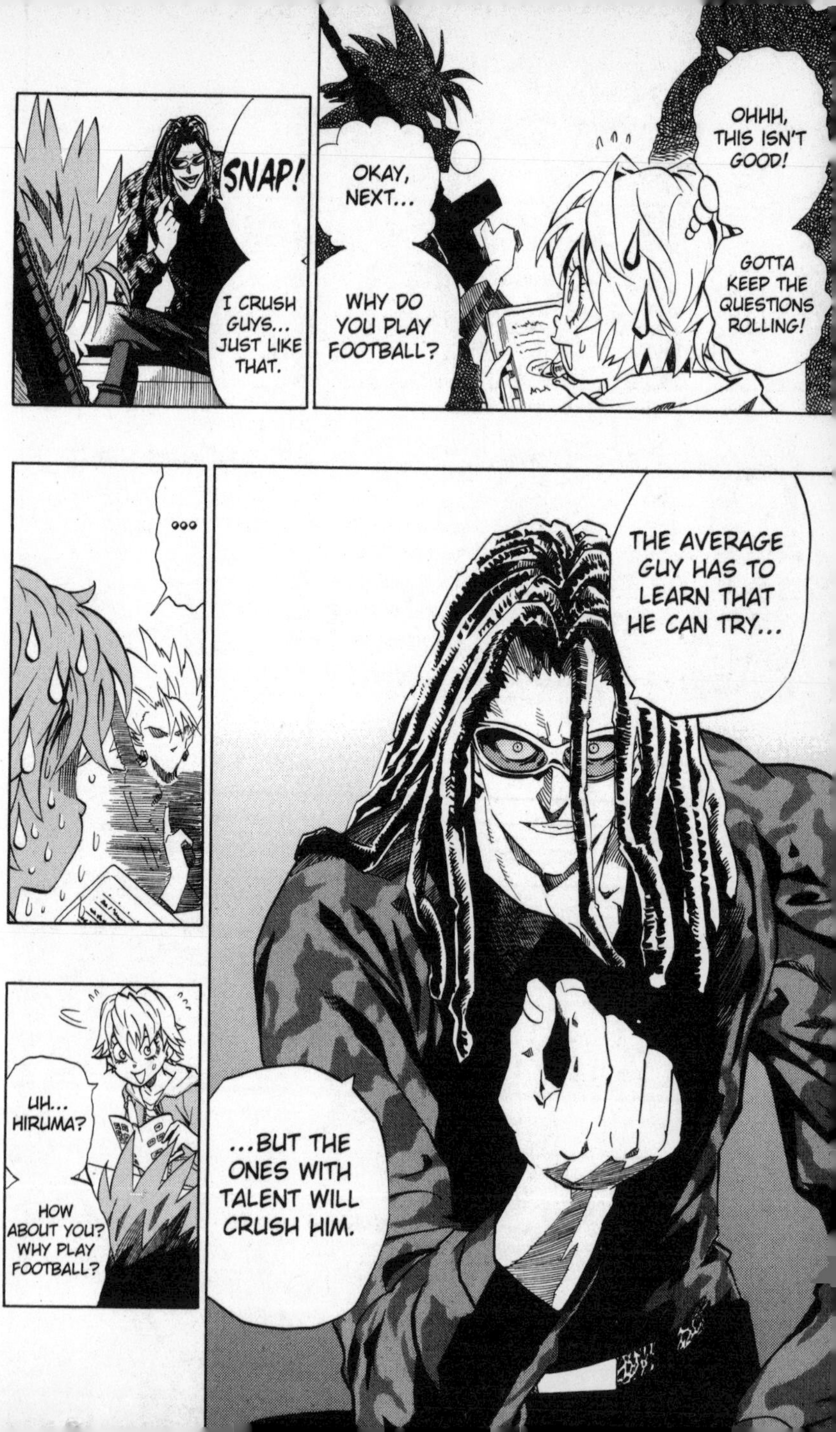
OHHH, THIS ISN'T GOOD!
GOTTA KEEP THE QUESTIONS ROLLING!
OKAY, NEXT...
WHY DO YOU PLAY FOOTBALL?
SNAP!
I CRUSH GUYS... JUST LIKE THAT.
THE AVERAGE GUY HAS TO LEARN THAT HE CAN TRY...
...BUT THE ONES WITH TALENT WILL CRUSH HIM.
...
UH... HIRUMA?
HOW ABOUT YOU? WHY PLAY FOOTBALL?

BECAUSE
IT'S FUN.

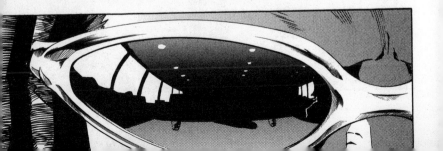

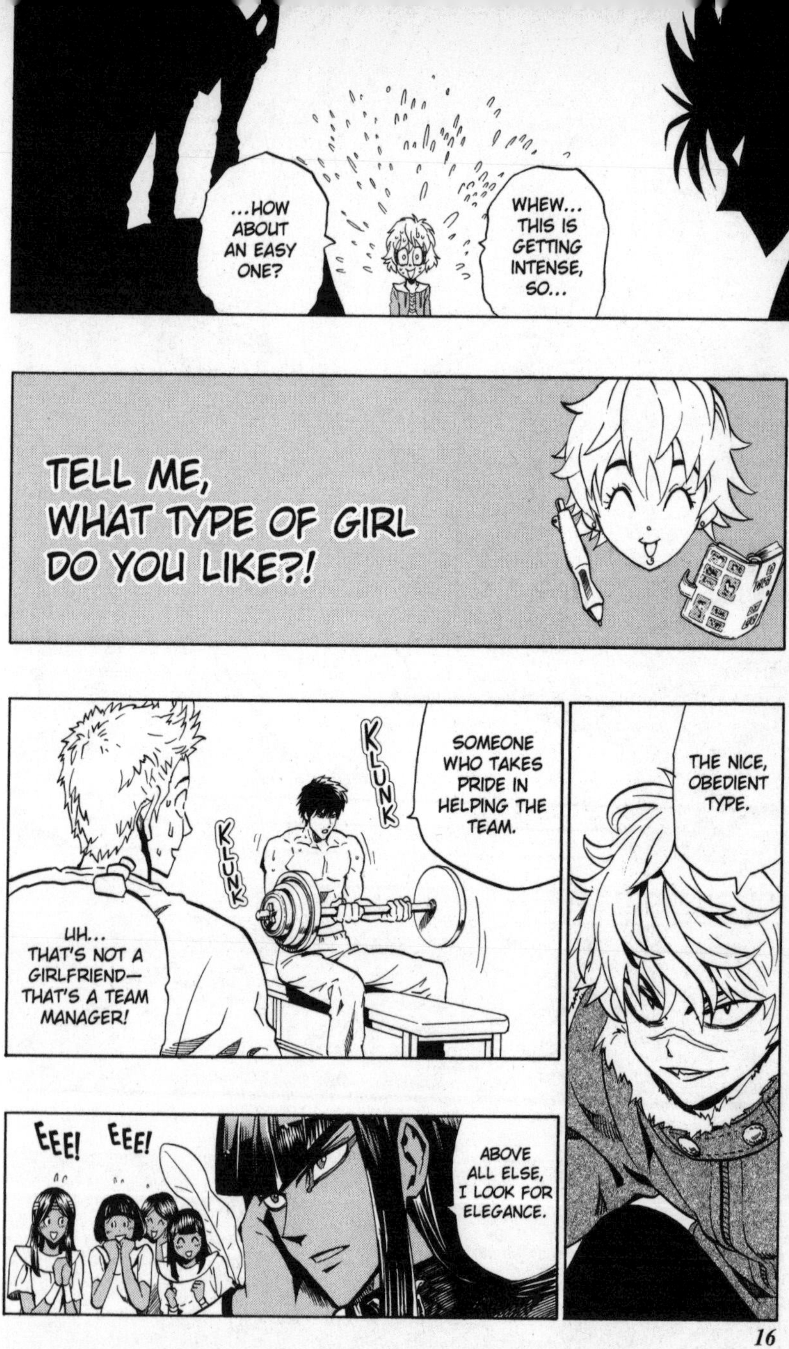
WHEW... THIS IS GETTING INTENSE, SO...
...HOW ABOUT AN EASY ONE?
TELL ME, WHAT TYPE OF GIRL DO YOU LIKE?!
THE NICE, OBEDIENT TYPE.
SOMEONE WHO TAKES PRIDE IN HELPING THE TEAM.
KLUNK
KLUNK
UH... THAT'S NOT A GIRLFRIEND— THAT'S A TEAM MANAGER!
ABOVE ALL ELSE, I LOOK FOR ELEGANCE.
EEE!
EEE!

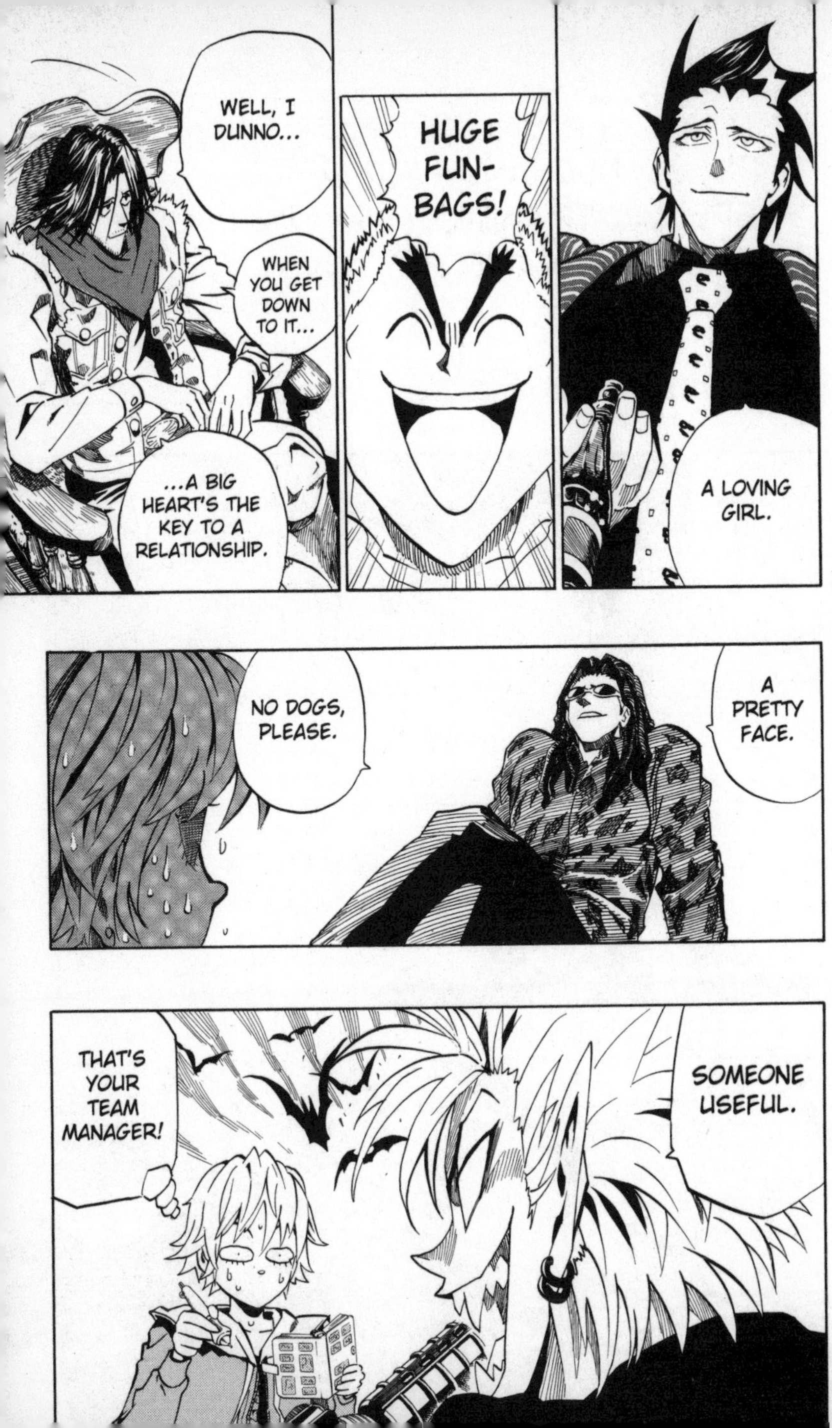
A LOVING GIRL.
HUGE FUN-BAGS!
WELL, I DUNNO...
WHEN YOU GET DOWN TO IT...
...A BIG HEART'S THE KEY TO A RELATIONSHIP.
A PRETTY FACE.
NO DOGS, PLEASE.
SOMEONE USEFUL.
THAT'S YOUR TEAM MANAGER!

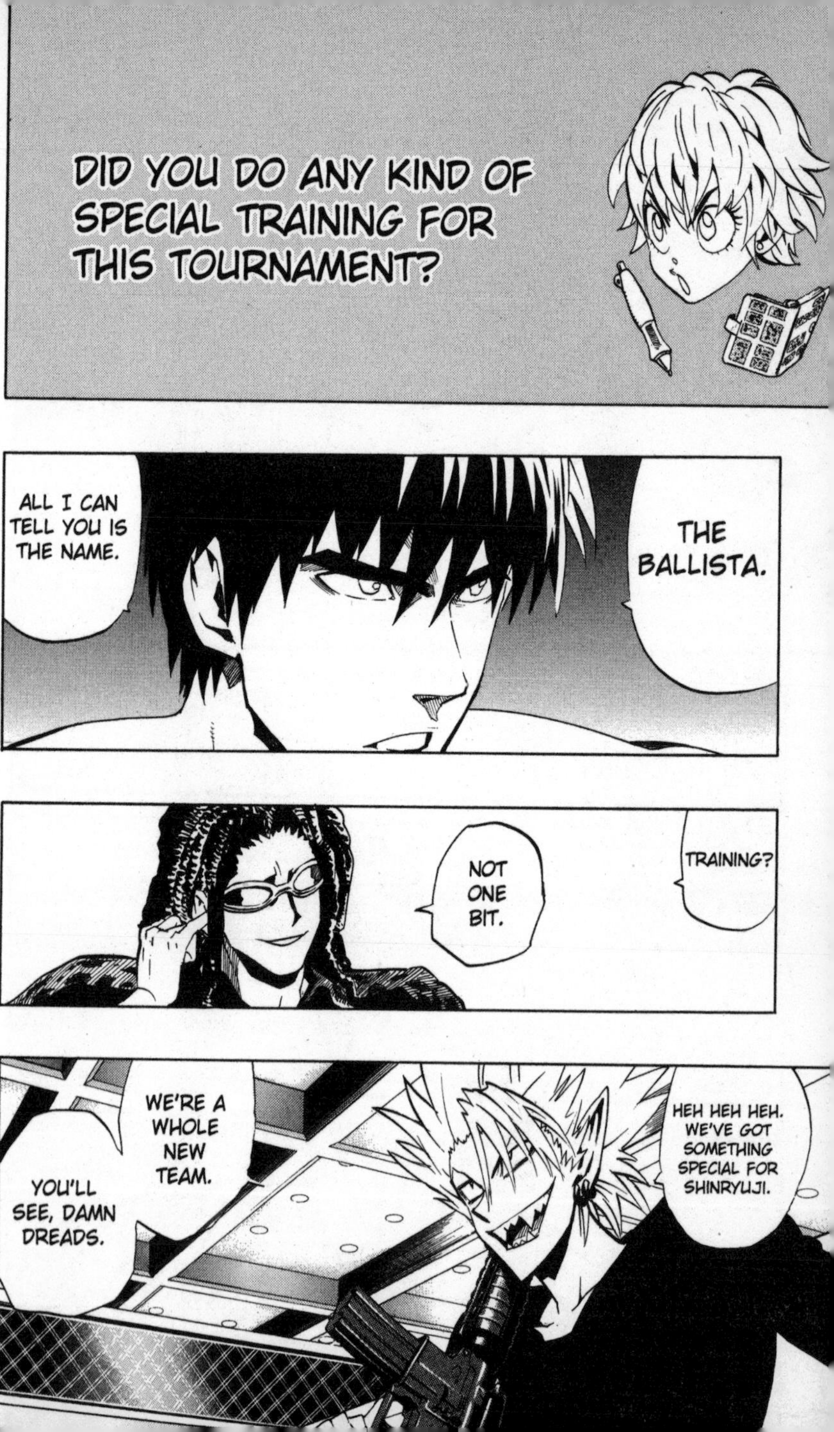
DID YOU DO ANY KIND OF SPECIAL TRAINING FOR THIS TOURNAMENT?
THE BALLISTA.
ALL I CAN TELL YOU IS THE NAME.
TRAINING?
NOT ONE BIT.
HEH HEH HEH. WE'VE GOT SOMETHING SPECIAL FOR SHINRYUJI.
WE'RE A WHOLE NEW TEAM.
YOU'LL SEE, DAMN DREADS.

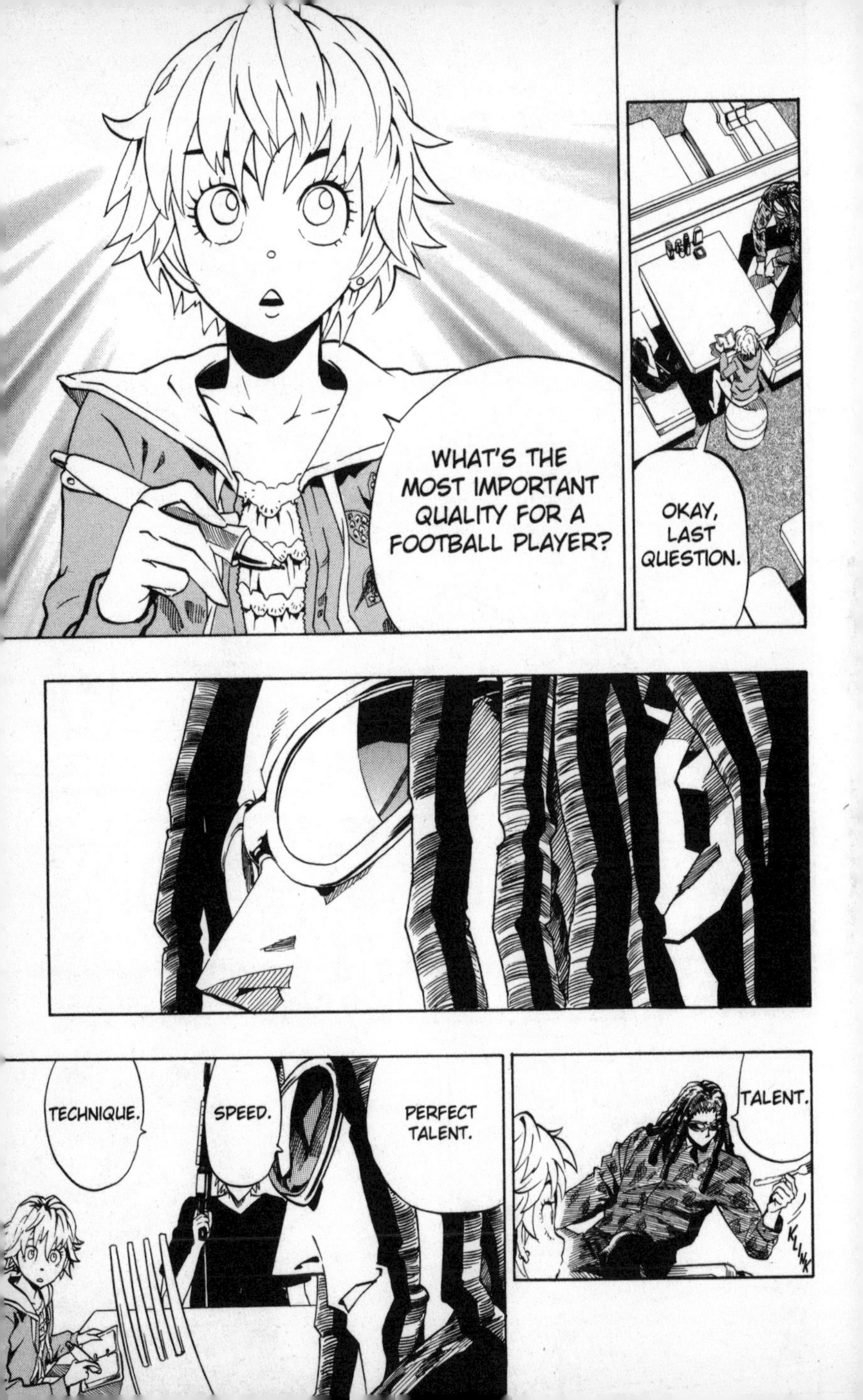
OKAY, LAST QUESTION.
WHAT'S THE MOST IMPORTANT QUALITY FOR A FOOTBALL PLAYER?
TALENT.
KLINK
PERFECT TALENT.
SPEED.
TECHNIQUE.

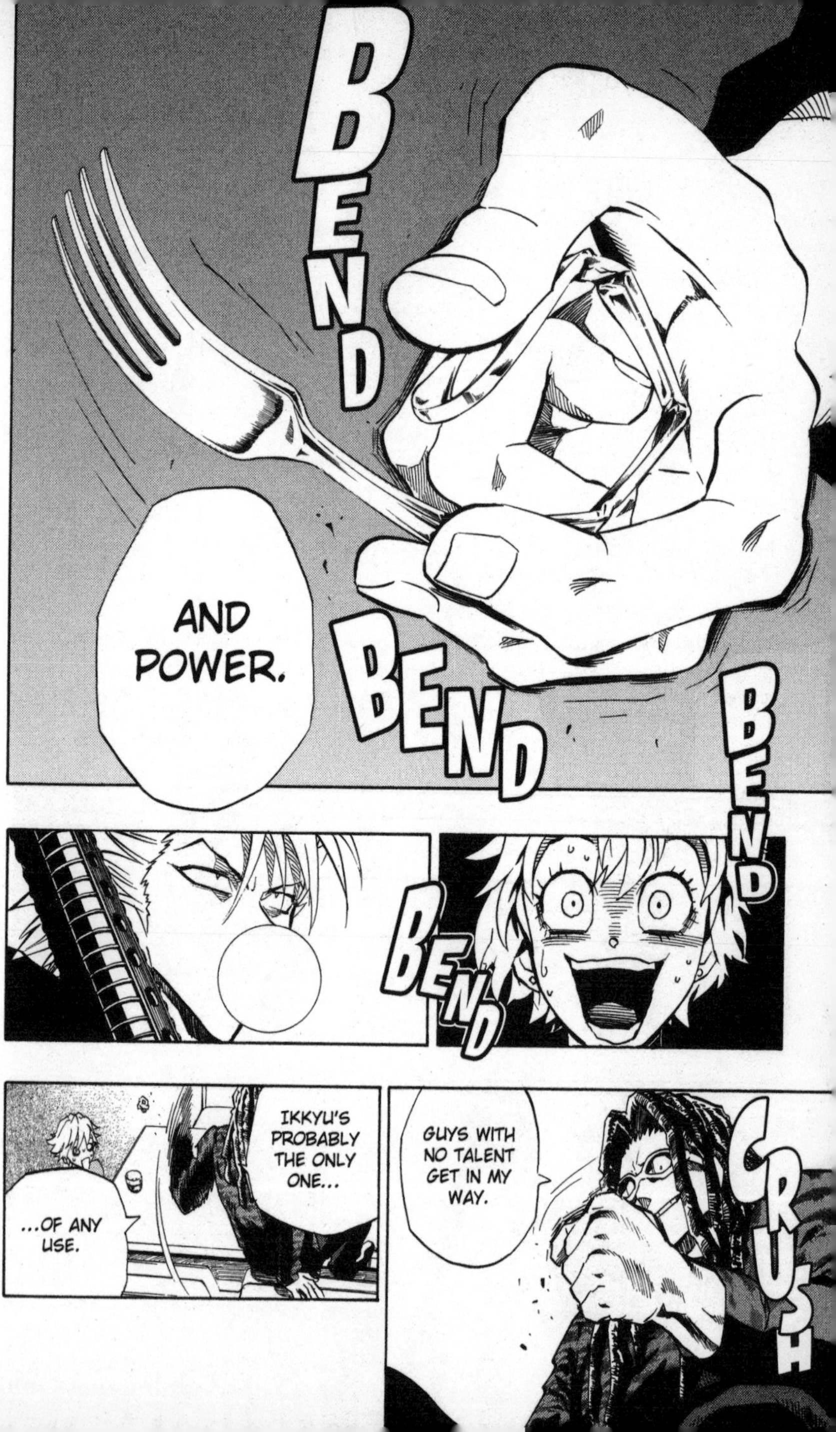
BEND
AND POWER.
BEND
BEND
BEND
GUYS WITH NO TALENT GET IN MY WAY.
CRUSH
IKKYU'S PROBABLY THE ONLY ONE...
...OF ANY USE.

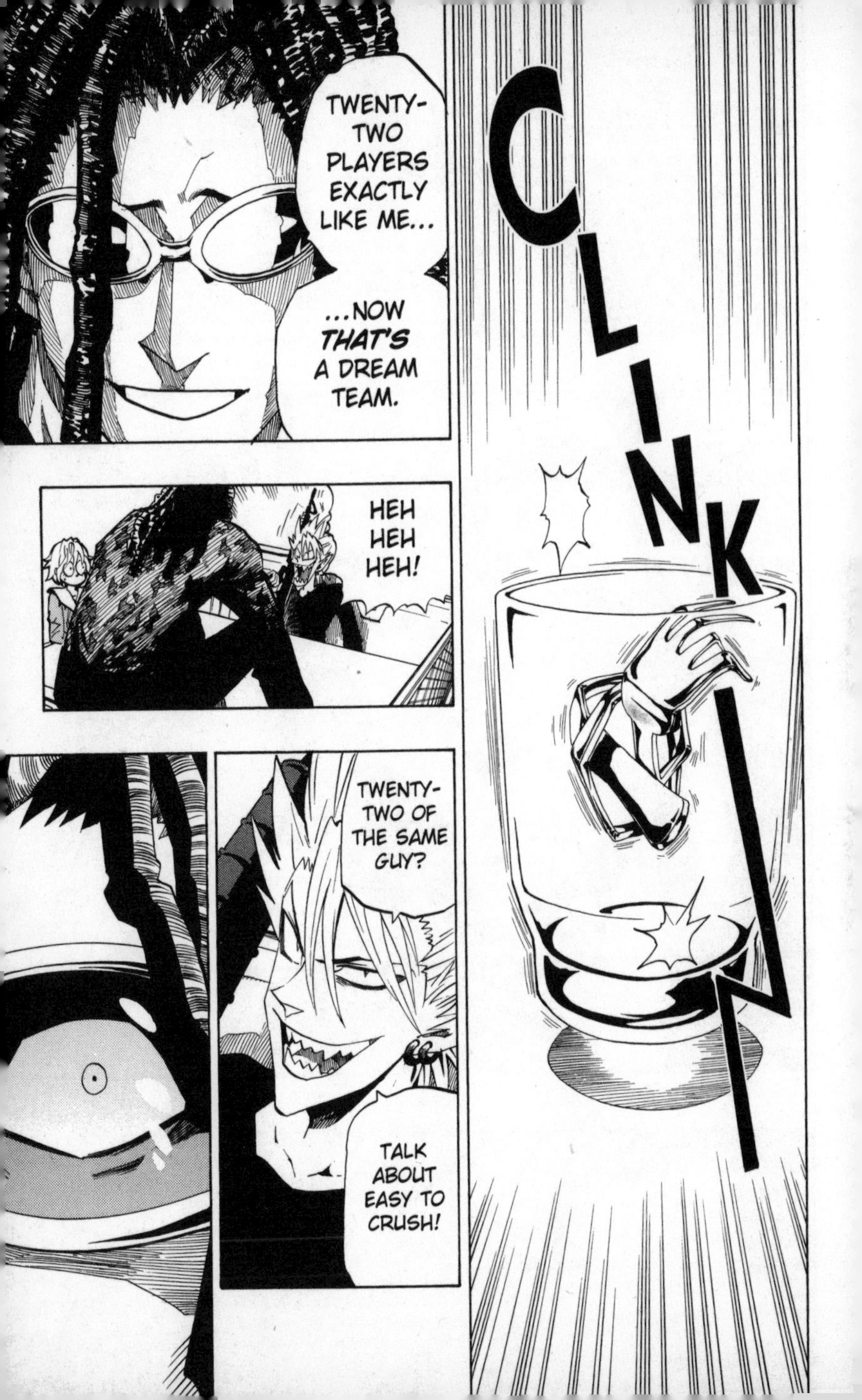
CLINK
TWENTY-TWO PLAYERS EXACTLY LIKE ME...
...NOW THAT'S A DREAM TEAM.
HEH HEH HEH!
TWENTY-TWO OF THE SAME GUY?
TALK ABOUT EASY TO CRUSH!

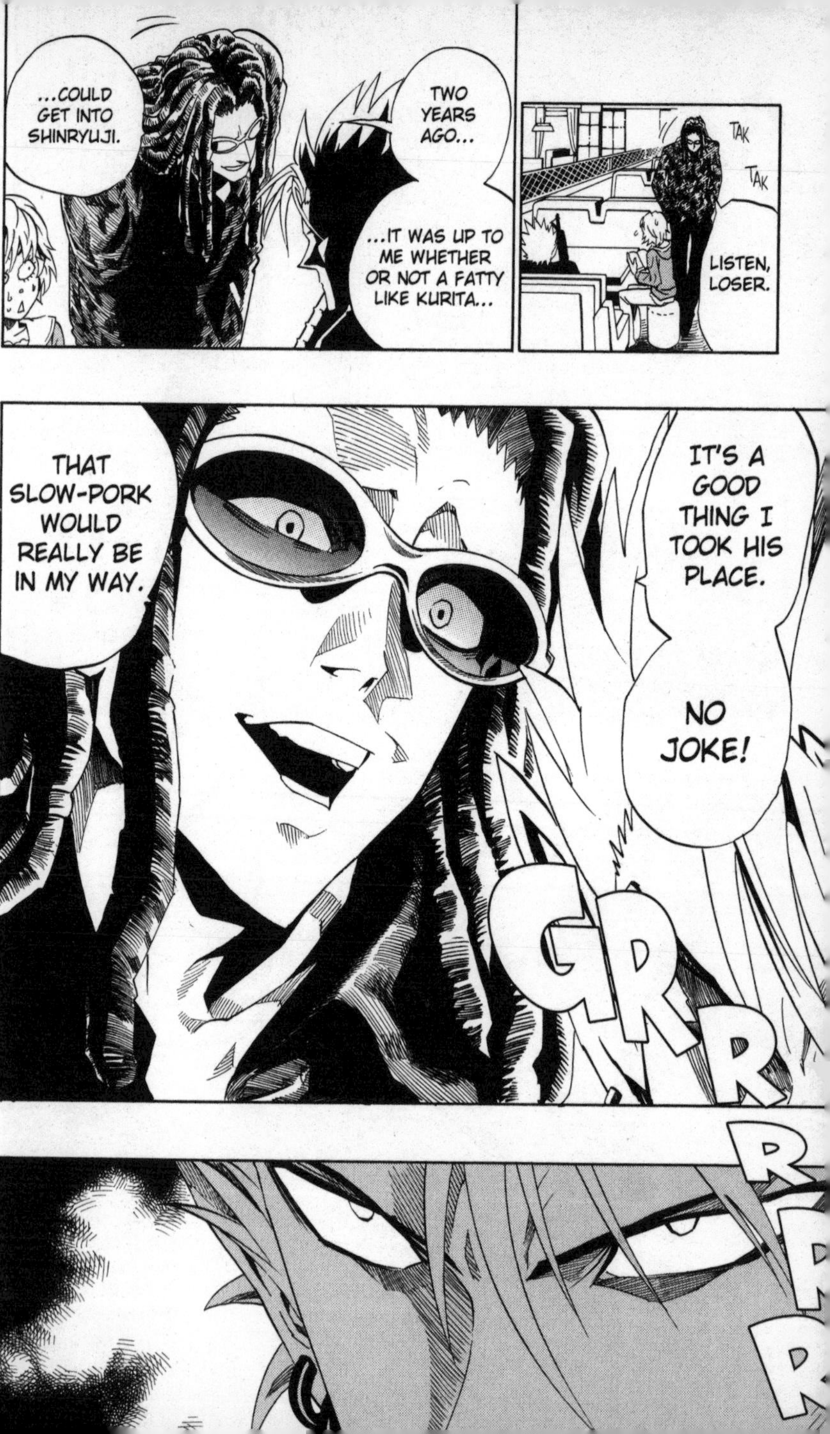
TAK
TAK
LISTEN, LOSER.
TWO YEARS AGO...
...IT WAS UP TO ME WHETHER OR NOT A FATTY LIKE KURITA...
...COULD GET INTO SHINRYUJI.
IT'S A GOOD THING I TOOK HIS PLACE.
THAT SLOW-PORK WOULD REALLY BE IN MY WAY.
NO JOKE!
GRRRRR

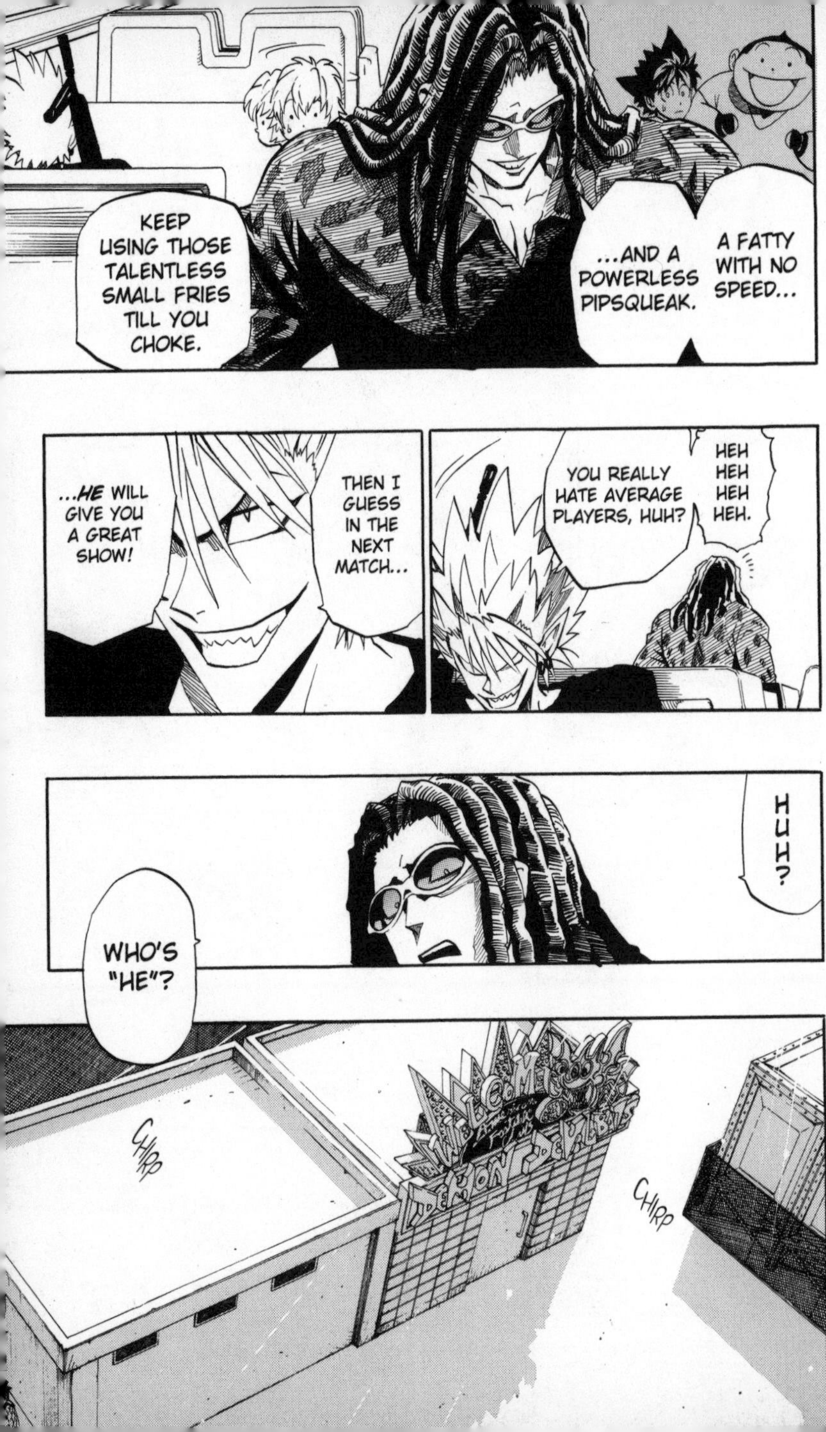
A FATTY WITH NO SPEED...
...AND A POWERLESS PIPSQUEAK.
KEEP USING THOSE TALENTLESS SMALL FRIES TILL YOU CHOKE.
HEH HEH HEH HEH.
YOU REALLY HATE AVERAGE PLAYERS, HUH?
THEN I GUESS IN THE NEXT MATCH...
...**HE** WILL GIVE YOU A GREAT SHOW!
HUH?
WHO'S "HE"?
CHIRP
CHIRP

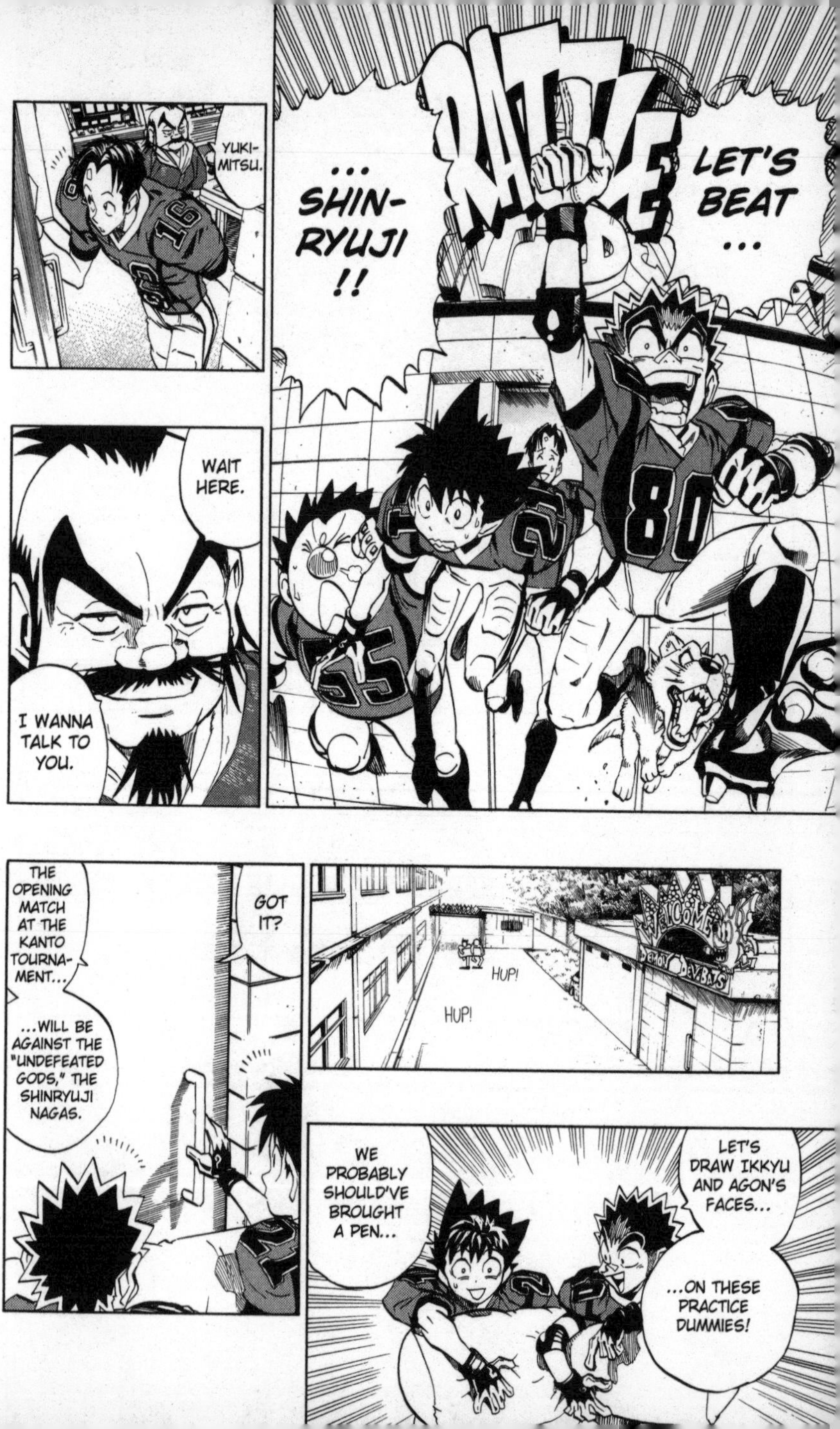
LET'S BEAT ...
... SHIN-RYUJI !!
YUKI-MITSU.
WAIT HERE.
I WANNA TALK TO YOU.
HUP!
HUP!
LET'S DRAW IKKYU AND AGON'S FACES...
...ON THESE PRACTICE DUMMIES!
WE PROBABLY SHOULD'VE BROUGHT A PEN...
GOT IT?
THE OPENING MATCH AT THE KANTO TOURNAMENT...
...WILL BE AGAINST THE "UNDEFEATED GODS," THE SHINRYUJI NAGAS.

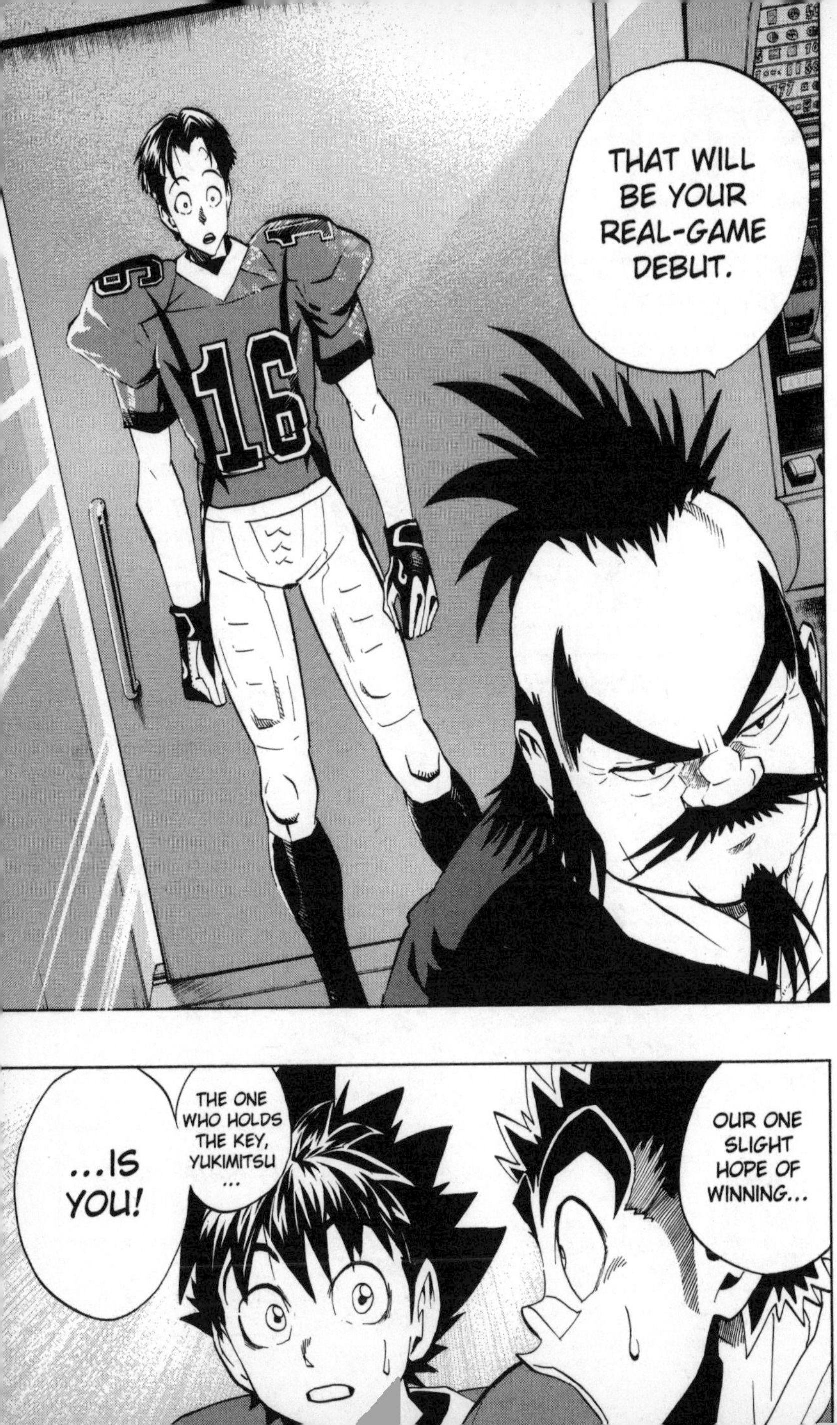
THAT WILL BE YOUR REAL-GAME DEBUT.
OUR ONE SLIGHT HOPE OF WINNING...
THE ONE WHO HOLDS THE KEY, YUKIMITSU...
...IS YOU!

RIKO KUMABUKURO'S INTERVIEW 8

# EXTRA QUESTION

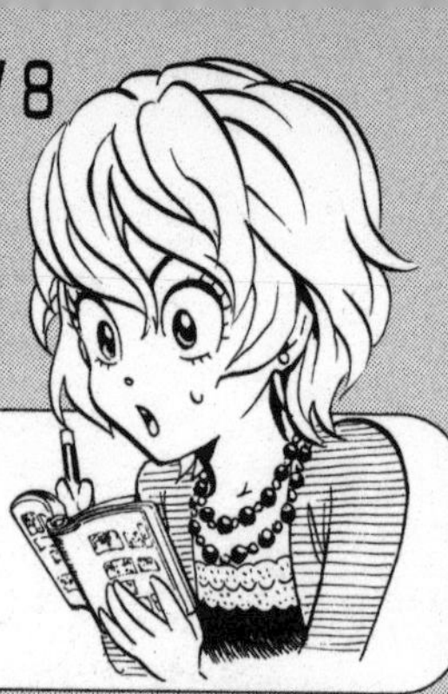

WHICH FOOTBALL PLAYER RESEMBLES YOU MOST, AND WHY?

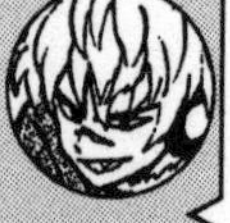

Kamiya

**KOTARO** (BANDO)

HE HAS LONG LEGS LIKE MINE, ALTHOUGH I'M MUCH BETTER LOOKING. OOPS! HA HA!

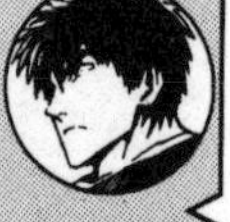

Shin

**AGON** (SHINRYUJI)

THE WAY HE'S BUILT, AND HIS BODY FAT PERCENTAGE.

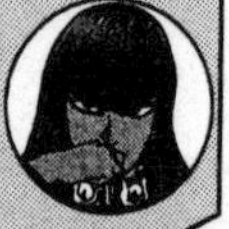

Harao

**BANBA** (TAIYO)

THOUGH NOT FROM A RICH FAMILY, HE TRANSCENDED HIS ORIGINS. LIKE ME, HE'S A CLASS ACT.

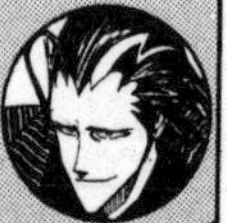

Maruko

**HIRUMA** (DEIMON)

HE KNOWS THAT POWER IS JUSTICE.

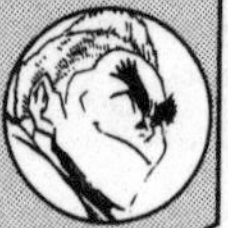

Iwashige

**ARNOLD SCHWARZENEGGER** (?!)

*RIKO'S NOTE: "I TOLD HIM ARNOLD DOESN'T PLAY FOOTBALL, BUT HE DIDN'T CARE."*

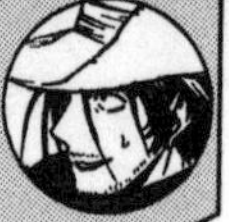

The Kid

AW, WHO'D WANNA LOOK LIKE ME?

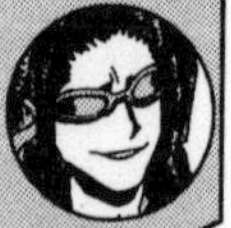

Agon

**IKKYU** (SHINRYUJI)

IF I HAVE TO NAME SOMEONE, IT'S HIM.

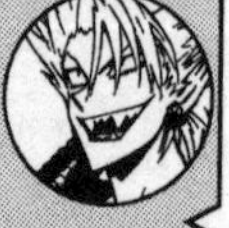

Hiruma

**TAKAMI** (OJO)

HEH HEH HEH! HE'S A SLY ONE WHO DOESN'T GIVE UP EASY.

## Chapter 171 Pieces of a Dream

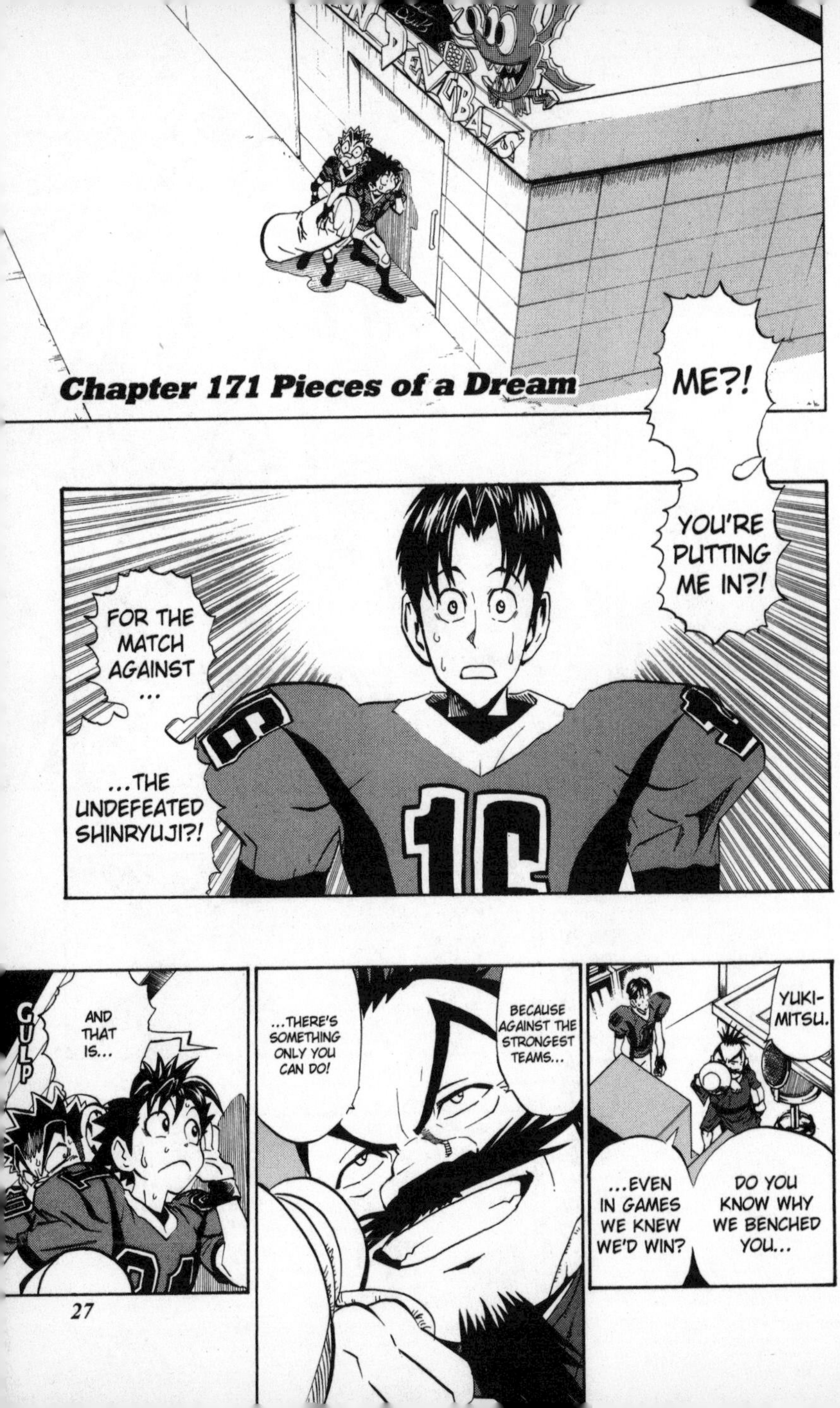
ME?!
YOU'RE PUTTING ME IN?!
FOR THE MATCH AGAINST ...
...THE UNDEFEATED SHINRYUJI?!
YUKI-MITSU.
DO YOU KNOW WHY WE BENCHED YOU...
...EVEN IN GAMES WE KNEW WE'D WIN?
BECAUSE AGAINST THE STRONGEST TEAMS...
...THERE'S SOMETHING ONLY YOU CAN DO!
AND THAT IS...
GULP

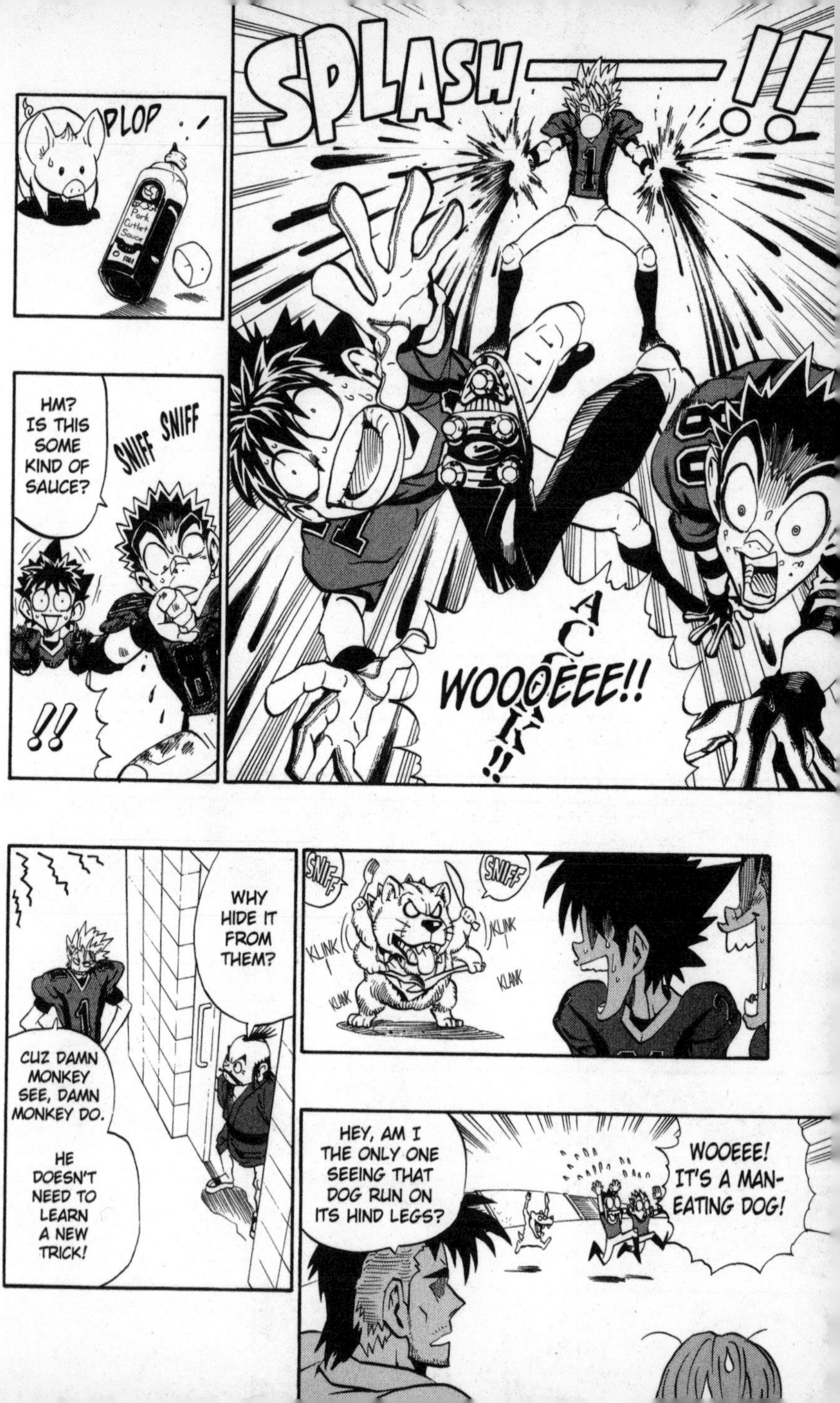
SPLASH——!!
WOOOEEE!!
ACK!!
PLOP
Pork Cutlet Sauce
SNIFF SNIFF
HM? IS THIS SOME KIND OF SAUCE?
!!
SNIFF
SNIFF
KLINK
KLINK
KLINK
KLINK
WOOEEE! IT'S A MAN-EATING DOG!
HEY, AM I THE ONLY ONE SEEING THAT DOG RUN ON ITS HIND LEGS?
WHY HIDE IT FROM THEM?
CUZ DAMN MONKEY SEE, DAMN MONKEY DO.
HE DOESN'T NEED TO LEARN A NEW TRICK!

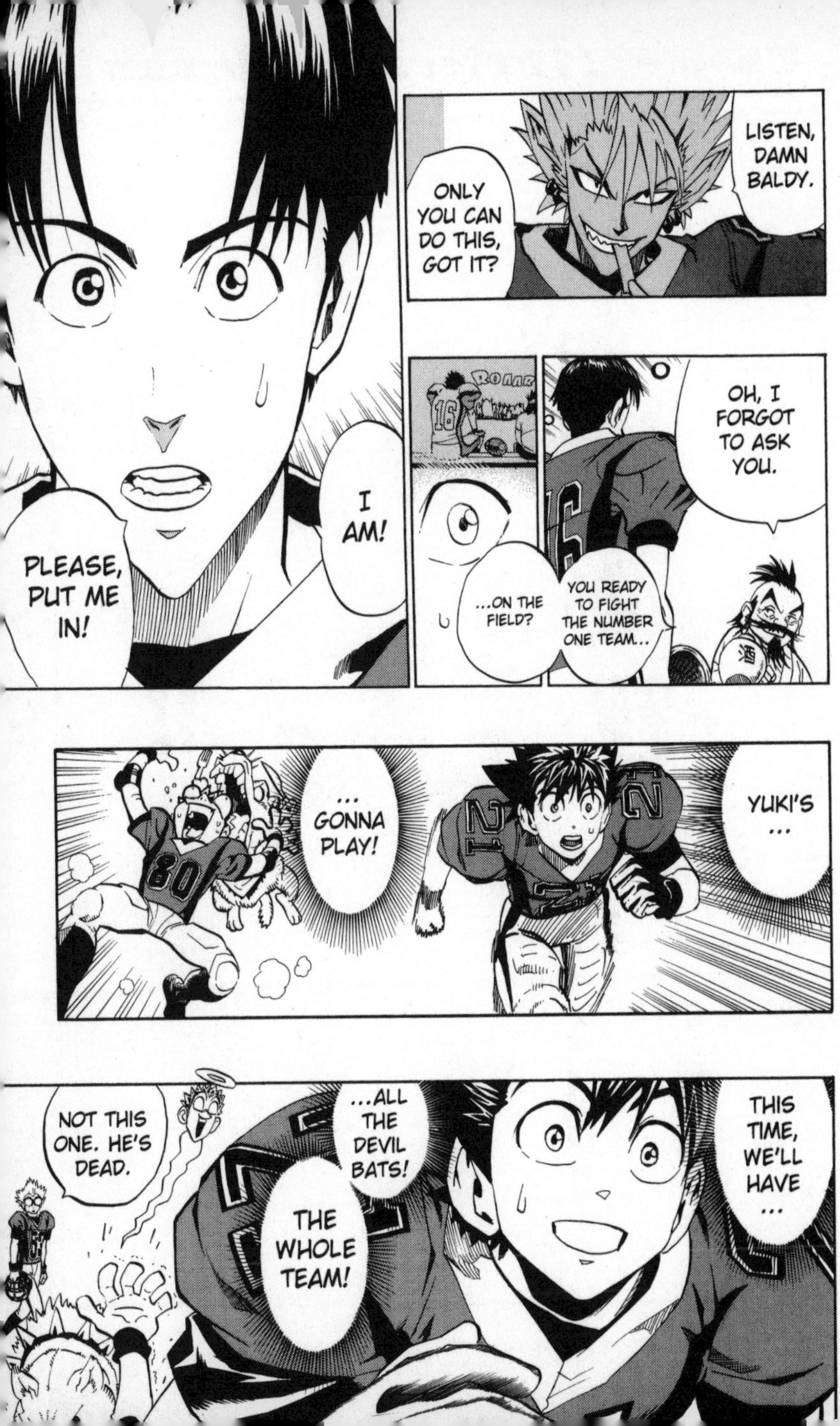
LISTEN, DAMN BALDY.
ONLY YOU CAN DO THIS, GOT IT?
OH, I FORGOT TO ASK YOU.
YOU READY TO FIGHT THE NUMBER ONE TEAM...
...ON THE FIELD?
I AM!
PLEASE, PUT ME IN!
YUKI'S ...
... GONNA PLAY!
THIS TIME, WE'LL HAVE ...
...ALL THE DEVIL BATS!
THE WHOLE TEAM!
NOT THIS ONE. HE'S DEAD.

# Chapter 171 Pieces of a Dream

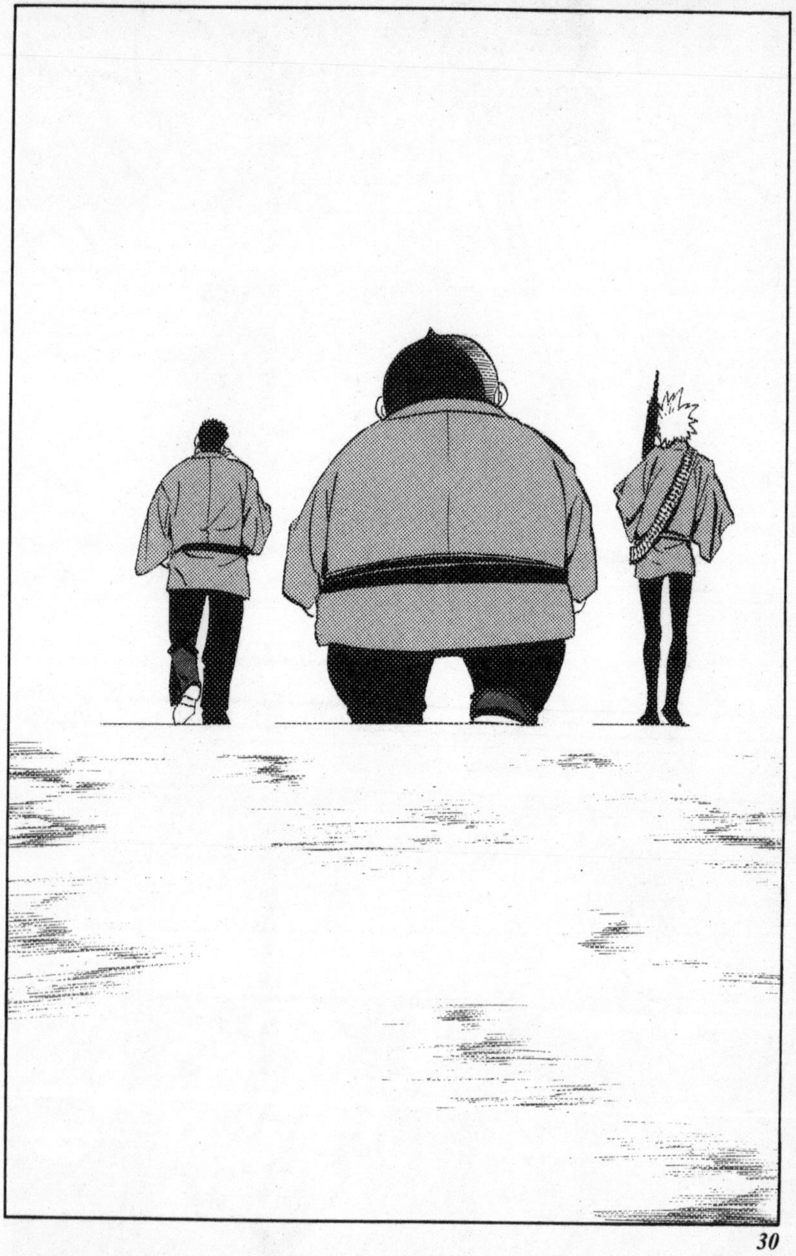

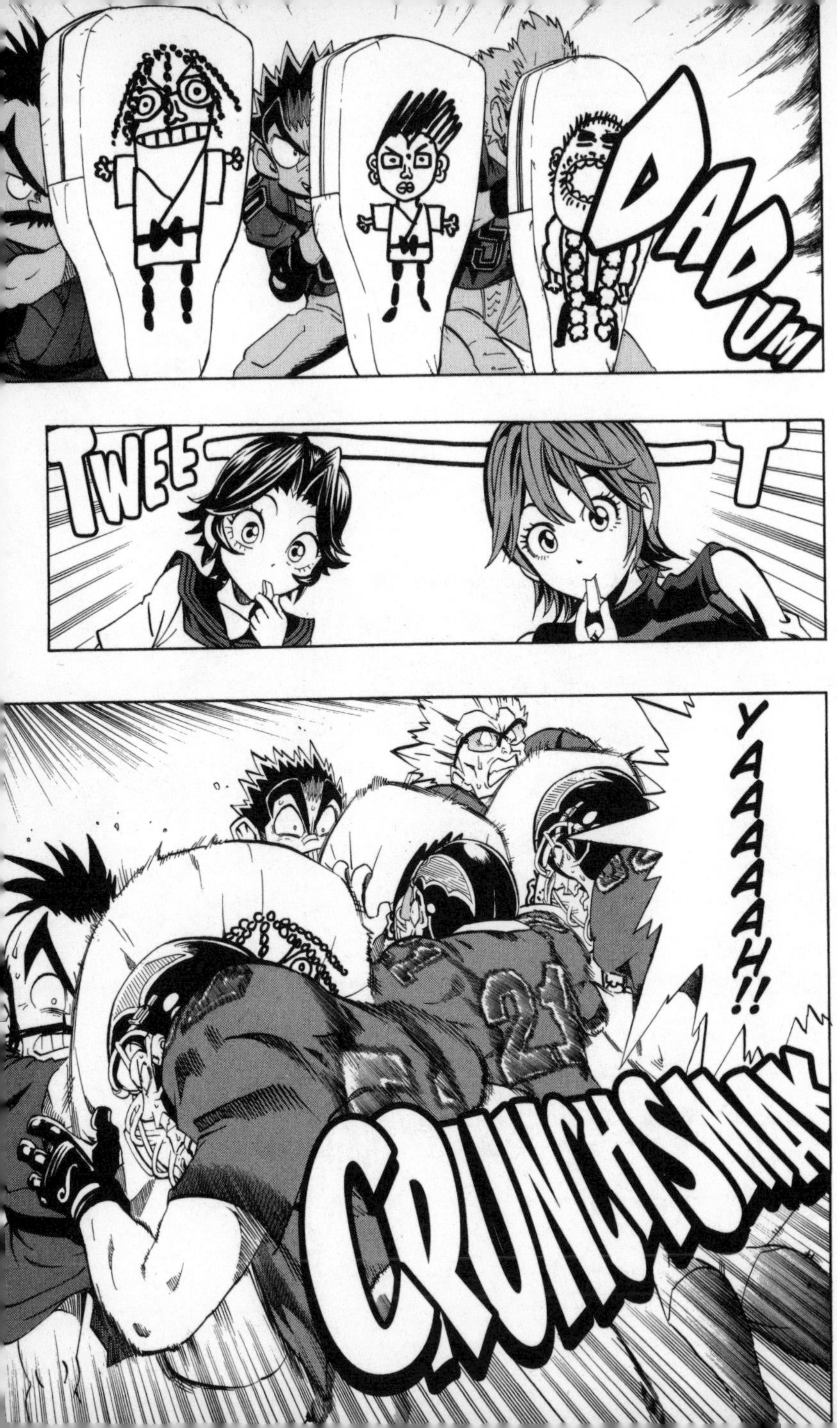
DADUM
TWEET
YAAAAAAH!!
CRUNCHSMAK

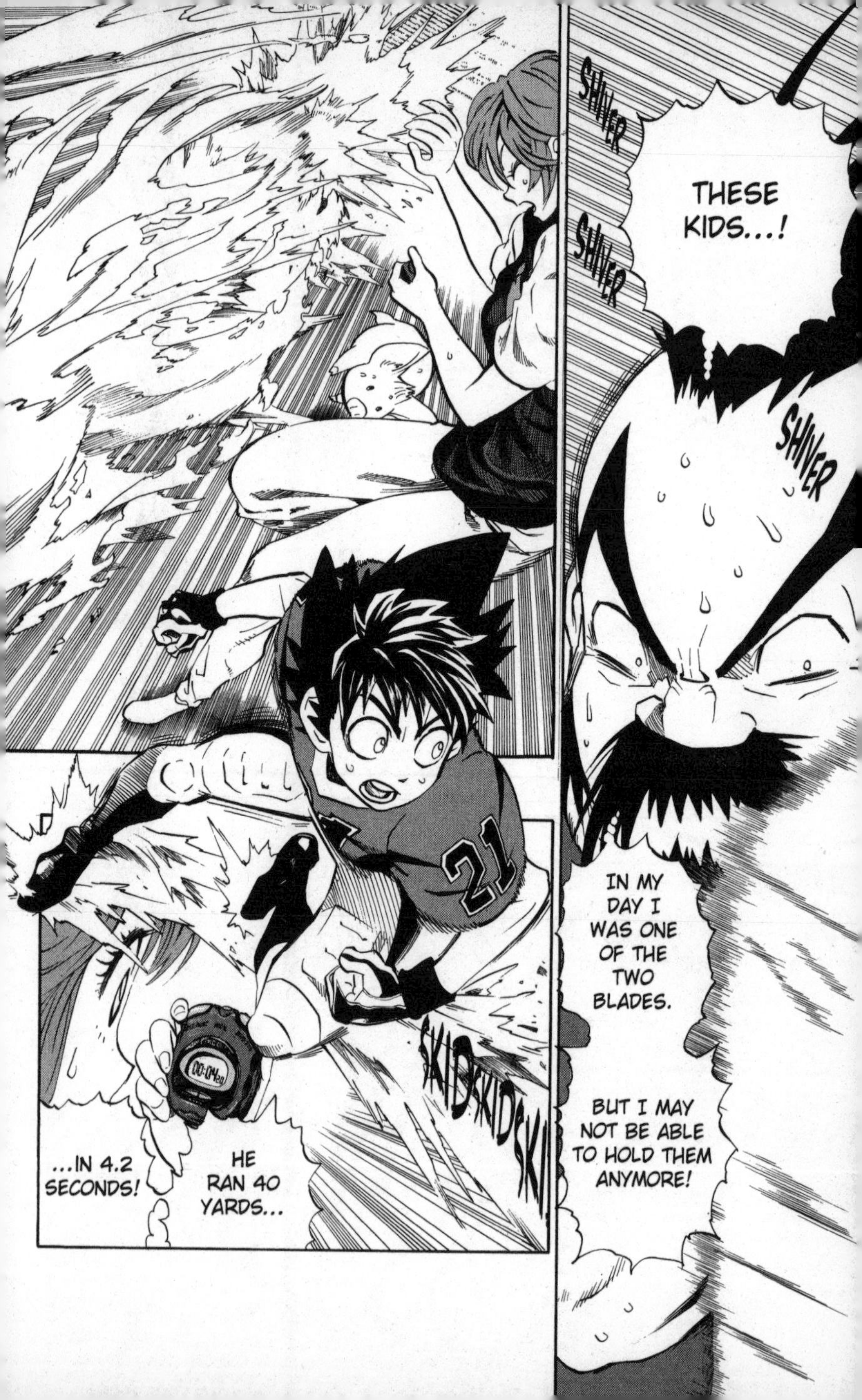
SHIVER
SHIVER
THESE KIDS...!
SHIVER
IN MY DAY I WAS ONE OF THE TWO BLADES.
BUT I MAY NOT BE ABLE TO HOLD THEM ANYMORE!
SKID SKID SKI
HE RAN 40 YARDS...
...IN 4.2 SECONDS!

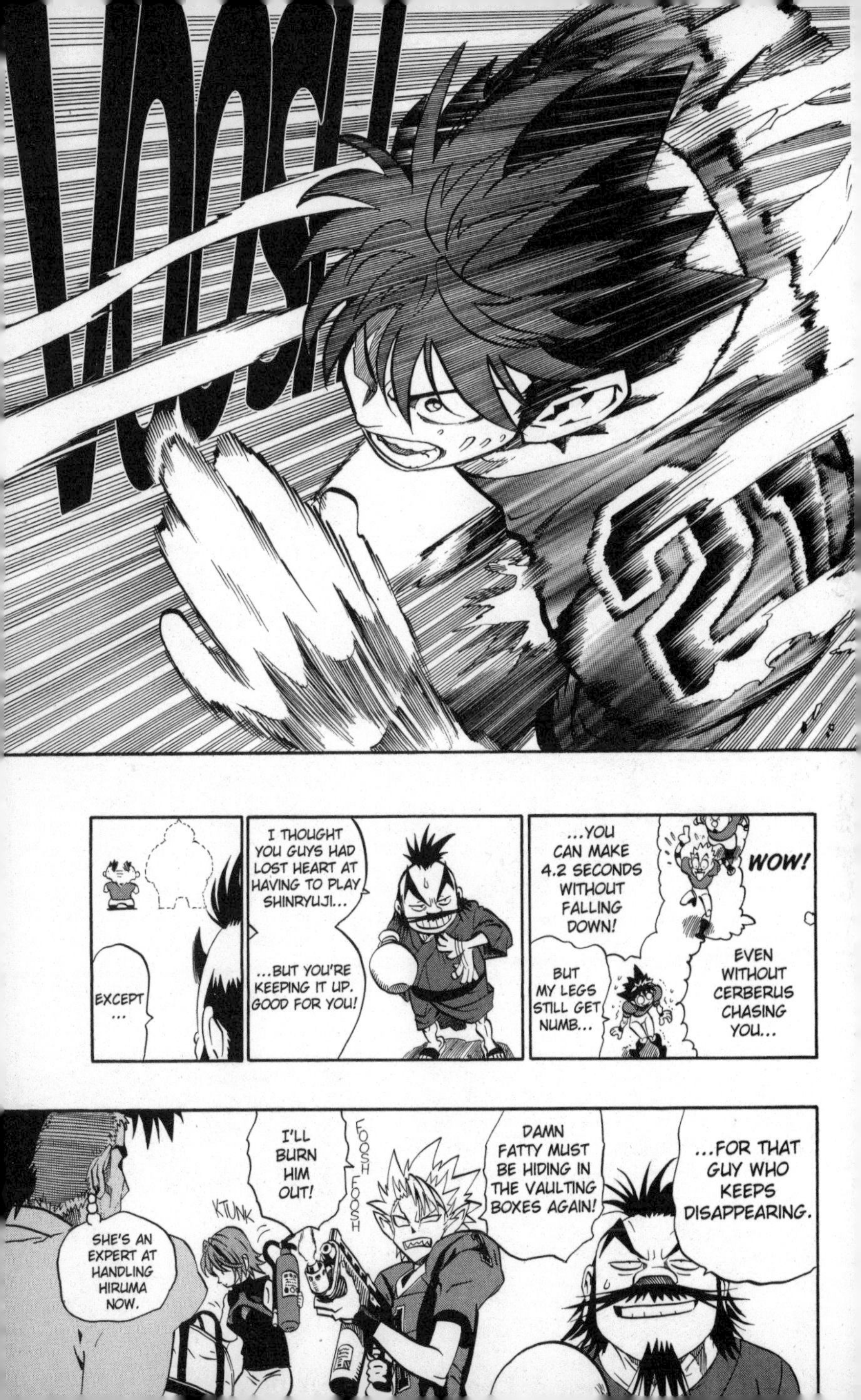
VOOSH
WOW!
EVEN WITHOUT CERBERUS CHASING YOU...
...YOU CAN MAKE 4.2 SECONDS WITHOUT FALLING DOWN!
BUT MY LEGS STILL GET NUMB...
I THOUGHT YOU GUYS HAD LOST HEART AT HAVING TO PLAY SHINRYUJI...
...BUT YOU'RE KEEPING IT UP. GOOD FOR YOU!
EXCEPT ...
...FOR THAT GUY WHO KEEPS DISAPPEARING.
DAMN FATTY MUST BE HIDING IN THE VAULTING BOXES AGAIN!
FOOSH FOOSH
I'LL BURN HIM OUT!
KTUNK
SHE'S AN EXPERT AT HANDLING HIRUMA NOW.

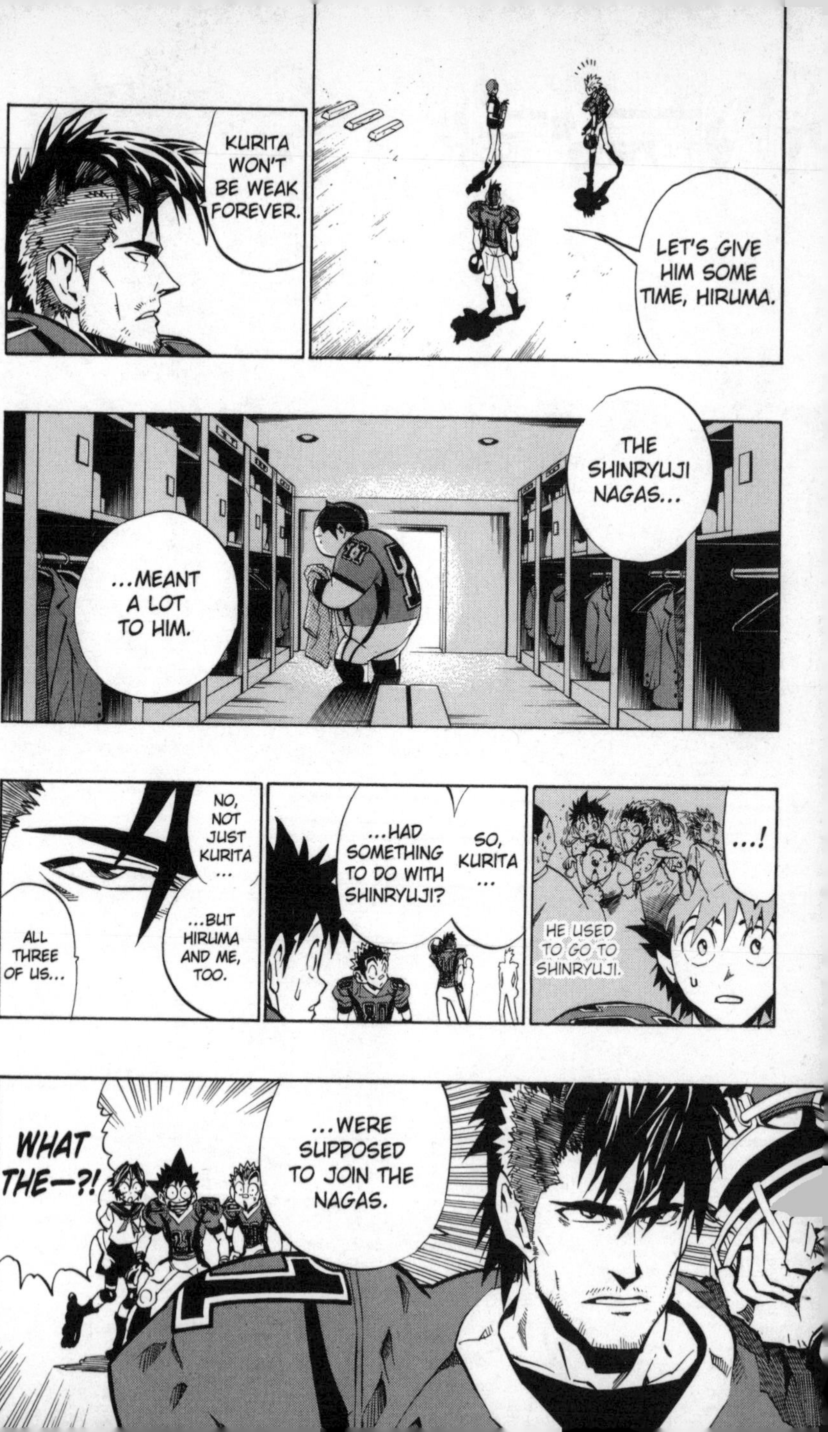
LET'S GIVE HIM SOME TIME, HIRUMA.
KURITA WON'T BE WEAK FOREVER.
THE SHINRYUJI NAGAS...
...MEANT A LOT TO HIM.
...!
HE USED TO GO TO SHINRYUJI.
SO, KURITA...
...HAD SOMETHING TO DO WITH SHINRYUJI?
NO, NOT JUST KURITA...
...BUT HIRUMA AND ME, TOO.
ALL THREE OF US...
...WERE SUPPOSED TO JOIN THE NAGAS.
WHAT THE—?!

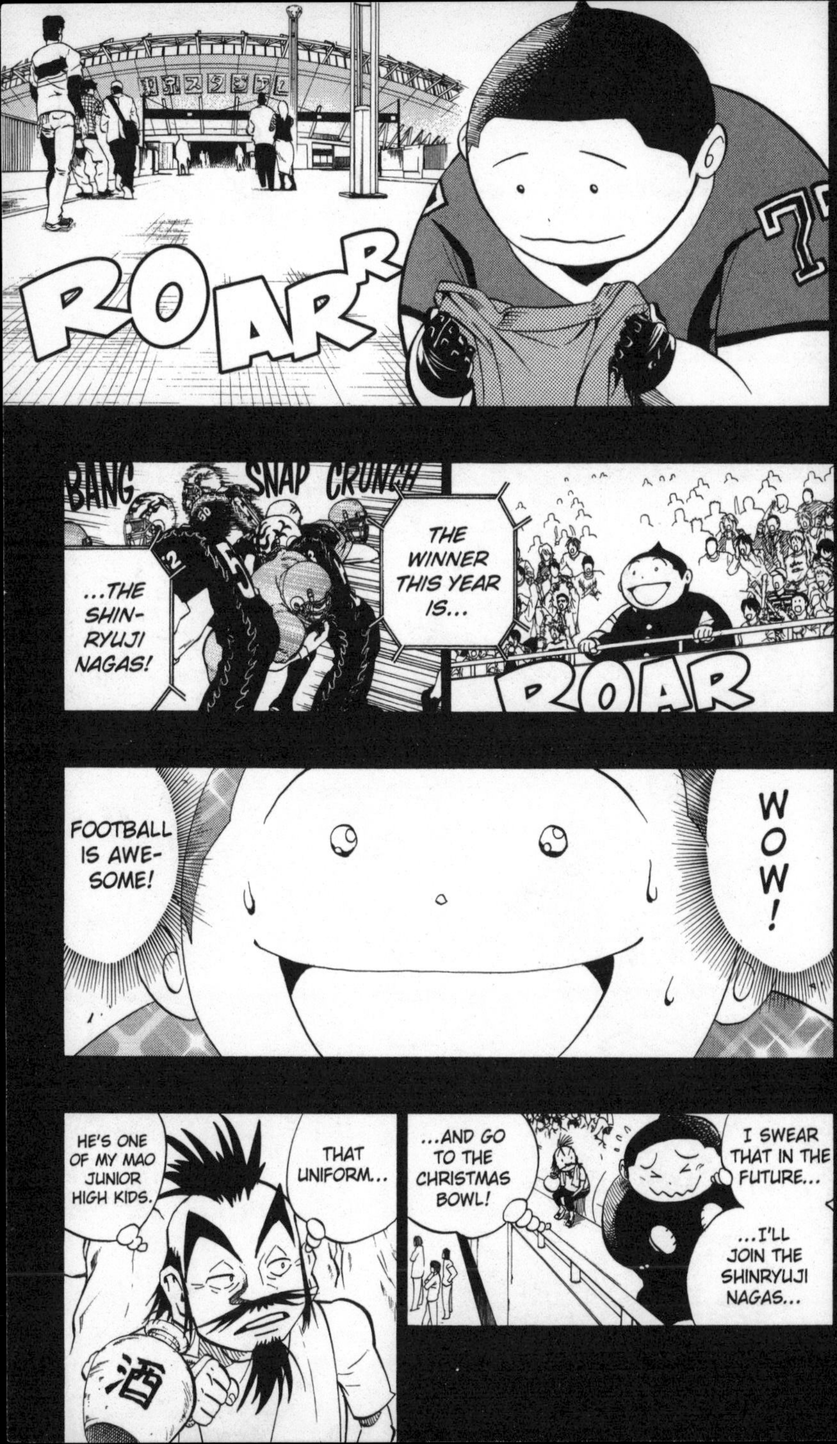

ROARR
THE WINNER THIS YEAR IS...
ROAR
BANG
SNAP
CRUNCH
...THE SHIN-RYUJI NAGAS!
WOW!
FOOTBALL IS AWE-SOME!
I SWEAR THAT IN THE FUTURE...
...I'LL JOIN THE SHINRYUJI NAGAS...
...AND GO TO THE CHRISTMAS BOWL!
THAT UNIFORM...
HE'S ONE OF MY MAO JUNIOR HIGH KIDS.
酒

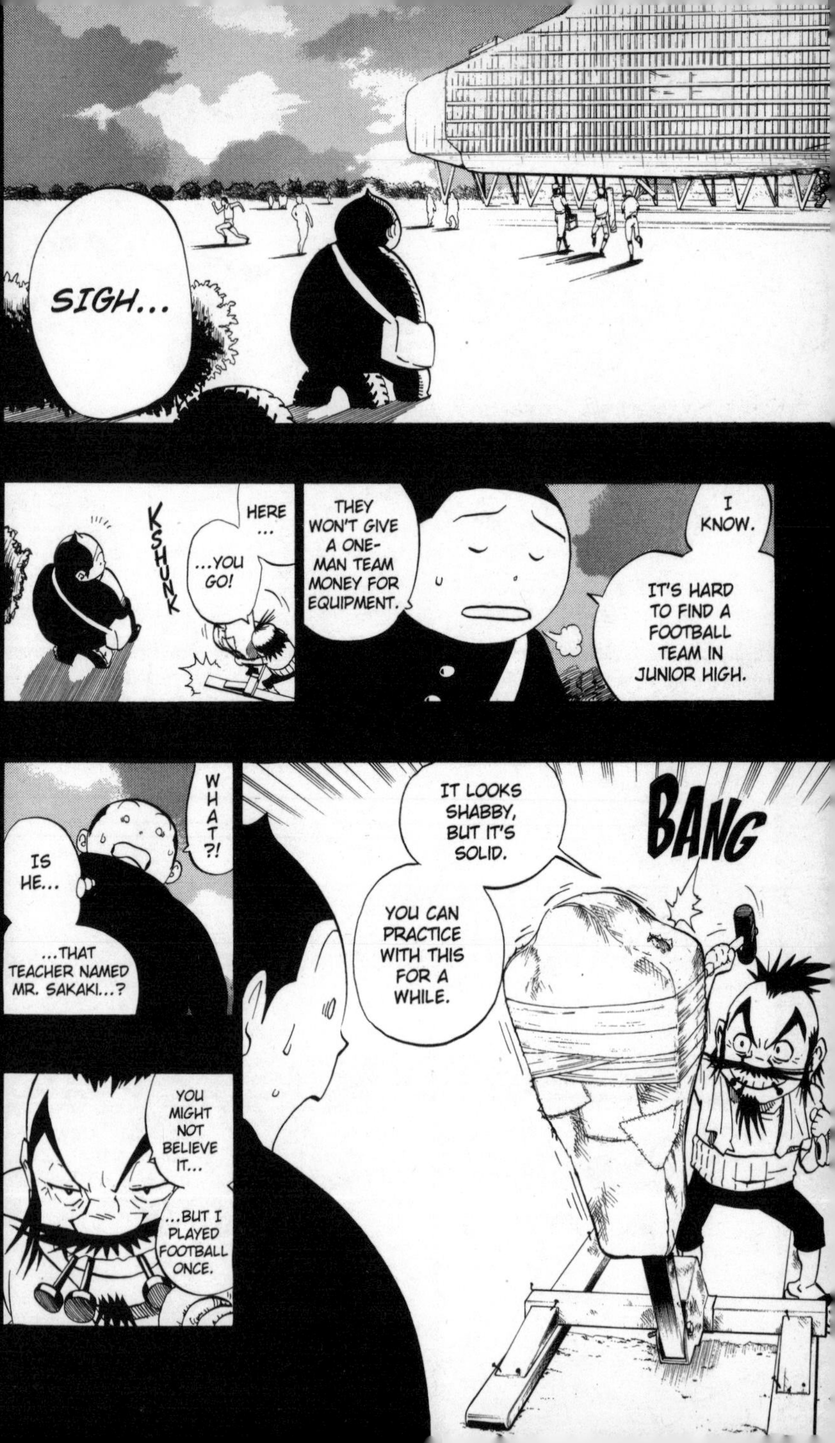
SIGH...
I KNOW.
IT'S HARD TO FIND A FOOTBALL TEAM IN JUNIOR HIGH.
THEY WON'T GIVE A ONE-MAN TEAM MONEY FOR EQUIPMENT.
KSHUNK
HERE...
...YOU GO!
BANG
IT LOOKS SHABBY, BUT IT'S SOLID.
YOU CAN PRACTICE WITH THIS FOR A WHILE.
WHAT?!
IS HE...
...THAT TEACHER NAMED MR. SAKAKI...?
YOU MIGHT NOT BELIEVE IT...
...BUT I PLAYED FOOTBALL ONCE.

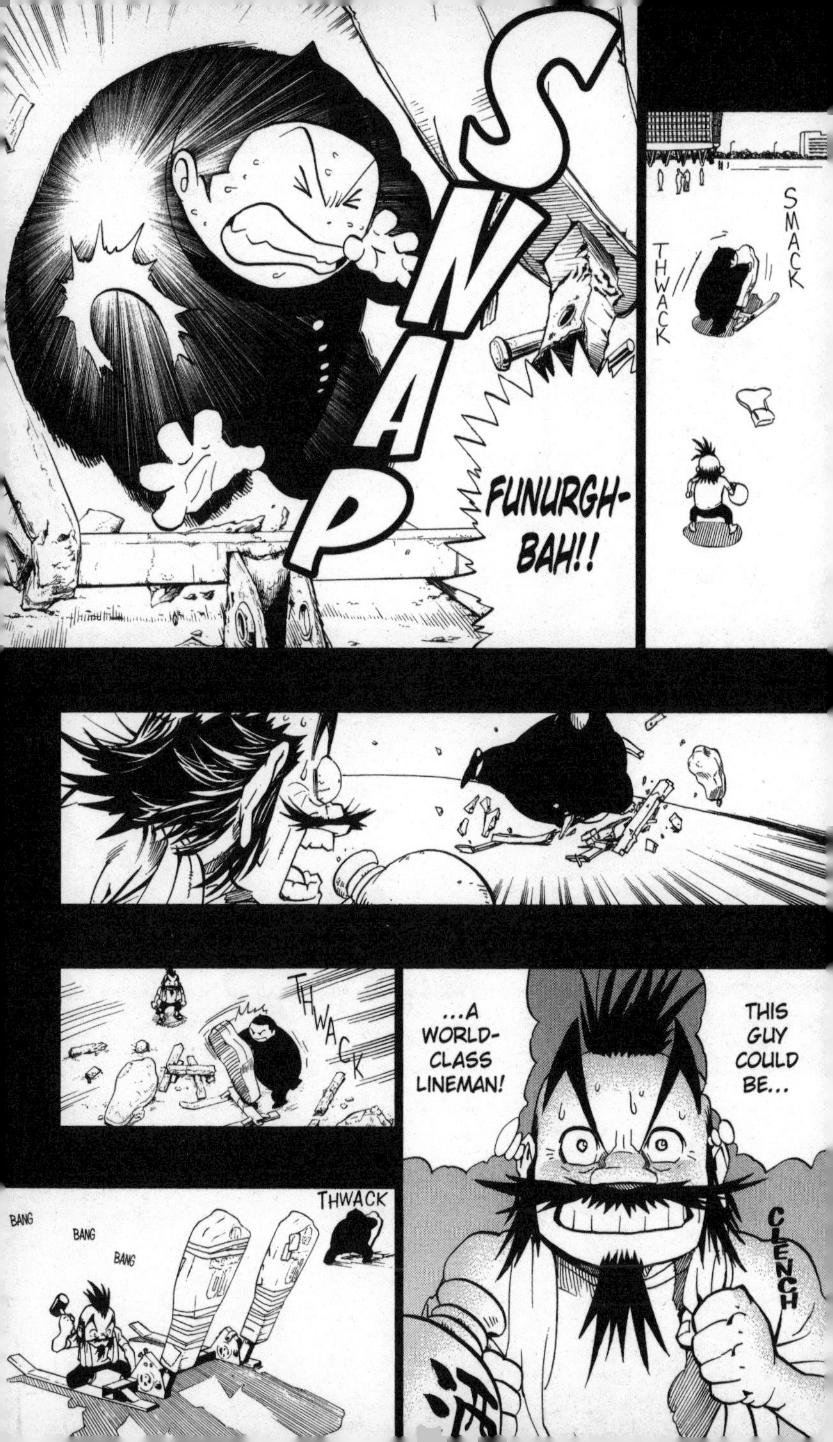
SMACK
THWACK
SNAP
FUNURGH-BAH!!
THIS GUY COULD BE...
...A WORLD-CLASS LINEMAN!
CLENCH
THWACK
THWACK
BANG
BANG
BANG

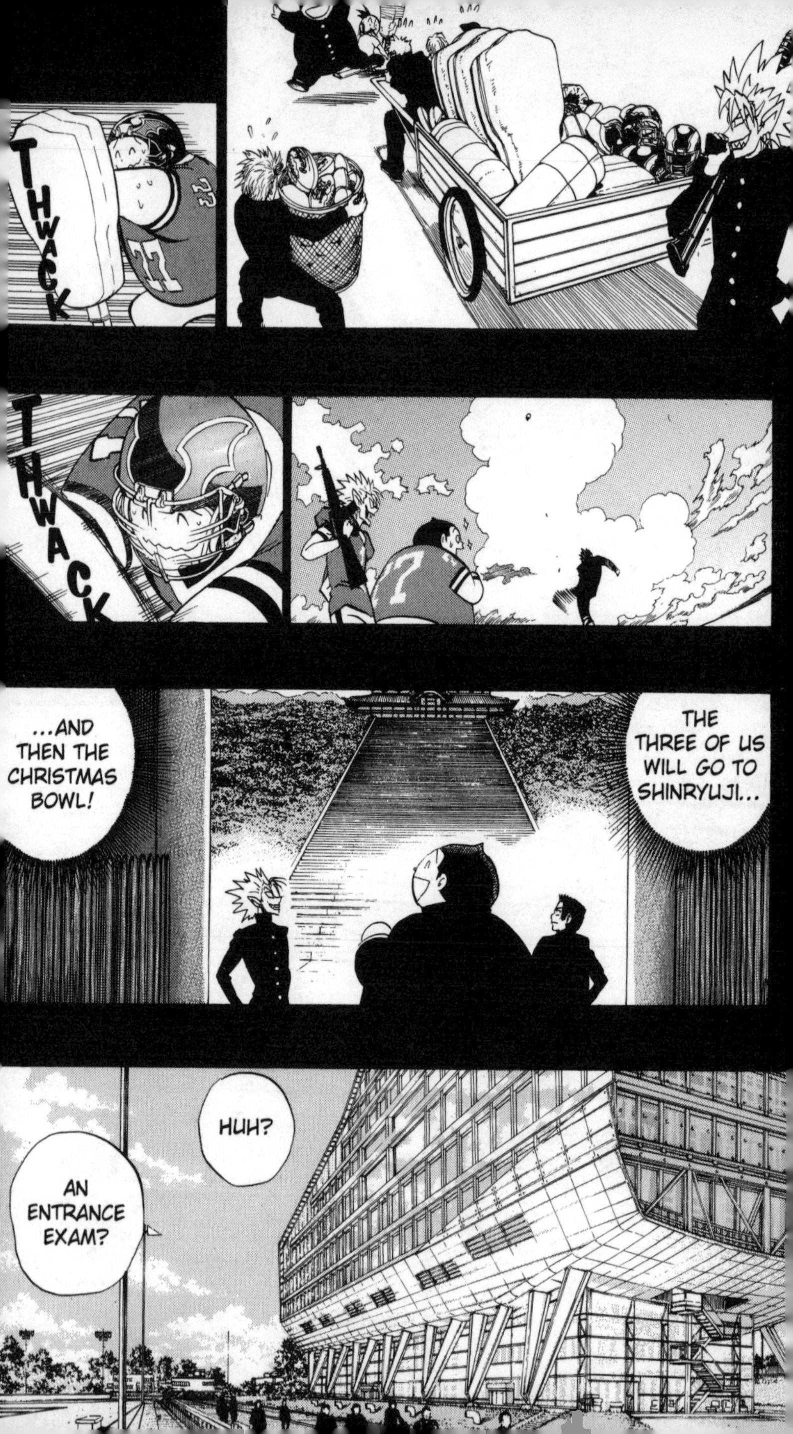
THWACK
THWACK
THE THREE OF US WILL GO TO SHINRYUJI...
...AND THEN THE CHRISTMAS BOWL!
HUH?
AN ENTRANCE EXAM?

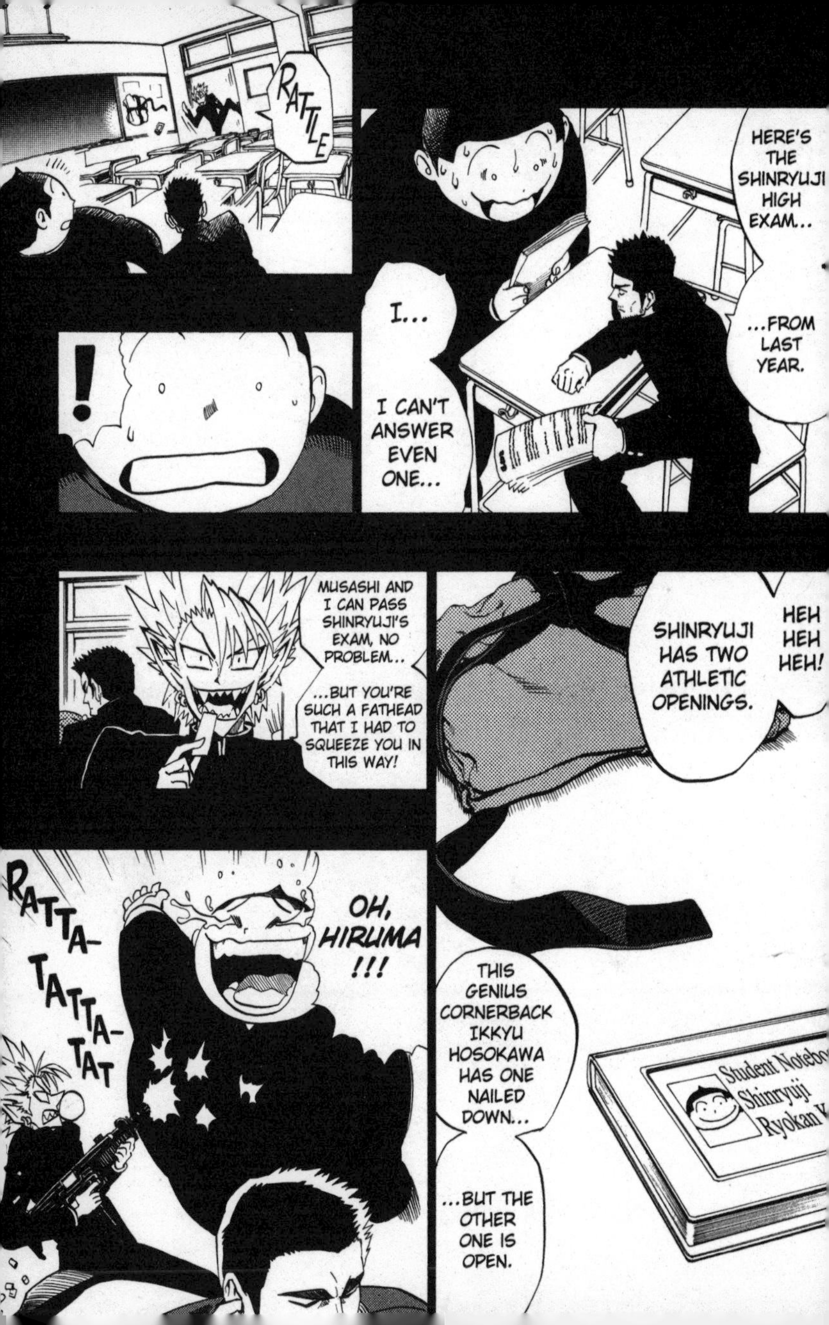
HERE'S THE SHINRYUJI HIGH EXAM...
...FROM LAST YEAR.
I...
I CAN'T ANSWER EVEN ONE...
RATTLE
!
HEH HEH HEH!
SHINRYUJI HAS TWO ATHLETIC OPENINGS.
THIS GENIUS CORNERBACK IKKYU HOSOKAWA HAS ONE NAILED DOWN...
...BUT THE OTHER ONE IS OPEN.
Shinryuji
MUSASHI AND I CAN PASS SHINRYUJI'S EXAM, NO PROBLEM...
...BUT YOU'RE SUCH A FATHEAD THAT I HAD TO SQUEEZE YOU IN THIS WAY!
OH, HIRUMA!!!
RATTA-TATTA-TAT

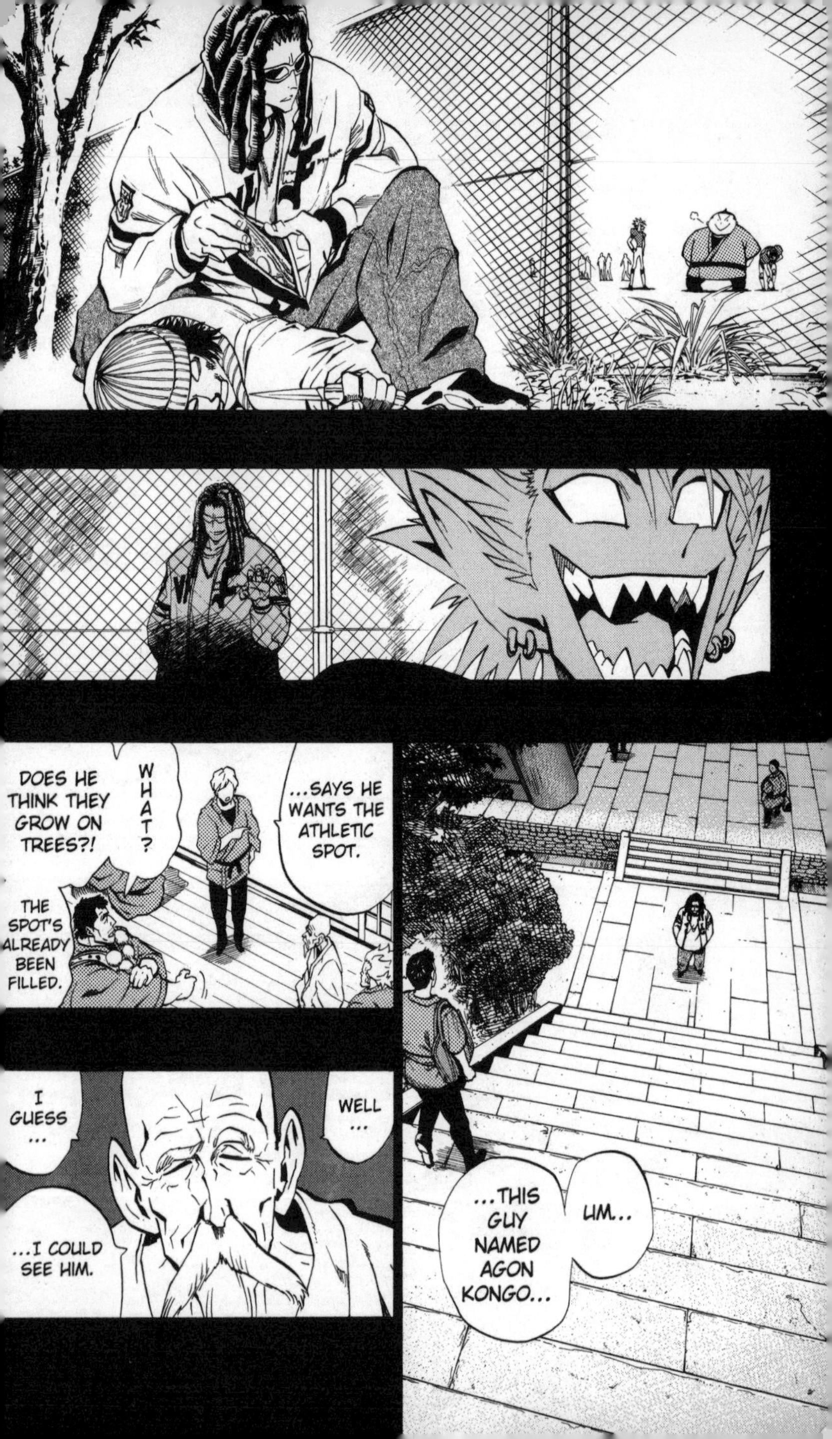
UM...
...THIS GUY NAMED AGON KONGO...
...SAYS HE WANTS THE ATHLETIC SPOT.
WHAT?
DOES HE THINK THEY GROW ON TREES?!
THE SPOT'S ALREADY BEEN FILLED.
WELL...
I GUESS...
...I COULD SEE HIM.

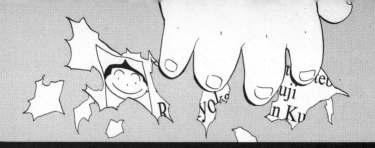

SWSH

WHAT A CREEPY FATSO!

FOR REAL?!

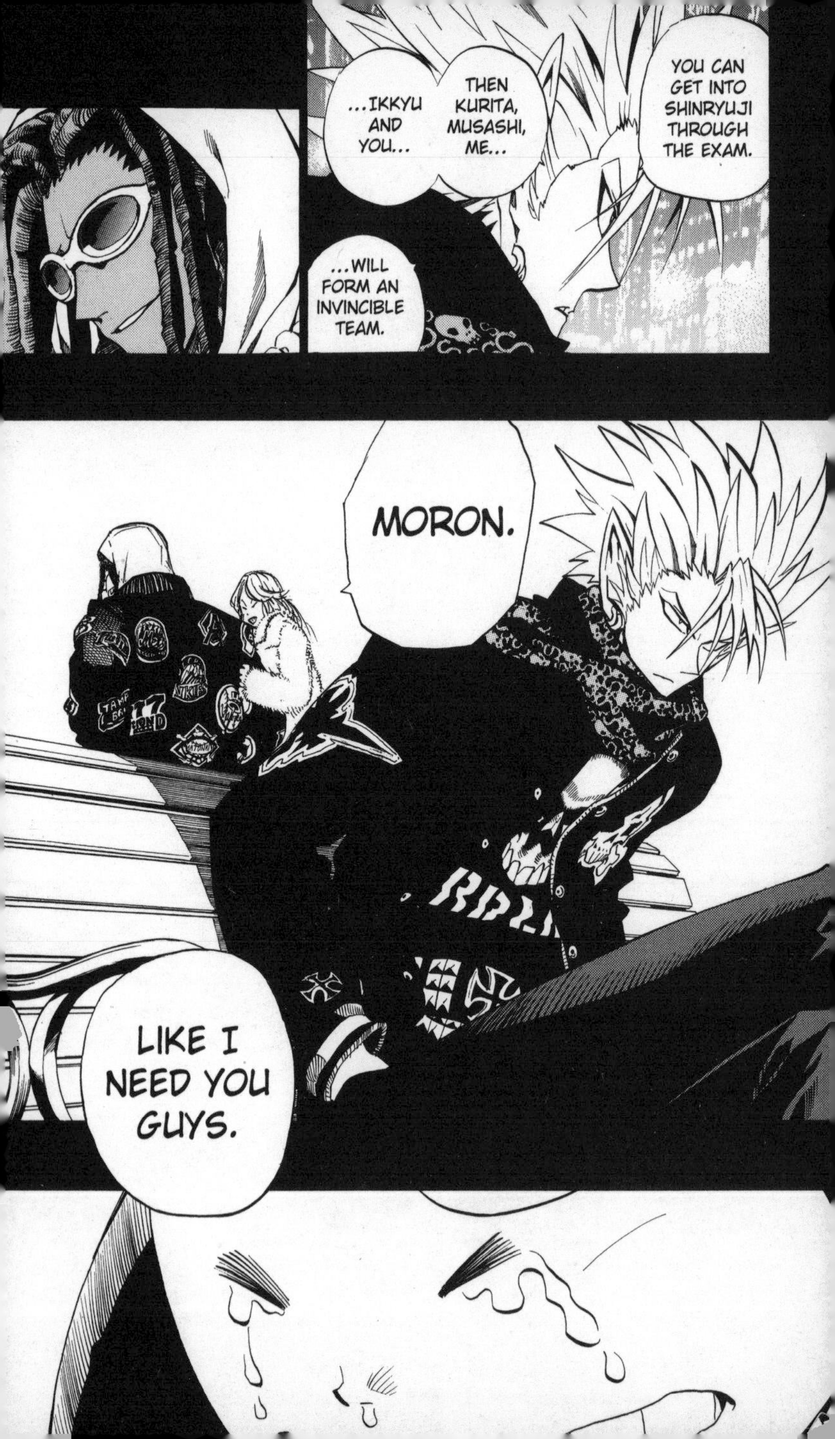
YOU CAN GET INTO SHINRYUJI THROUGH THE EXAM.
THEN KURITA, MUSASHI, ME...
...IKKYU AND YOU...
...WILL FORM AN INVINCIBLE TEAM.
MORON.
LIKE I NEED YOU GUYS.

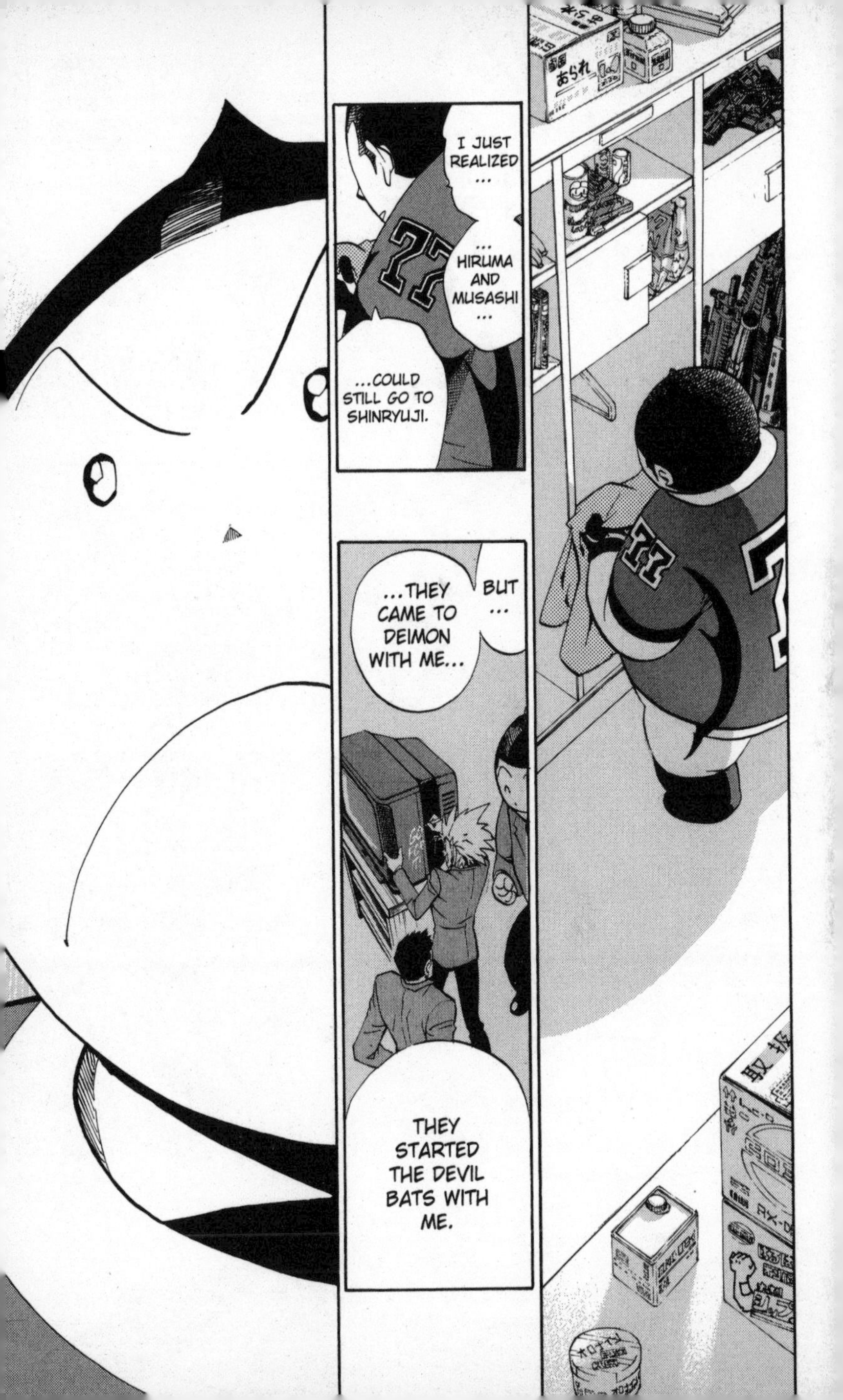
I JUST REALIZED ...
... HIRUMA AND MUSASHI ...
...COULD STILL GO TO SHINRYUJI.
BUT ...
...THEY CAME TO DEIMON WITH ME...
THEY STARTED THE DEVIL BATS WITH ME.

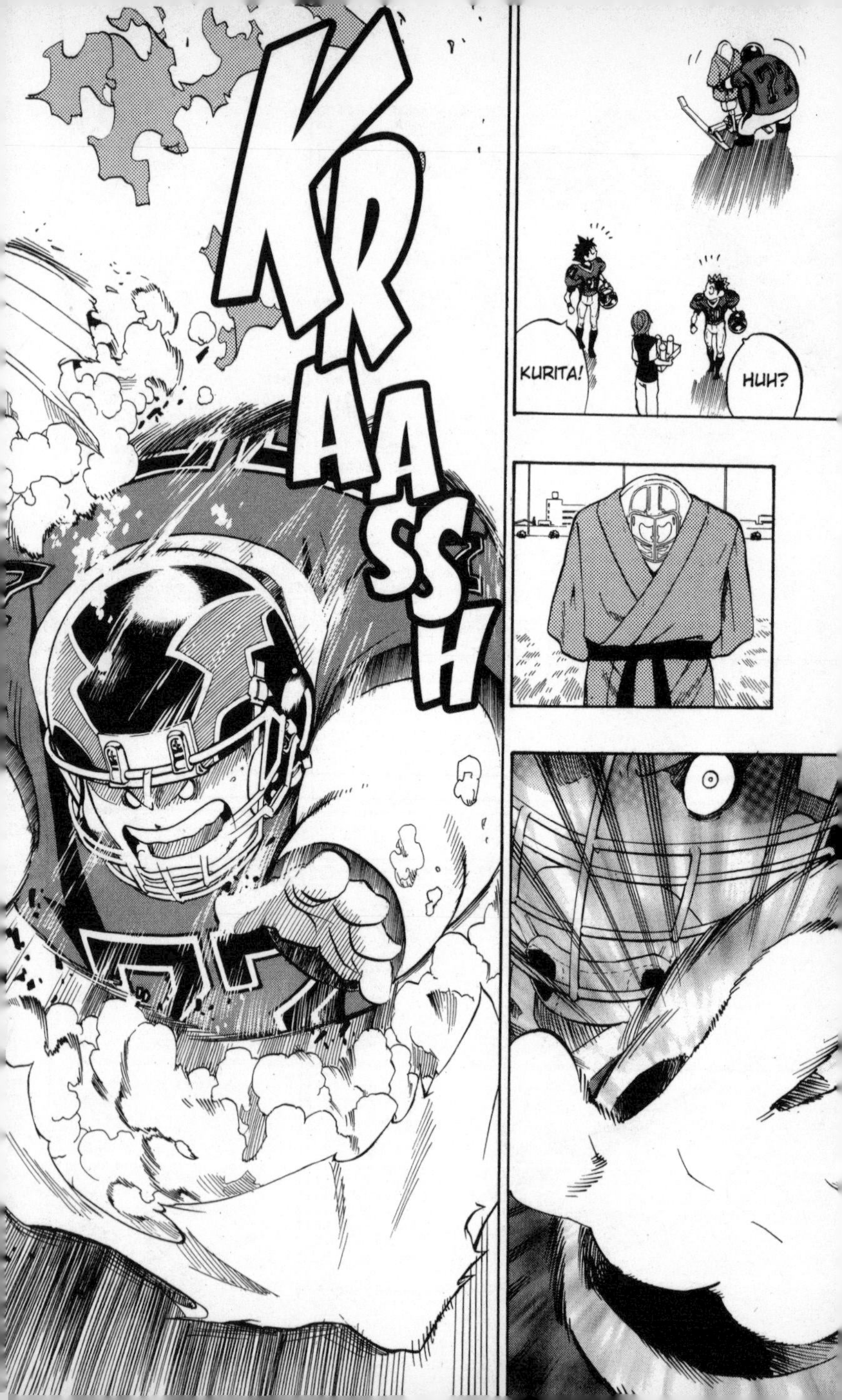
KURITA!
HUH?
KRAASH

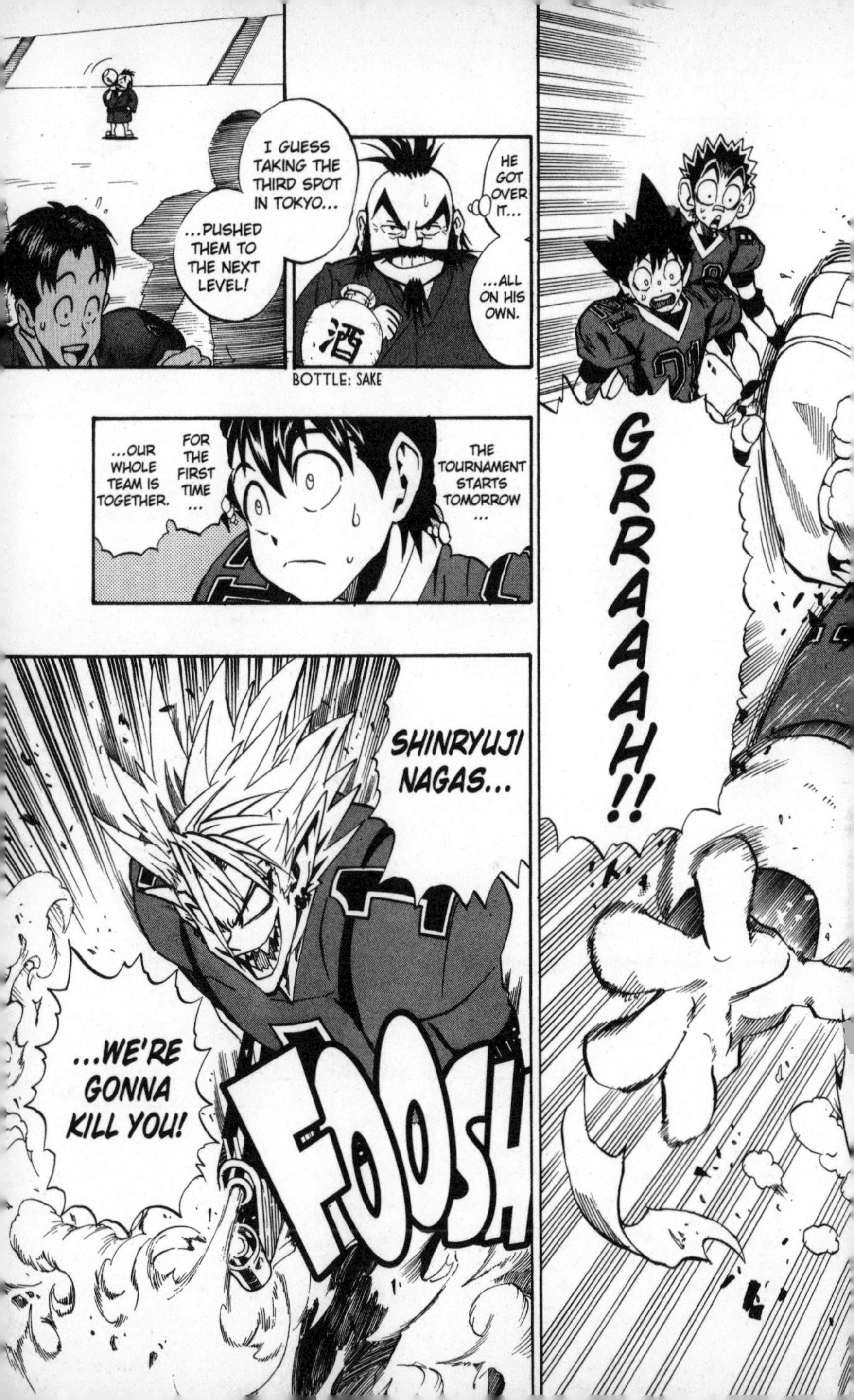
GRRAAAAH!!
HE GOT OVER IT...
...ALL ON HIS OWN.
I GUESS TAKING THE THIRD SPOT IN TOKYO...
...PUSHED THEM TO THE NEXT LEVEL!
酒
BOTTLE: SAKE
THE TOURNAMENT STARTS TOMORROW...
FOR THE FIRST TIME...
...OUR WHOLE TEAM IS TOGETHER.
SHINRYUJI NAGAS...
FOOSH
...WE'RE GONNA KILL YOU!

RIKO KUMABUKURO'S INTERVIEW 8

# EXTRA QUESTION

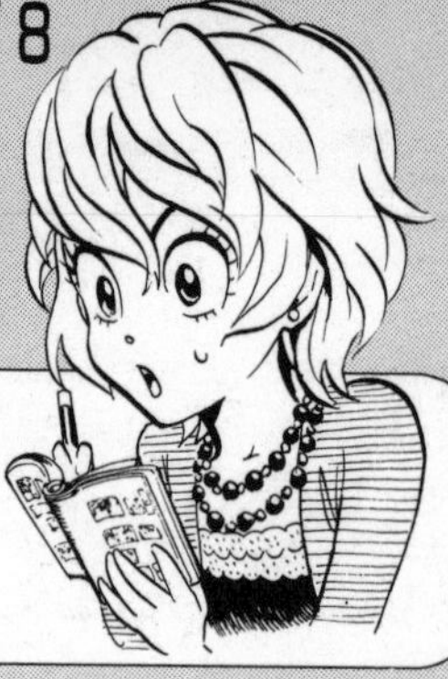

WHAT'S THE MOST YOU'VE EVER PAID FOR SOMETHING?

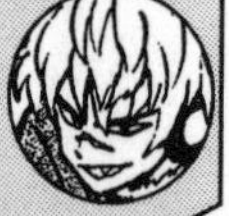

Kamiya

FOR RARE SHOES.

$1,500 [150,000 YEN]

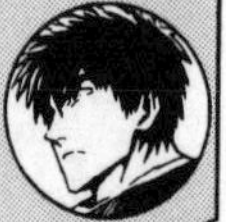

Shin

FOR BREAKING A VENDING MACHINE.

$200 [20,000 YEN]

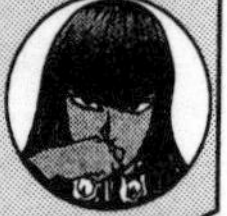

Harao

FOR A RACING CAMEL.

$300,000 [30,000,000 YEN]

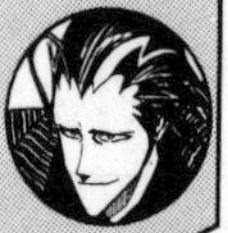

Maruko

FOR AN ARMANI SUIT.

$2,500 [250,000 YEN]

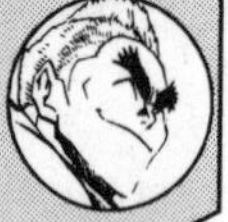

Iwashige

FOR DUMBBELLS.

$400 [40,000 YEN]

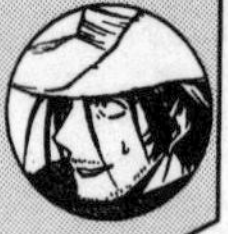

The Kid

FOR A FRIDGE FOR MY BACHELOR PAD.

$300 [30,000 YEN]

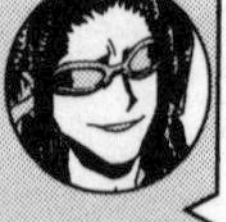

Agon

I ALWAYS MAKE SOME GIRL PAY, SO I'VE NEVER BOUGHT ANYTHING EXPENSIVE.

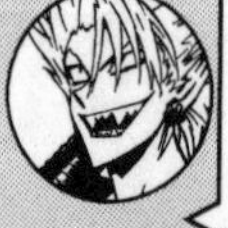

Hiruma

FOR AN ISLAND.

$?

# Chapter 172 The Lion and the Rabbit

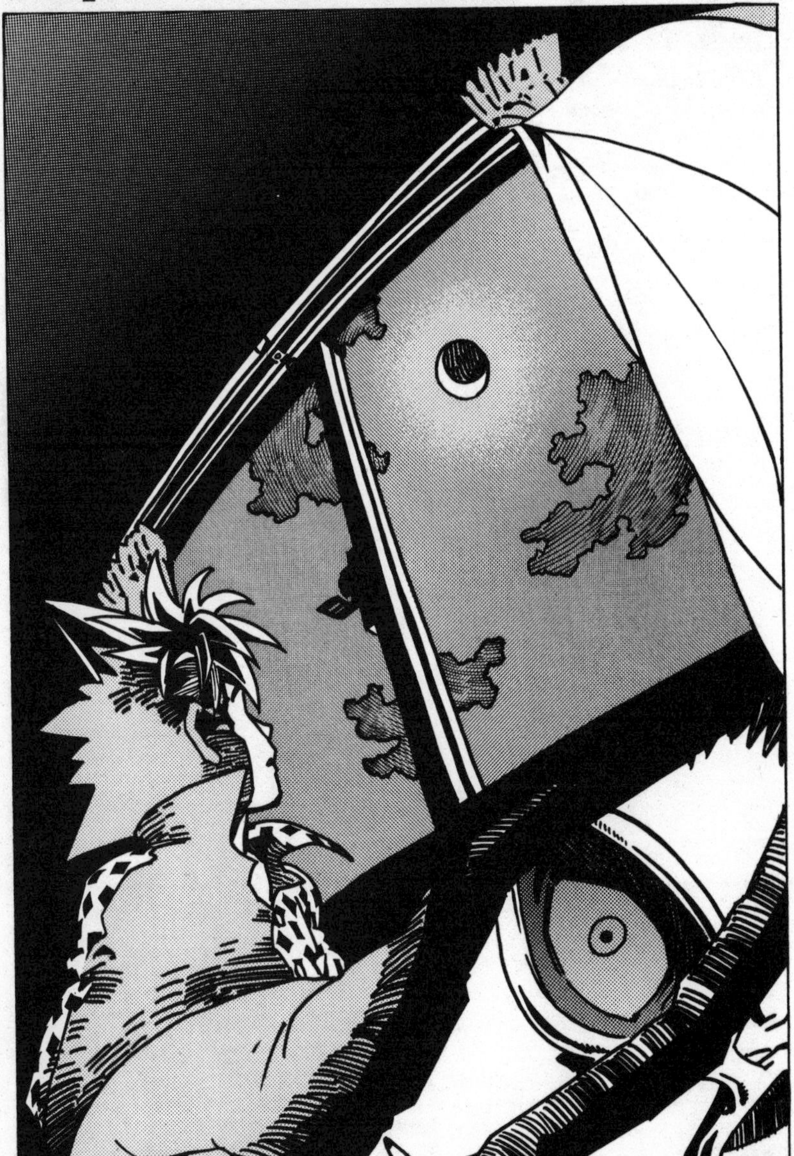

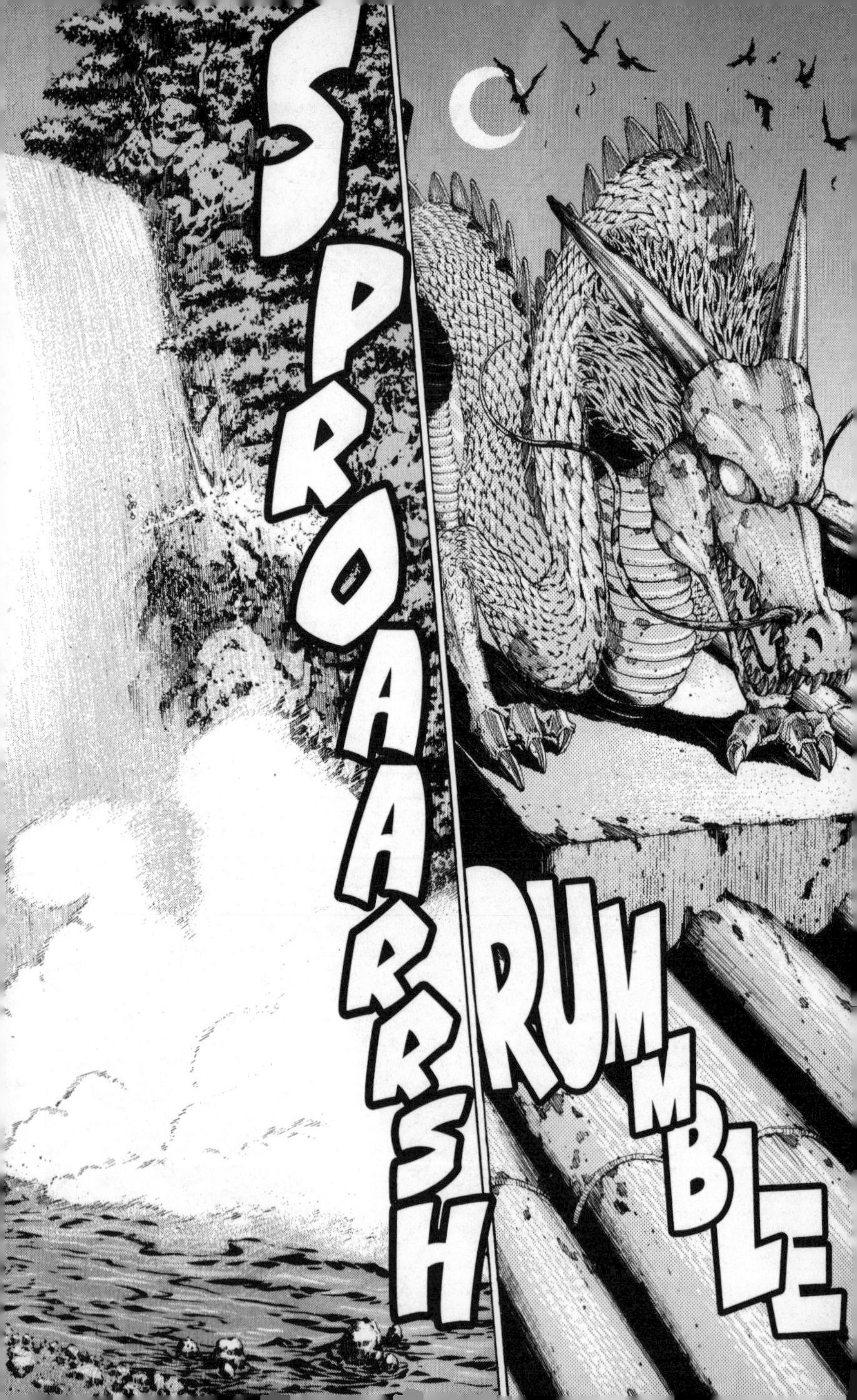
RUMMBLE
SPROAARRSH

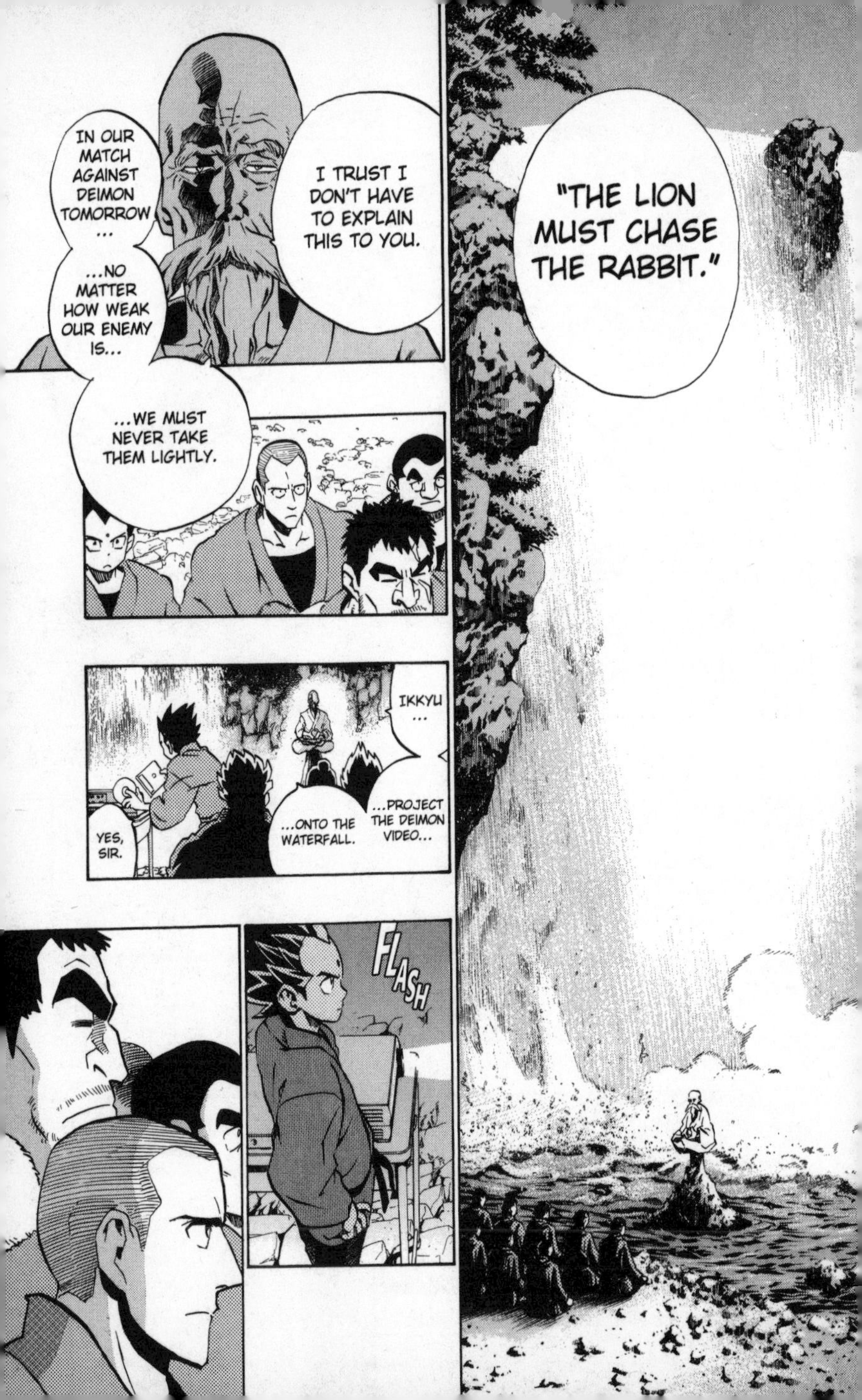
"THE LION MUST CHASE THE RABBIT."
I TRUST I DON'T HAVE TO EXPLAIN THIS TO YOU.
IN OUR MATCH AGAINST DEIMON TOMORROW...
...NO MATTER HOW WEAK OUR ENEMY IS...
...WE MUST NEVER TAKE THEM LIGHTLY.
IKKYU...
...PROJECT THE DEIMON VIDEO...
...ONTO THE WATERFALL.
YES, SIR.
FLASH

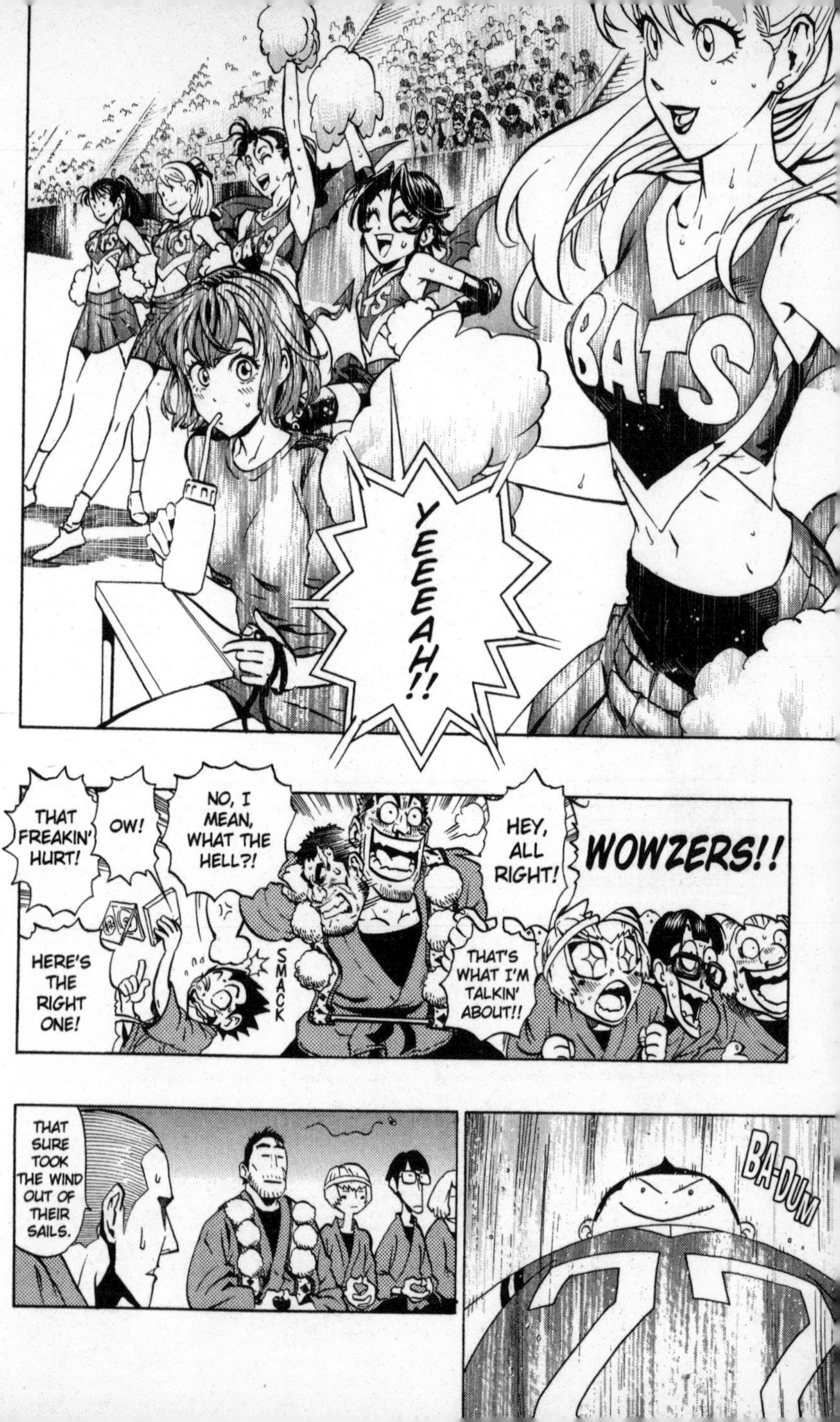
YEEEAH!!
WOWZERS!!
HEY, ALL RIGHT!
THAT'S WHAT I'M TALKIN' ABOUT!!
NO, I MEAN, WHAT THE HELL?!
SMACK
OW!
THAT FREAKIN' HURT!
HERE'S THE RIGHT ONE!
BA-DUM
THAT SURE TOOK THE WIND OUT OF THEIR SAILS.

READ THIS WAY

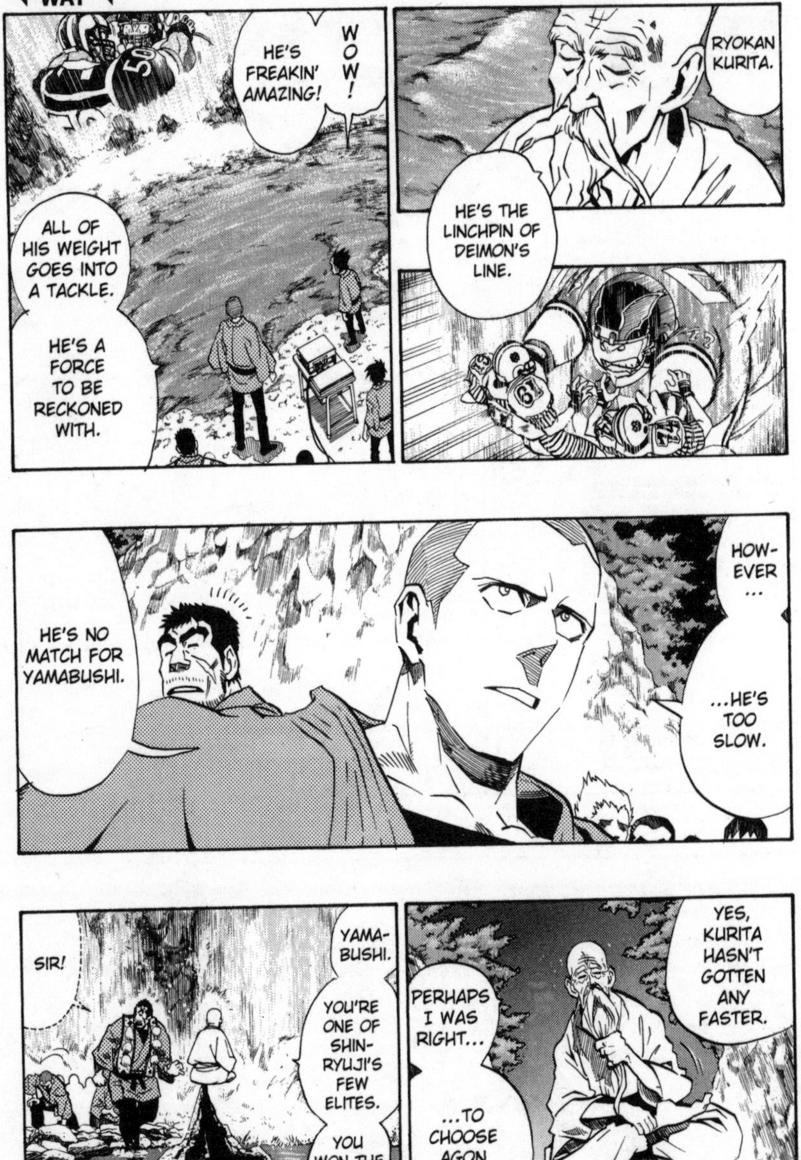
RYOKAN KURITA.
HE'S THE LINCHPIN OF DEIMON'S LINE.
WOW!
HE'S FREAKIN' AMAZING!
ALL OF HIS WEIGHT GOES INTO A TACKLE.
HE'S A FORCE TO BE RECKONED WITH.
HOW-EVER...
...HE'S TOO SLOW.
HE'S NO MATCH FOR YAMABUSHI.
YES, KURITA HASN'T GOTTEN ANY FASTER.
PERHAPS I WAS RIGHT...
...TO CHOOSE AGON INSTEAD.
YAMA-BUSHI.
YOU'RE ONE OF SHIN-RYUJI'S FEW ELITES.
YOU WON THE ATHLETIC SPOT.
SIR!

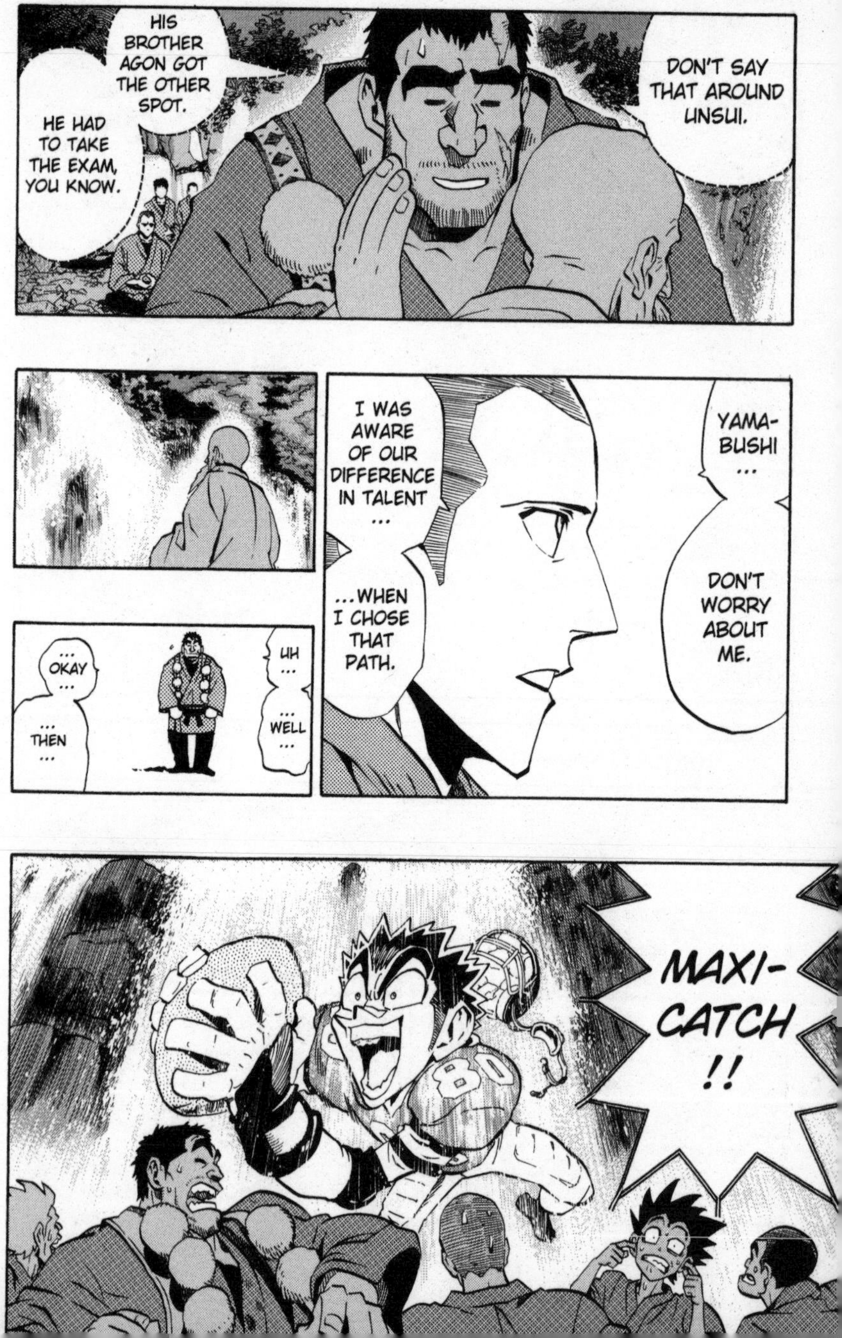
DON'T SAY THAT AROUND UNSUI.
HIS BROTHER AGON GOT THE OTHER SPOT.
HE HAD TO TAKE THE EXAM, YOU KNOW.
YAMA-BUSHI ...
DON'T WORRY ABOUT ME.
I WAS AWARE OF OUR DIFFERENCE IN TALENT ...
...WHEN I CHOSE THAT PATH.
UH ...
... WELL ...
... OKAY ...
... THEN ...
MAXI-CATCH !!

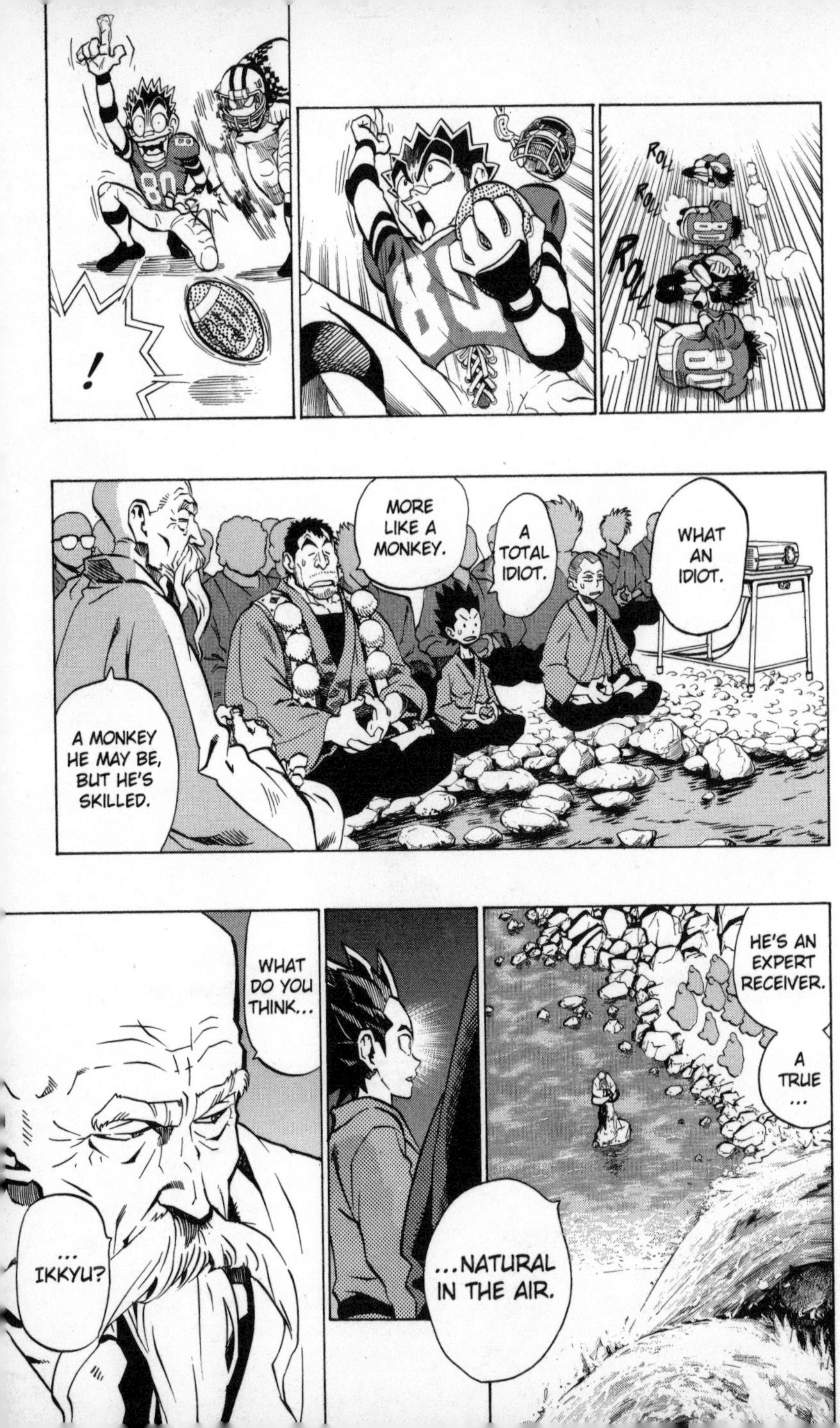
ROLL
ROLL
ROLL
!
WHAT AN IDIOT.
A TOTAL IDIOT.
MORE LIKE A MONKEY.
A MONKEY HE MAY BE, BUT HE'S SKILLED.
HE'S AN EXPERT RECEIVER.
A TRUE ...
...NATURAL IN THE AIR.
WHAT DO YOU THINK...
...IKKYU?

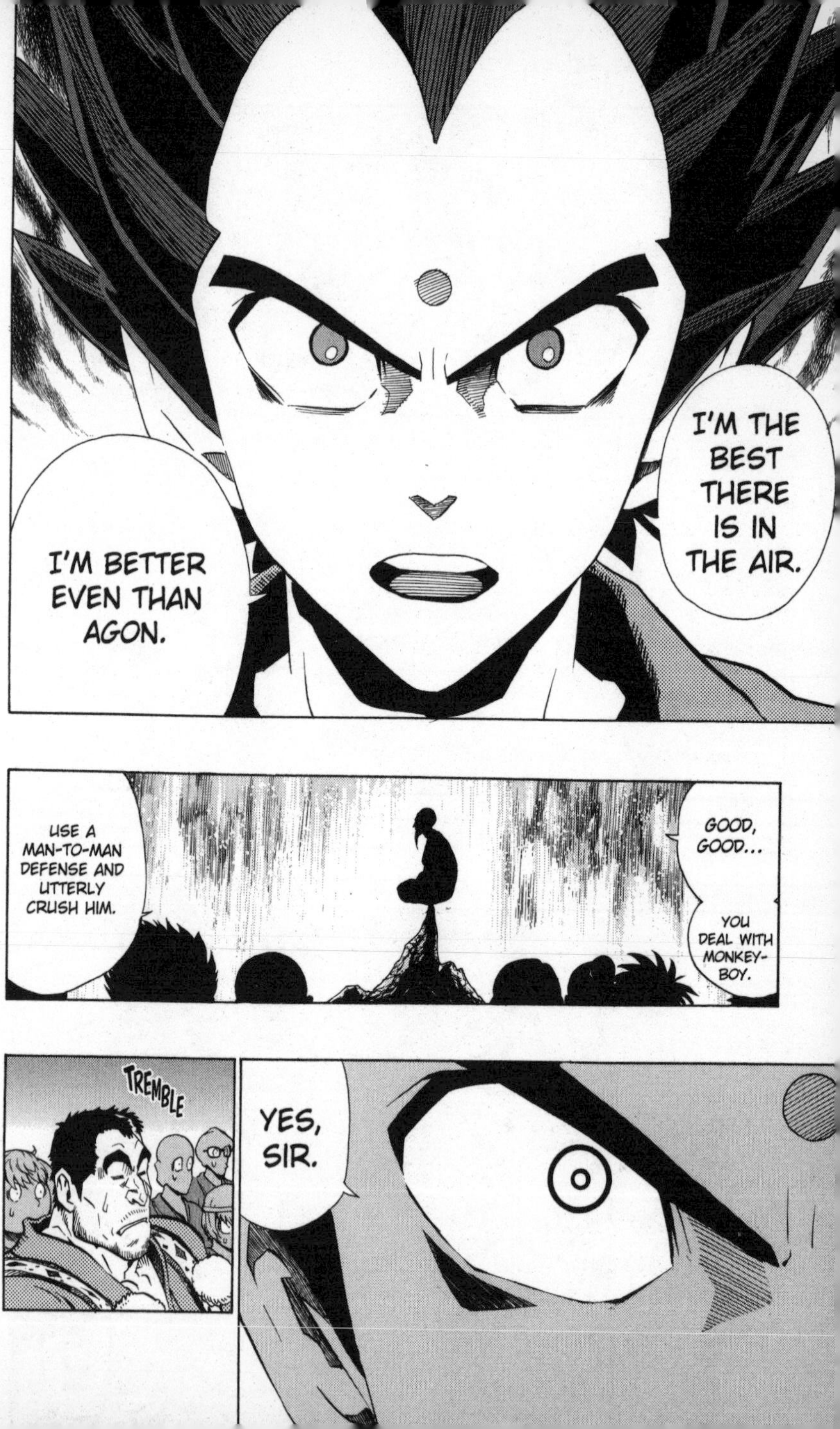
I'M THE BEST THERE IS IN THE AIR.
I'M BETTER EVEN THAN AGON.
GOOD, GOOD...
YOU DEAL WITH MONKEY-BOY.
USE A MAN-TO-MAN DEFENSE AND UTTERLY CRUSH HIM.
YES, SIR.
TREMBLE

READ THIS WAY

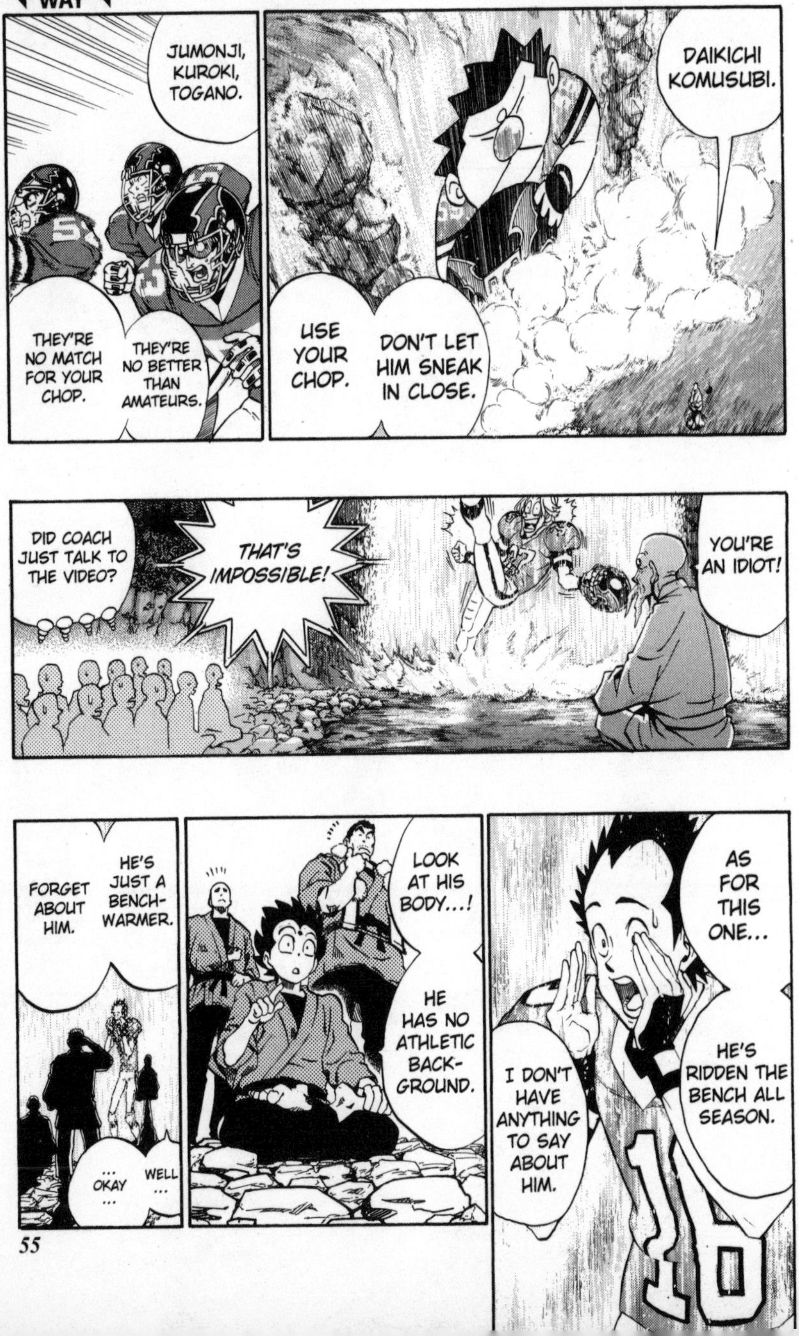

DAIKICHI KOMUSUBI.
DON'T LET HIM SNEAK IN CLOSE.
USE YOUR CHOP.
JUMONJI, KUROKI, TOGANO.
THEY'RE NO BETTER THAN AMATEURS.
THEY'RE NO MATCH FOR YOUR CHOP.
YOU'RE AN IDIOT!
THAT'S IMPOSSIBLE!
DID COACH JUST TALK TO THE VIDEO?
AS FOR THIS ONE...
HE'S RIDDEN THE BENCH ALL SEASON.
I DON'T HAVE ANYTHING TO SAY ABOUT HIM.
LOOK AT HIS BODY...!
HE HAS NO ATHLETIC BACKGROUND.
HE'S JUST A BENCH-WARMER.
FORGET ABOUT HIM.
WELL...
...OKAY...

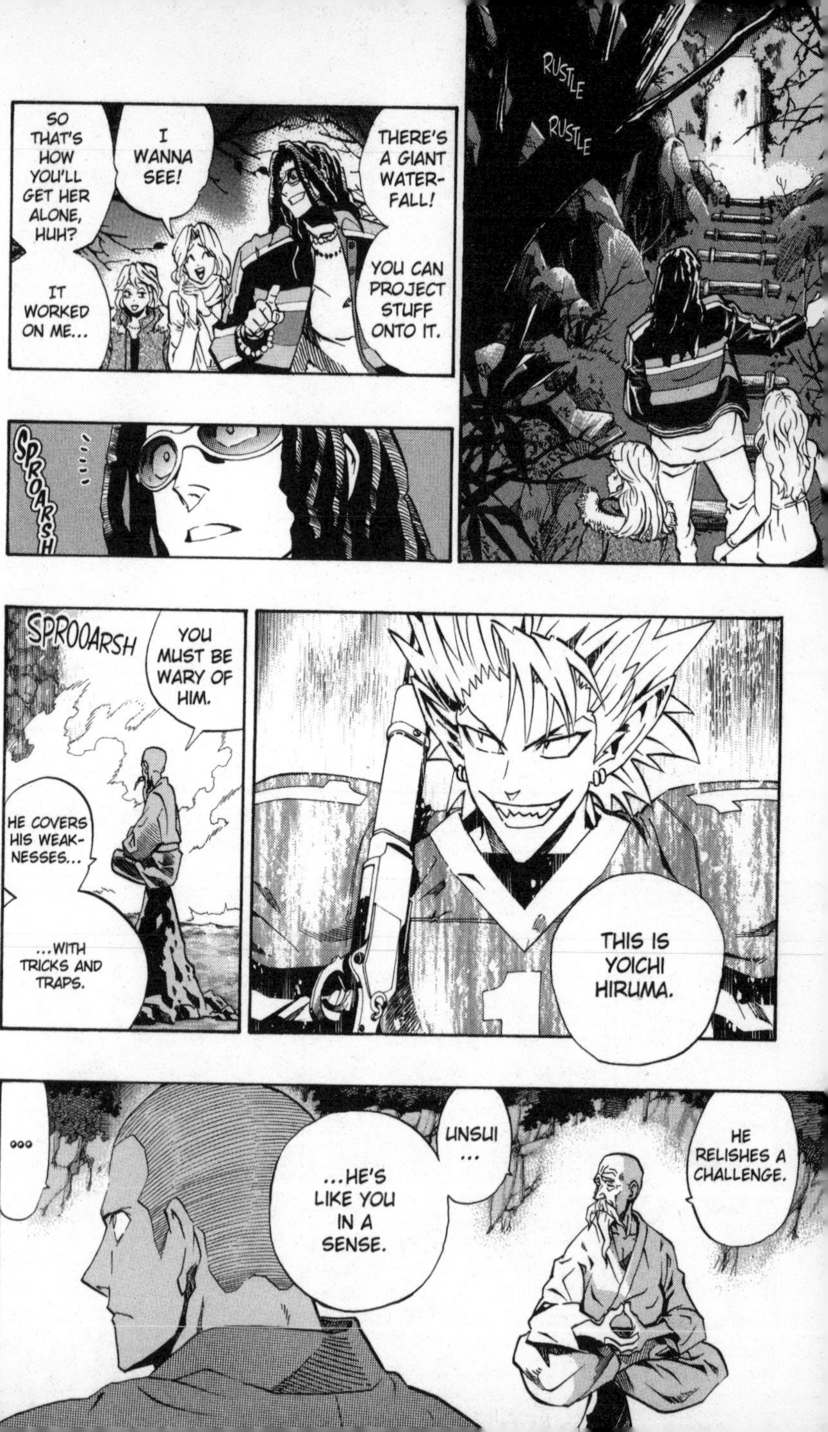
RUSTLE
RUSTLE
THERE'S A GIANT WATER-FALL!
YOU CAN PROJECT STUFF ONTO IT.
I WANNA SEE!
SO THAT'S HOW YOU'LL GET HER ALONE, HUH?
IT WORKED ON ME...
...
SPROARSH
THIS IS YOICHI HIRUMA.
YOU MUST BE WARY OF HIM.
SPROOARSH
HE COVERS HIS WEAK-NESSES...
...WITH TRICKS AND TRAPS.
HE RELISHES A CHALLENGE.
UNSUI...
...HE'S LIKE YOU IN A SENSE.
...

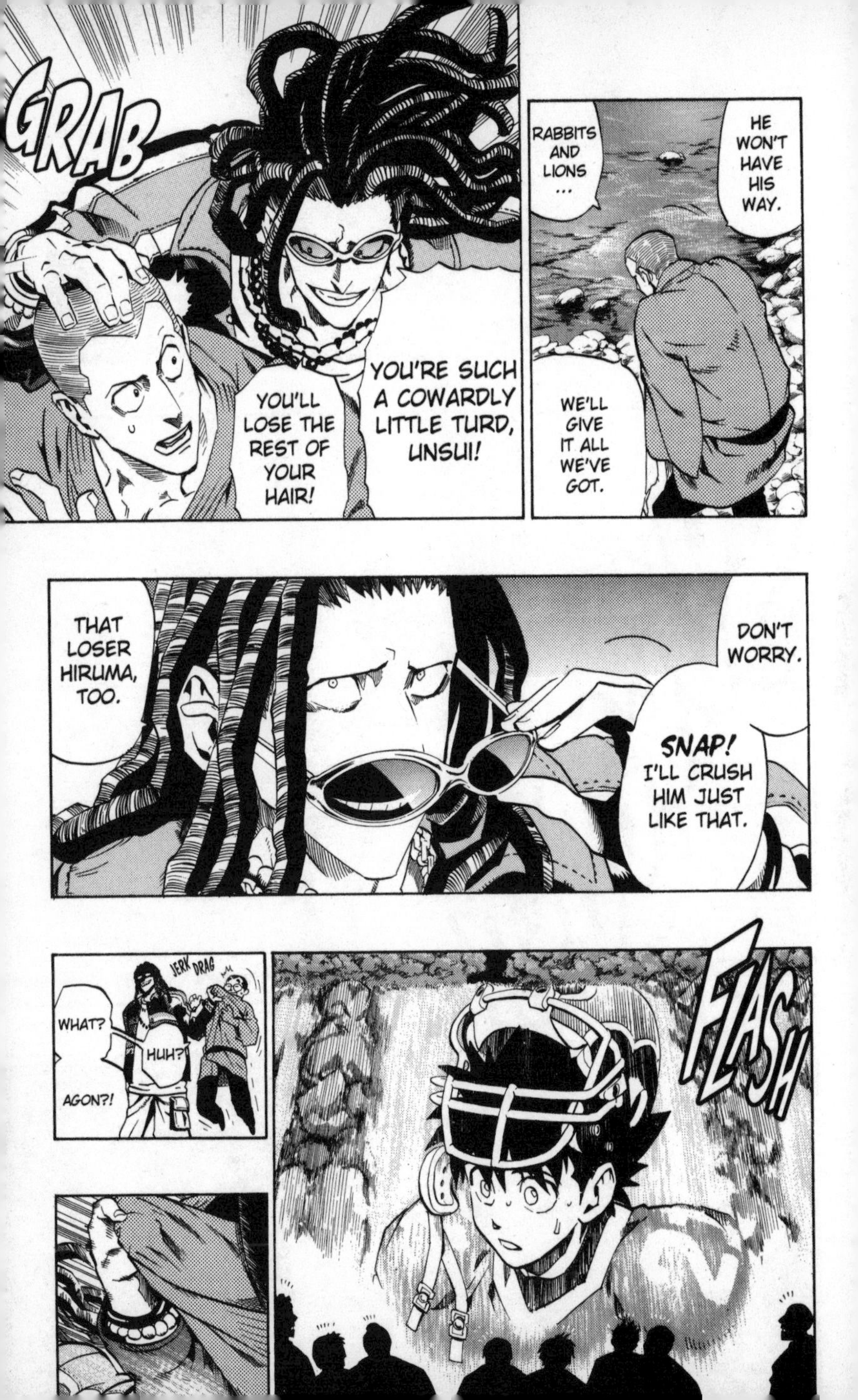
HE WON'T HAVE HIS WAY.
RABBITS AND LIONS ...
WE'LL GIVE IT ALL WE'VE GOT.
GRAB
YOU'RE SUCH A COWARDLY LITTLE TURD, UNSUI!
YOU'LL LOSE THE REST OF YOUR HAIR!
DON'T WORRY.
THAT LOSER HIRUMA, TOO.
SNAP! I'LL CRUSH HIM JUST LIKE THAT.
FLASH
JERK
DRAG
WHAT?
HUH?
AGON?!

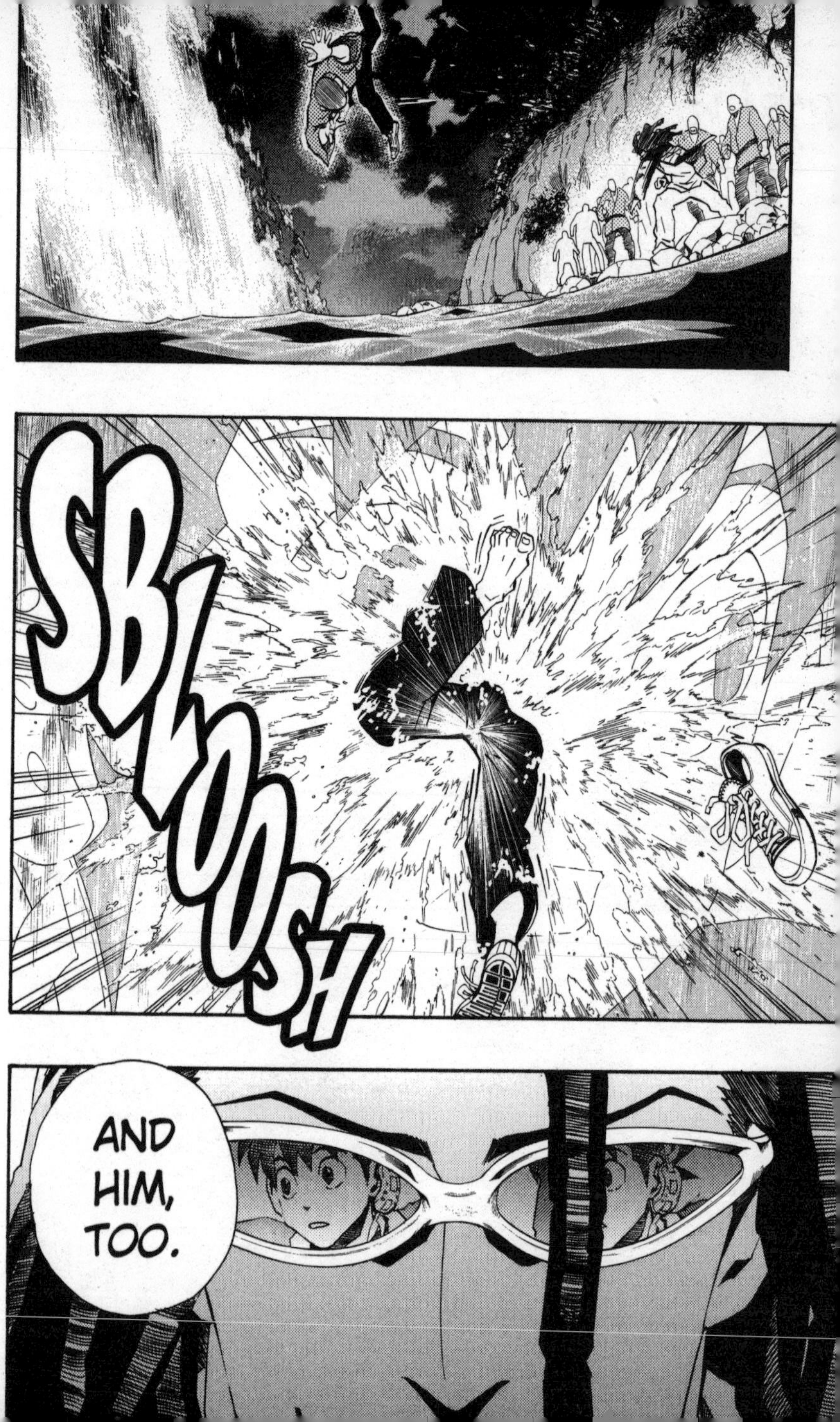
SBLOOOSH
AND HIM, TOO.

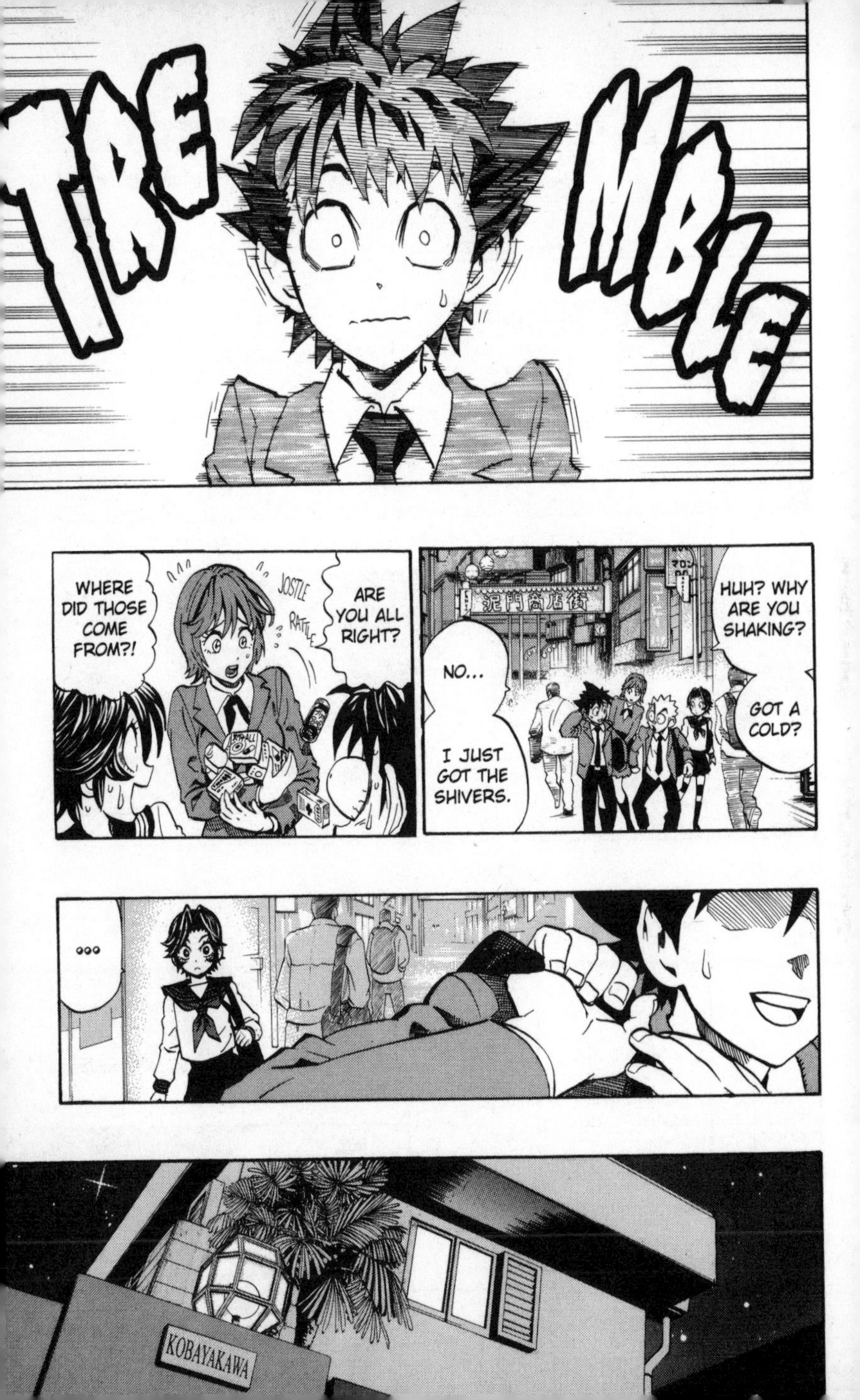
TREMBLE
泥門商店街
HUH? WHY ARE YOU SHAKING?
GOT A COLD?
NO...
I JUST GOT THE SHIVERS.
ARE YOU ALL RIGHT?
JOSTLE
RATTLE
WHERE DID THOSE COME FROM?!
...
KOBAYAKAWA

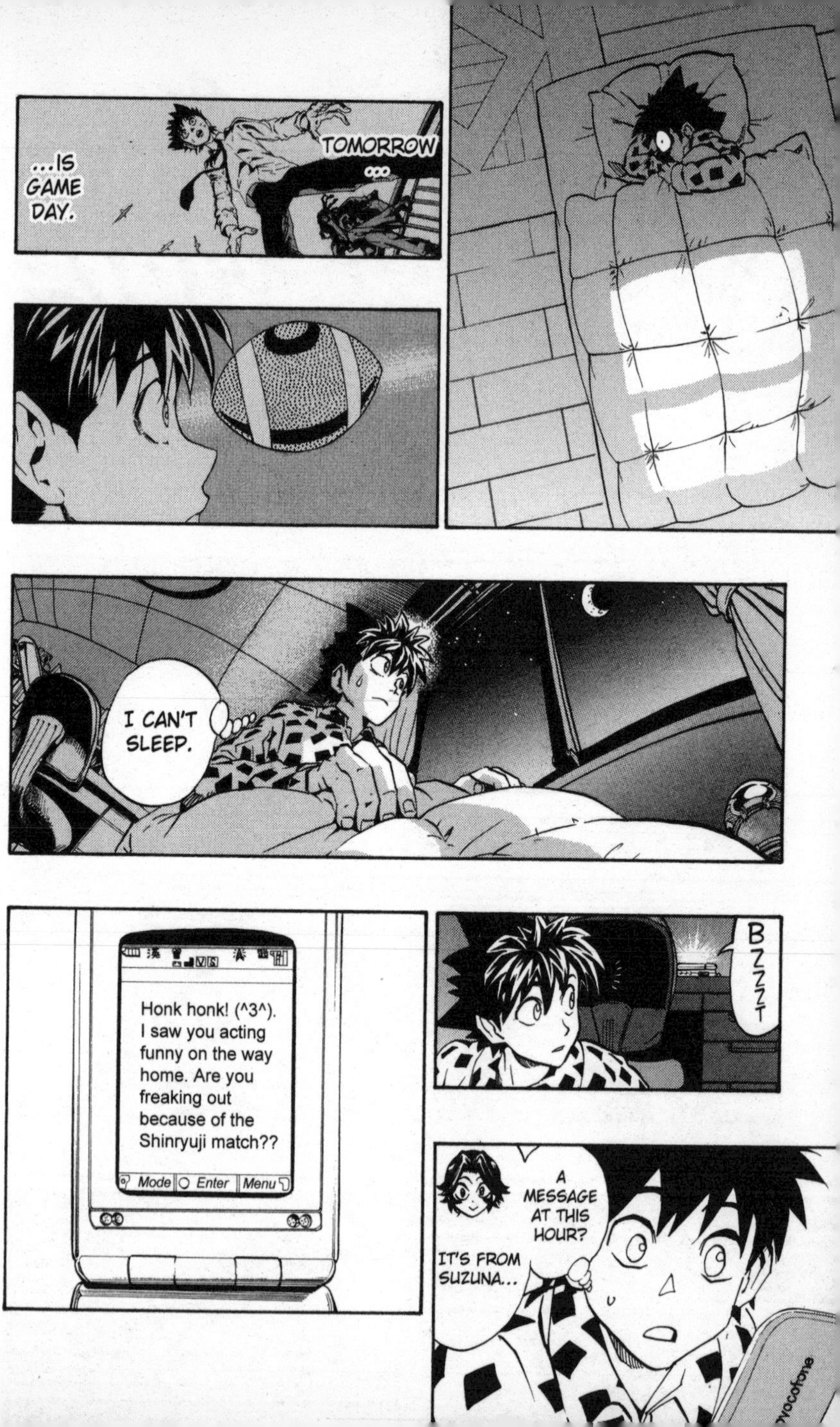
TOMORROW...
...IS GAME DAY.
I CAN'T SLEEP.
BZZZT
A MESSAGE AT THIS HOUR?
IT'S FROM SUZUNA...
vocofone
Honk honk! (^3^). I saw you acting funny on the way home. Are you freaking out because of the Shinryuji match??
Mode
Enter
Menu

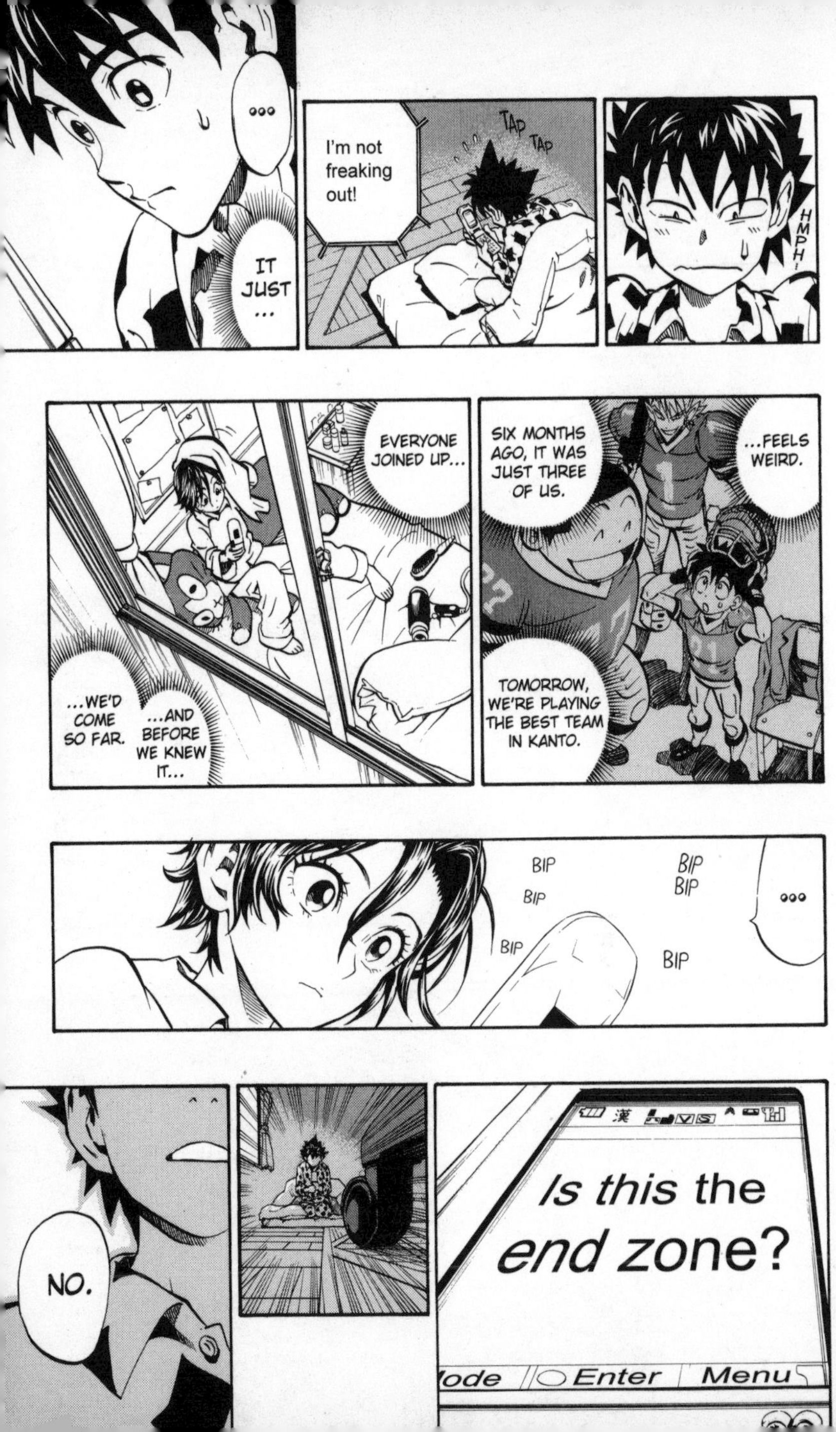
HMPH!
TAP TAP
I'm not freaking out!
...
IT JUST ...
...FEELS WEIRD.
SIX MONTHS AGO, IT WAS JUST THREE OF US.
TOMORROW, WE'RE PLAYING THE BEST TEAM IN KANTO.
EVERYONE JOINED UP...
...AND BEFORE WE KNEW IT...
...WE'D COME SO FAR.
...
BIP BIP
BIP
BIP
BIP
BIP
Is this the end zone?
ode
Enter
Menu
NO.

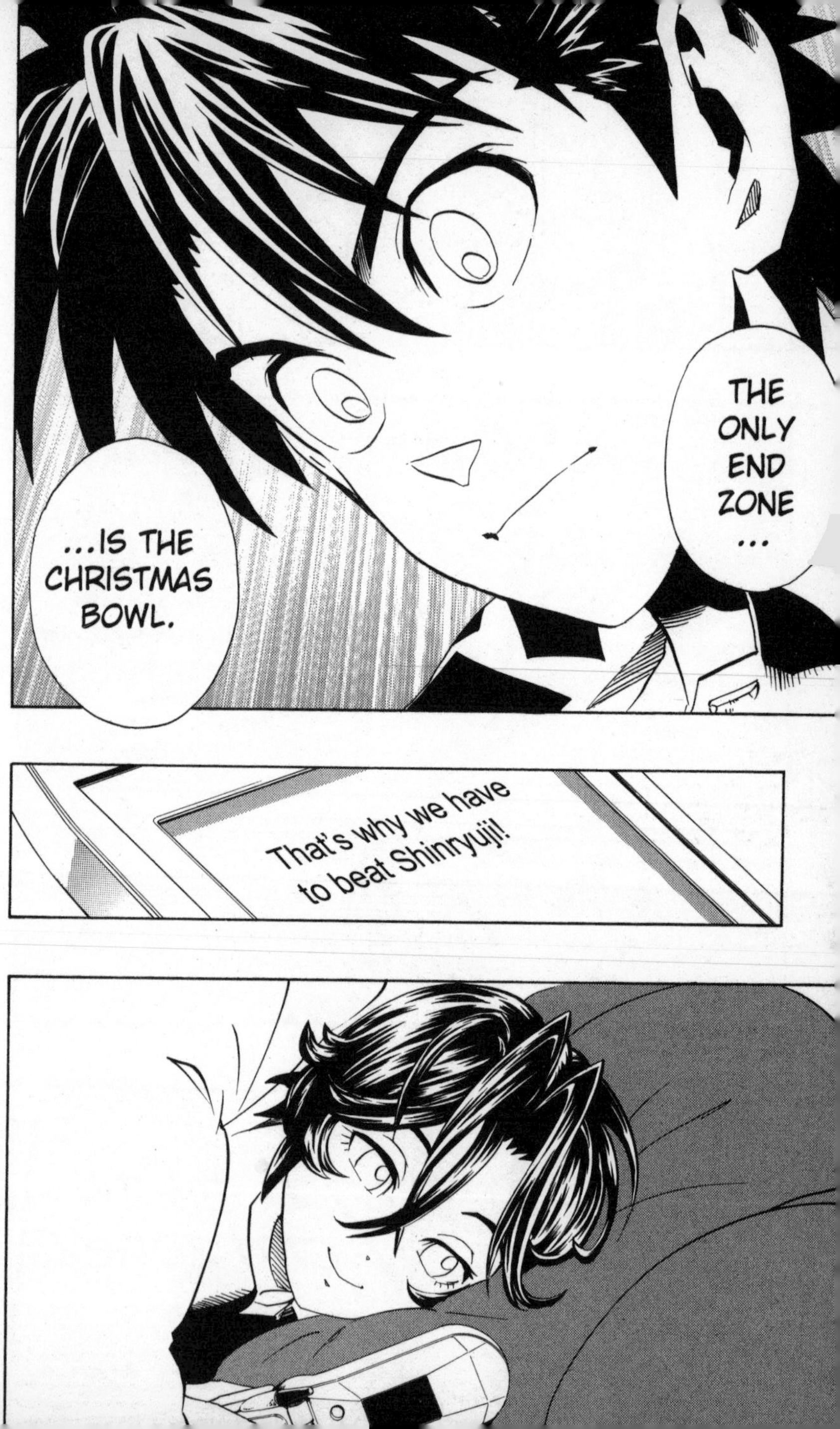
THE ONLY END ZONE ...
...IS THE CHRISTMAS BOWL.
That's why we have to beat Shinryuji!

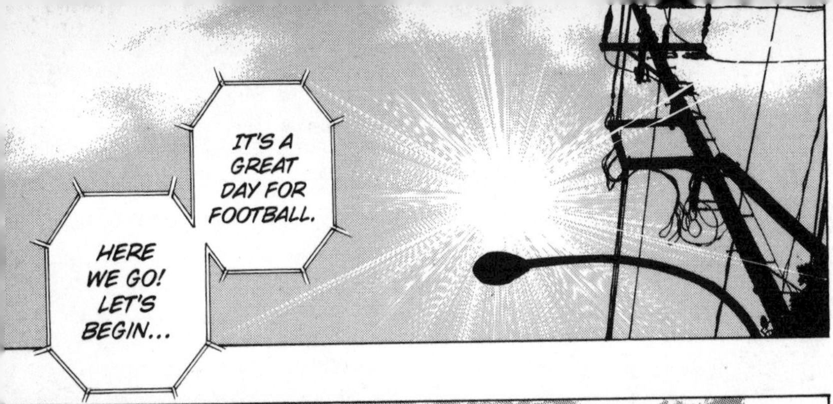
IT'S A GREAT DAY FOR FOOTBALL.
HERE WE GO! LET'S BEGIN...
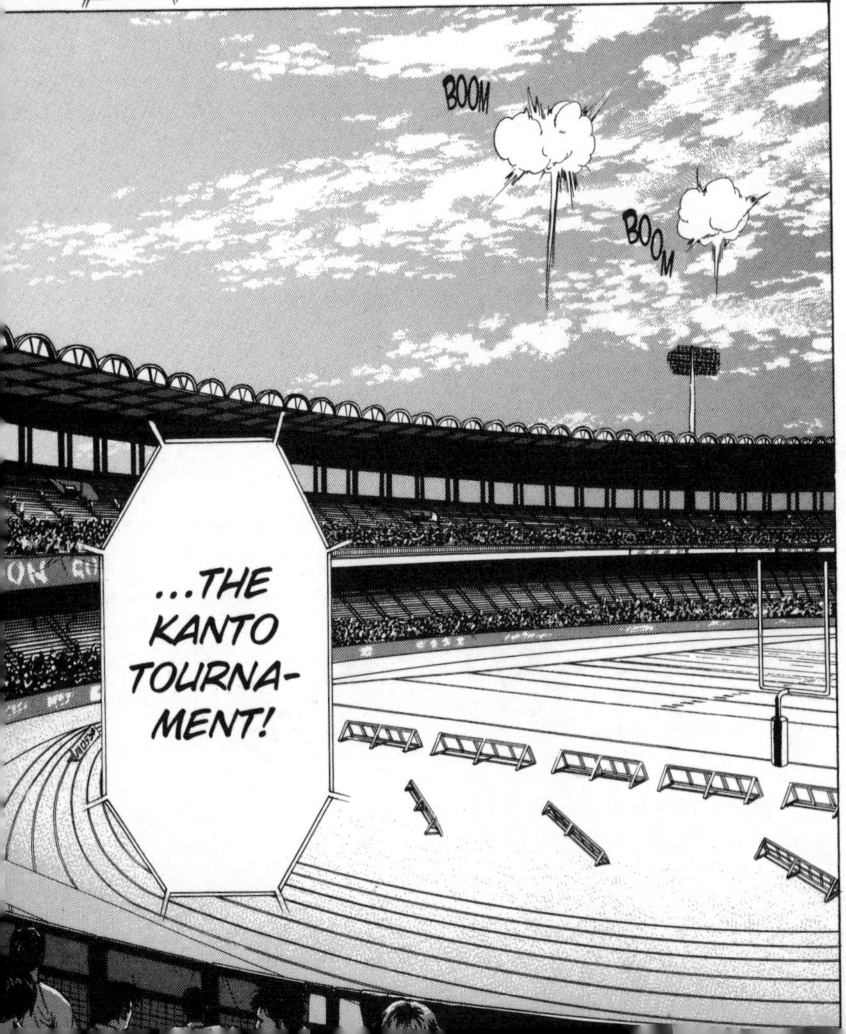
BOOM
BOOM
...THE KANTO TOURNAMENT!

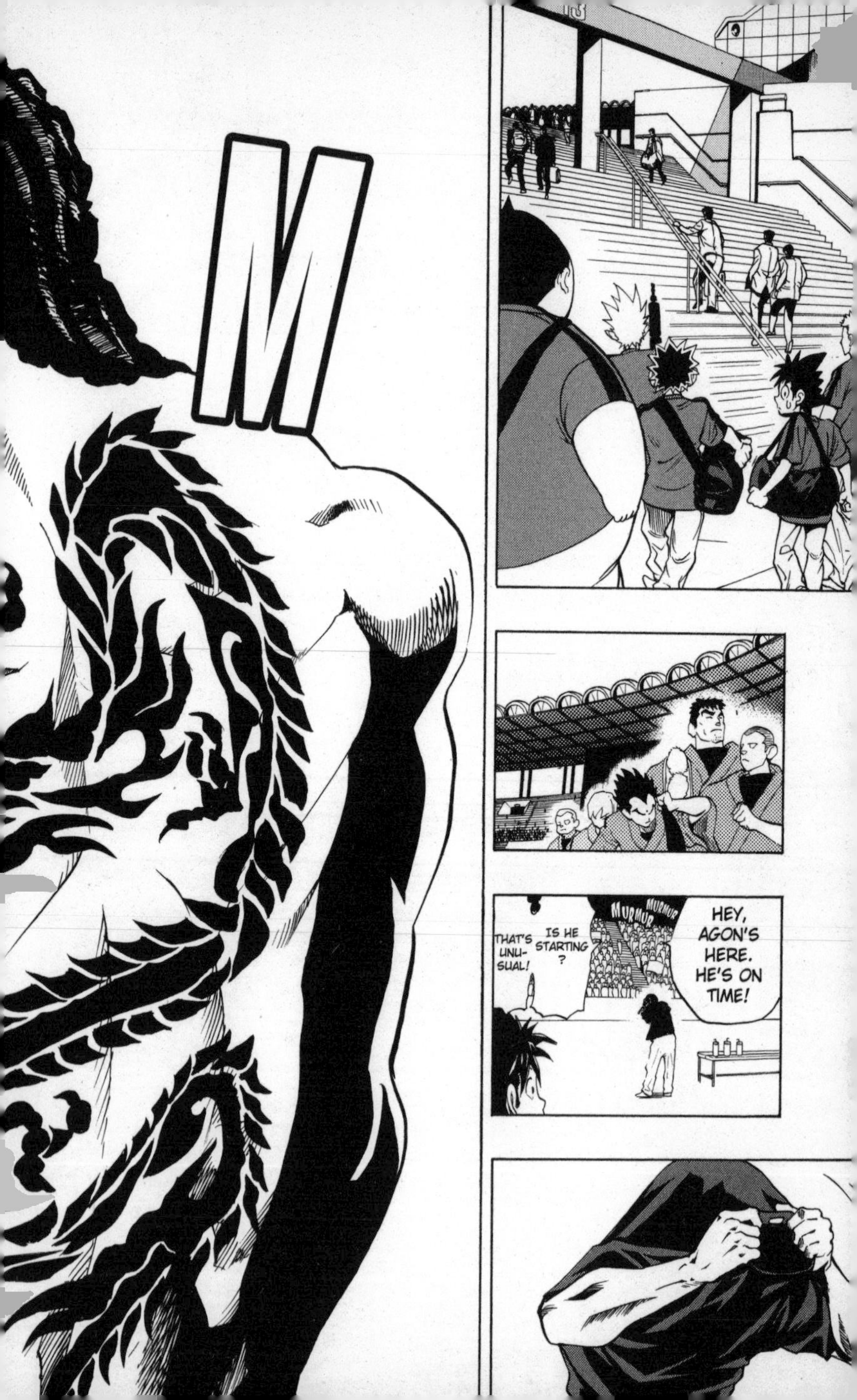
MURMUR MURMUR
HEY, AGON'S HERE. HE'S ON TIME!
IS HE STARTING?
THAT'S UNU-SUAL!
M

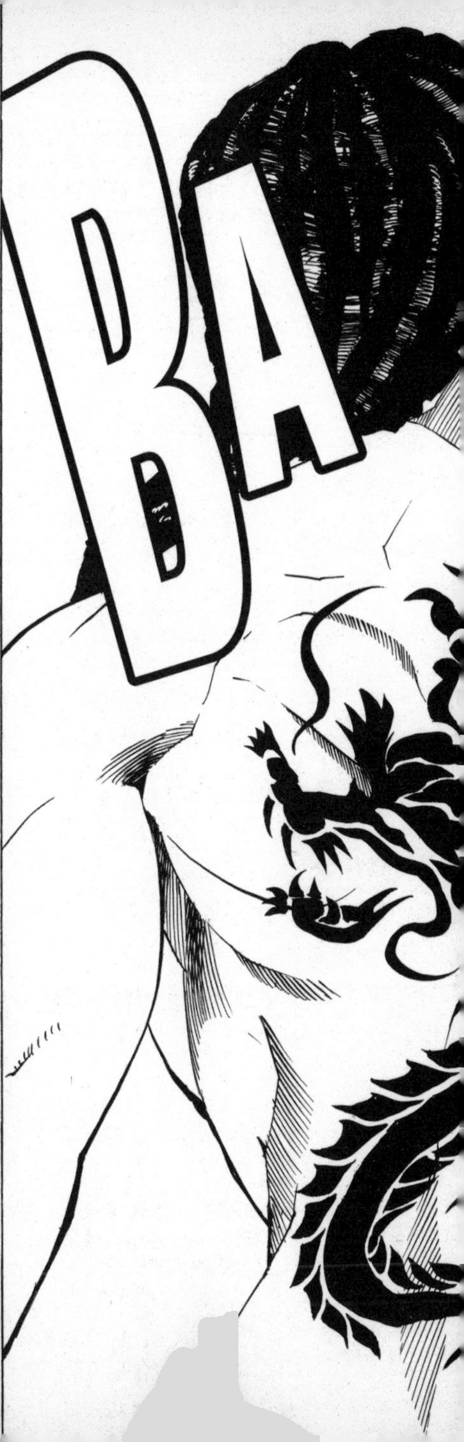
BA

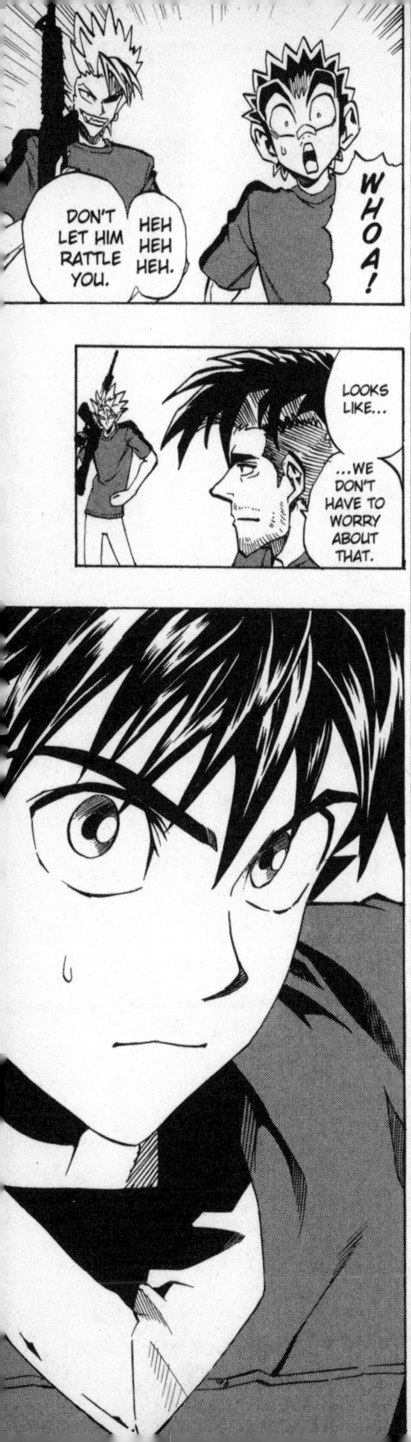
WHOA!
HEH HEH HEH.
DON'T LET HIM RATTLE YOU.
LOOKS LIKE...
...WE DON'T HAVE TO WORRY ABOUT THAT.

RIKO KUMABUKURO'S INTERVIEW 8

# EXTRA QUESTION

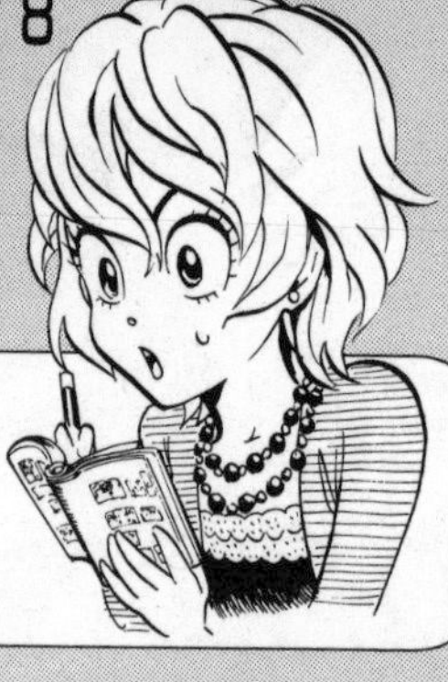

IF TODAY WERE THE LAST DAY ON EARTH, HOW WOULD YOU SPEND IT?

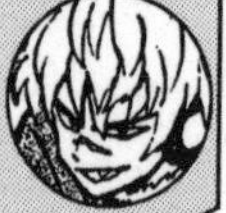

Kamiya

SPEND ALL MY MONEY JUST FOR FUN.

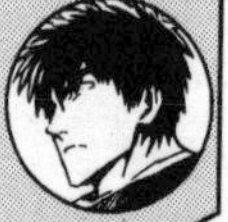

Shin

FIGURE OUT WHAT'S LEFT TO DO, AND PUSH MY LIMITS.

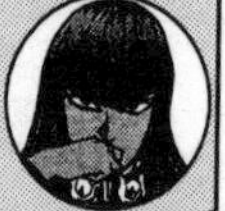

Harao

MEDITATE, AND WAIT FOR THE END IN PEACE.

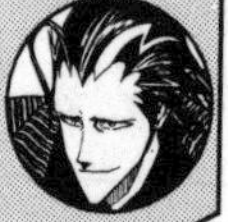

Maruko

I'D TRY TO MEET ALL KINDS OF PEOPLE.

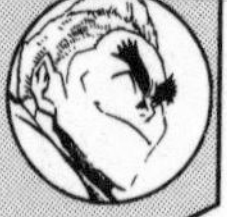

Iwashige

EAT UNTIL I BURST!

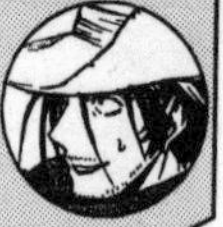

The Kid

AW, JUST KICK AROUND LIKE ANY OTHER DAY.

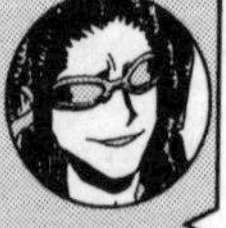

Agon

*NOTE FROM RIKO: HIS ANSWER WAS UNPRINTABLE!*

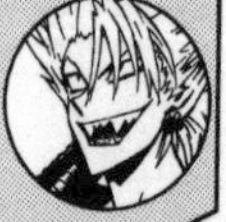

Hiruma

DEVISE SOME WAY TO KEEP THE EARTH AROUND ANOTHER DAY.

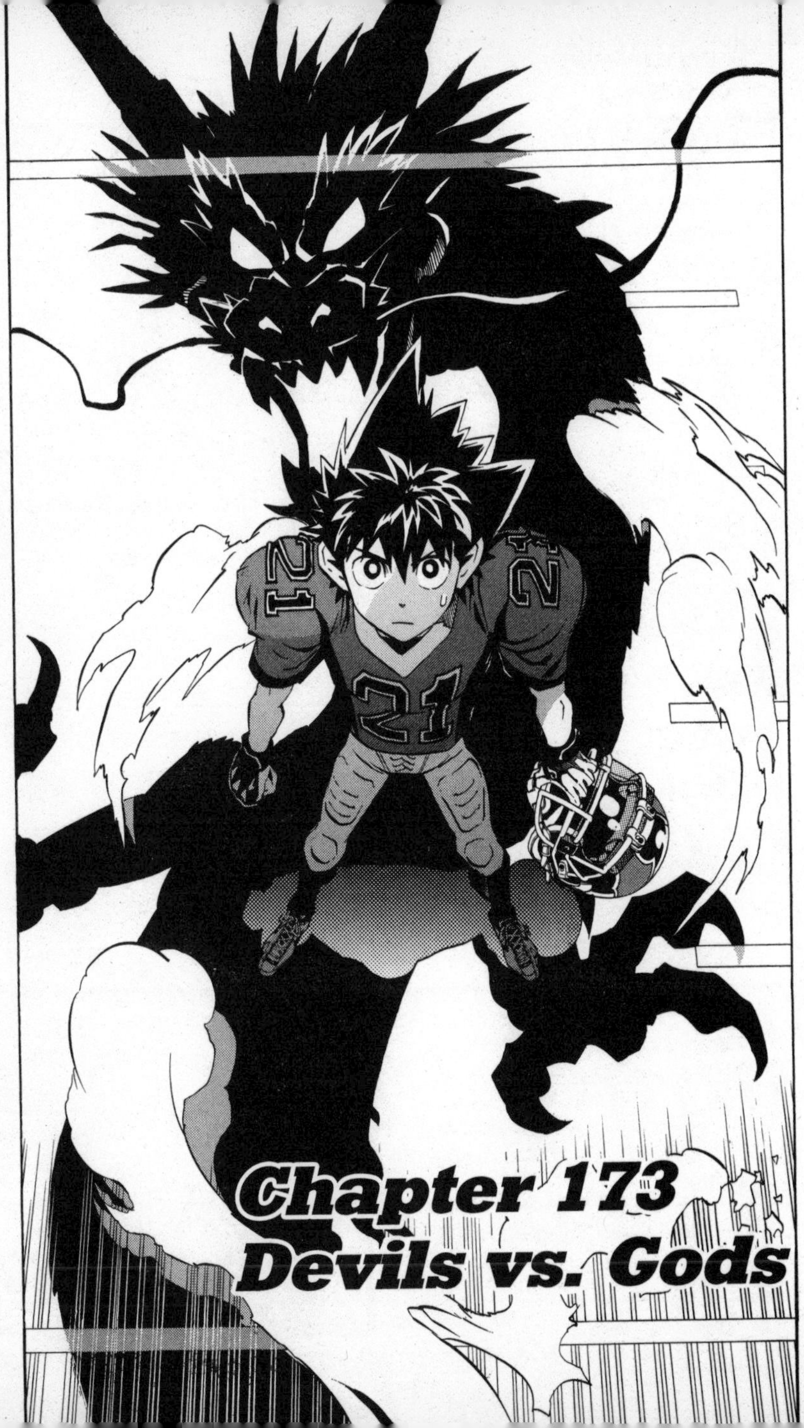
Chapter 173
Devils vs. Gods

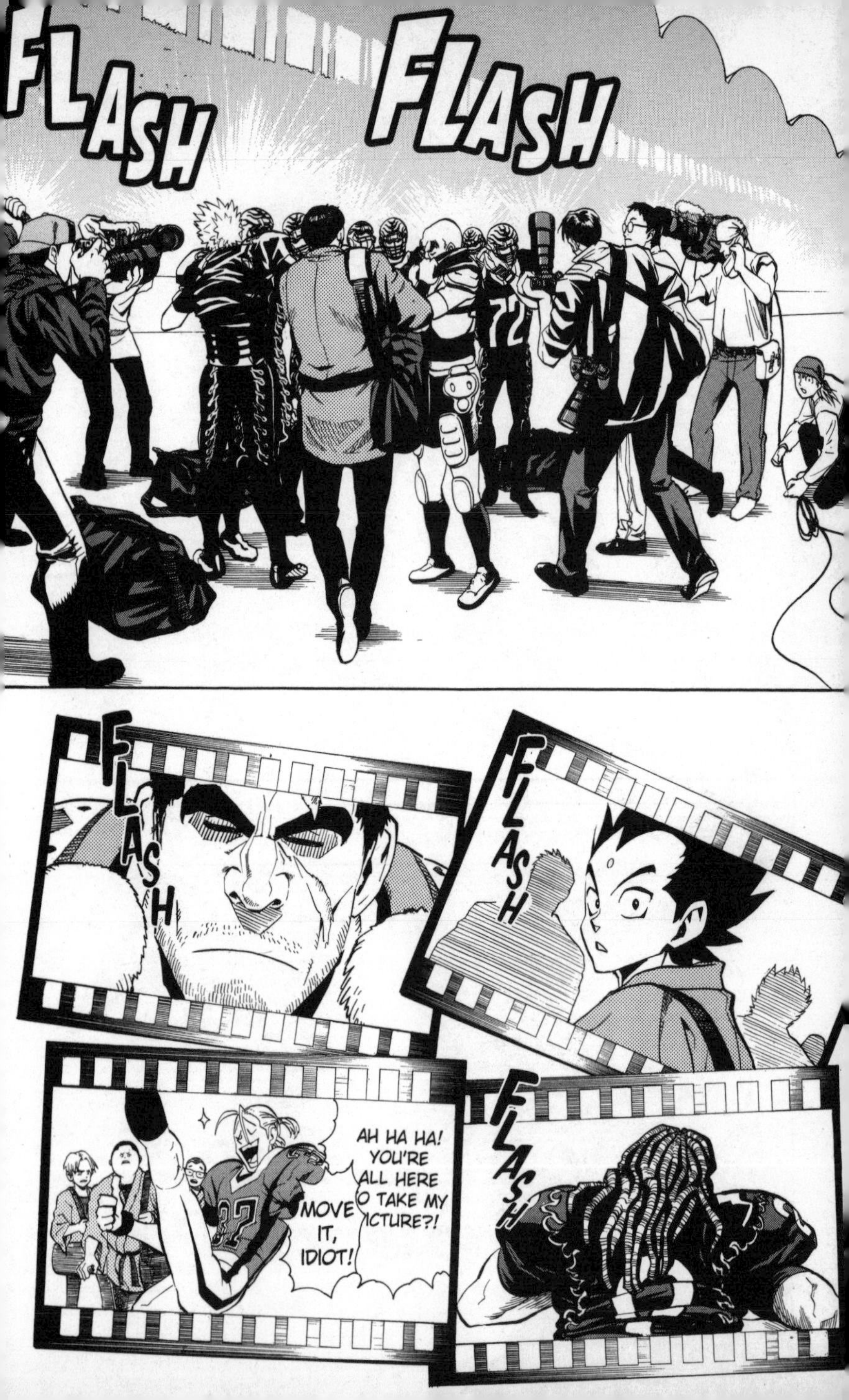
FLASH
FLASH
FLASH
FLASH
FLASH
AH HA HA! YOU'RE ALL HERE O TAKE MY ICTURE?!
MOVE IT, IDIOT!

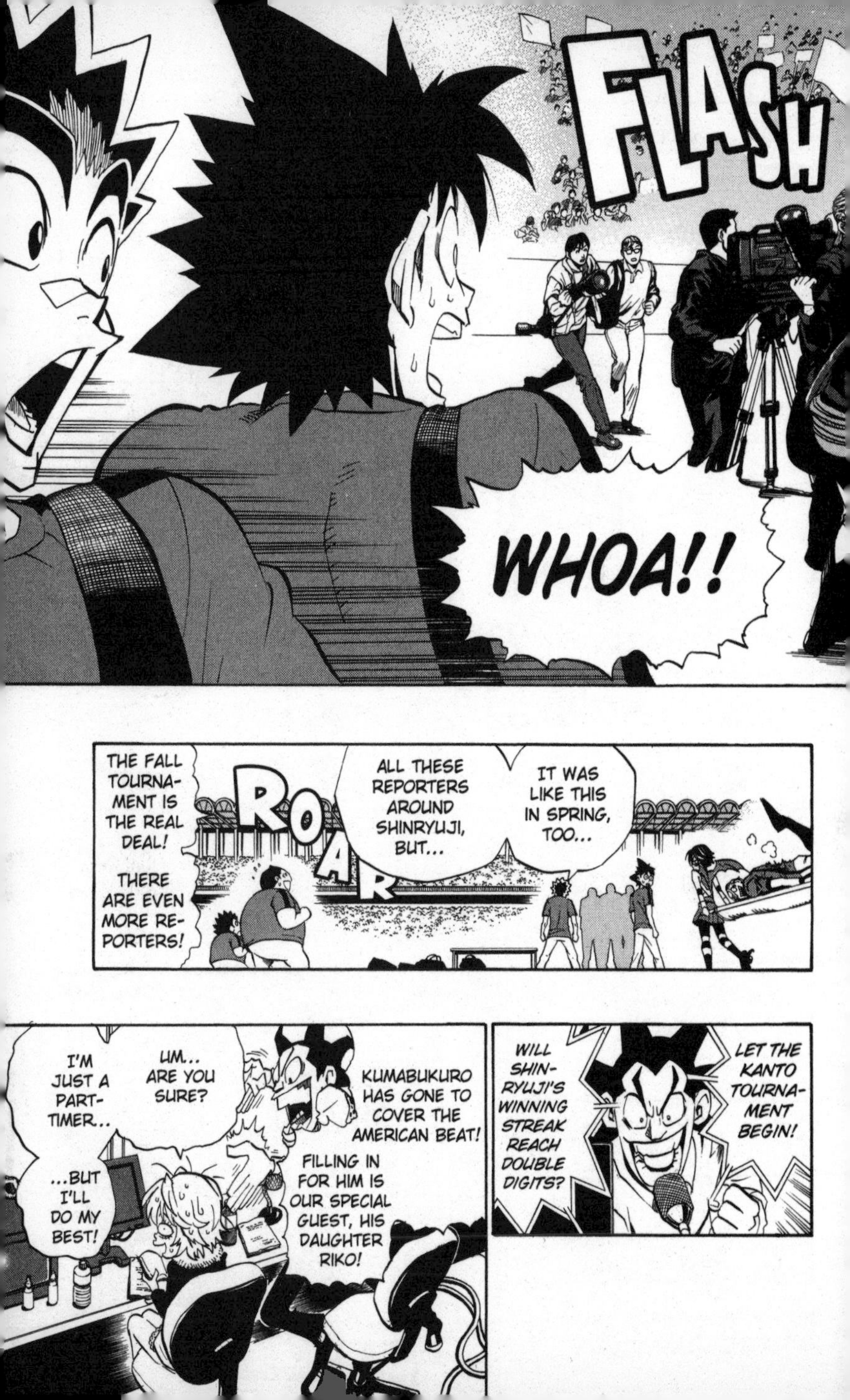
FLASH
WHOA!!
IT WAS LIKE THIS IN SPRING, TOO...
ALL THESE REPORTERS AROUND SHINRYUJI, BUT...
ROAR
THE FALL TOURNAMENT IS THE REAL DEAL!
THERE ARE EVEN MORE REPORTERS!
LET THE KANTO TOURNAMENT BEGIN!
WILL SHINRYUJI'S WINNING STREAK REACH DOUBLE DIGITS?
KUMABUKURO HAS GONE TO COVER THE AMERICAN BEAT!
FILLING IN FOR HIM IS OUR SPECIAL GUEST, HIS DAUGHTER RIKO!
UM... ARE YOU SURE?
I'M JUST A PART-TIMER...
...BUT I'LL DO MY BEST!

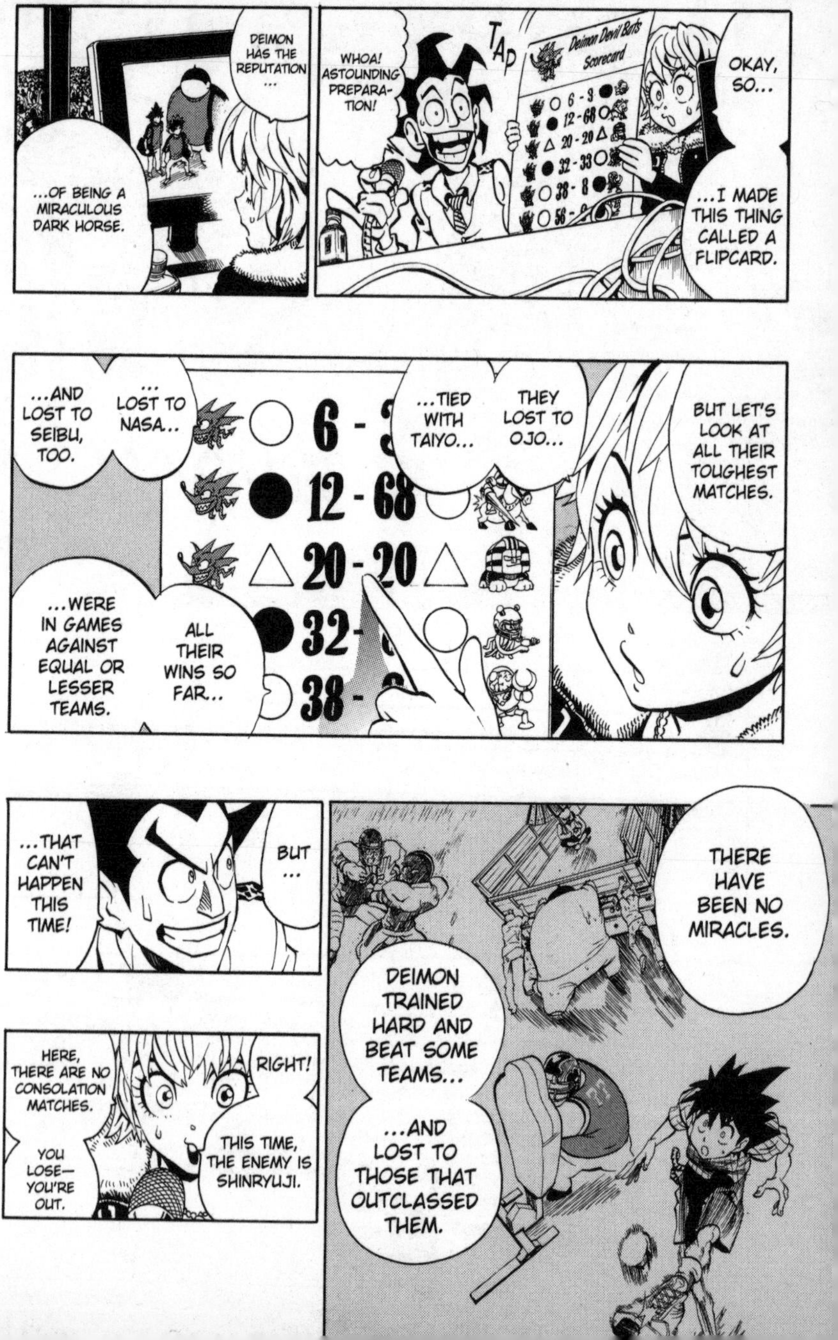
OKAY, SO...
...I MADE THIS THING CALLED A FLIPCARD.
TAP
Deimon Devil Bats Scorecard
6 - 3
12 - 68
20 - 20
32 - 33
38 - 8
WHOA! ASTOUNDING PREPARA-TION!
DEIMON HAS THE REPUTATION...
...OF BEING A MIRACULOUS DARK HORSE.
BUT LET'S LOOK AT ALL THEIR TOUGHEST MATCHES.
THEY LOST TO OJO...
...TIED WITH TAIYO...
...LOST TO NASA...
...AND LOST TO SEIBU, TOO.
12 - 68
20 - 20
ALL THEIR WINS SO FAR...
...WERE IN GAMES AGAINST EQUAL OR LESSER TEAMS.
THERE HAVE BEEN NO MIRACLES.
DEIMON TRAINED HARD AND BEAT SOME TEAMS...
...AND LOST TO THOSE THAT OUTCLASSED THEM.
BUT...
...THAT CAN'T HAPPEN THIS TIME!
RIGHT!
THIS TIME, THE ENEMY IS SHINRYUJI.
HERE, THERE ARE NO CONSOLATION MATCHES.
YOU LOSE—YOU'RE OUT.

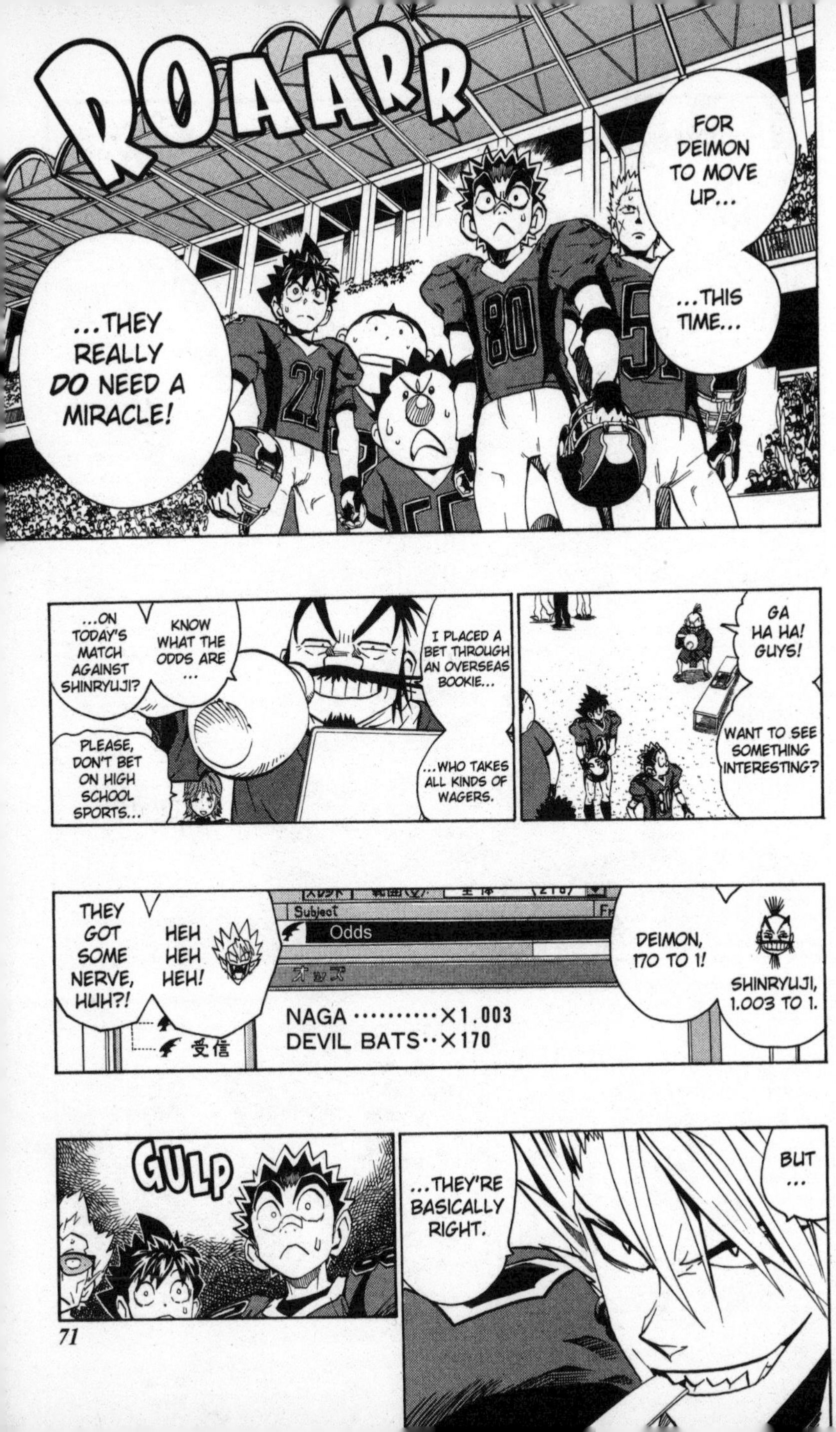
ROAARR
FOR DEIMON TO MOVE UP...
...THIS TIME...
...THEY REALLY DO NEED A MIRACLE!
GA HA HA! GUYS!
WANT TO SEE SOMETHING INTERESTING?
I PLACED A BET THROUGH AN OVERSEAS BOOKIE...
...WHO TAKES ALL KINDS OF WAGERS.
KNOW WHAT THE ODDS ARE...
...ON TODAY'S MATCH AGAINST SHINRYUJI?
PLEASE, DON'T BET ON HIGH SCHOOL SPORTS...
SHINRYUJI, 1.003 TO 1.
DEIMON, 170 TO 1!
Subject
Odds
オッズ
NAGA ··········×1.003
DEVIL BATS··×170
受信
HEH HEH HEH!
THEY GOT SOME NERVE, HUH?!
BUT...
...THEY'RE BASICALLY RIGHT.
GULP

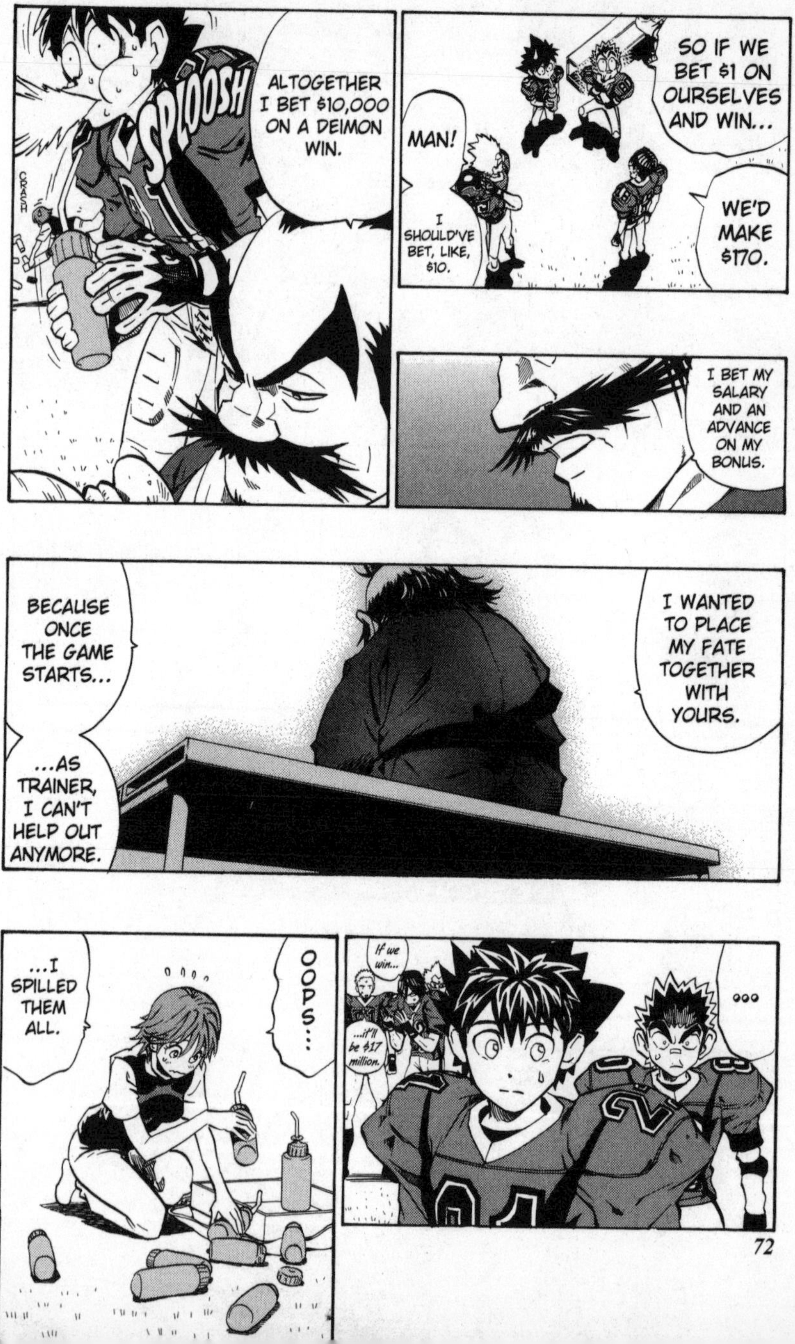
SO IF WE BET $1 ON OURSELVES AND WIN...
WE'D MAKE $170.
MAN!
I SHOULD'VE BET, LIKE, $10.
I BET MY SALARY AND AN ADVANCE ON MY BONUS.
ALTOGETHER I BET $10,000 ON A DEIMON WIN.
SPLOOSH
CRASH
I WANTED TO PLACE MY FATE TOGETHER WITH YOURS.
BECAUSE ONCE THE GAME STARTS...
...AS TRAINER, I CAN'T HELP OUT ANYMORE.
...
If we win...
...it'll be $17 million.
OOPS...
...I SPILLED THEM ALL.

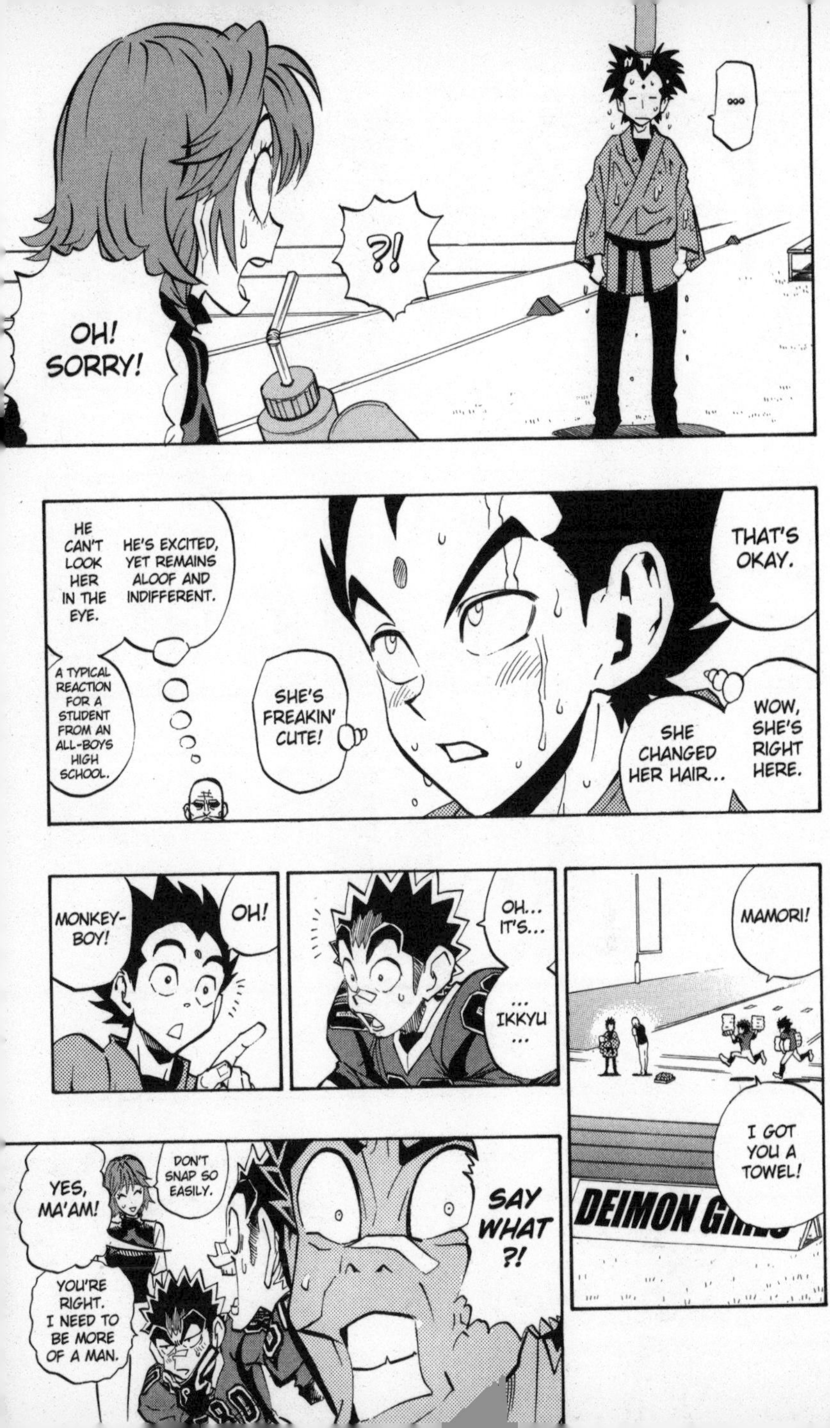
...
?!
OH! SORRY!
THAT'S OKAY.
WOW, SHE'S RIGHT HERE.
SHE CHANGED HER HAIR...
SHE'S FREAKIN' CUTE!
HE'S EXCITED, YET REMAINS ALOOF AND INDIFFERENT.
HE CAN'T LOOK HER IN THE EYE.
A TYPICAL REACTION FOR A STUDENT FROM AN ALL-BOYS HIGH SCHOOL.
MAMORI!
I GOT YOU A TOWEL!
DEIMON GIR
OH... IT'S...
... IKKYU ...
OH!
MONKEY-BOY!
SAY WHAT ?!
DON'T SNAP SO EASILY.
YES, MA'AM!
YOU'RE RIGHT. I NEED TO BE MORE OF A MAN.

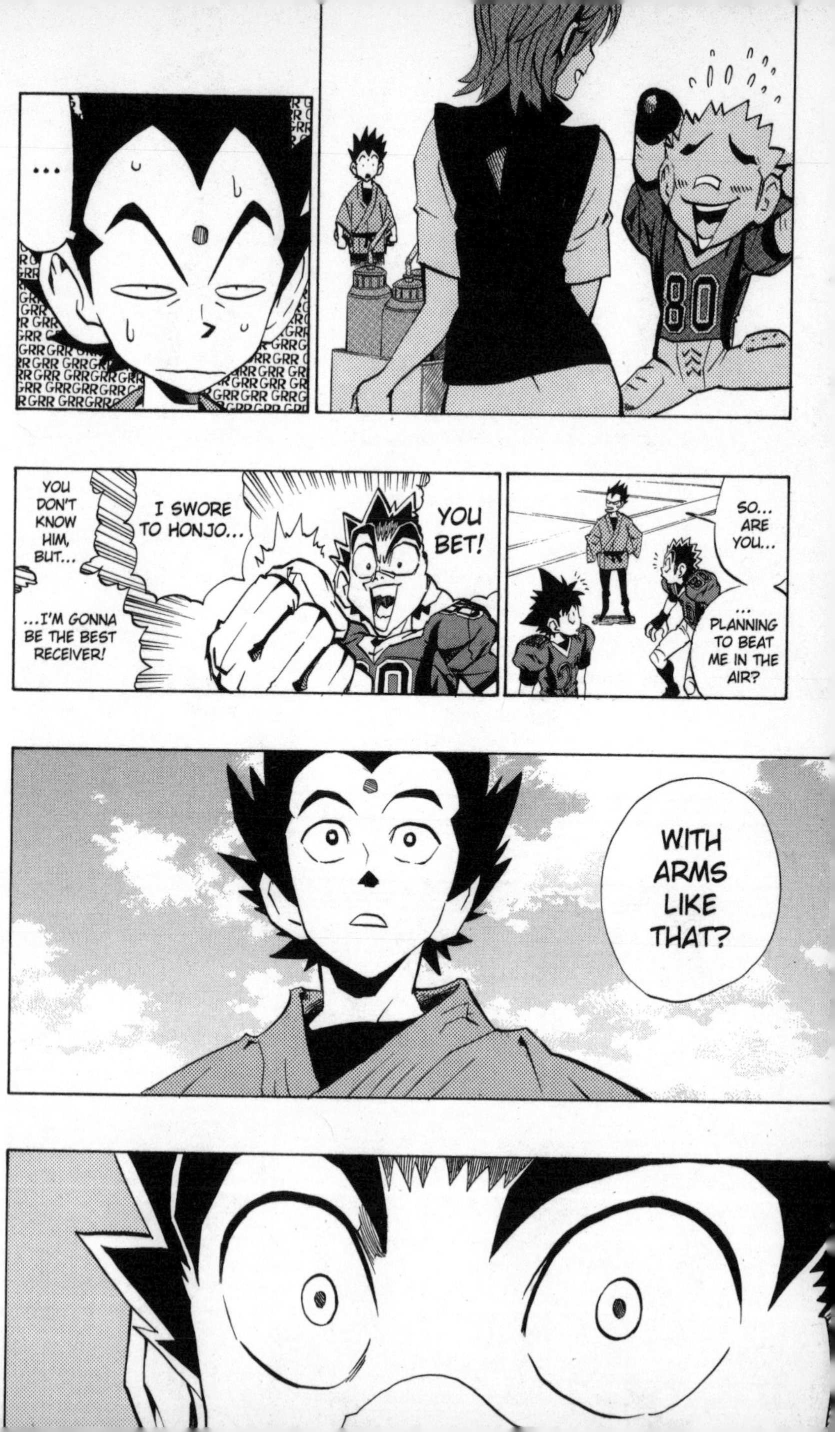
...
GRR GRR GRR
SO... ARE YOU...
...PLANNING TO BEAT ME IN THE AIR?
YOU BET!
I SWORE TO HONJO...
YOU DON'T KNOW HIM, BUT...
...I'M GONNA BE THE BEST RECEIVER!
WITH ARMS LIKE THAT?

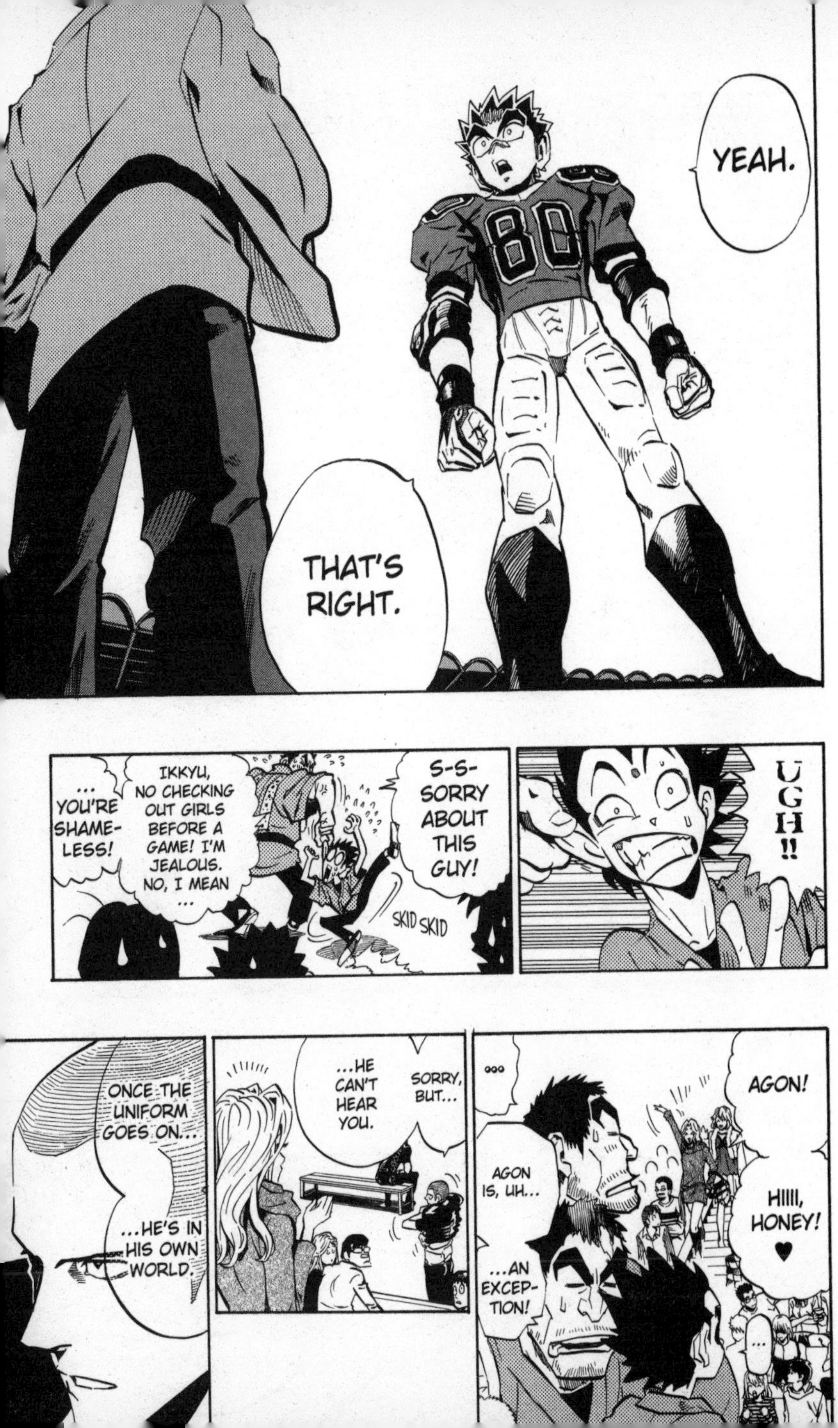
YEAH.
THAT'S RIGHT.
UGH!!
S-S-SORRY ABOUT THIS GUY!
SKID SKID
IKKYU, NO CHECKING OUT GIRLS BEFORE A GAME! I'M JEALOUS. NO, I MEAN ...
... YOU'RE SHAME-LESS!
AGON!
HIIII, HONEY! ♥
...
AGON IS, UH...
...AN EXCEP-TION!
...
SORRY, BUT...
...HE CAN'T HEAR YOU.
ONCE THE UNIFORM GOES ON...
...HE'S IN HIS OWN WORLD.

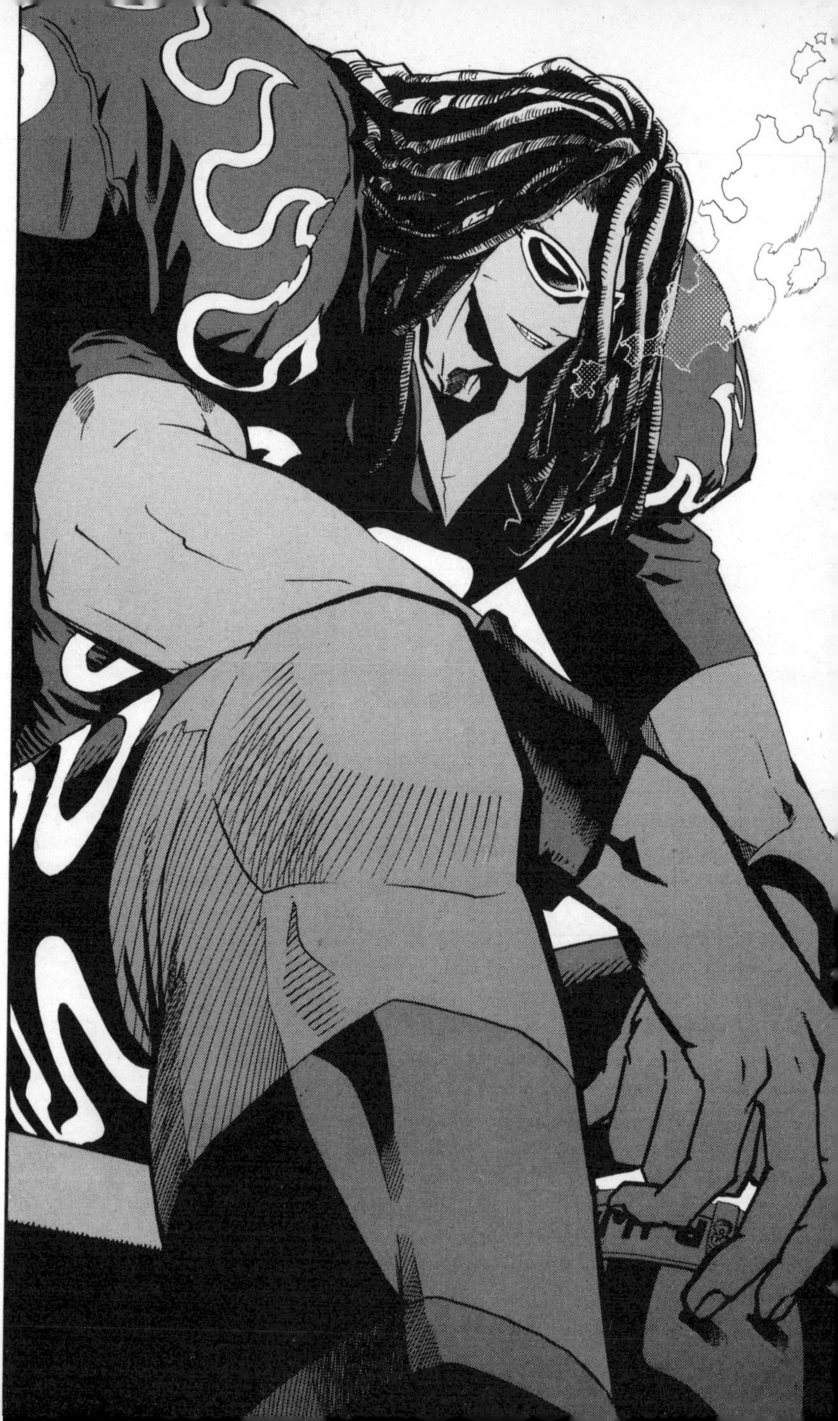

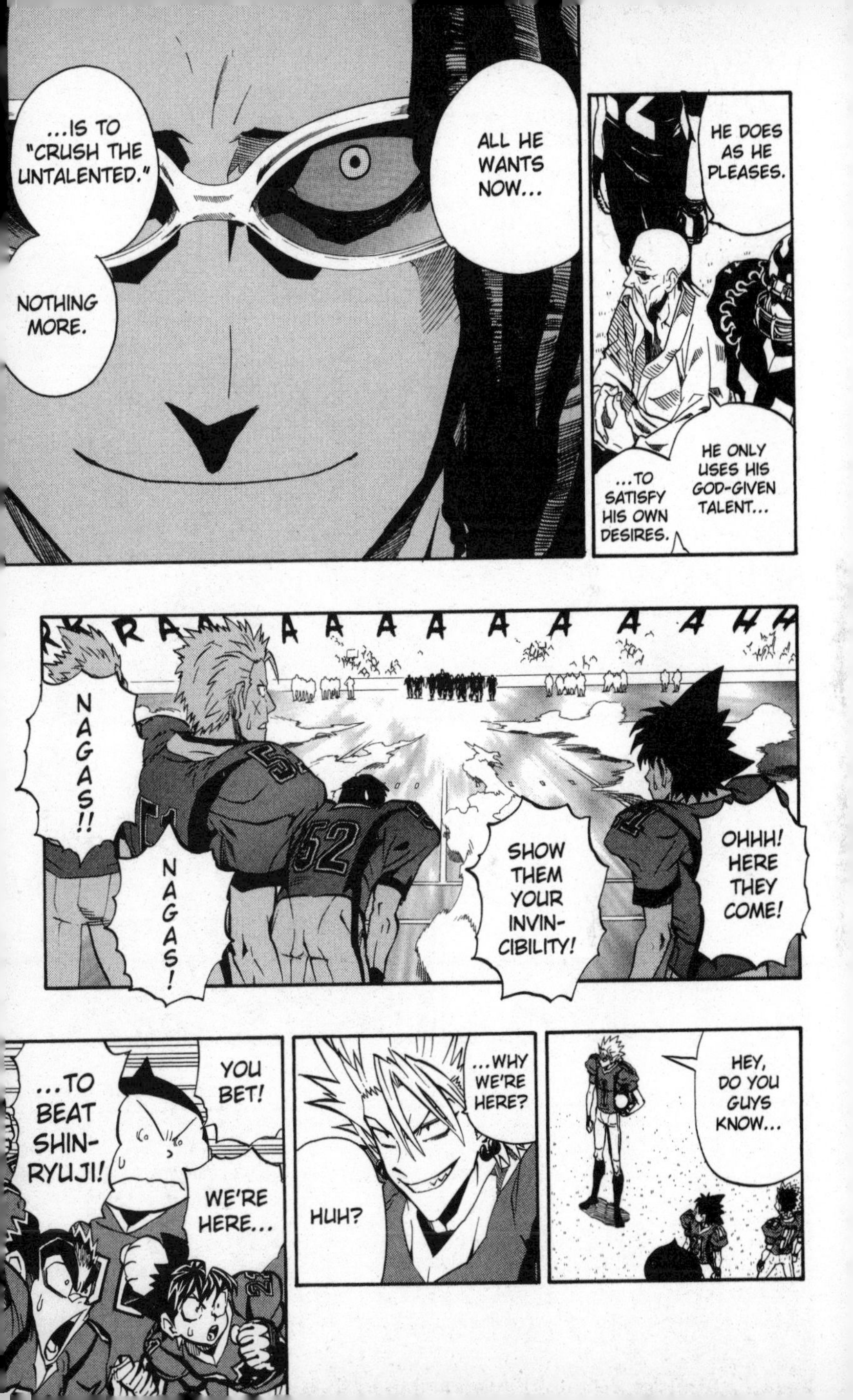
HE DOES AS HE PLEASES.
HE ONLY USES HIS GOD-GIVEN TALENT...
...TO SATISFY HIS OWN DESIRES.
ALL HE WANTS NOW...
...IS TO "CRUSH THE UNTALENTED."
NOTHING MORE.
RRAAAAAAAAAAAHH
OHHH! HERE THEY COME!
SHOW THEM YOUR INVIN-CIBILITY!
NAGAS!!
NAGAS!
HEY, DO YOU GUYS KNOW...
...WHY WE'RE HERE?
HUH?
YOU BET!
WE'RE HERE...
...TO BEAT SHIN-RYUJI!

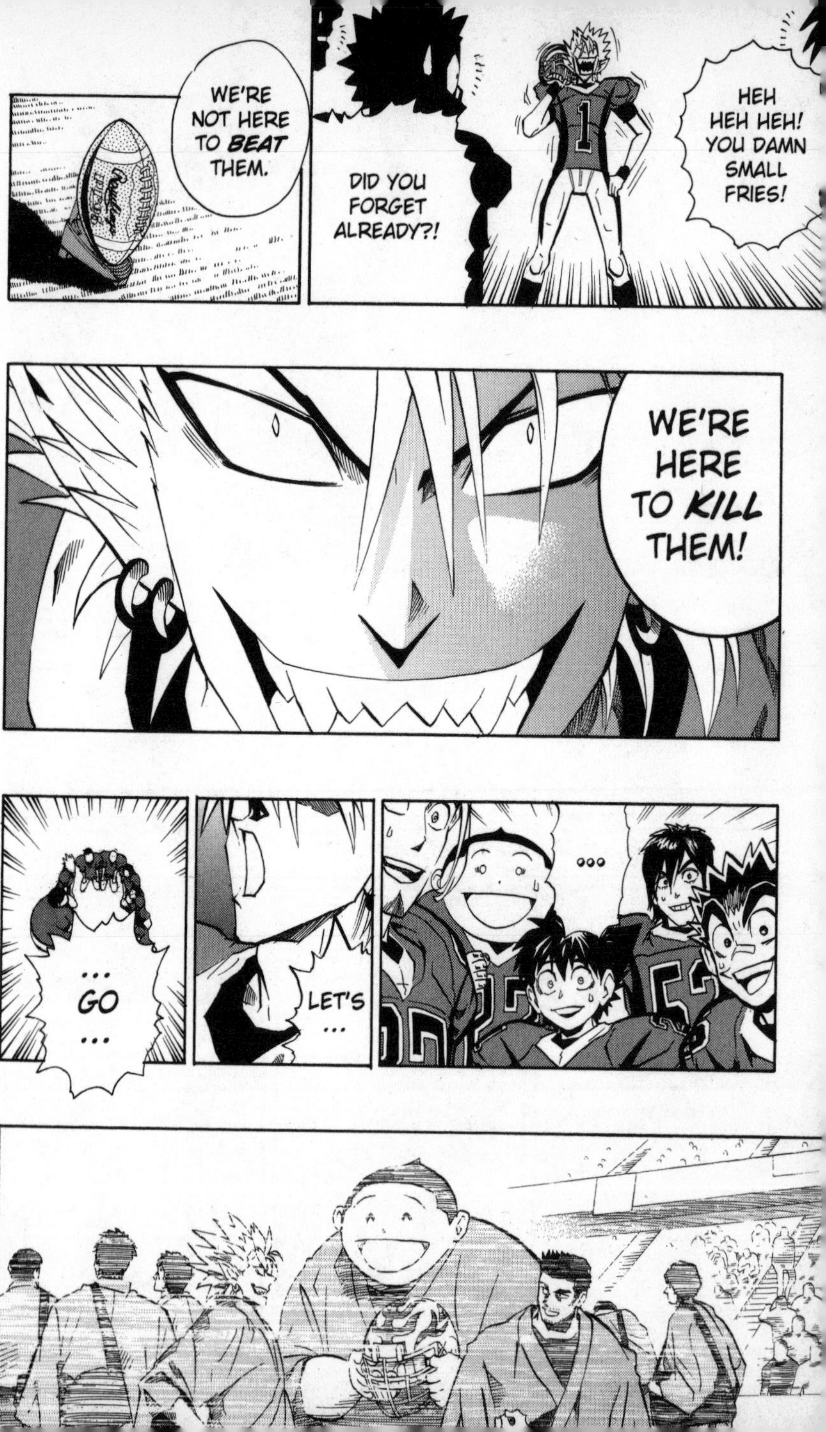
HEH HEH HEH! YOU DAMN SMALL FRIES!
DID YOU FORGET ALREADY?!
WE'RE NOT HERE TO *BEAT* THEM.
WE'RE HERE TO *KILL* THEM!
...
LET'S ...
... GO ...

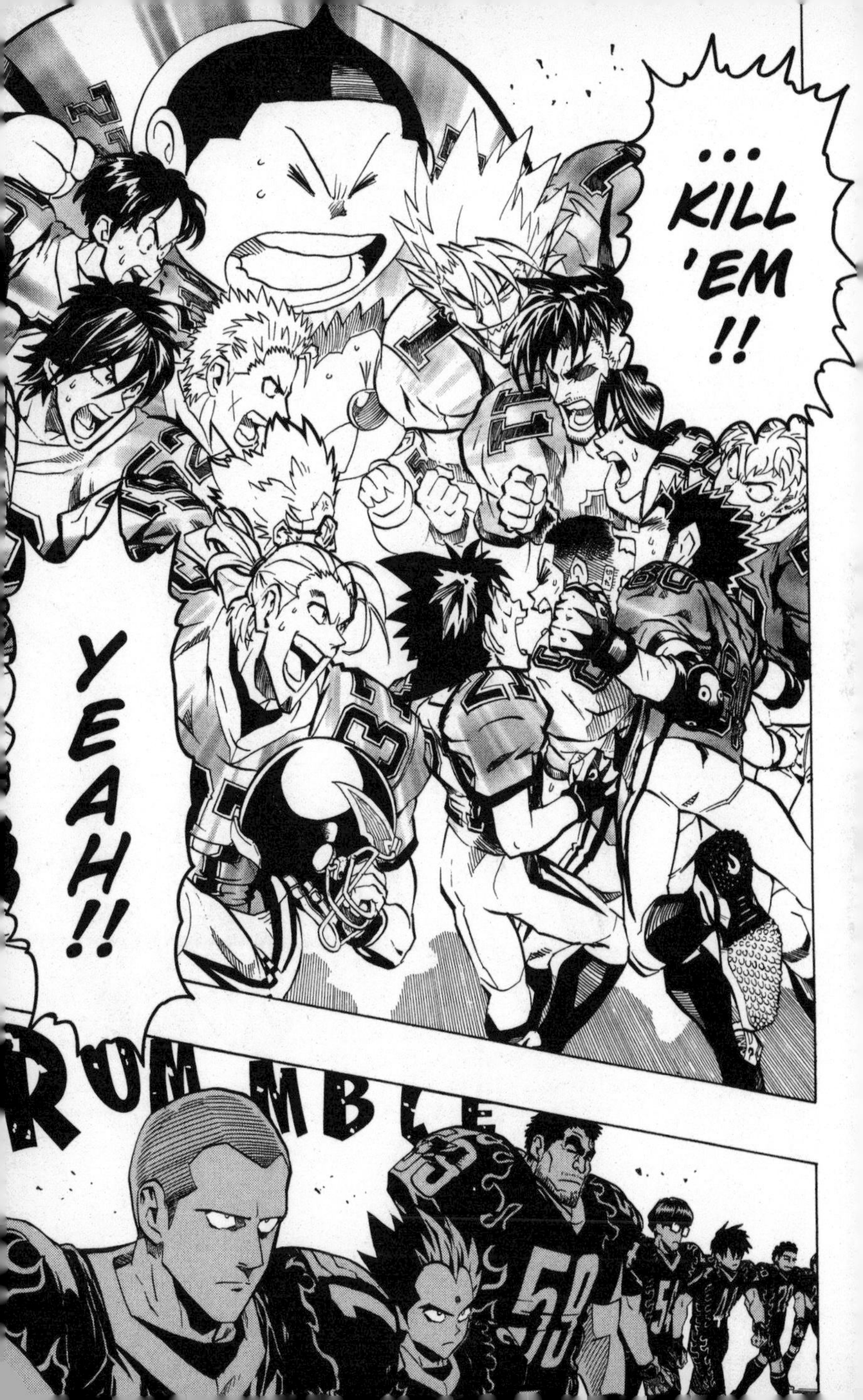
...KILL 'EM!!
YEAH!!
RUMMBLE

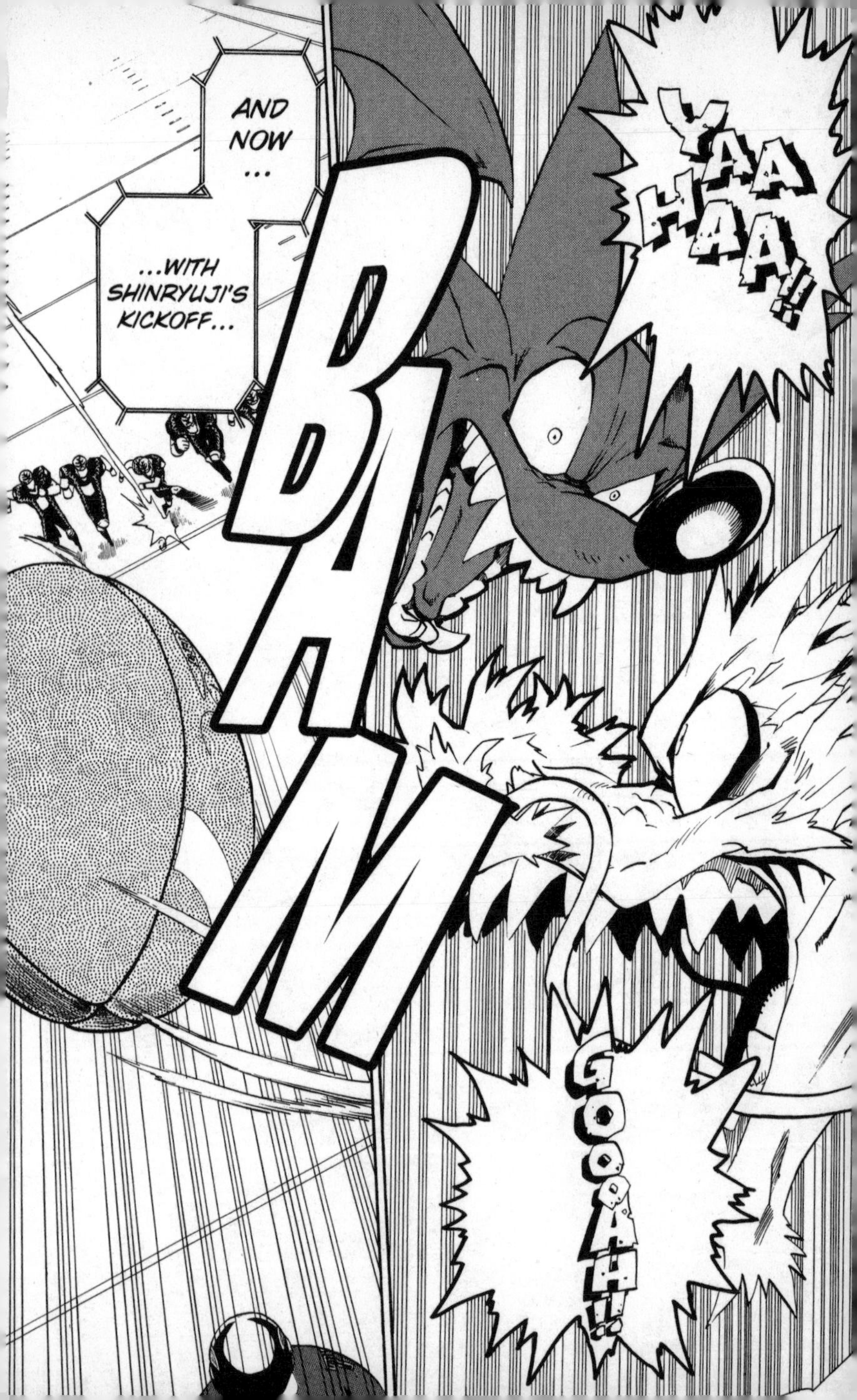
YAA HAA!!
AND NOW ...
...WITH SHINRYUJI'S KICKOFF...
BAM
GOOOAH!!

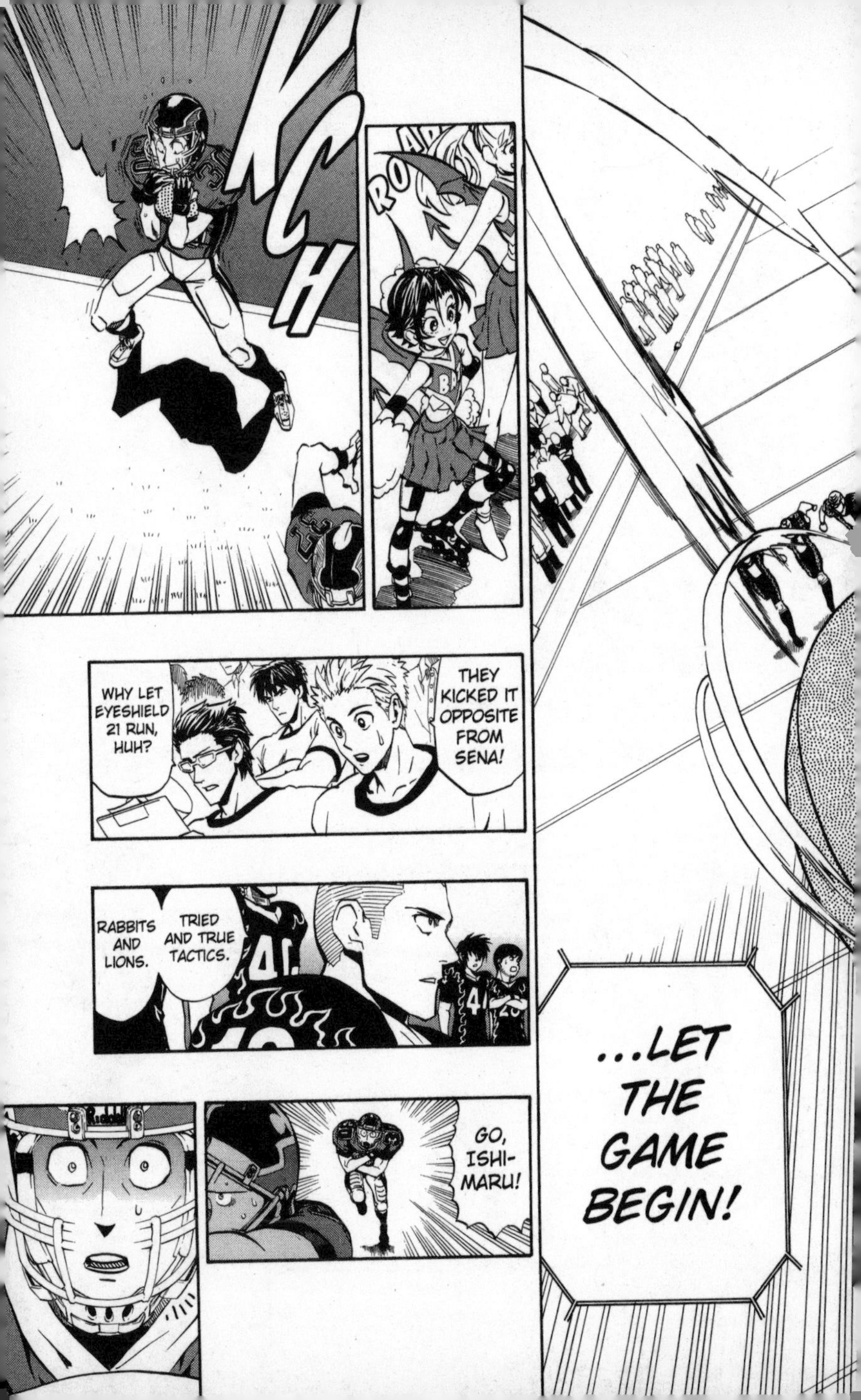
...LET THE GAME BEGIN!
ROAR
KCH
THEY KICKED IT OPPOSITE FROM SENA!
WHY LET EYESHIELD 21 RUN, HUH?
TRIED AND TRUE TACTICS.
RABBITS AND LIONS.
GO, ISHI-MARU!

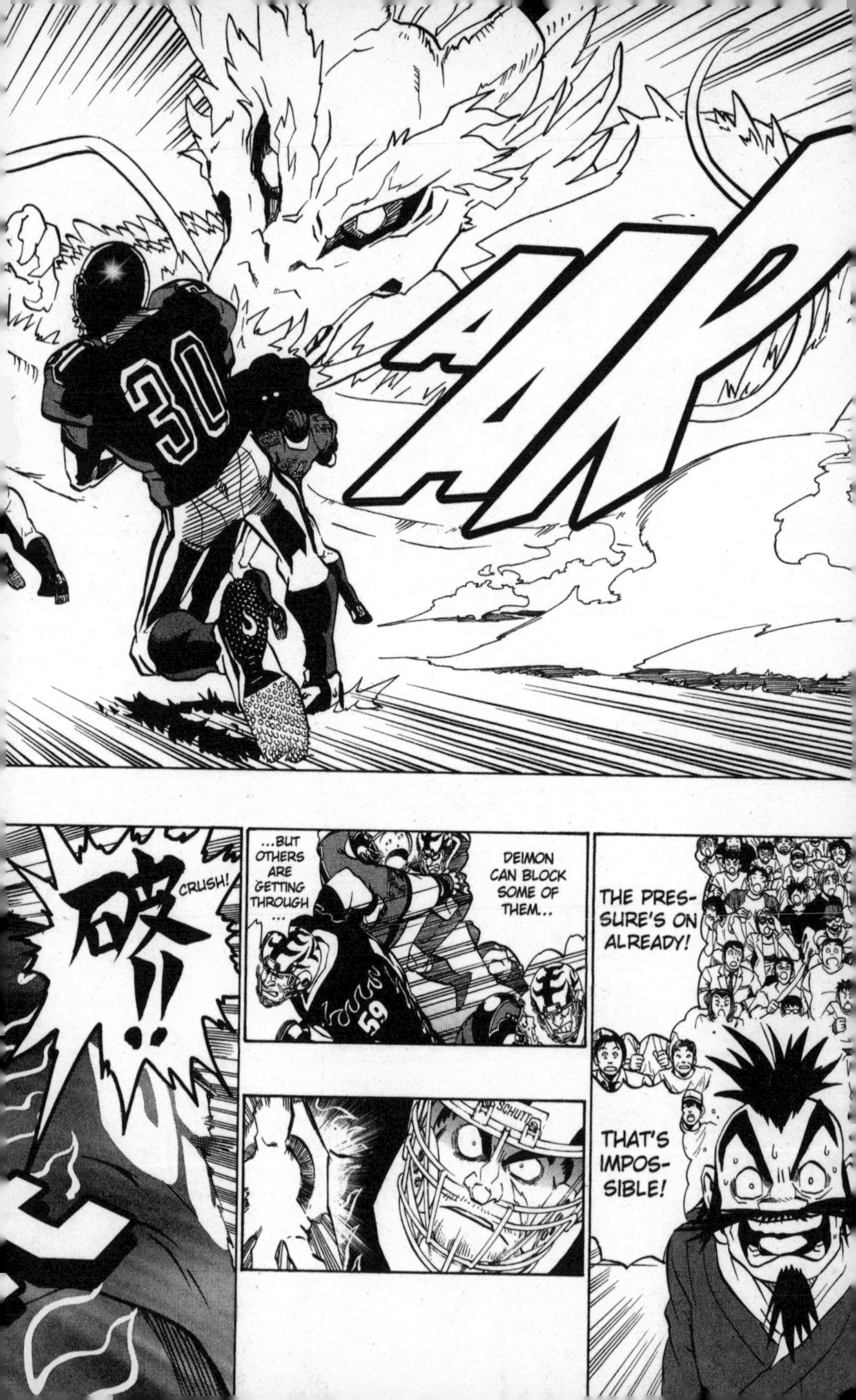
THE PRES-SURE'S ON ALREADY!
THAT'S IMPOS-SIBLE!
DEIMON CAN BLOCK SOME OF THEM...
...BUT OTHERS ARE GETTING THROUGH...
SCHUTT
破!!
CRUSH!

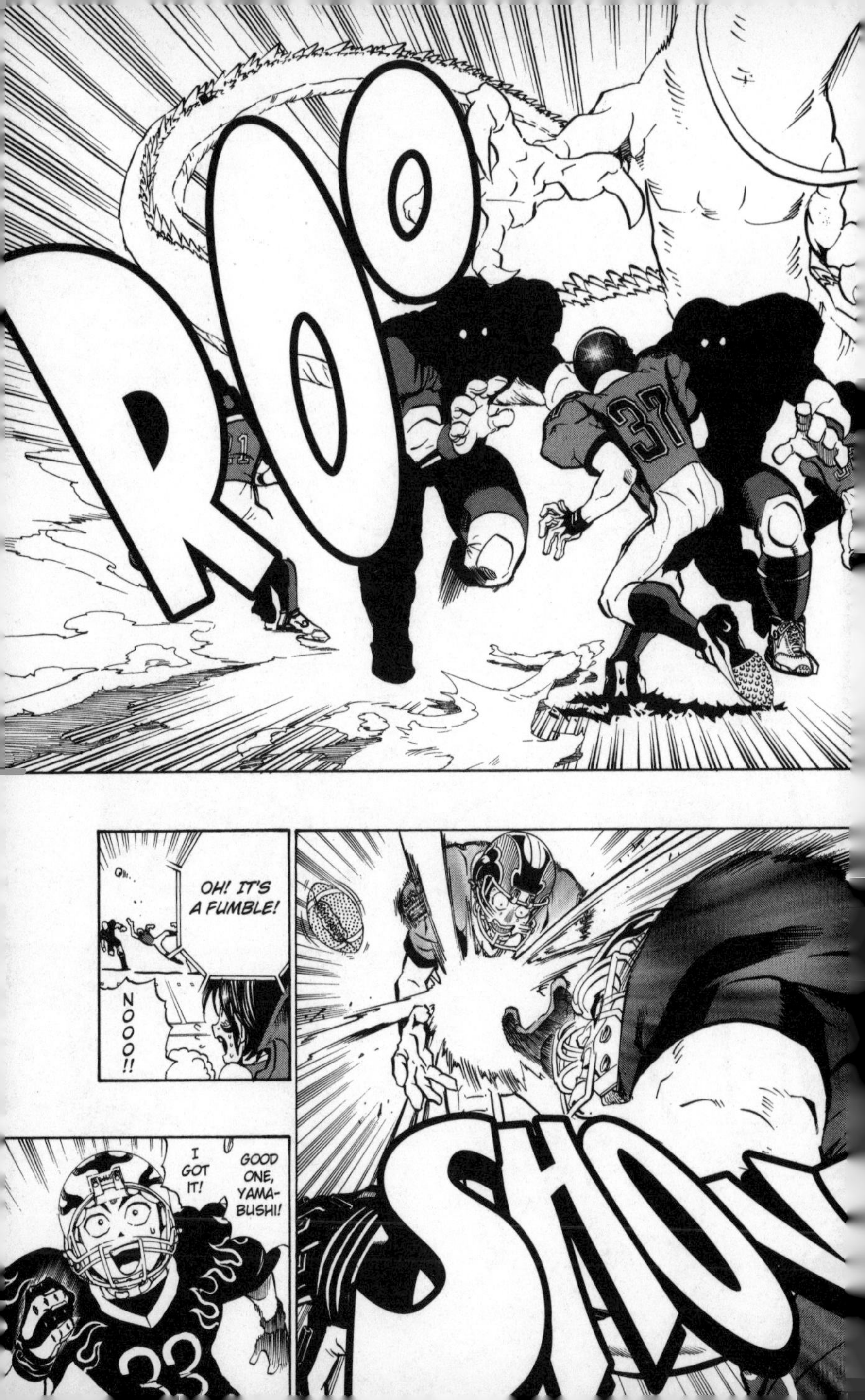
ROO
37
SHO
OH! IT'S A FUMBLE!
NOOOO!!
GOOD ONE, YAMA-BUSHI!
I GOT IT!
33

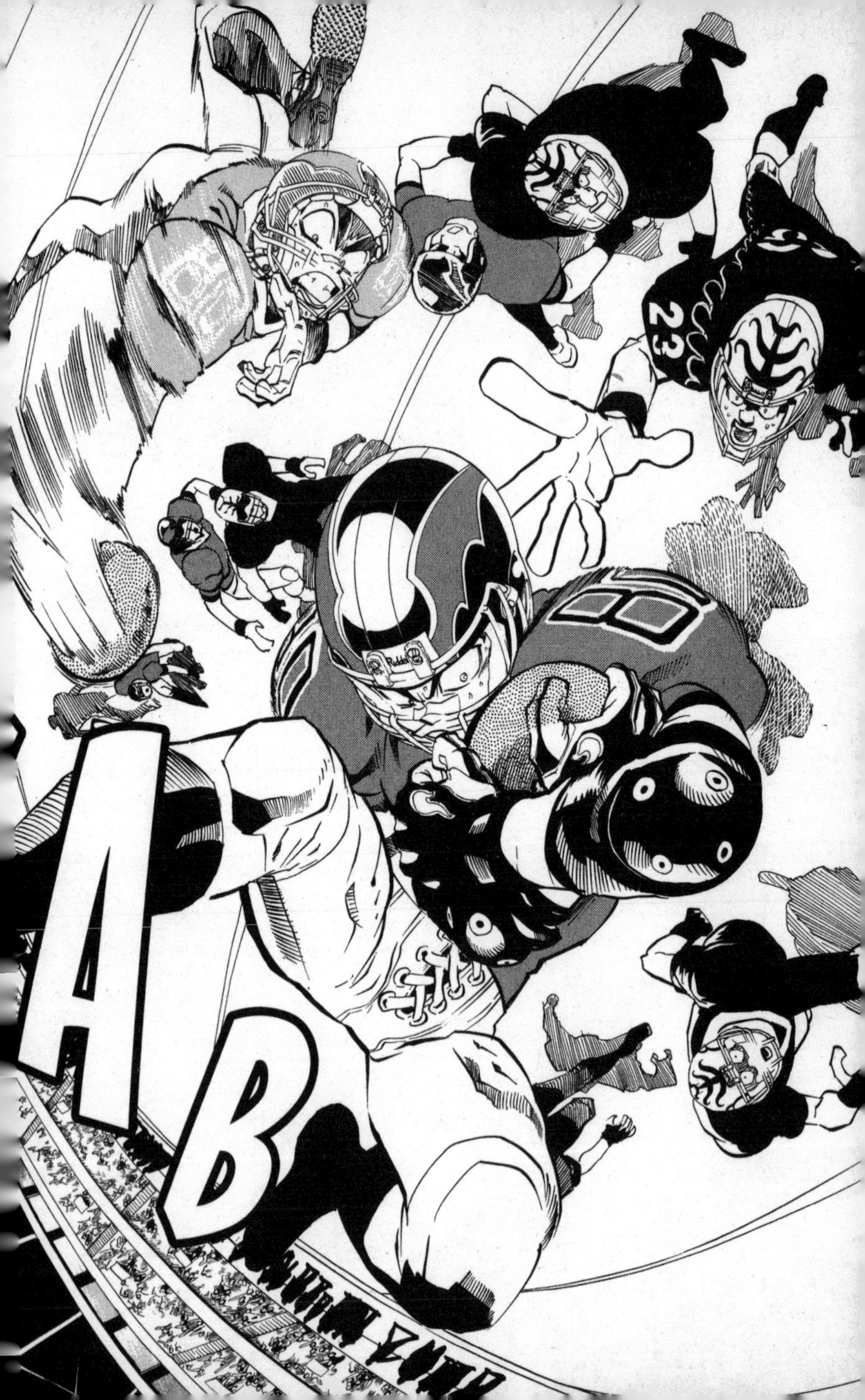

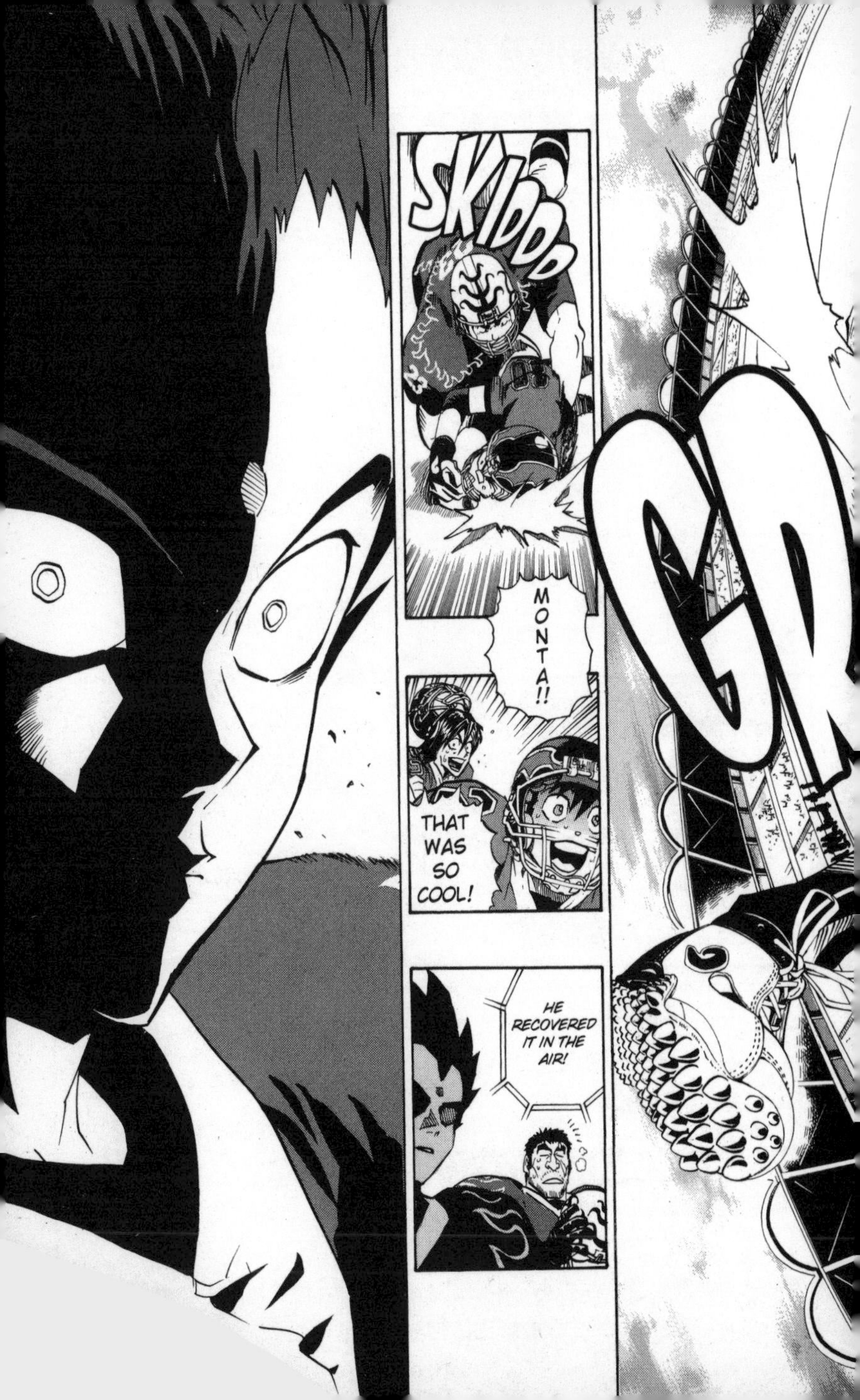
GR
SKIDDD
MONTA!!
THAT WAS SO COOL!
HE RECOVERED IT IN THE AIR!

**SURE BETS**

# WHO'S GONNA WIN?!

# DEIMON VS. SHINRYUJI

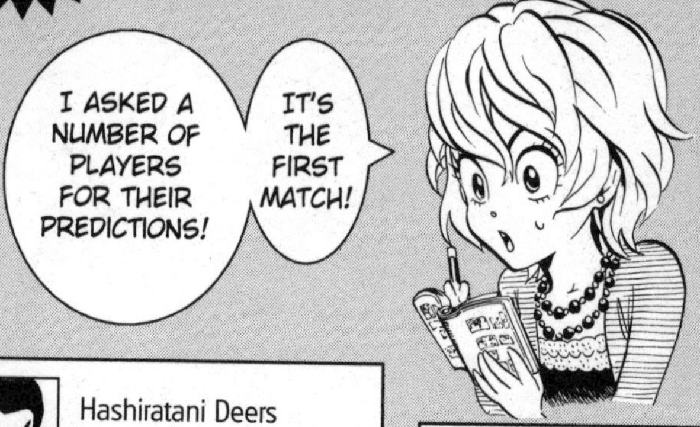
IT'S THE FIRST MATCH!
I ASKED A NUMBER OF PLAYERS FOR THEIR PREDICTIONS!

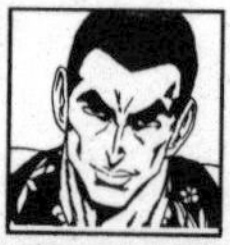

Hashiratani Deers

**Onihei Yamamoto**

| ODDS: | | |
|---|---|---|
| | DEIMON | 0.1% |
| | SHINRYUJI | 99.9% |

THE DIFFERENCE BETWEEN THE TWO TEAMS IS TOO GREAT. I GIVE DEIMON 0.1% ON THE MINISCULE CHANCE THAT KURITA MAY BE EVENLY MATCHED WITH YAMABUSHI. OTHER THAN THAT, AGON AND IKKYU ARE TOO GOOD. DEIMON BARELY STANDS A CHANCE.

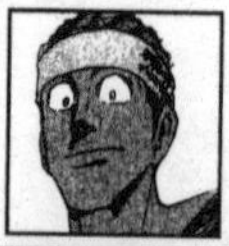

Nasa Aliens

**Panther**

| ODDS: | | |
|---|---|---|
| | DEIMON | 100% |
| | SHINRYUJI | 0% |

I DON'T KNOW ABOUT FOOTBALL IN JAPAN...BUT DEIMON'S GOT SENA, SO THEY'RE NOT GONNA LOSE!

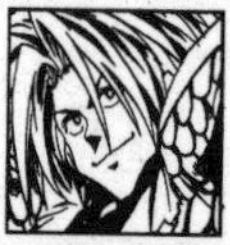

Kyoshin Poseidons

**Kengo Mizumachi**

| ODDS: | | |
|---|---|---|
| | DEIMON | 10% |
| | SHINRYUJI | 90% |

WELL, SHINRYUJI'S PRETTY STRONG! THEY SPRAINED MY ARM, BUT I'M TRAINING HARD SO I CAN GET REVENGE!

SENA PROMISED KAKEI THAT HE WOULDN'T LOSE UNTIL HE MEETS THE REAL EYESHIELD.

A GUY THAT SPIRITED CAN TURN THINGS AROUND, NO MATTER WHAT!

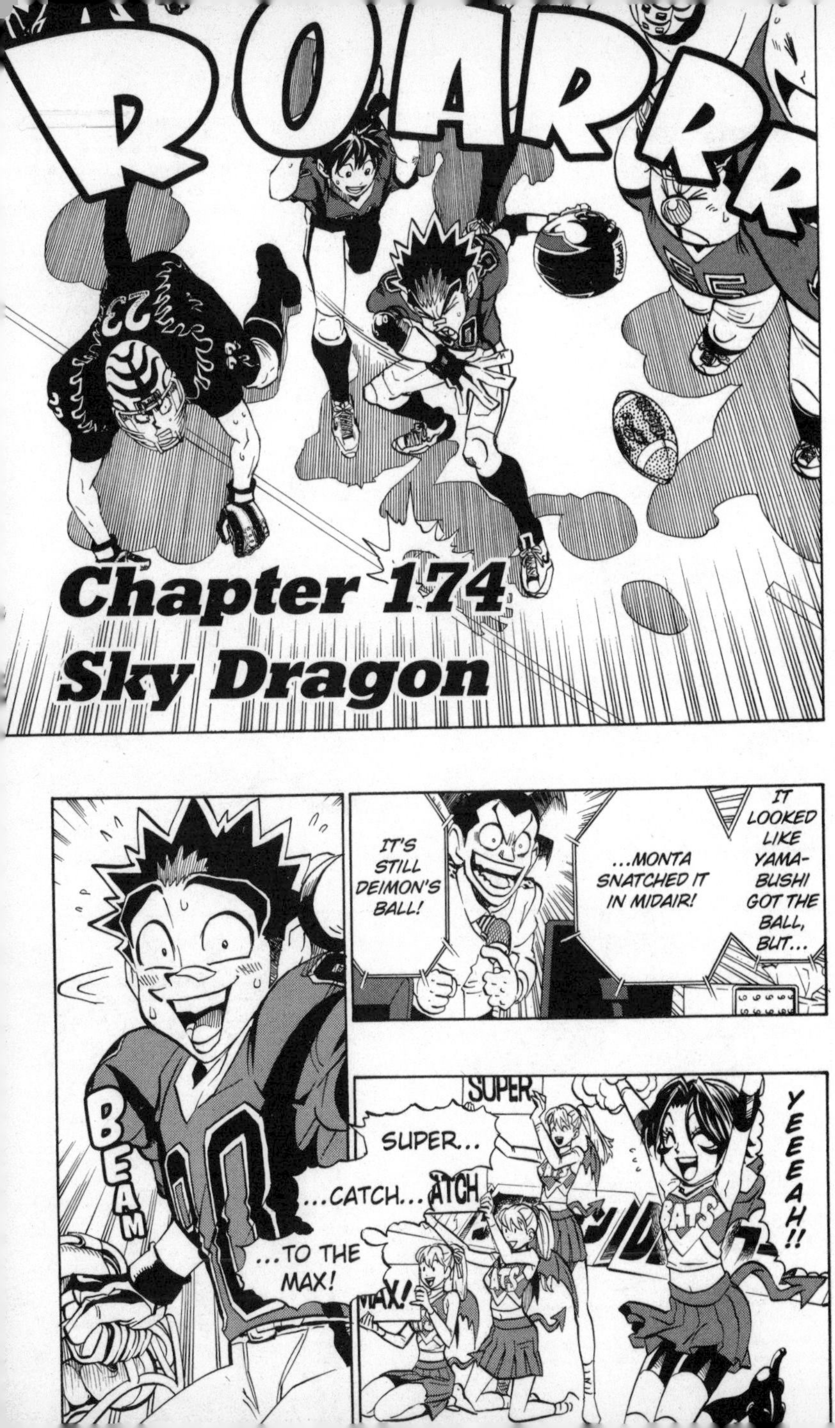
ROARR
Chapter 174
Sky Dragon
IT LOOKED LIKE YAMA-BUSHI GOT THE BALL, BUT...
...MONTA SNATCHED IT IN MIDAIR!
IT'S STILL DEIMON'S BALL!
YEEEAH!!
SUPER
SUPER...
...CATCH...
ATCH
...TO THE MAX!
MAX!
BEAM

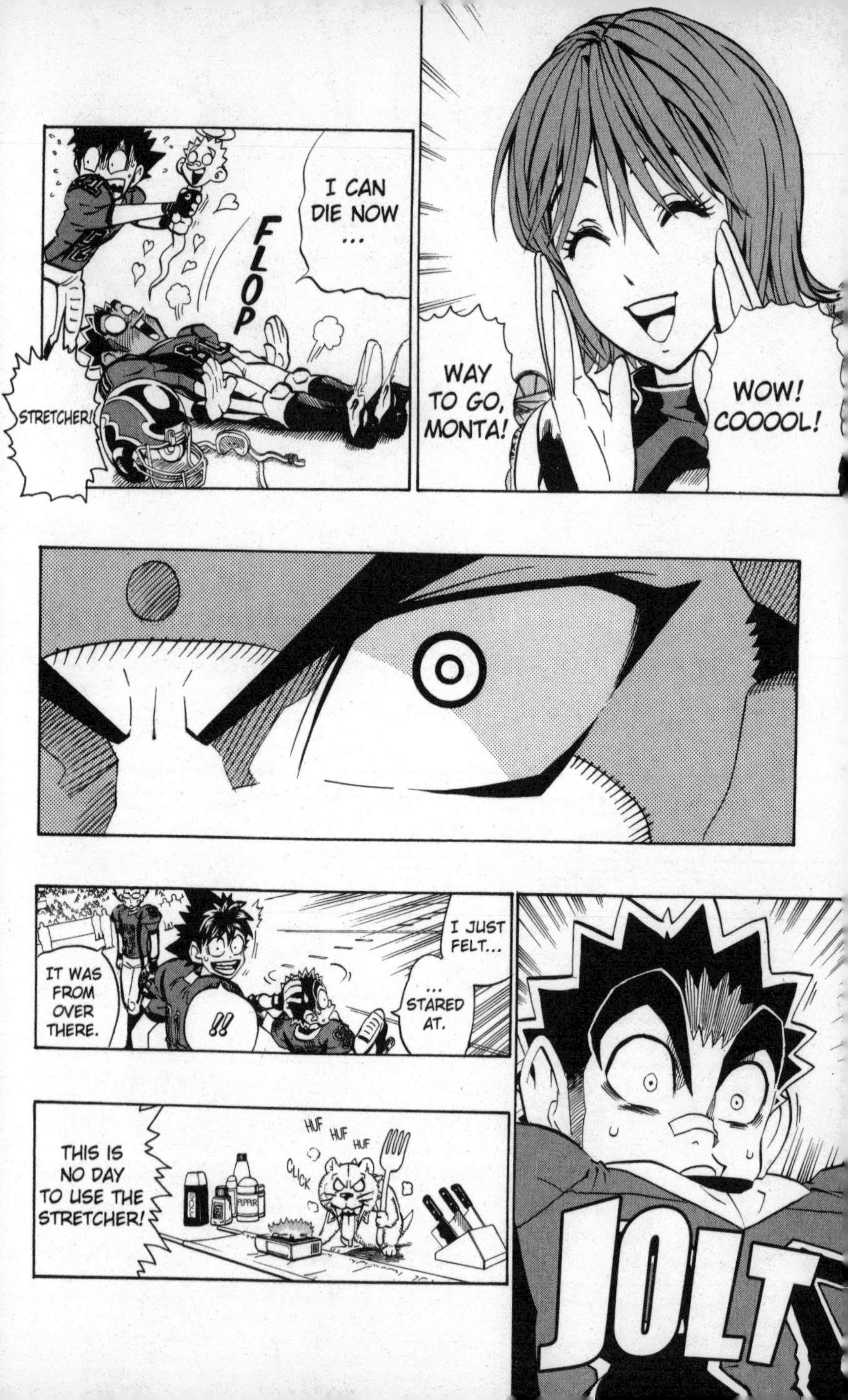
WOW! COOOOL!
WAY TO GO, MONTA!
I CAN DIE NOW ...
FLOP
STRETCHER!
JOLT
I JUST FELT...
... STARED AT.
!!
IT WAS FROM OVER THERE.
HUF HUF HUF
CLICK
THIS IS NO DAY TO USE THE STRETCHER!

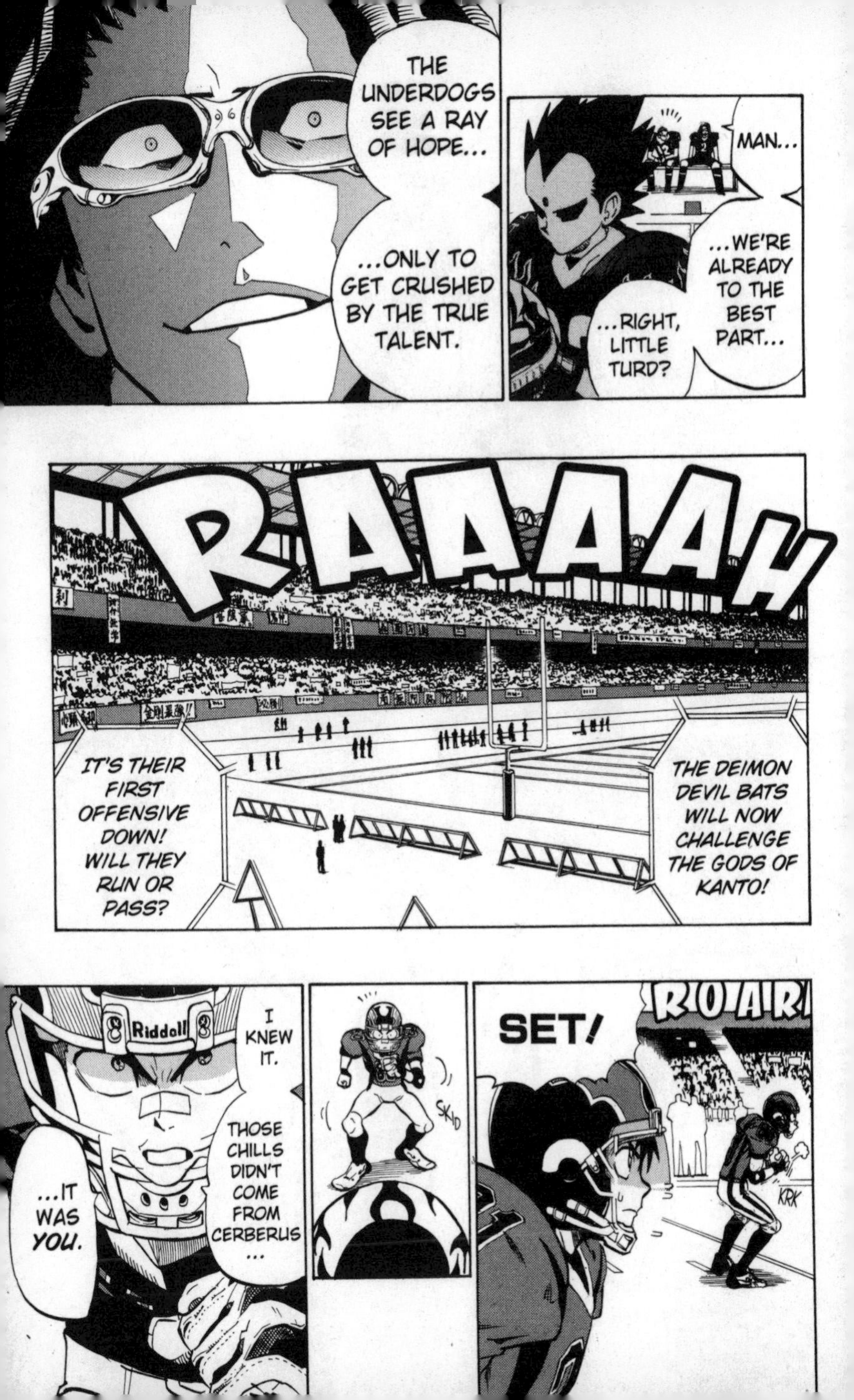
MAN...
...WE'RE ALREADY TO THE BEST PART...
...RIGHT, LITTLE TURD?
THE UNDERDOGS SEE A RAY OF HOPE...
...ONLY TO GET CRUSHED BY THE TRUE TALENT.
RAAAAH
THE DEIMON DEVIL BATS WILL NOW CHALLENGE THE GODS OF KANTO!
IT'S THEIR FIRST OFFENSIVE DOWN! WILL THEY RUN OR PASS?
ROAR
SET!
KRK
SKID
Riddell
I KNEW IT.
THOSE CHILLS DIDN'T COME FROM CERBERUS...
...IT WAS YOU.

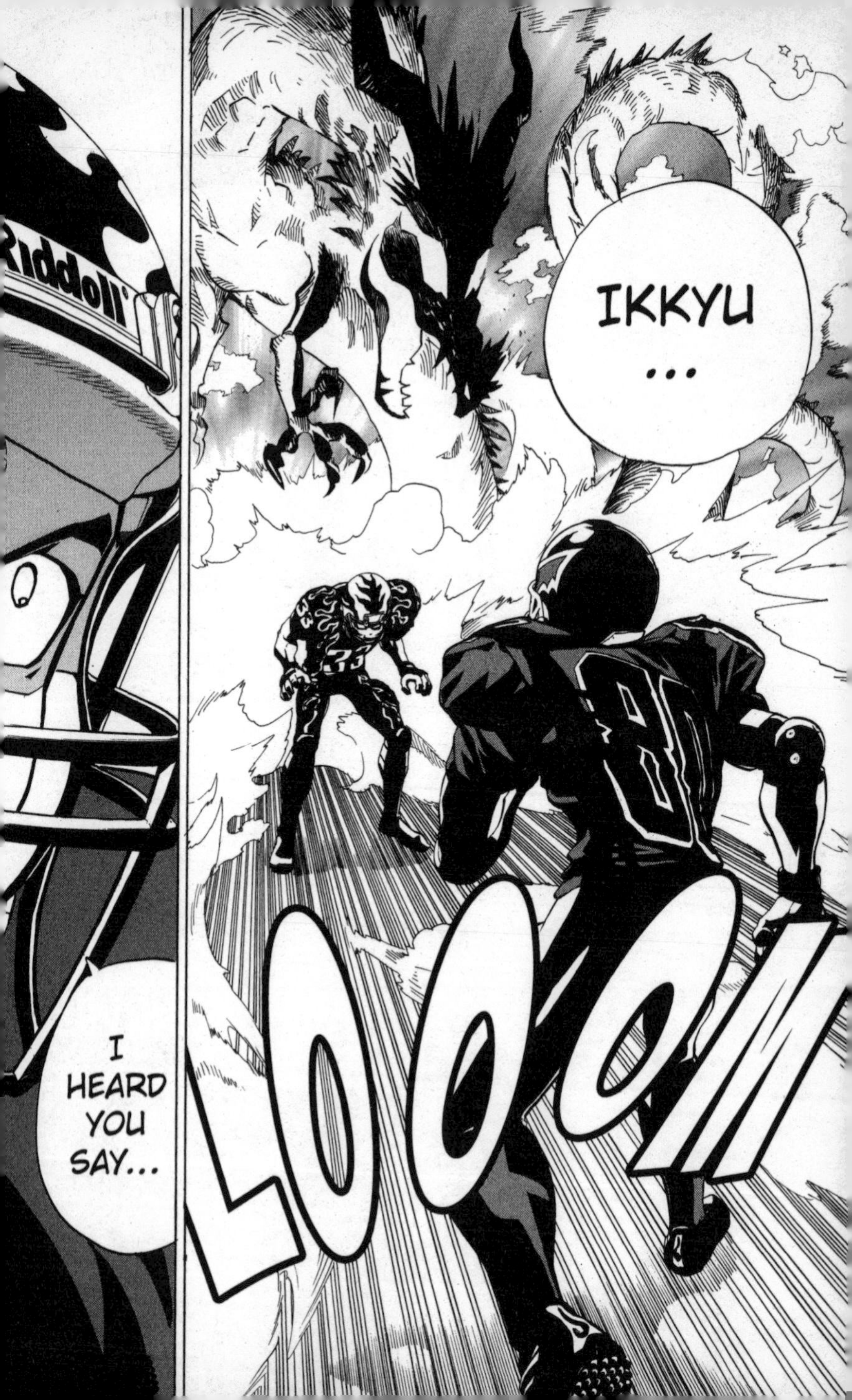
IKKYU ...
LOOOM
I HEARD YOU SAY...

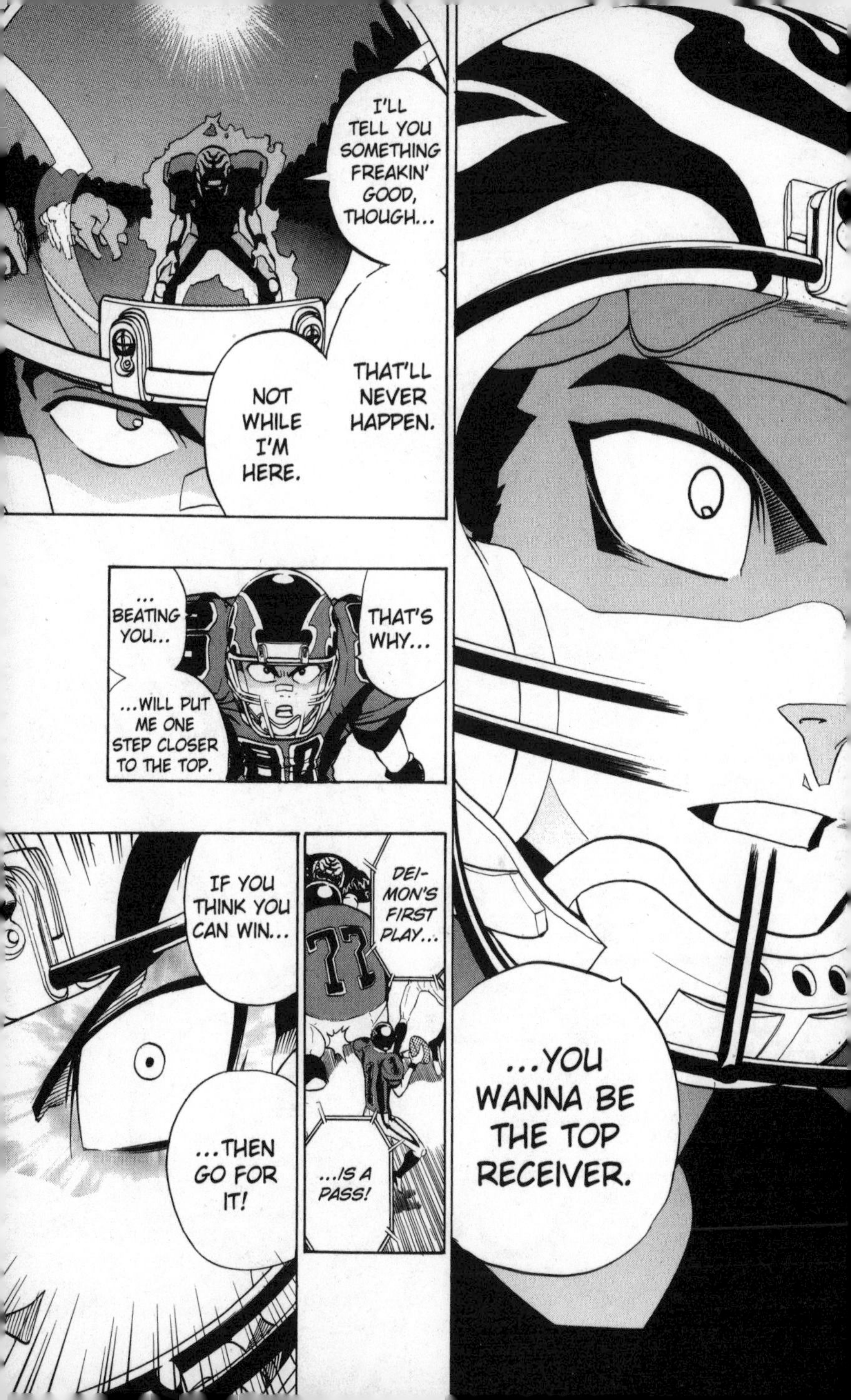
I'LL TELL YOU SOMETHING FREAKIN' GOOD, THOUGH...
...YOU WANNA BE THE TOP RECEIVER.
THAT'LL NEVER HAPPEN.
NOT WHILE I'M HERE.
THAT'S WHY...
...BEATING YOU...
...WILL PUT ME ONE STEP CLOSER TO THE TOP.
DEI-MON'S FIRST PLAY...
...IS A PASS!
IF YOU THINK YOU CAN WIN...
...THEN GO FOR IT!

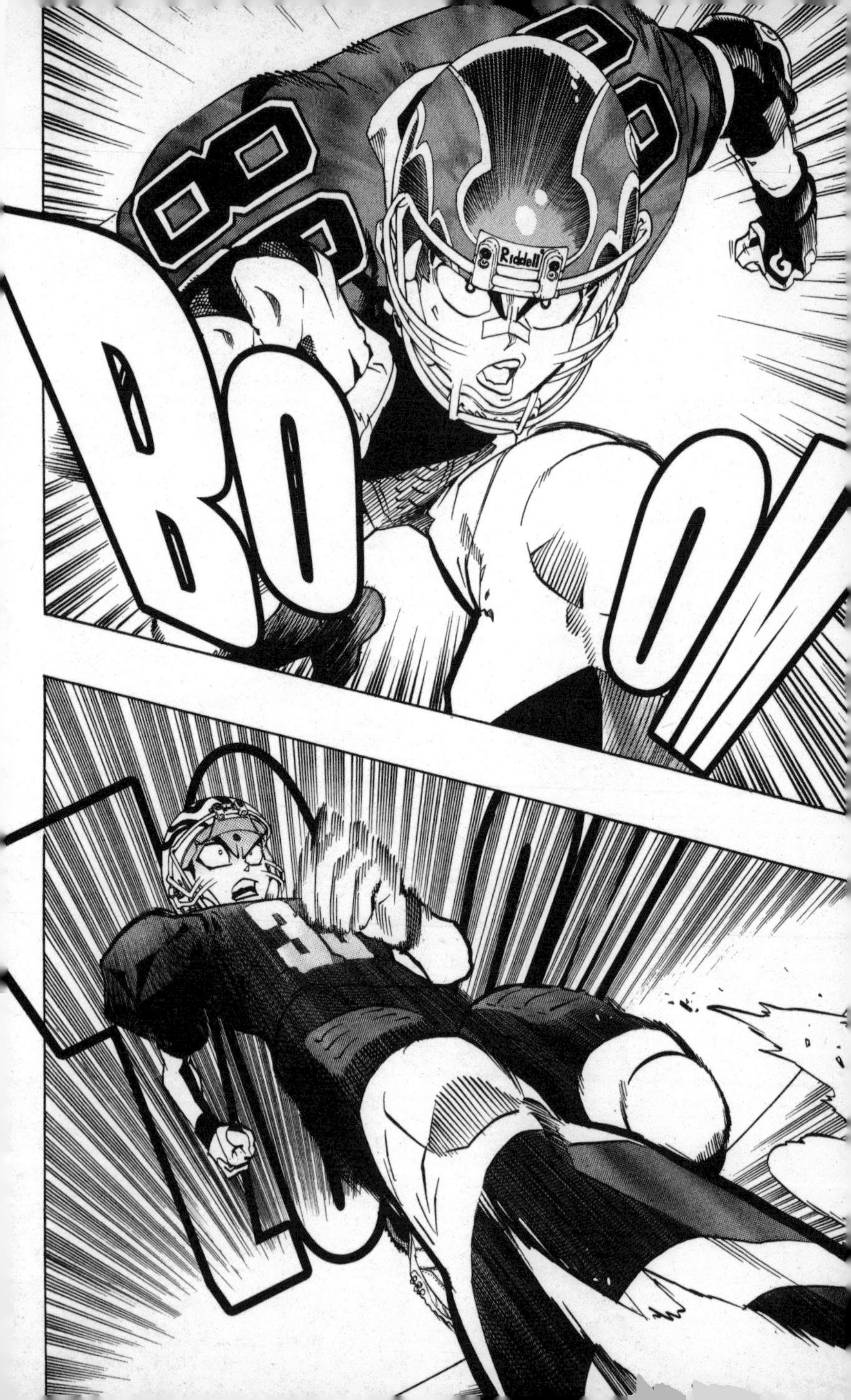
Riddell
BO
O

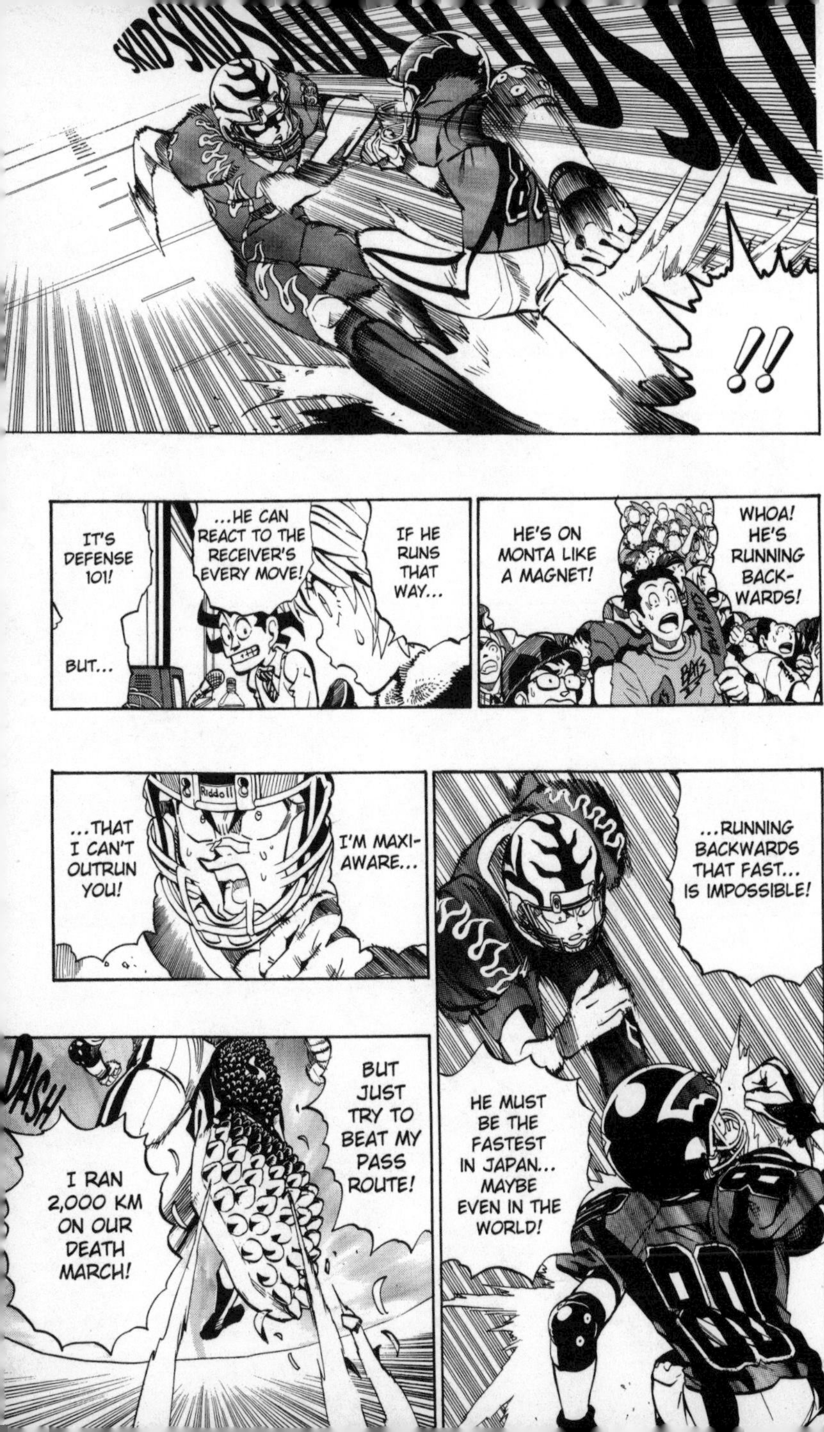
SKIDSKIDSKIDSKIDSKID
!!
WHOA! HE'S RUNNING BACKWARDS!
HE'S ON MONTA LIKE A MAGNET!
IF HE RUNS THAT WAY...
...HE CAN REACT TO THE RECEIVER'S EVERY MOVE!
IT'S DEFENSE 101!
BUT...
...RUNNING BACKWARDS THAT FAST... IS IMPOSSIBLE!
HE MUST BE THE FASTEST IN JAPAN... MAYBE EVEN IN THE WORLD!
I'M MAXI-AWARE...
...THAT I CAN'T OUTRUN YOU!
BUT JUST TRY TO BEAT MY PASS ROUTE!
I RAN 2,000 KM ON OUR DEATH MARCH!
DASH

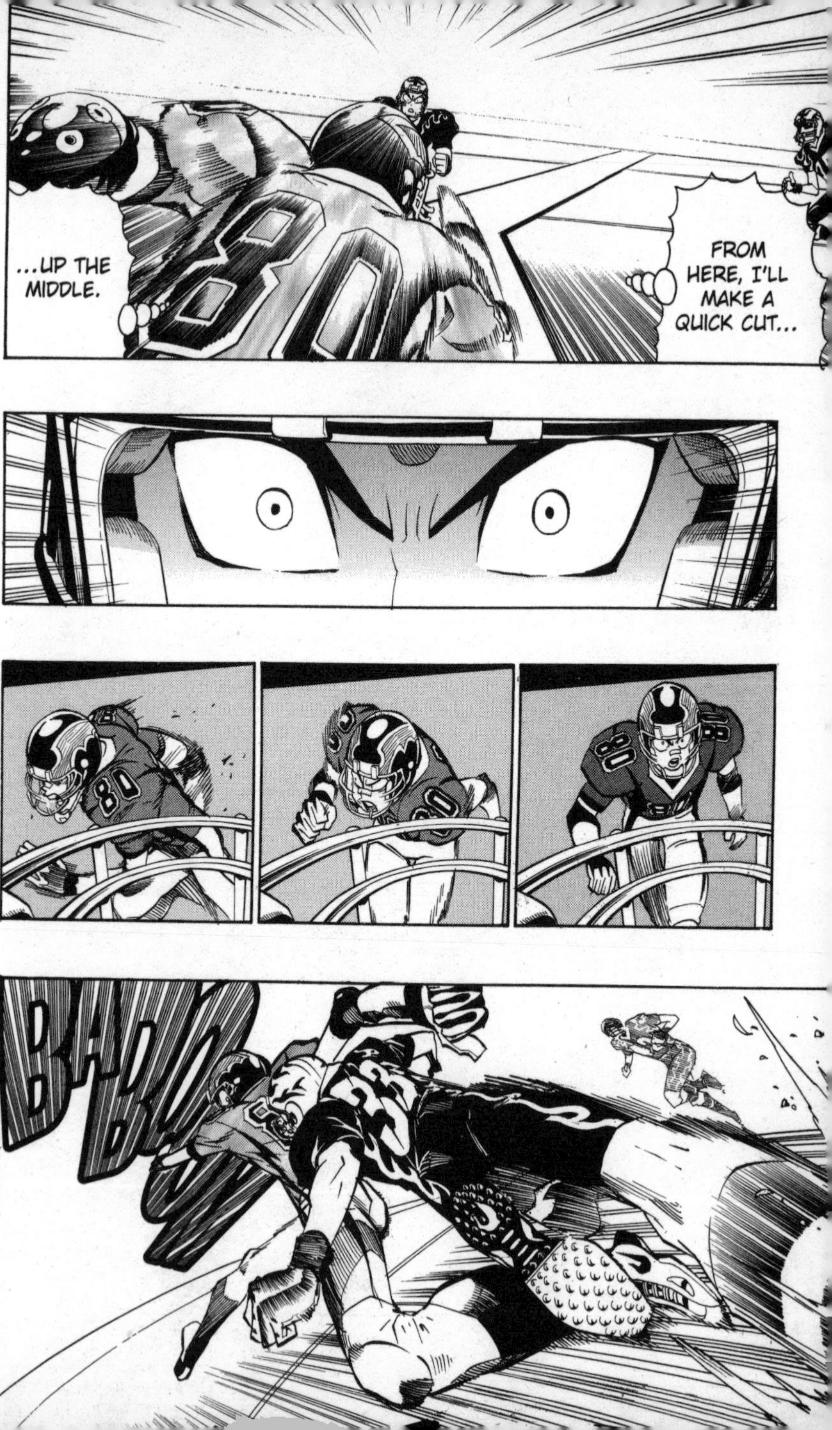
FROM HERE, I'LL MAKE A QUICK CUT...
...UP THE MIDDLE.

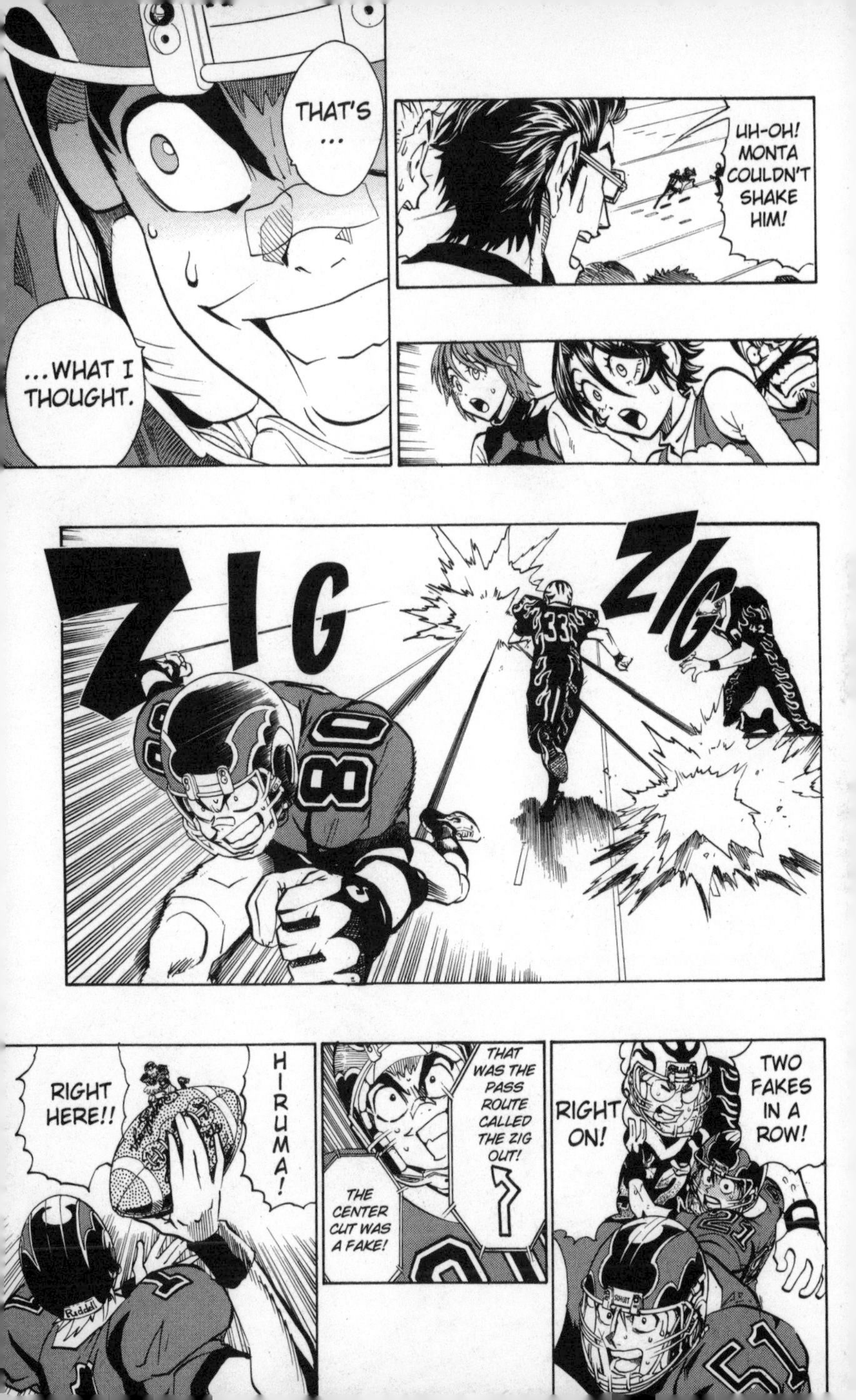
UH-OH! MONTA COULDN'T SHAKE HIM!
THAT'S ...
...WHAT I THOUGHT.
ZIG
ZIG
TWO FAKES IN A ROW!
RIGHT ON!
THAT WAS THE PASS ROUTE CALLED THE ZIG OUT!
THE CENTER CUT WAS A FAKE!
HIRUMA!
RIGHT HERE!!

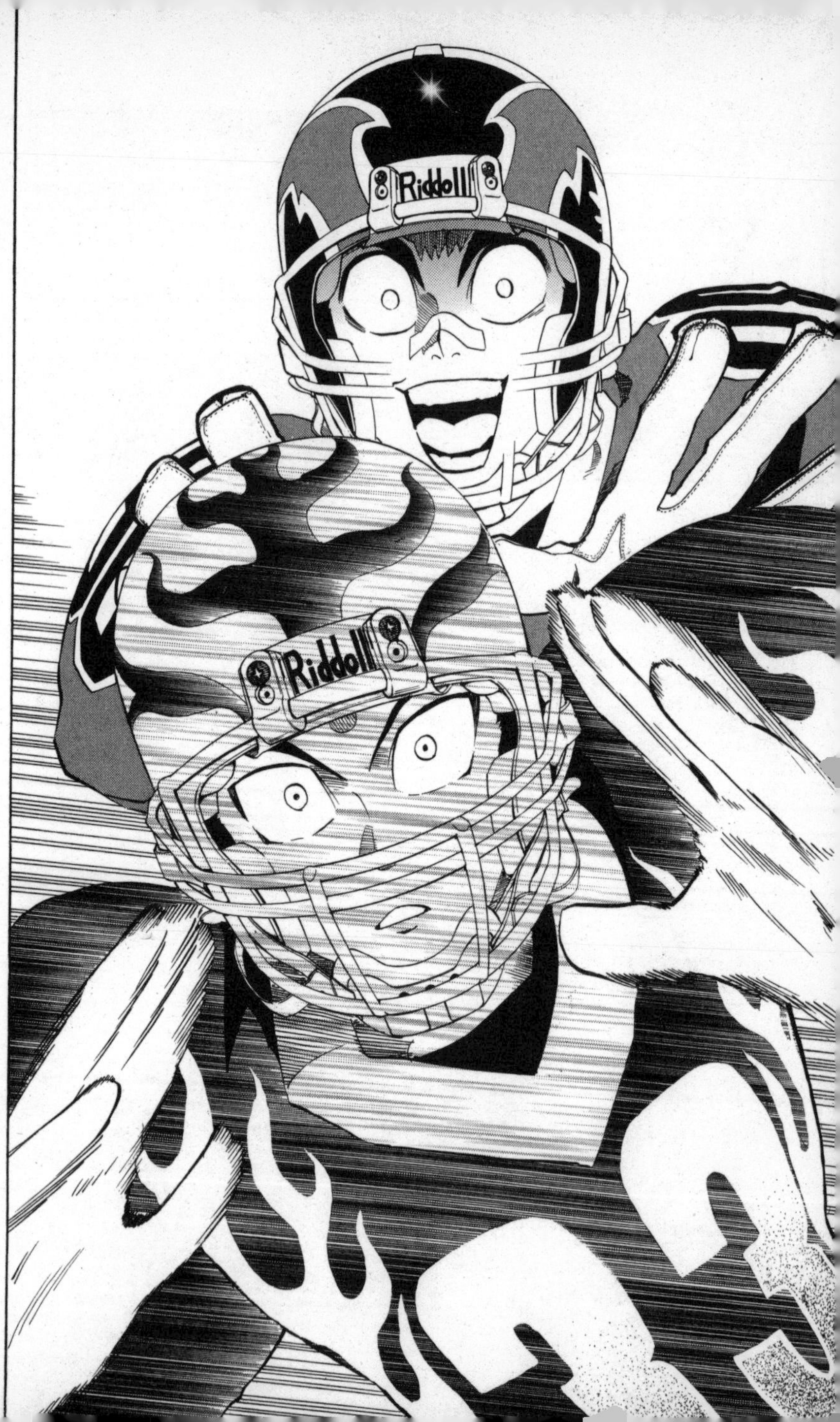
Riddoll
Riddoll

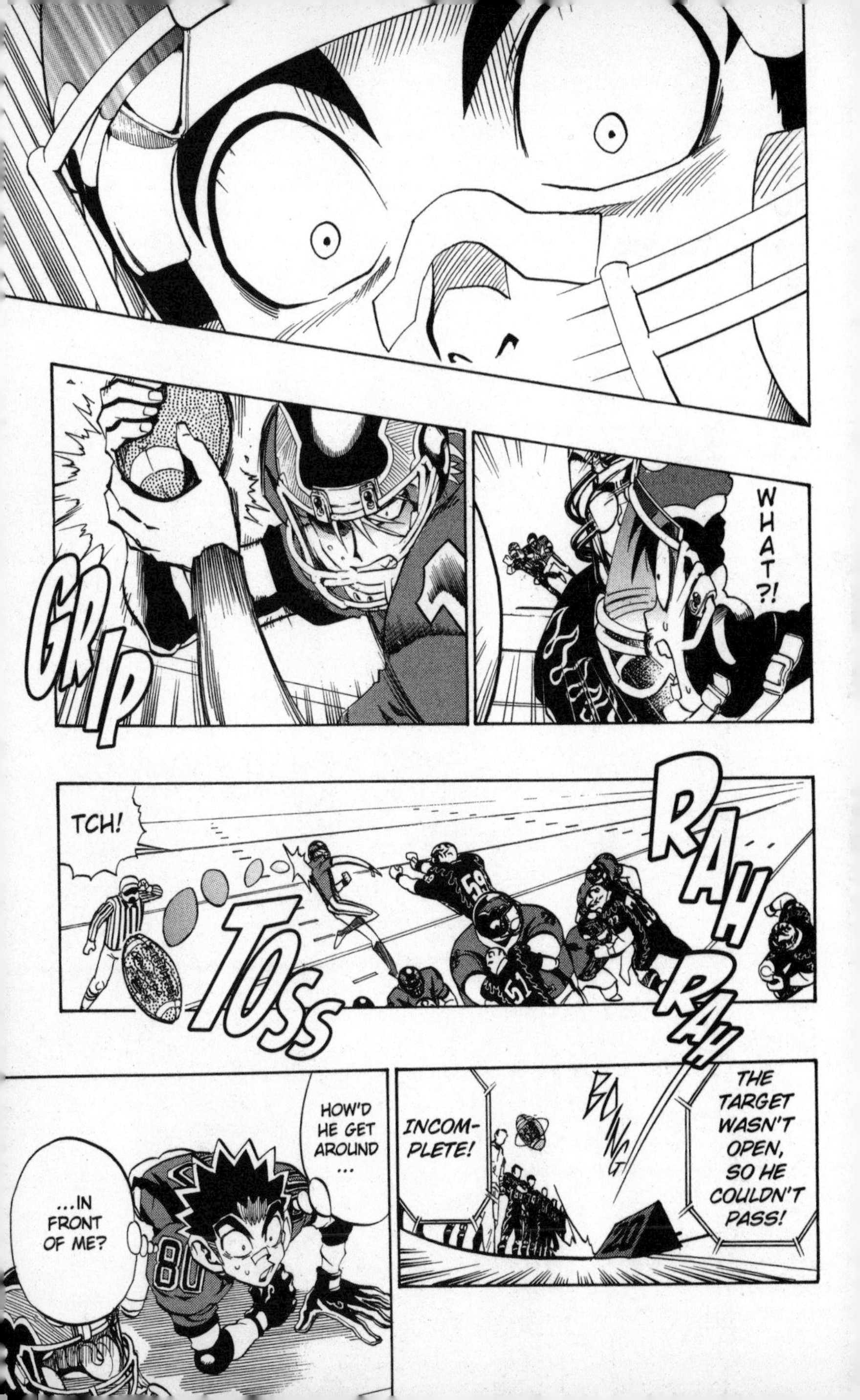
WHAT?!
GRIP
RAH RAH
TCH!
TOSS
THE TARGET WASN'T OPEN, SO HE COULDN'T PASS!
BOING
INCOMPLETE!
HOW'D HE GET AROUND...
...IN FRONT OF ME?

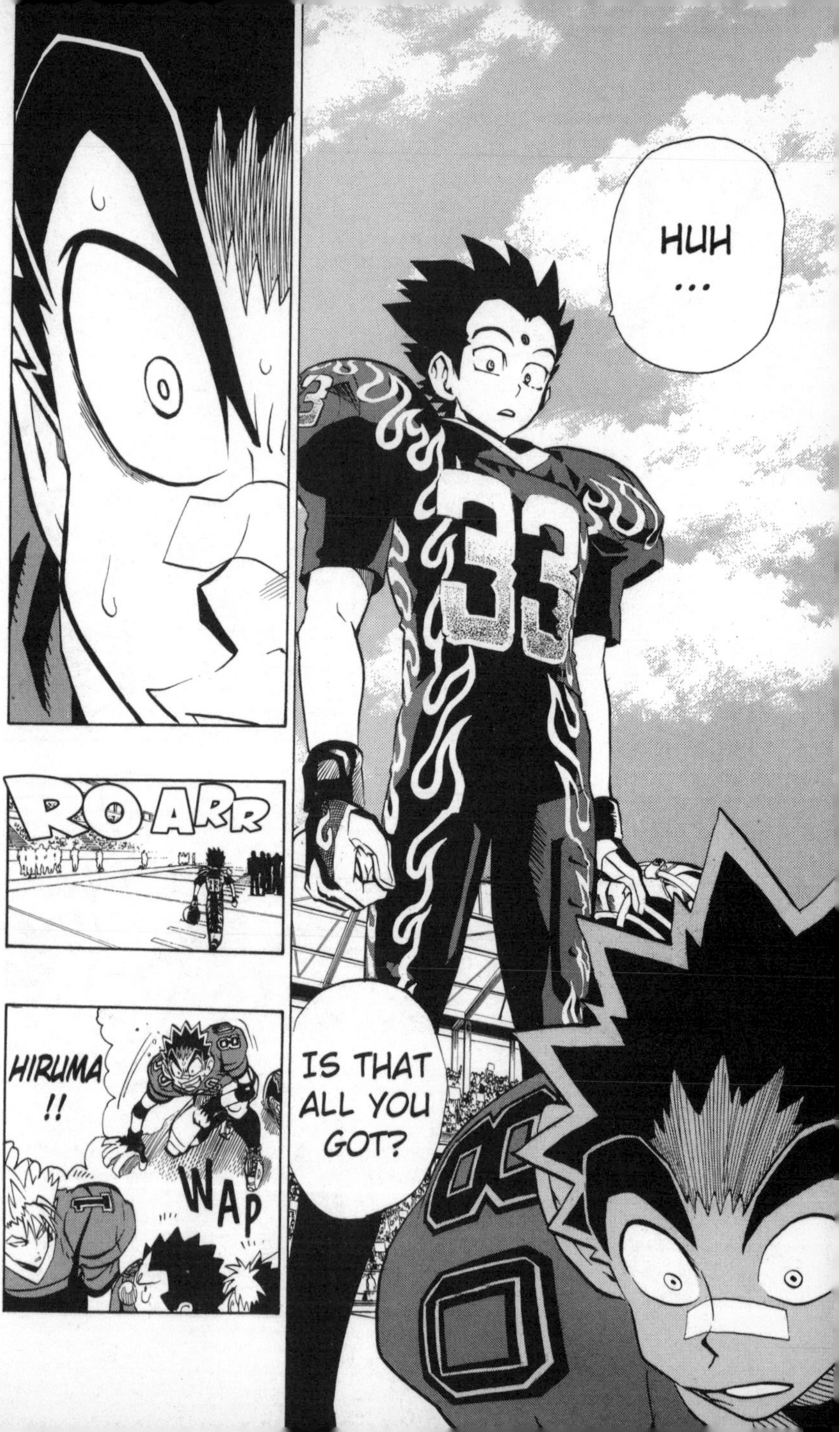
HUH...
IS THAT ALL YOU GOT?
RO-ARR
HIRUMA!!
WAP

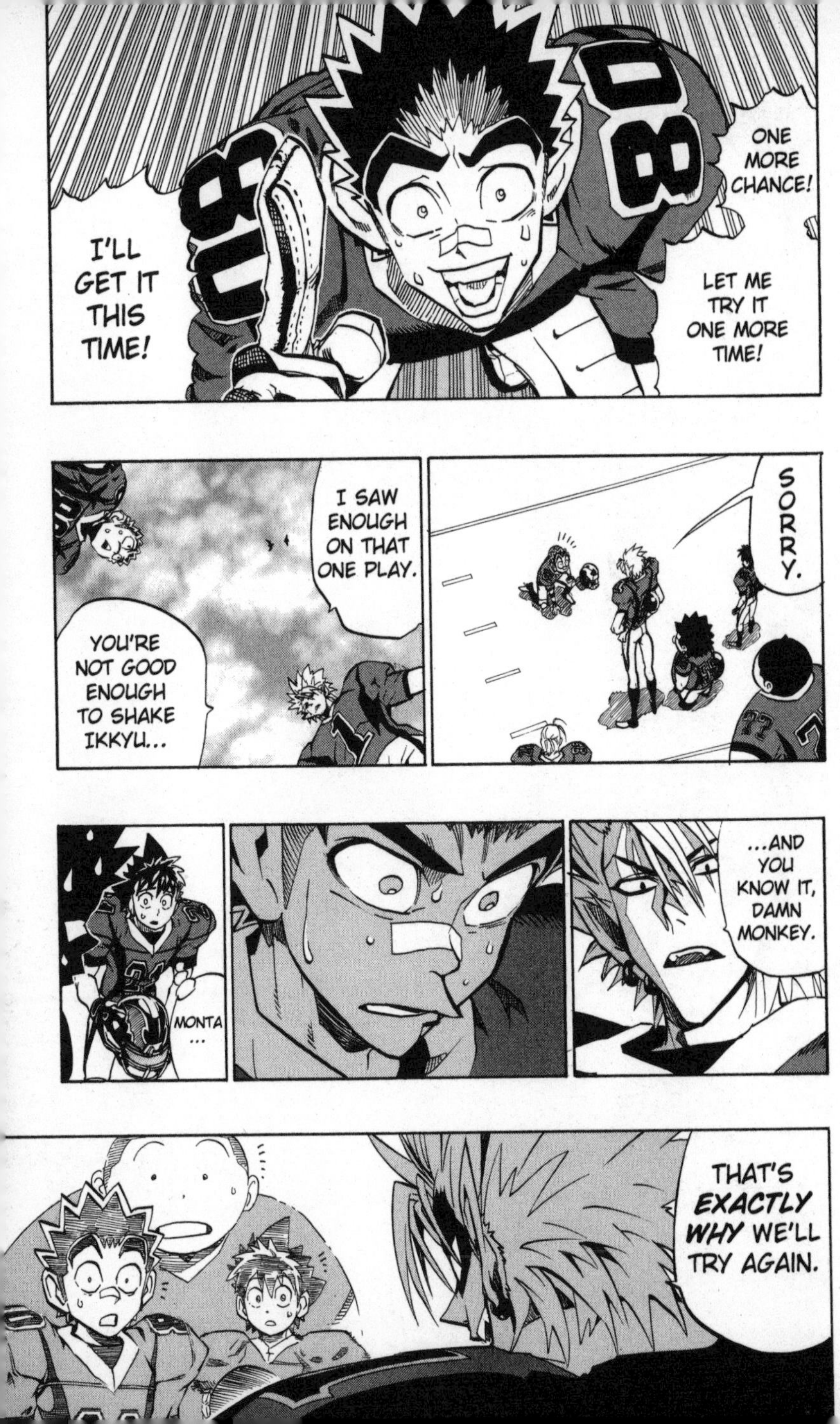
ONE MORE CHANCE!
LET ME TRY IT ONE MORE TIME!
I'LL GET IT THIS TIME!
SORRY.
I SAW ENOUGH ON THAT ONE PLAY.
YOU'RE NOT GOOD ENOUGH TO SHAKE IKKYU...
...AND YOU KNOW IT, DAMN MONKEY.
MONTA ...
THAT'S *EXACTLY WHY* WE'LL TRY AGAIN.

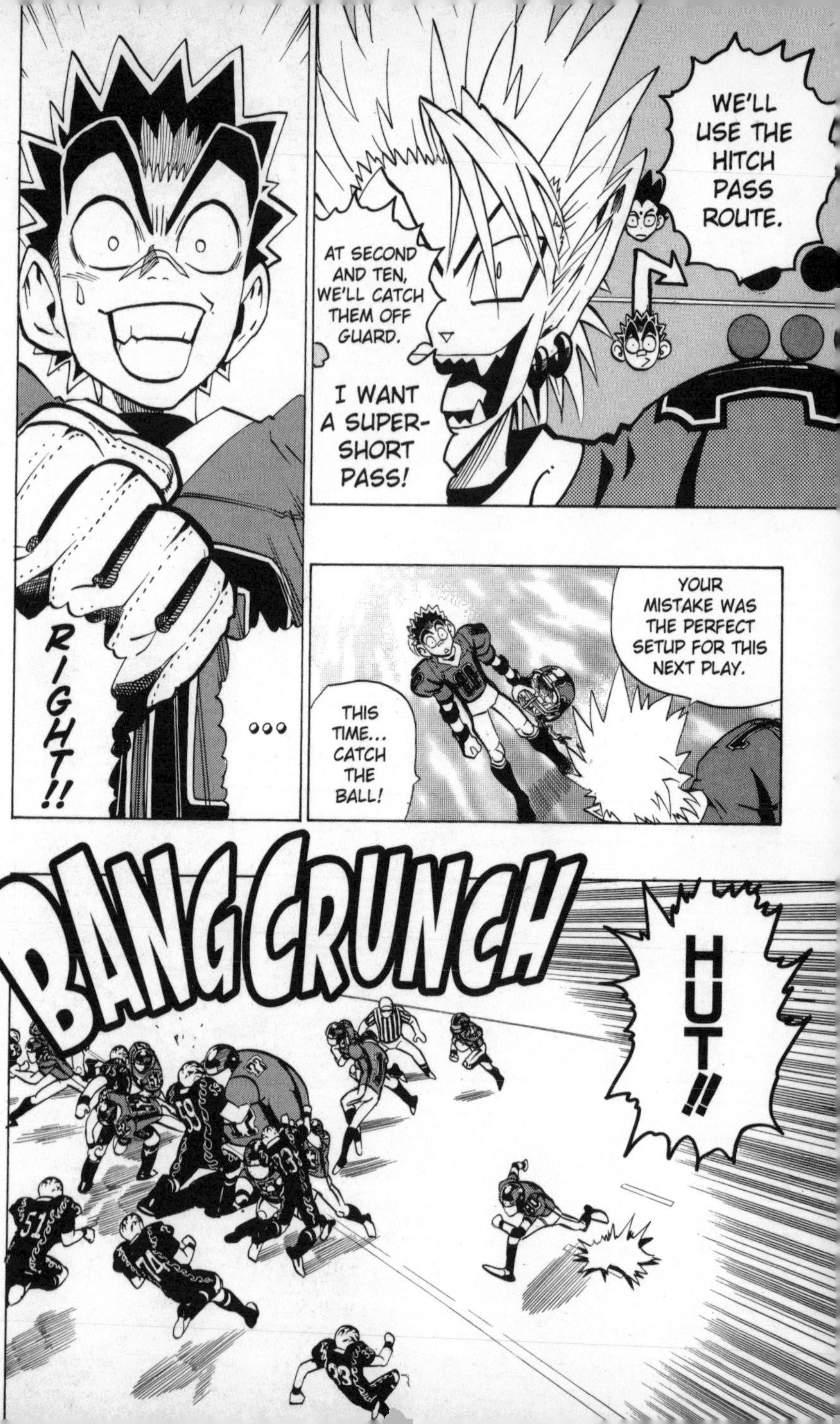
WE'LL USE THE HITCH PASS ROUTE.
AT SECOND AND TEN, WE'LL CATCH THEM OFF GUARD.
I WANT A SUPER-SHORT PASS!
YOUR MISTAKE WAS THE PERFECT SETUP FOR THIS NEXT PLAY.
THIS TIME... CATCH THE BALL!
RIGHT!!
...
HUT!!
BANG CRUNCH

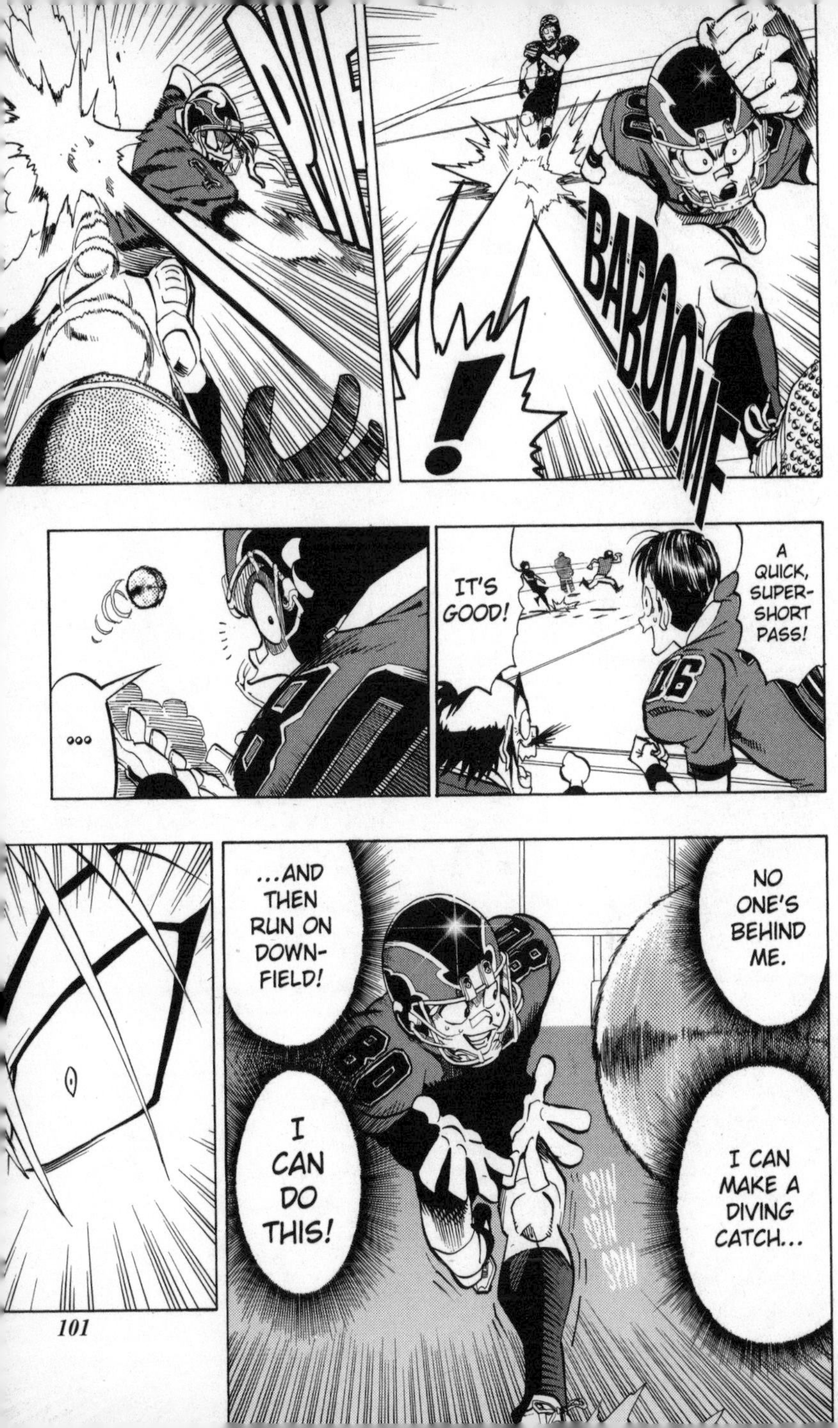
BABOOM
!
A QUICK, SUPER-SHORT PASS!
IT'S GOOD!
...
NO ONE'S BEHIND ME.
I CAN MAKE A DIVING CATCH...
...AND THEN RUN ON DOWNFIELD!
I CAN DO THIS!
SPIN SPIN SPIN

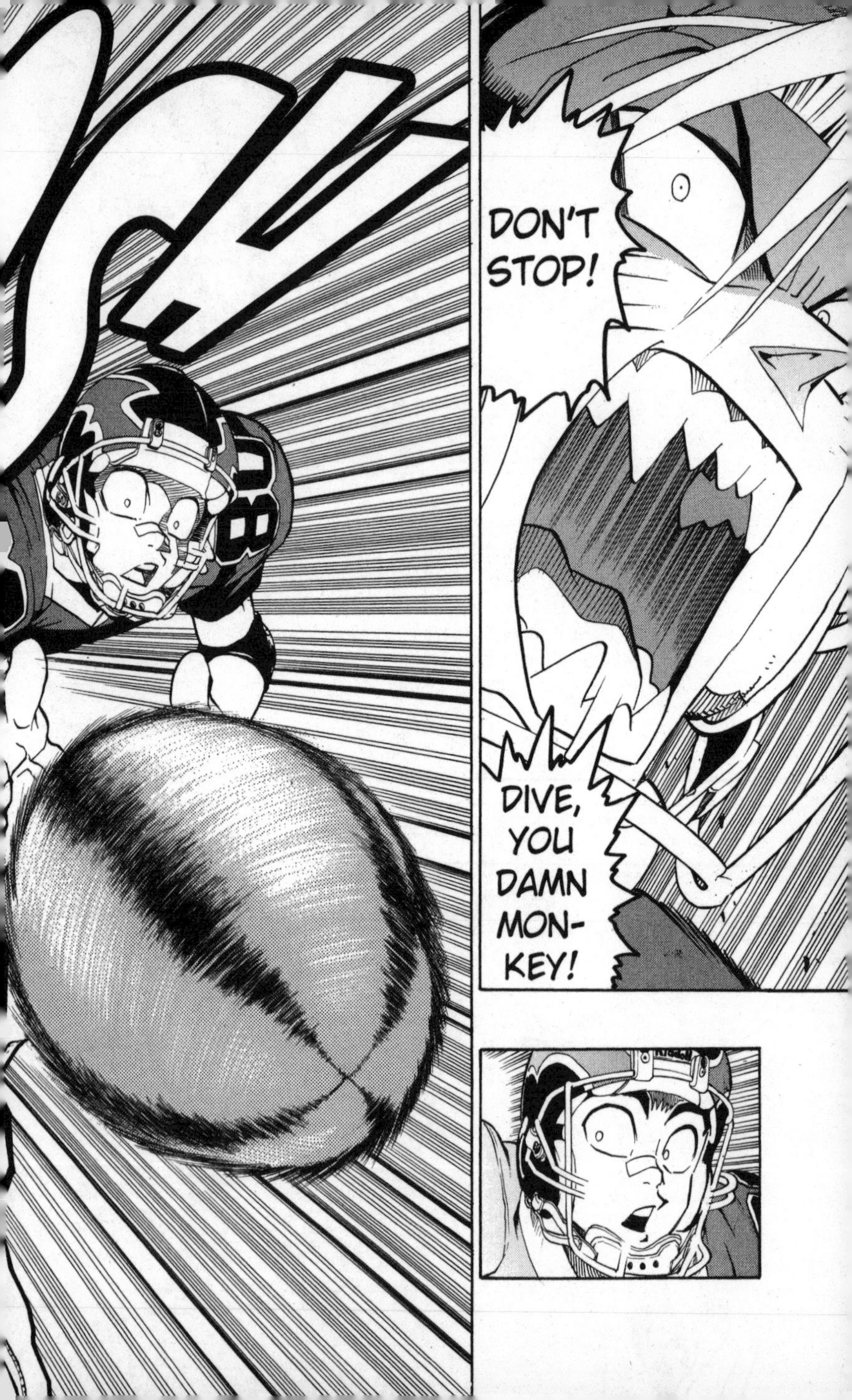
DON'T STOP!
DIVE, YOU DAMN MON-KEY!

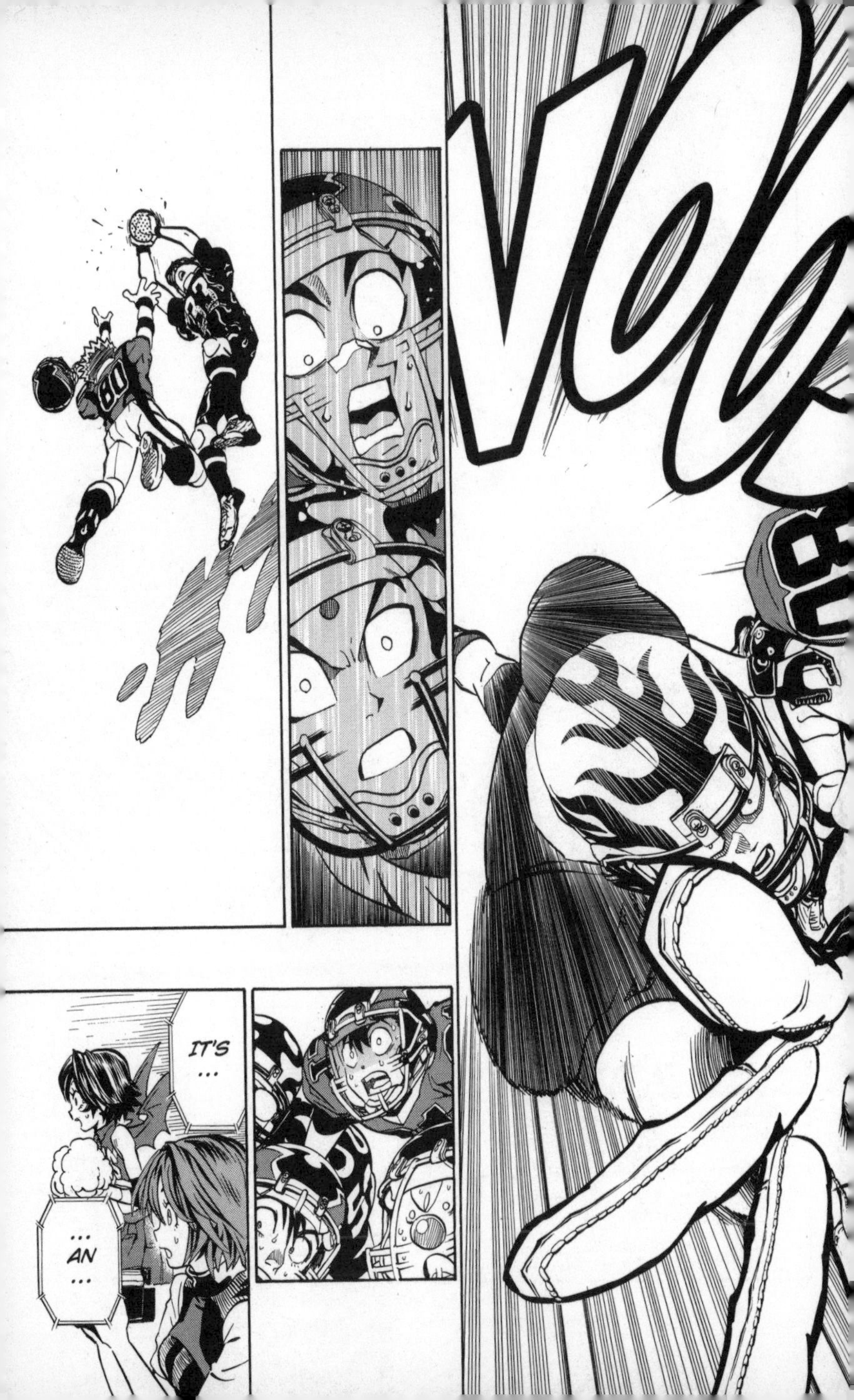
IT'S ...
... AN ...

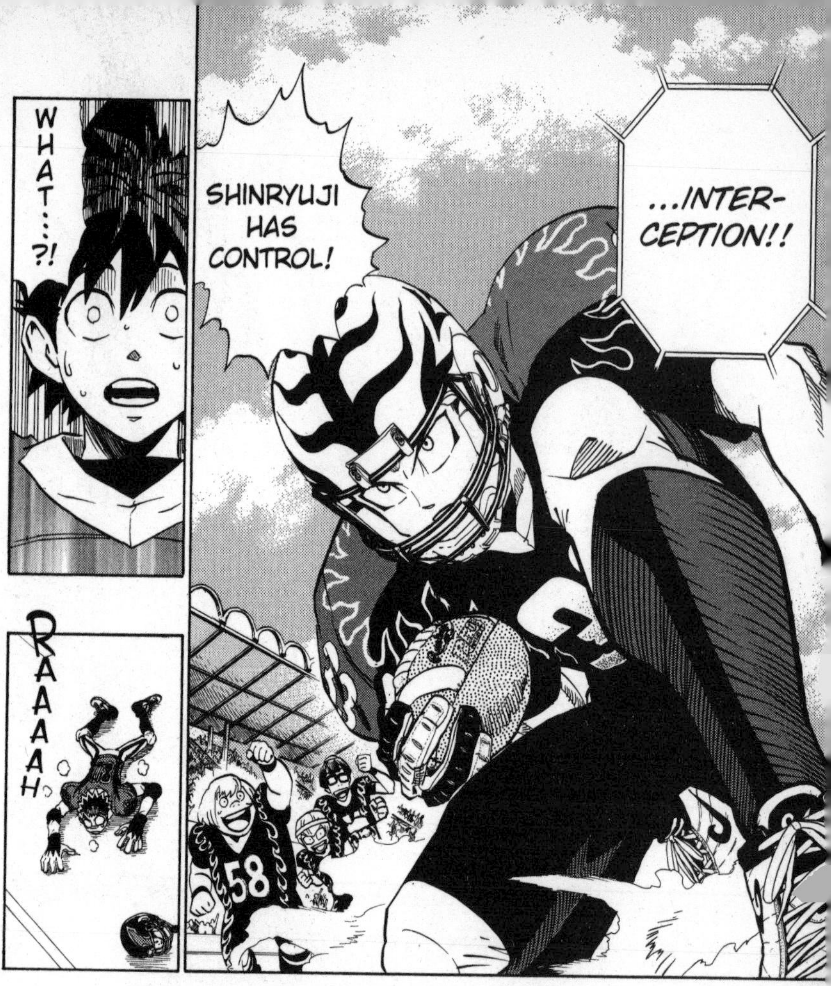
...INTER-CEPTION!!
SHINRYUJI HAS CONTROL!
WHAT...?!
RAAAAAH

※ INTERCEPTION = CATCHING THE OPPONENT'S BALL IN MIDAIR

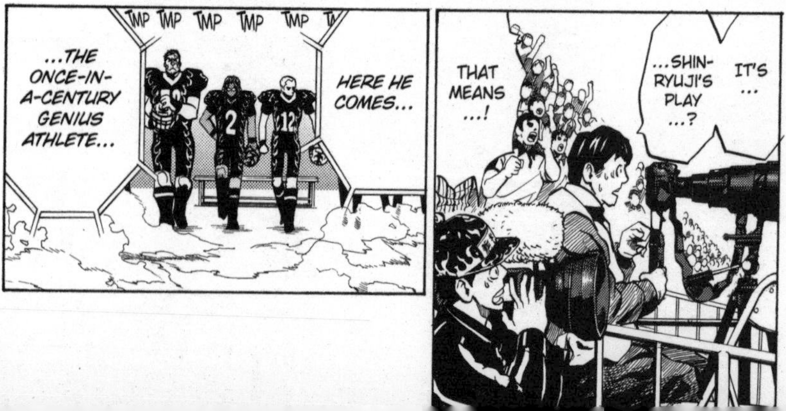
IT'S ...
...SHIN-RYUJI'S PLAY ...?
THAT MEANS ...!
TMP TMP TMP TMP TMP
HERE HE COMES...
...THE ONCE-IN-A-CENTURY GENIUS ATHLETE...

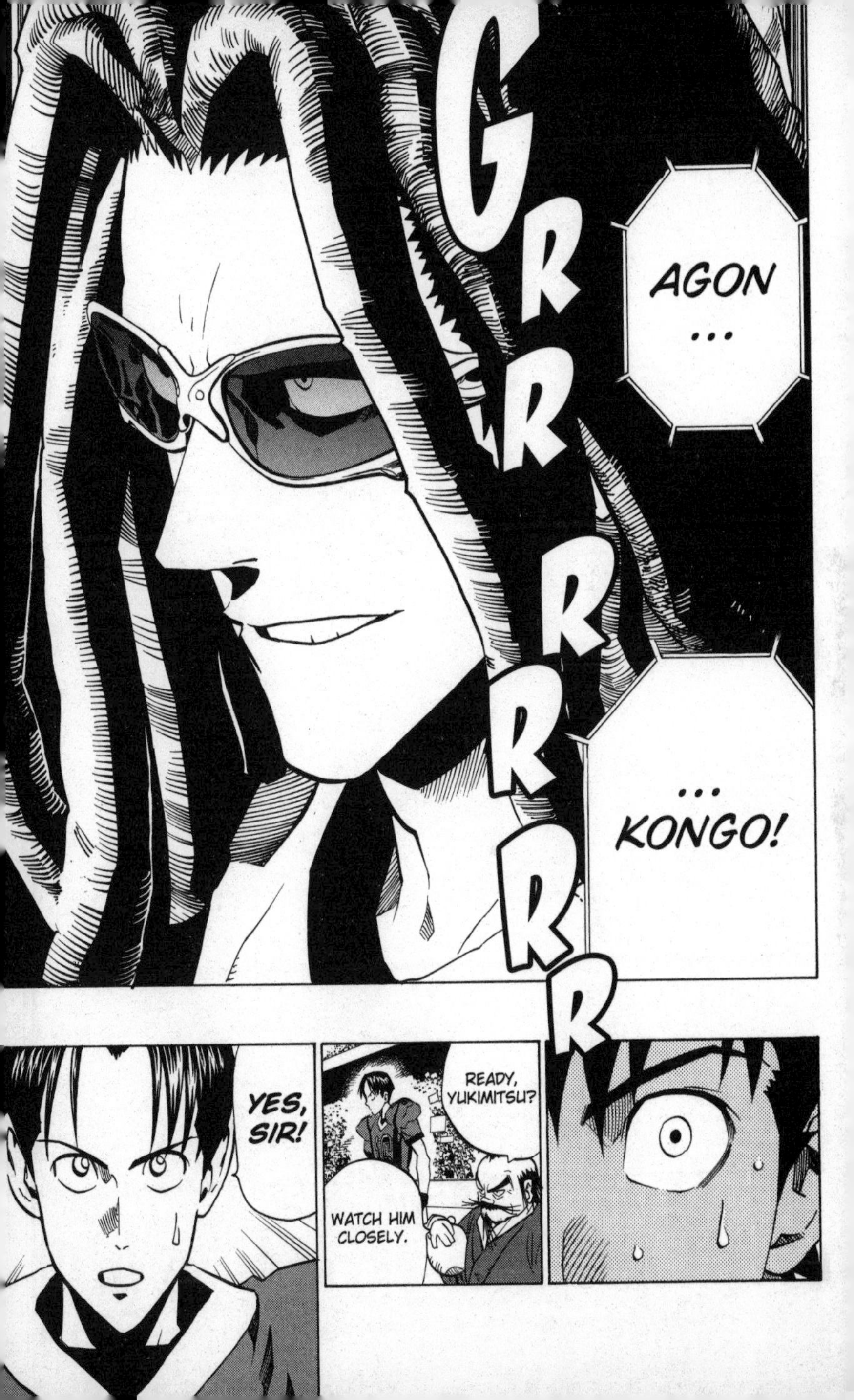
AGON ...
... KONGO!
GRRRRRRR
READY, YUKIMITSU?
WATCH HIM CLOSELY.
YES, SIR!

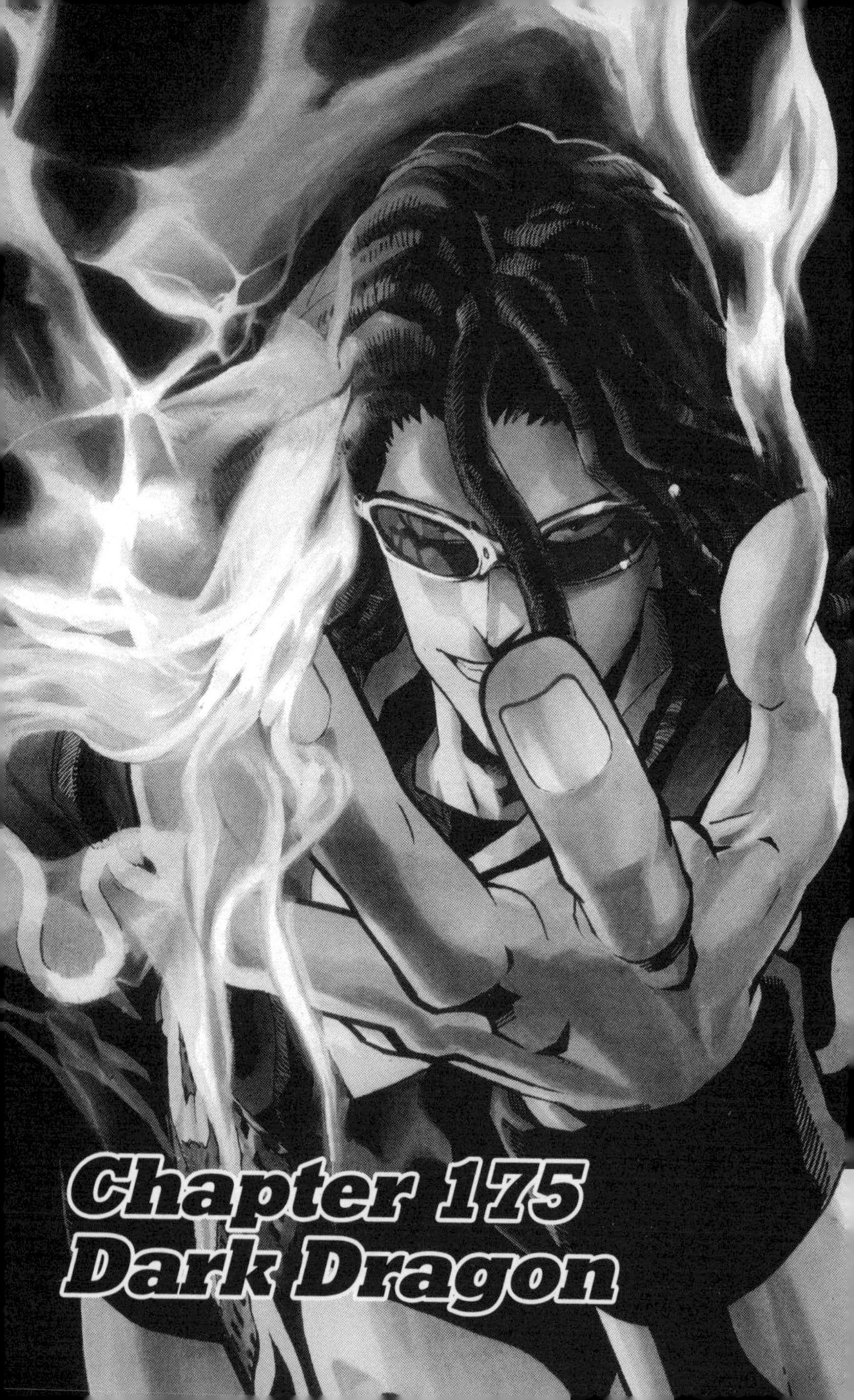
Chapter 175
Dark Dragon

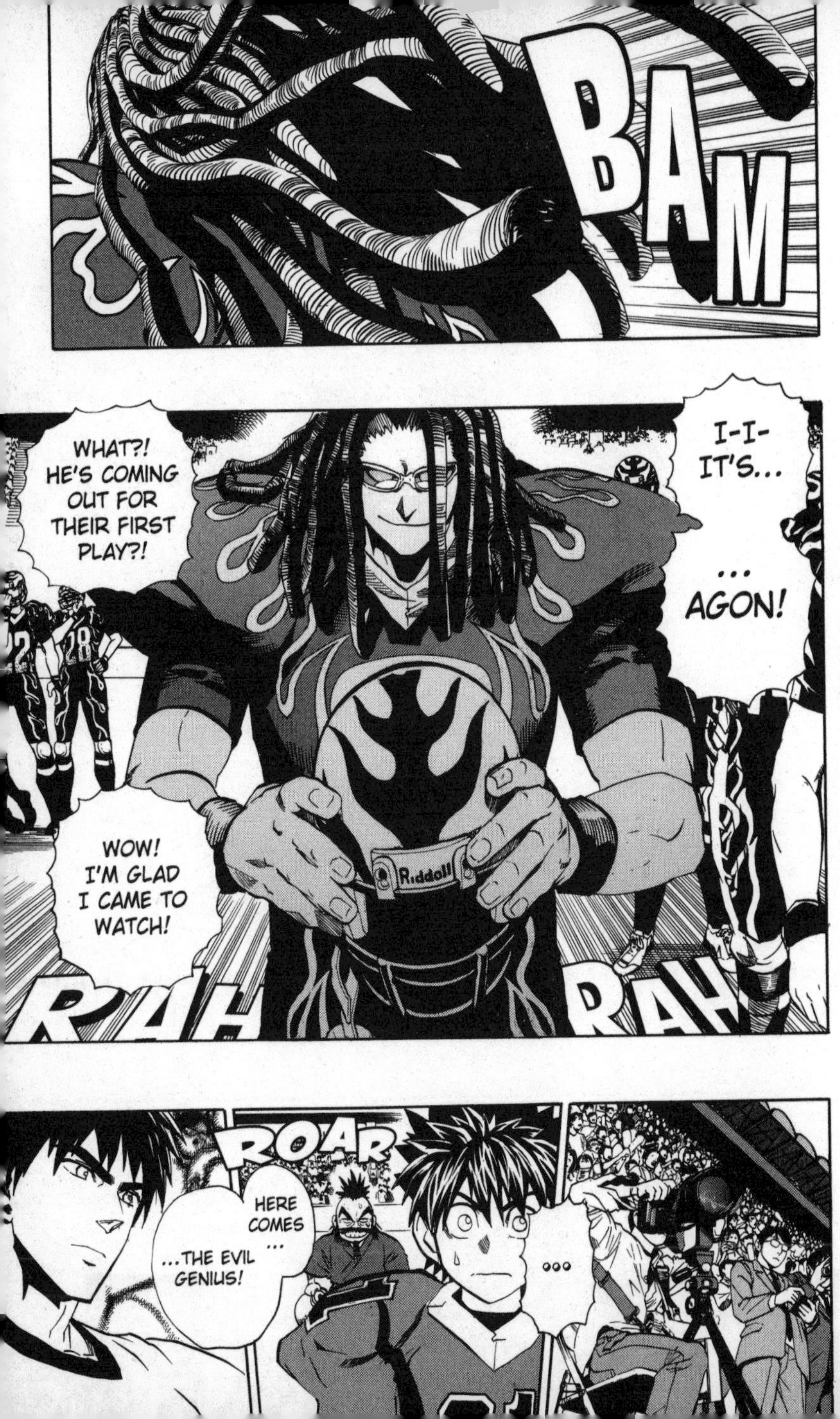
BAM
I-I- IT'S... ...AGON!
WHAT?! HE'S COMING OUT FOR THEIR FIRST PLAY?!
WOW! I'M GLAD I CAME TO WATCH!
RAH
RAH
ROAR
...
HERE COMES ...
...THE EVIL GENIUS!

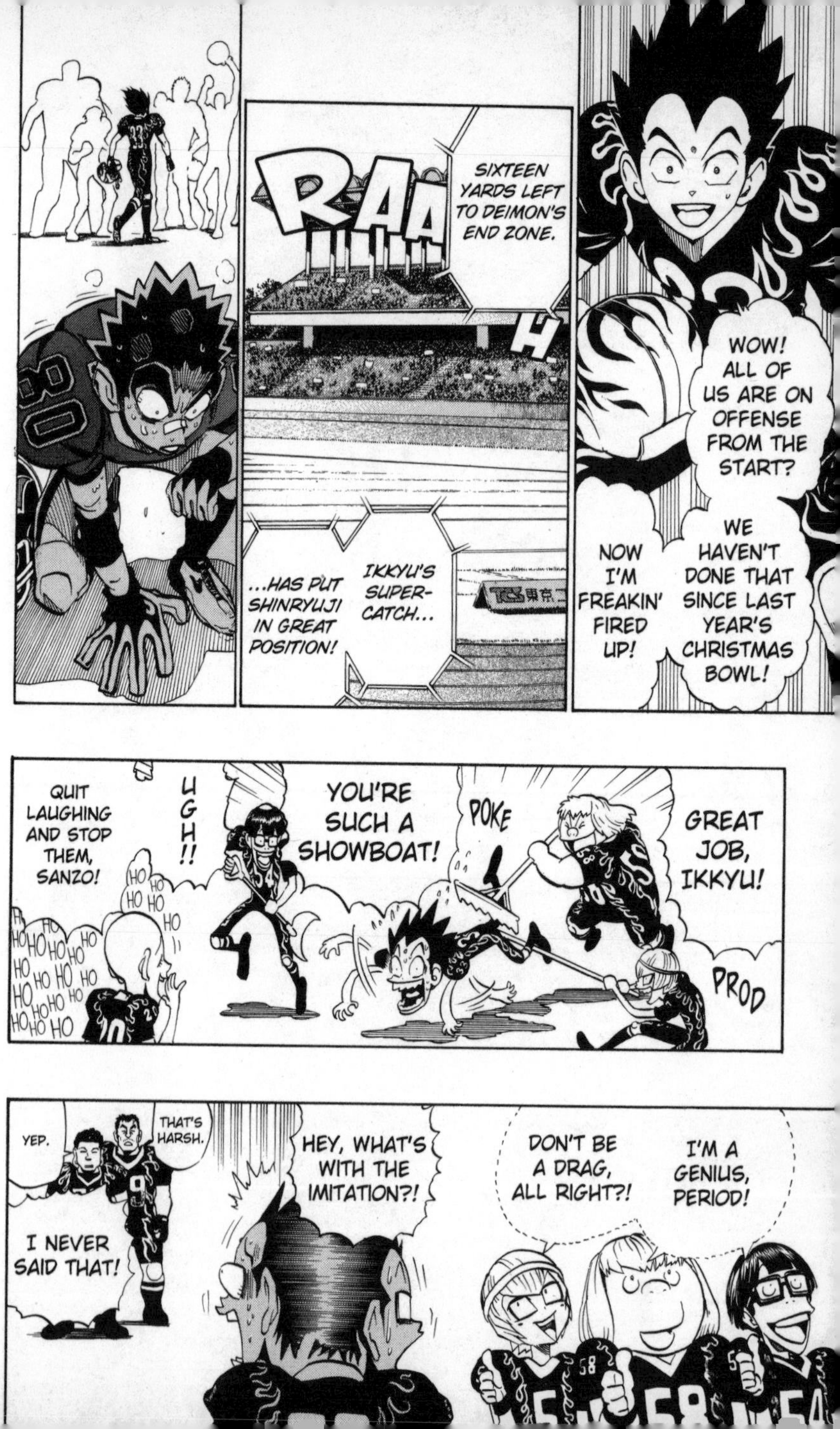
WOW! ALL OF US ARE ON OFFENSE FROM THE START?
WE HAVEN'T DONE THAT SINCE LAST YEAR'S CHRISTMAS BOWL!
NOW I'M FREAKIN' FIRED UP!
RAAAH
SIXTEEN YARDS LEFT TO DEIMON'S END ZONE.
IKKYU'S SUPER-CATCH...
...HAS PUT SHINRYUJI IN GREAT POSITION!
GREAT JOB, IKKYU!
PROD
POKE
YOU'RE SUCH A SHOWBOAT!
UGH!!
QUIT LAUGHING AND STOP THEM, SANZO!
HO HO HO HO HO
I'M A GENIUS, PERIOD!
DON'T BE A DRAG, ALL RIGHT?!
HEY, WHAT'S WITH THE IMITATION?!
THAT'S HARSH.
YEP.
I NEVER SAID THAT!

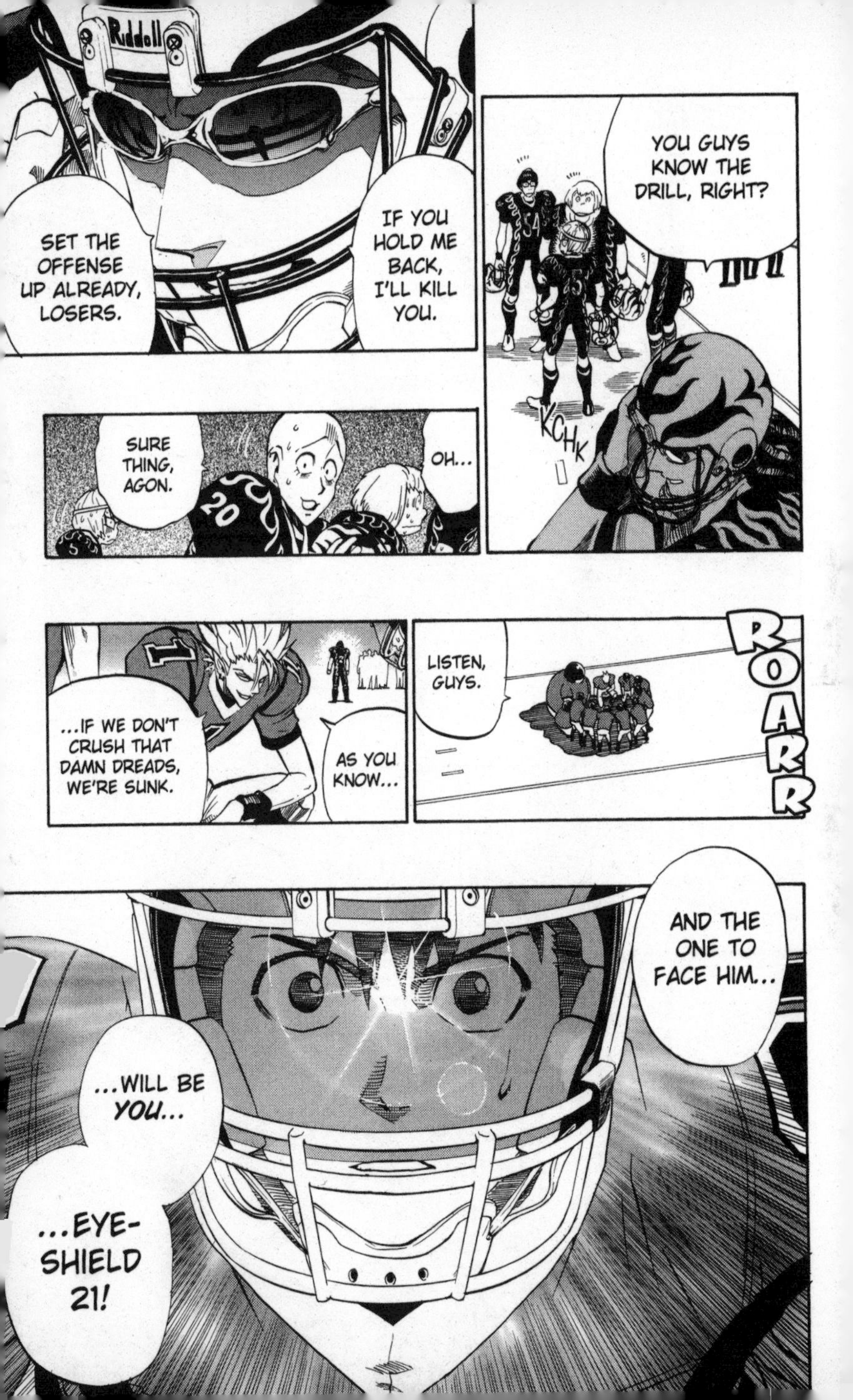
YOU GUYS KNOW THE DRILL, RIGHT?
KCHK
IF YOU HOLD ME BACK, I'LL KILL YOU.
SET THE OFFENSE UP ALREADY, LOSERS.
OH...
SURE THING, AGON.
ROARR
LISTEN, GUYS.
AS YOU KNOW...
...IF WE DON'T CRUSH THAT DAMN DREADS, WE'RE SUNK.
AND THE ONE TO FACE HIM...
...WILL BE *YOU*...
...EYE-SHIELD 21!

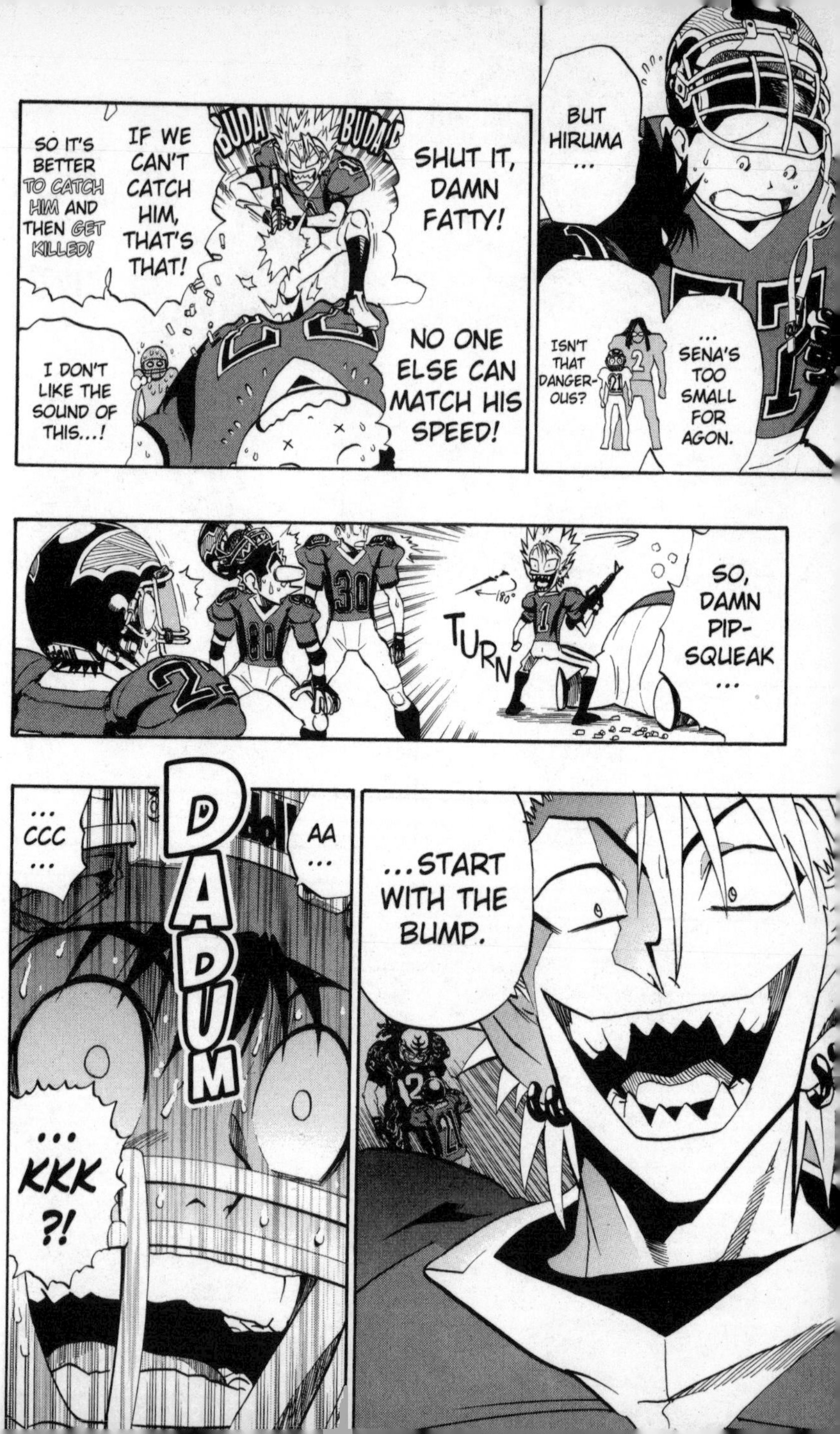
BUT HIRUMA ...
... SENA'S TOO SMALL FOR AGON.
ISN'T THAT DANGER-OUS?
SHUT IT, DAMN FATTY!
BUDA BUDA
IF WE CAN'T CATCH HIM, THAT'S THAT!
SO IT'S BETTER TO CATCH HIM AND THEN GET KILLED!
NO ONE ELSE CAN MATCH HIS SPEED!
I DON'T LIKE THE SOUND OF THIS...!
SO, DAMN PIP-SQUEAK ...
180°
TURN
...START WITH THE BUMP.
AA ...
DADUM
... CCC ...
... KKK ?!

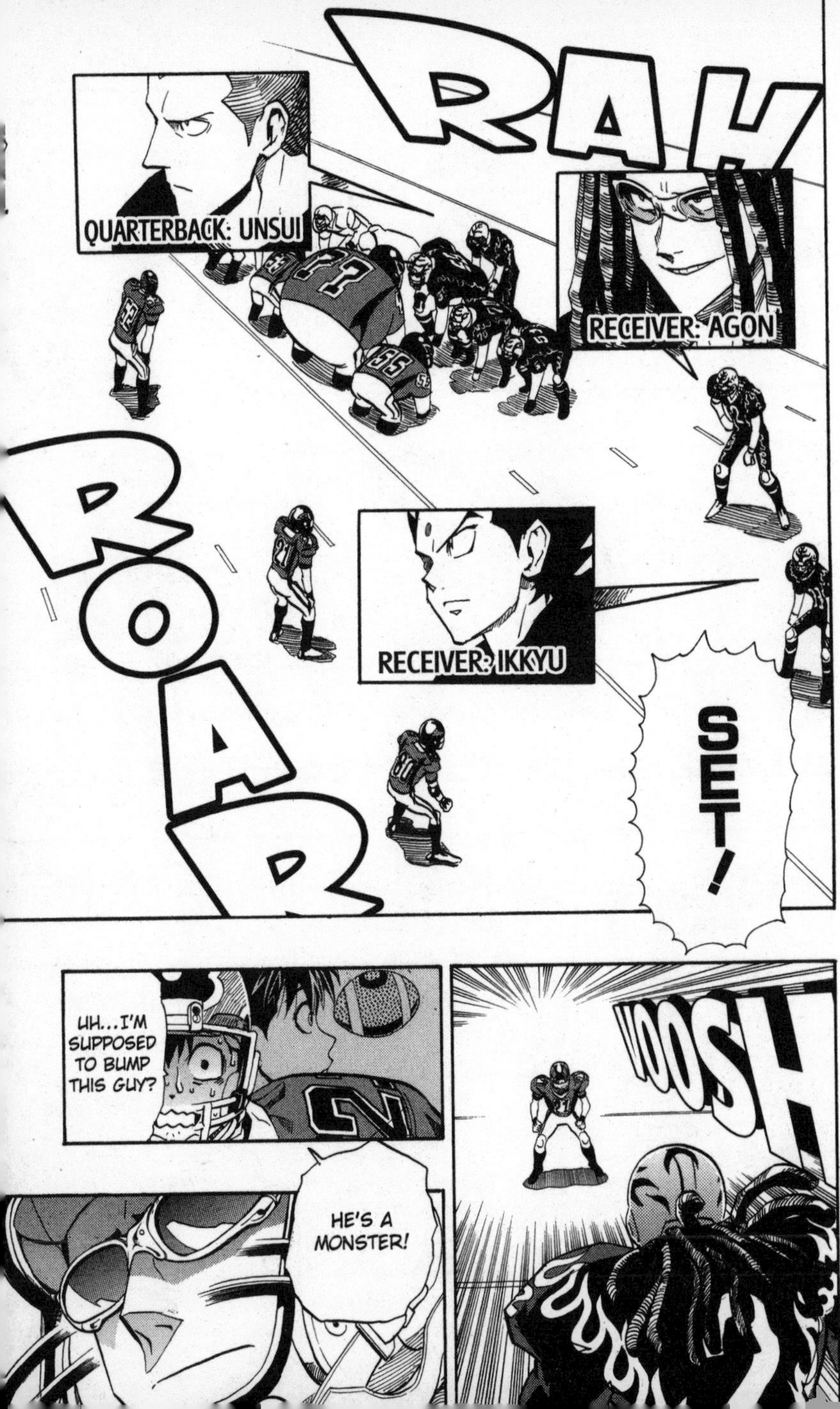
RAH
RECEIVER: AGON
QUARTERBACK: UNSUI
ROAR
RECEIVER: IKKYU
SET!
VOOSH
UH...I'M SUPPOSED TO BUMP THIS GUY?
HE'S A MONSTER!

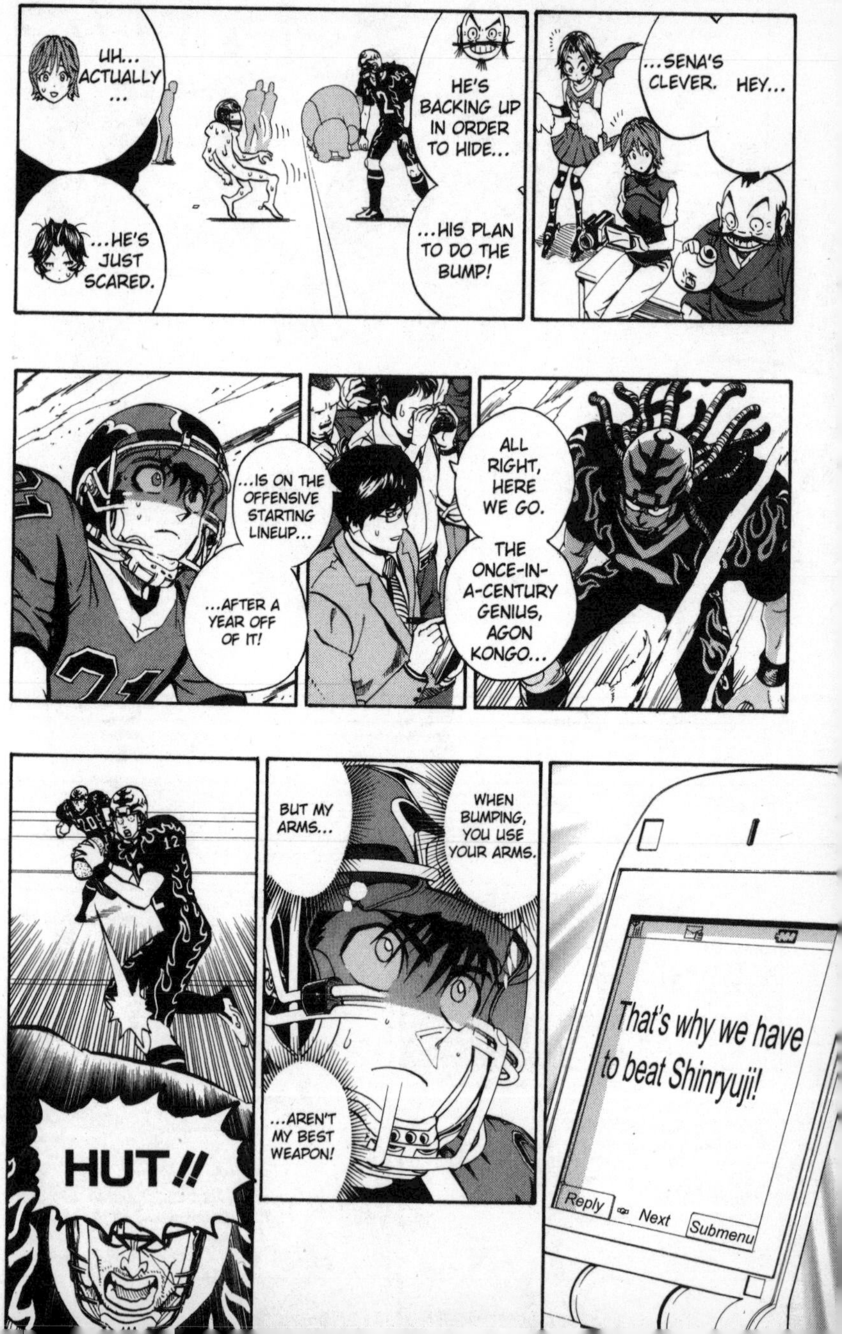
...SENA'S CLEVER. HEY...
HE'S BACKING UP IN ORDER TO HIDE...
...HIS PLAN TO DO THE BUMP!
UH... ACTUALLY...
...HE'S JUST SCARED.
ALL RIGHT, HERE WE GO.
THE ONCE-IN-A-CENTURY GENIUS, AGON KONGO...
...IS ON THE OFFENSIVE STARTING LINEUP...
...AFTER A YEAR OFF OF IT!
That's why we have to beat Shinryuji!
Reply
Next
Submenu
WHEN BUMPING, YOU USE YOUR ARMS.
BUT MY ARMS...
...AREN'T MY BEST WEAPON!
HUT!!

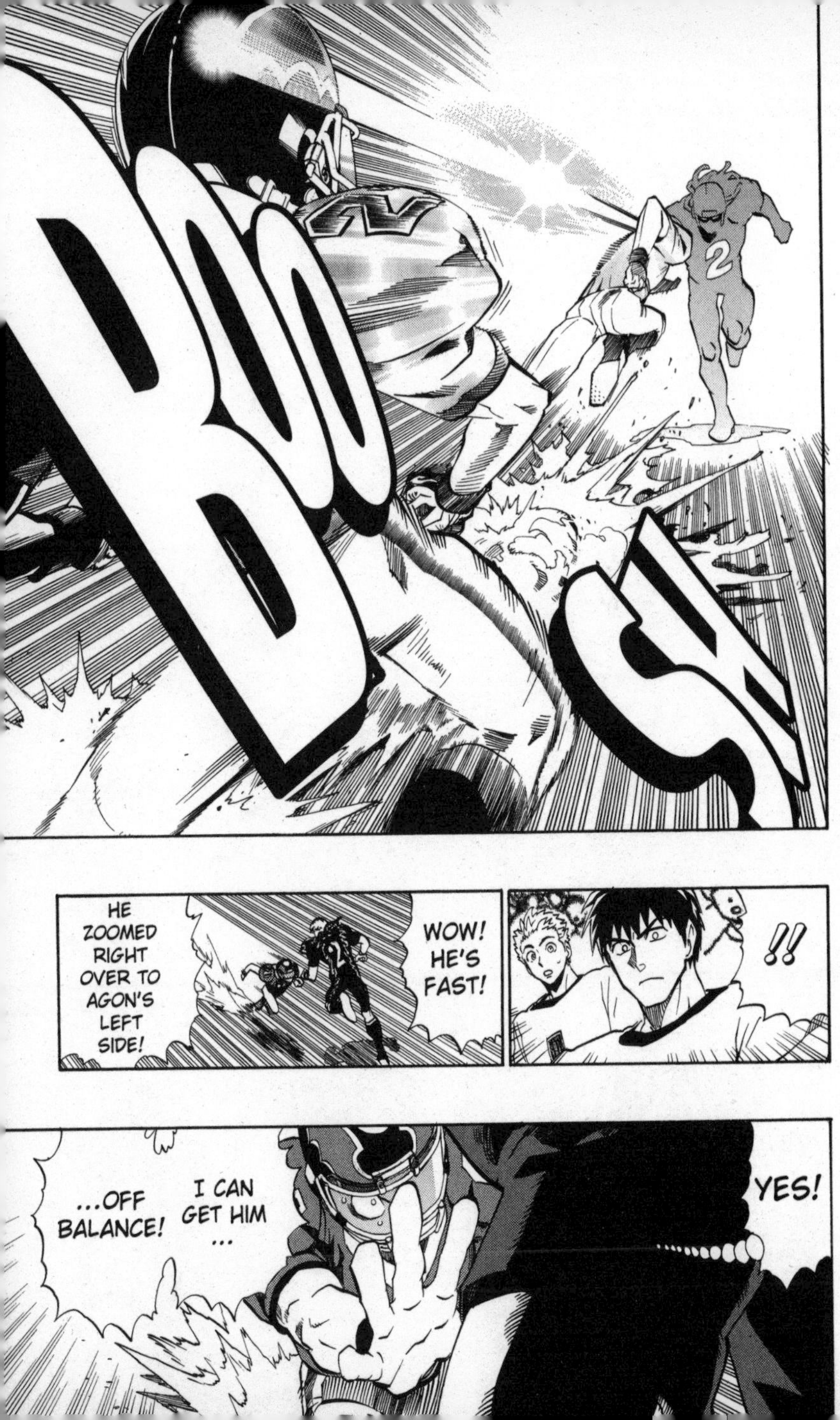
!!
WOW! HE'S FAST!
HE ZOOMED RIGHT OVER TO AGON'S LEFT SIDE!
YES!
I CAN GET HIM ...
...OFF BALANCE!

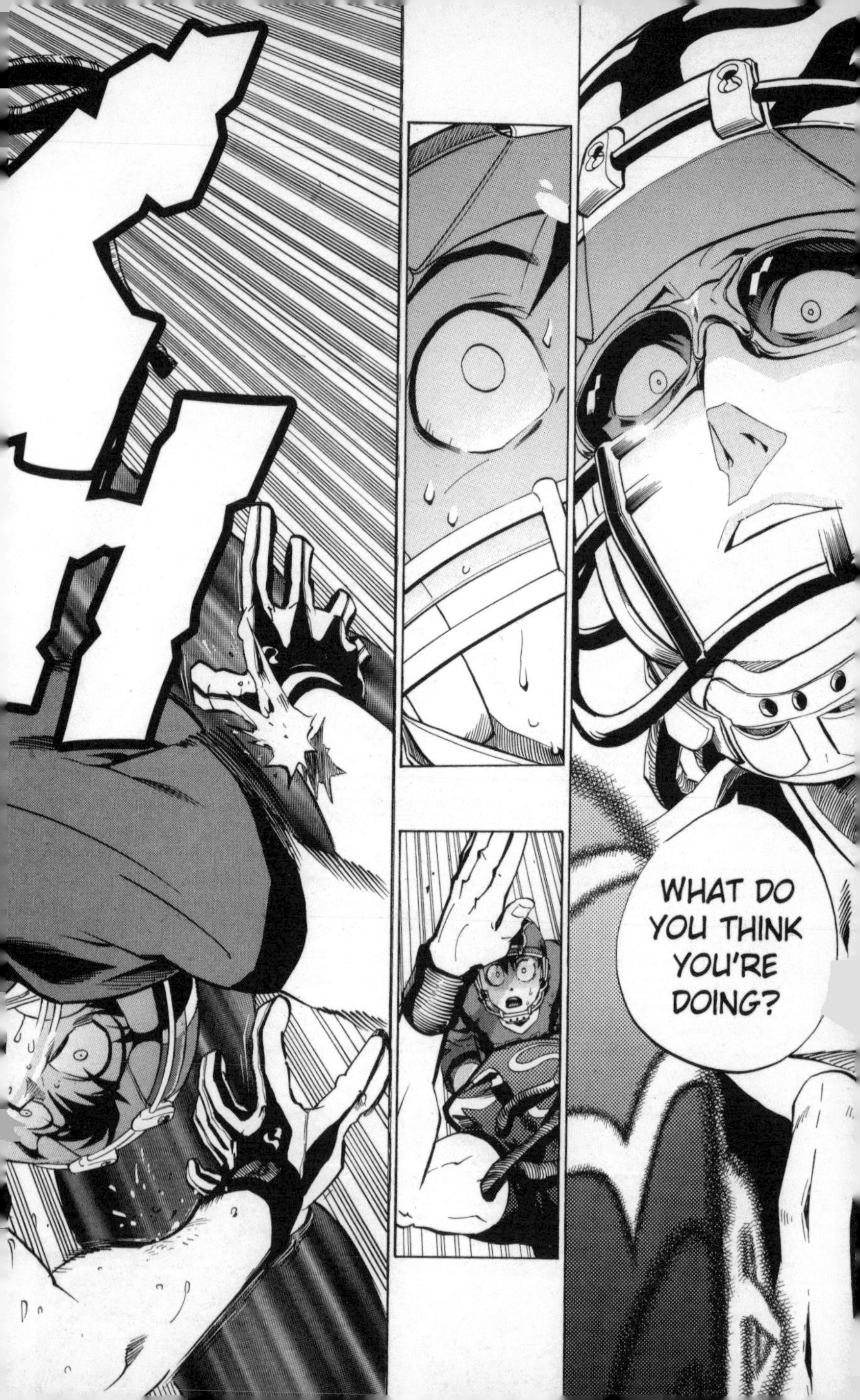
WHAT DO YOU THINK YOU'RE DOING?

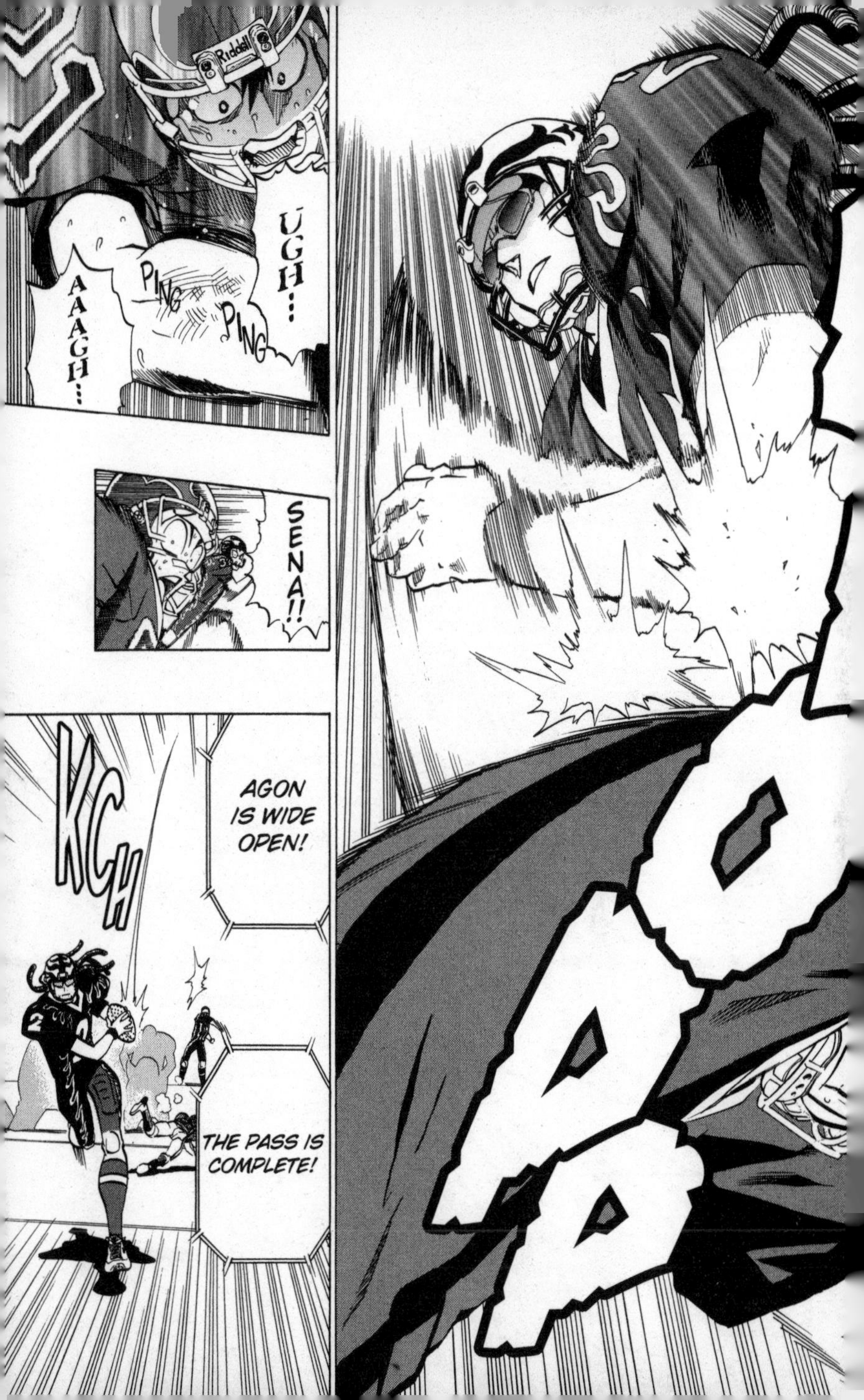
UGH...
PING PING
AAAGH...
SENA!!
KCH
AGON IS WIDE OPEN!
THE PASS IS COMPLETE!

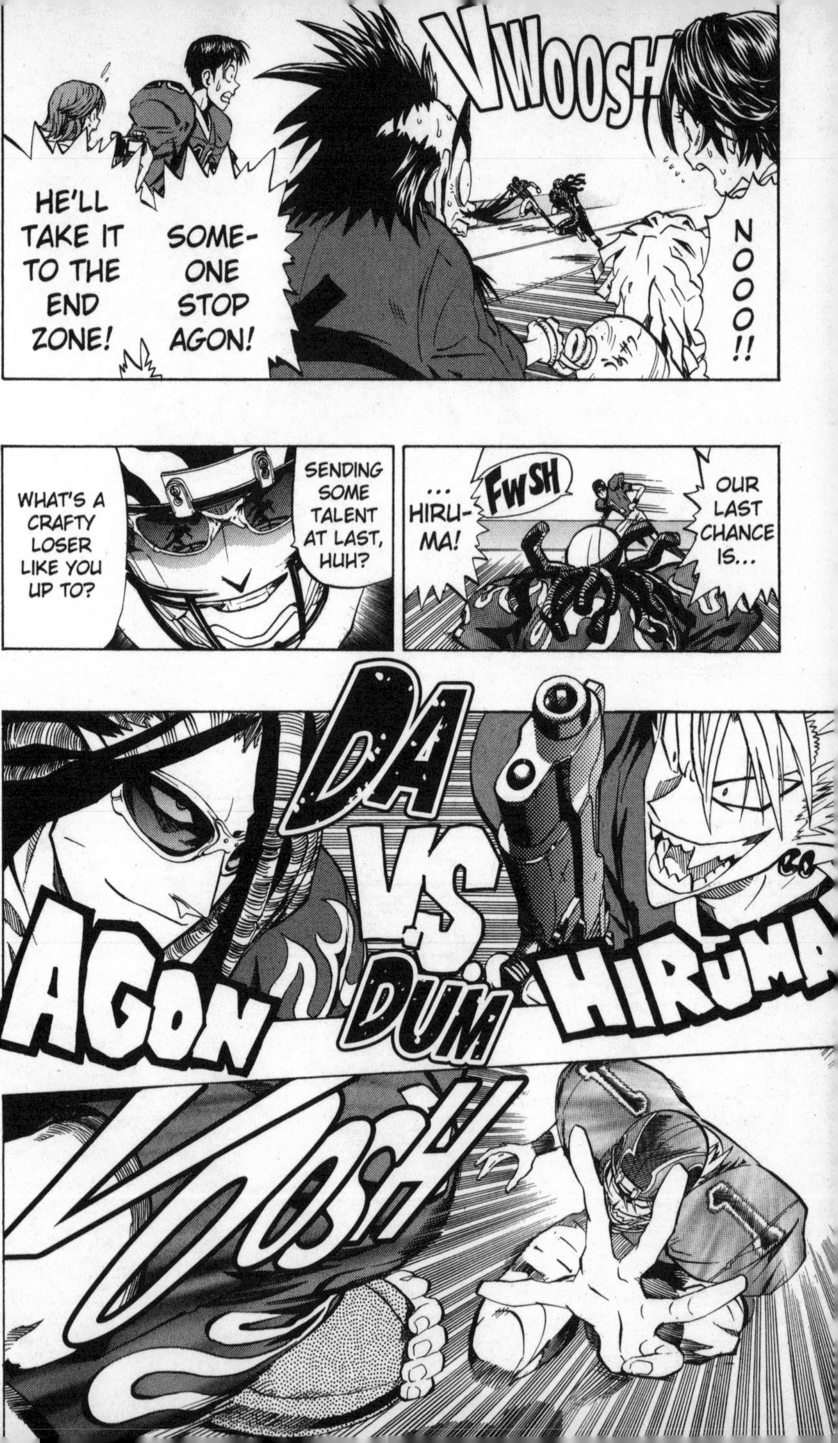
VWOOSH
NOOOO!!
SOME-ONE STOP AGON!
HE'LL TAKE IT TO THE END ZONE!
OUR LAST CHANCE IS...
FWSH
...HIRU-MA!
SENDING SOME TALENT AT LAST, HUH?
WHAT'S A CRAFTY LOSER LIKE YOU UP TO?
HIRUMA
DA VS. DUM
AGON
WOSH

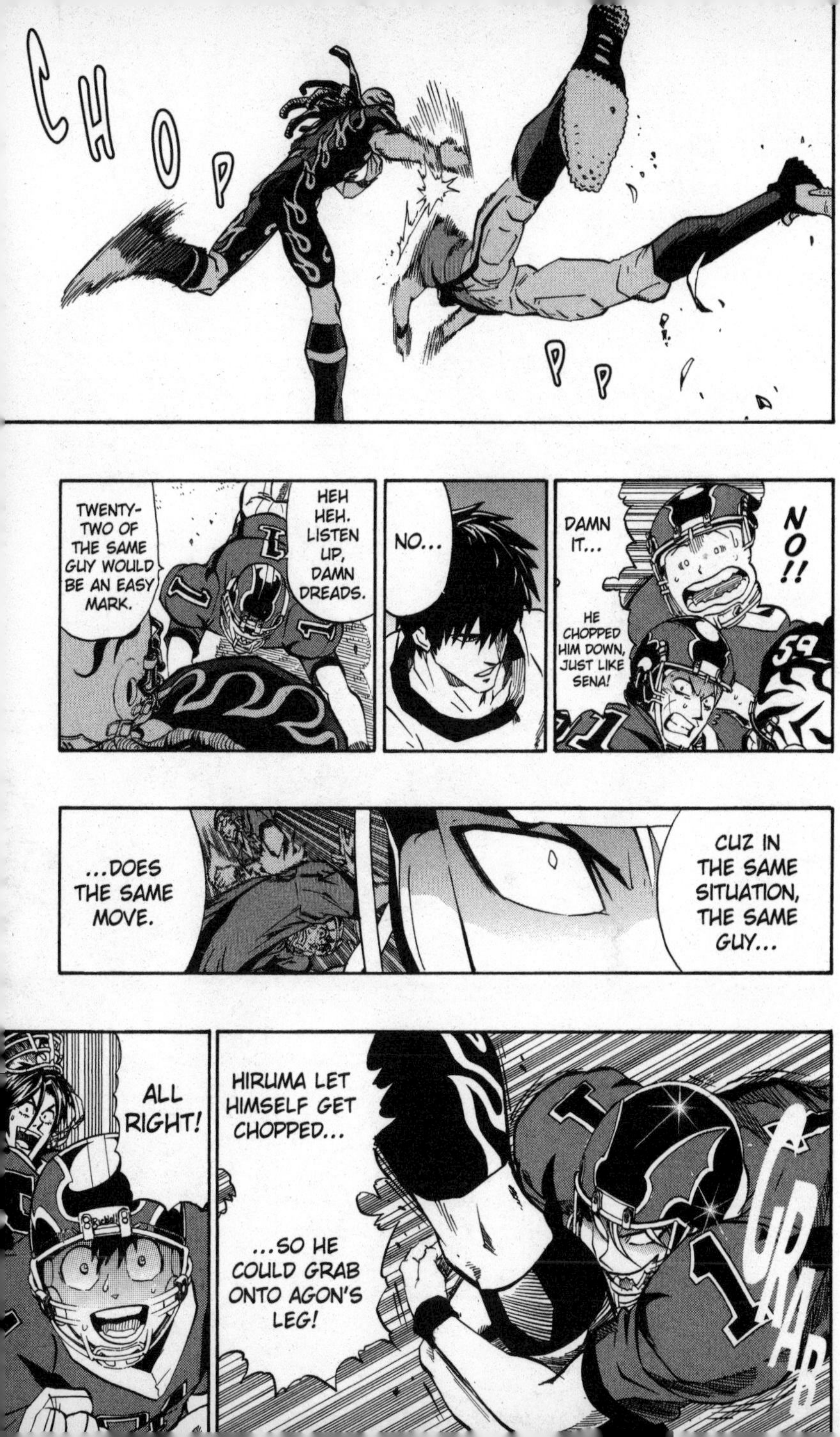
CHOP
PP
NO!!
DAMN IT...
HE CHOPPED HIM DOWN, JUST LIKE SENA!
NO...
HEH HEH. LISTEN UP, DAMN DREADS.
TWENTY-TWO OF THE SAME GUY WOULD BE AN EASY MARK.
CUZ IN THE SAME SITUATION, THE SAME GUY...
...DOES THE SAME MOVE.
HIRUMA LET HIMSELF GET CHOPPED...
...SO HE COULD GRAB ONTO AGON'S LEG!
GRAB
ALL RIGHT!

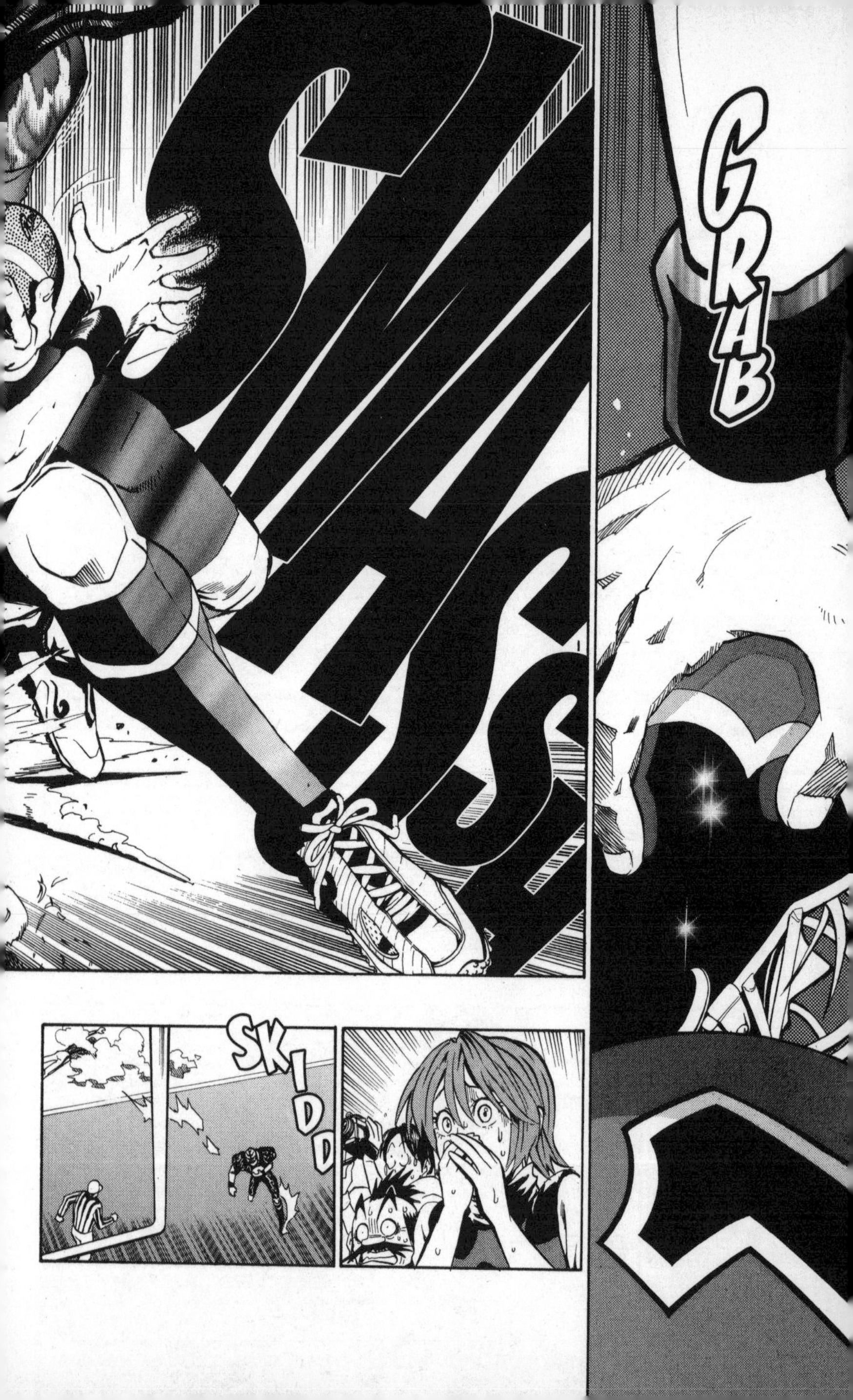
GRAB
SKIDD

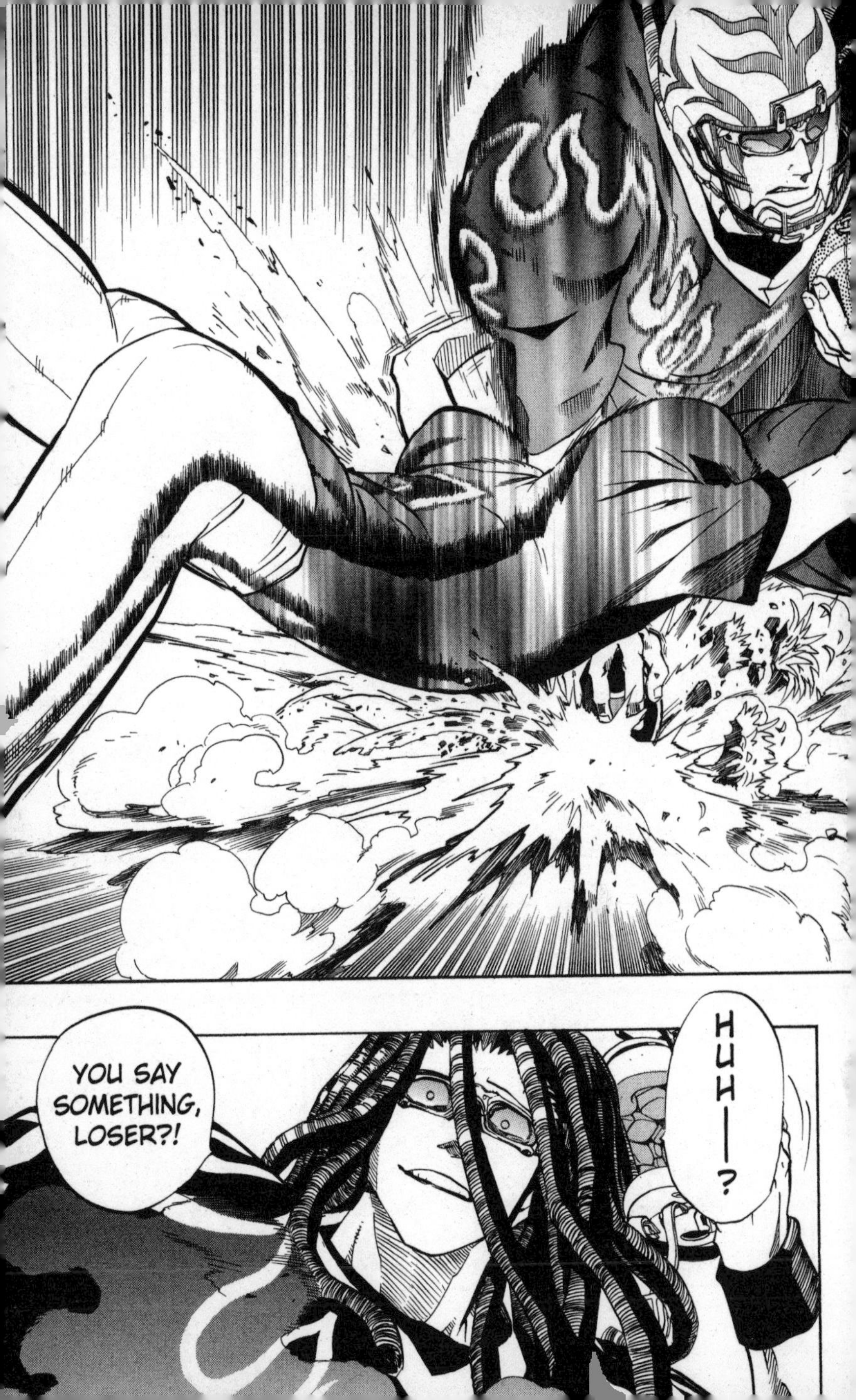
HUH—?
YOU SAY SOMETHING, LOSER?!

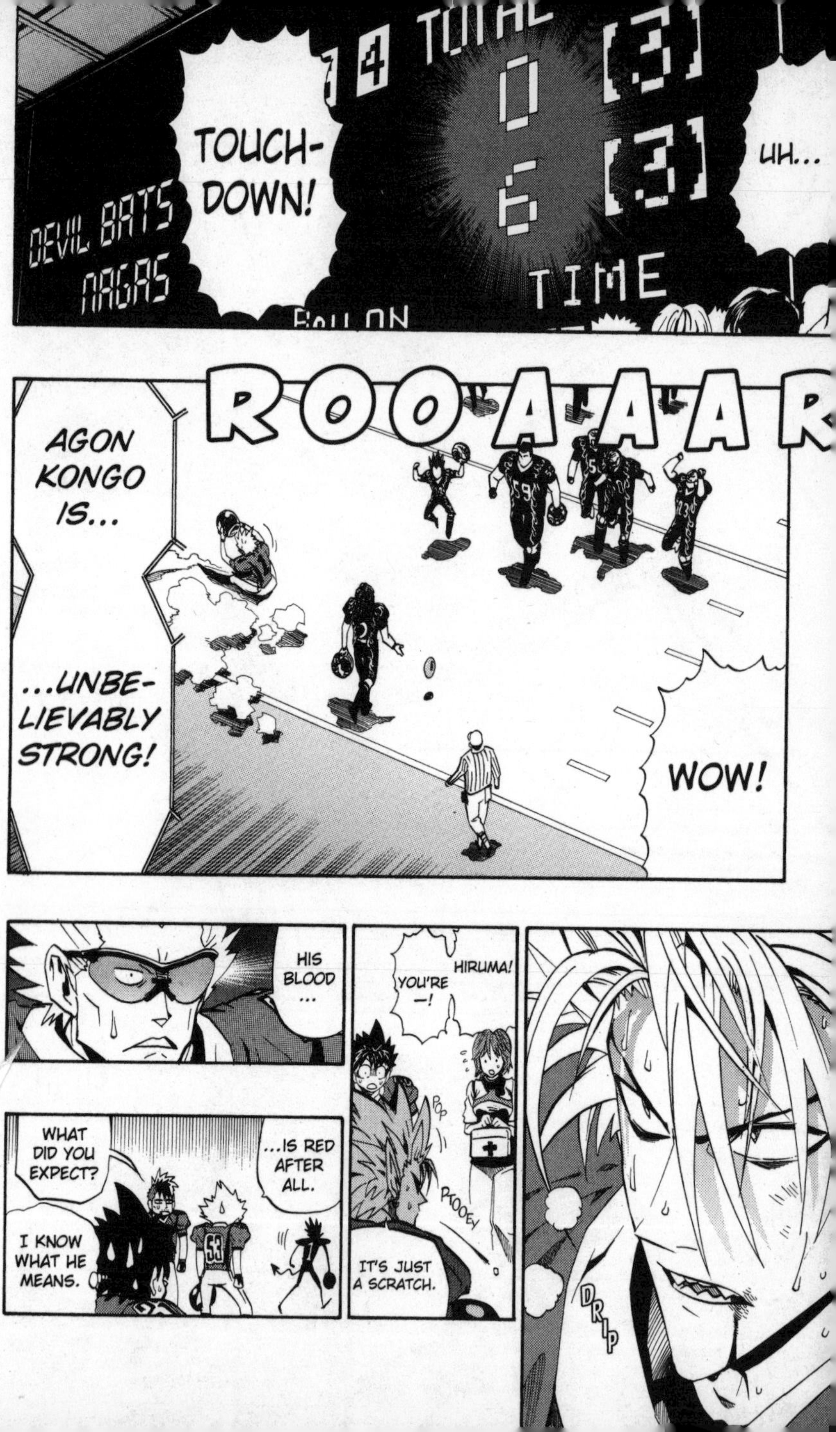
TOUCH-DOWN!
UH...
DEVIL BATS
NAGAS
TOTAL
TIME
BALL ON
ROOAAAR
AGON KONGO IS...
...UNBE-LIEVABLY STRONG!
WOW!
DRIP
HIRUMA!
YOU'RE—!
POP
PTOOEY
IT'S JUST A SCRATCH.
HIS BLOOD...
...IS RED AFTER ALL.
WHAT DID YOU EXPECT?
I KNOW WHAT HE MEANS.

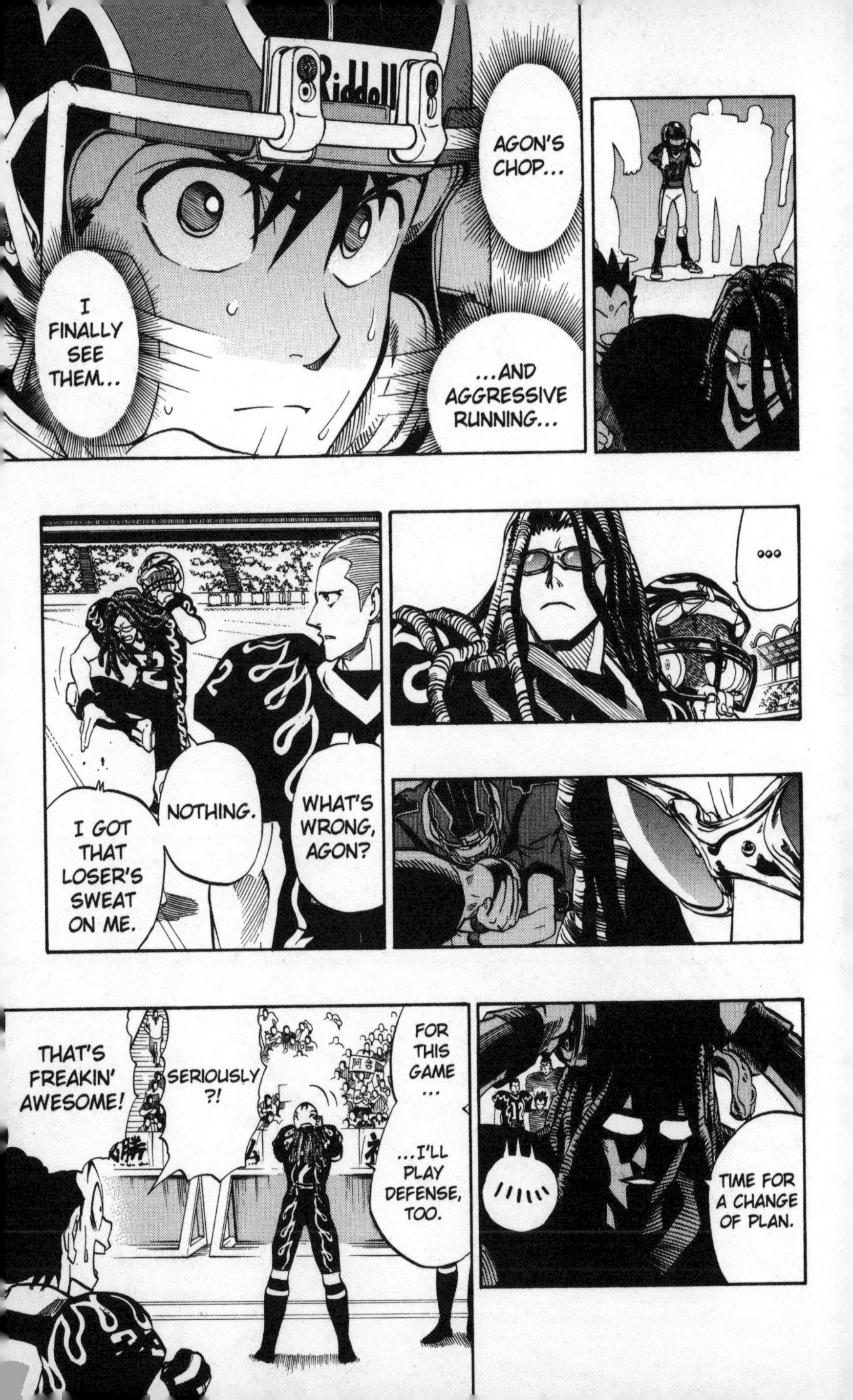
AGON'S CHOP...
...AND AGGRESSIVE RUNNING...
I FINALLY SEE THEM...
...
WHAT'S WRONG, AGON?
NOTHING.
I GOT THAT LOSER'S SWEAT ON ME.
TIME FOR A CHANGE OF PLAN.
FOR THIS GAME...
...I'LL PLAY DEFENSE, TOO.
SERIOUSLY?!
THAT'S FREAKIN' AWESOME!

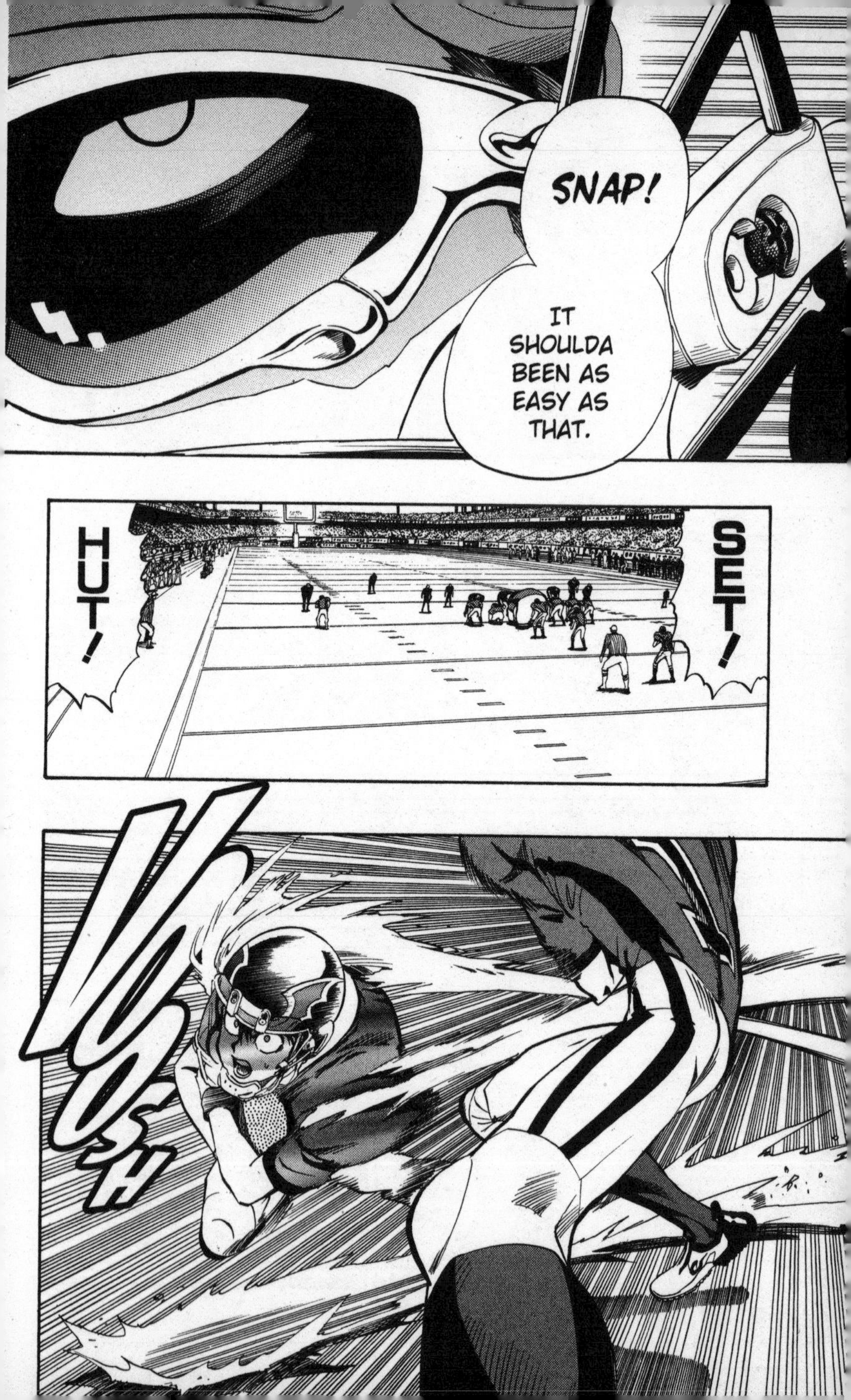
SNAP!
IT SHOULDA BEEN AS EASY AS THAT.
SET!
HUT!
VOOSH

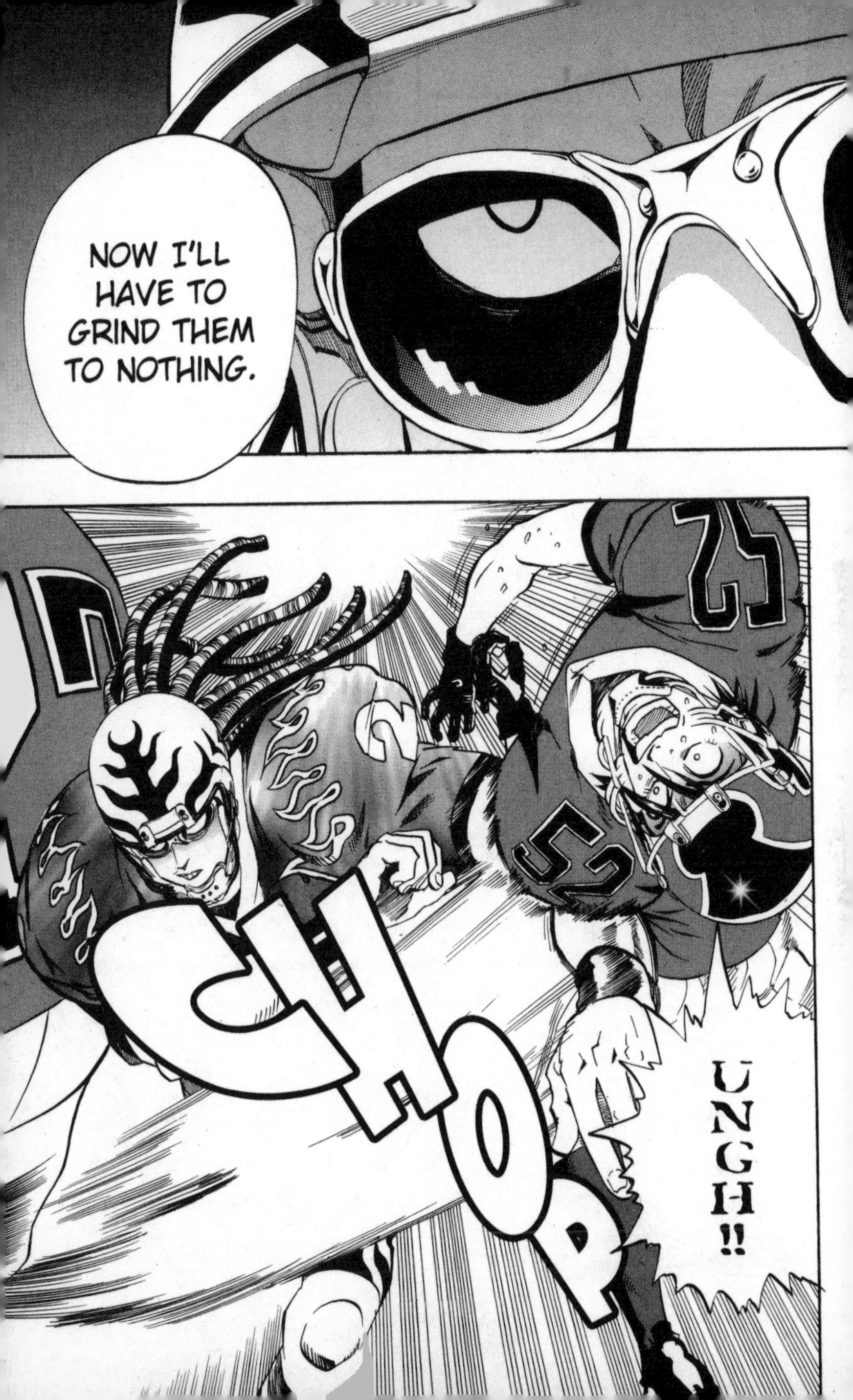
NOW I'LL HAVE TO GRIND THEM TO NOTHING.
CHOP
UNGH!!

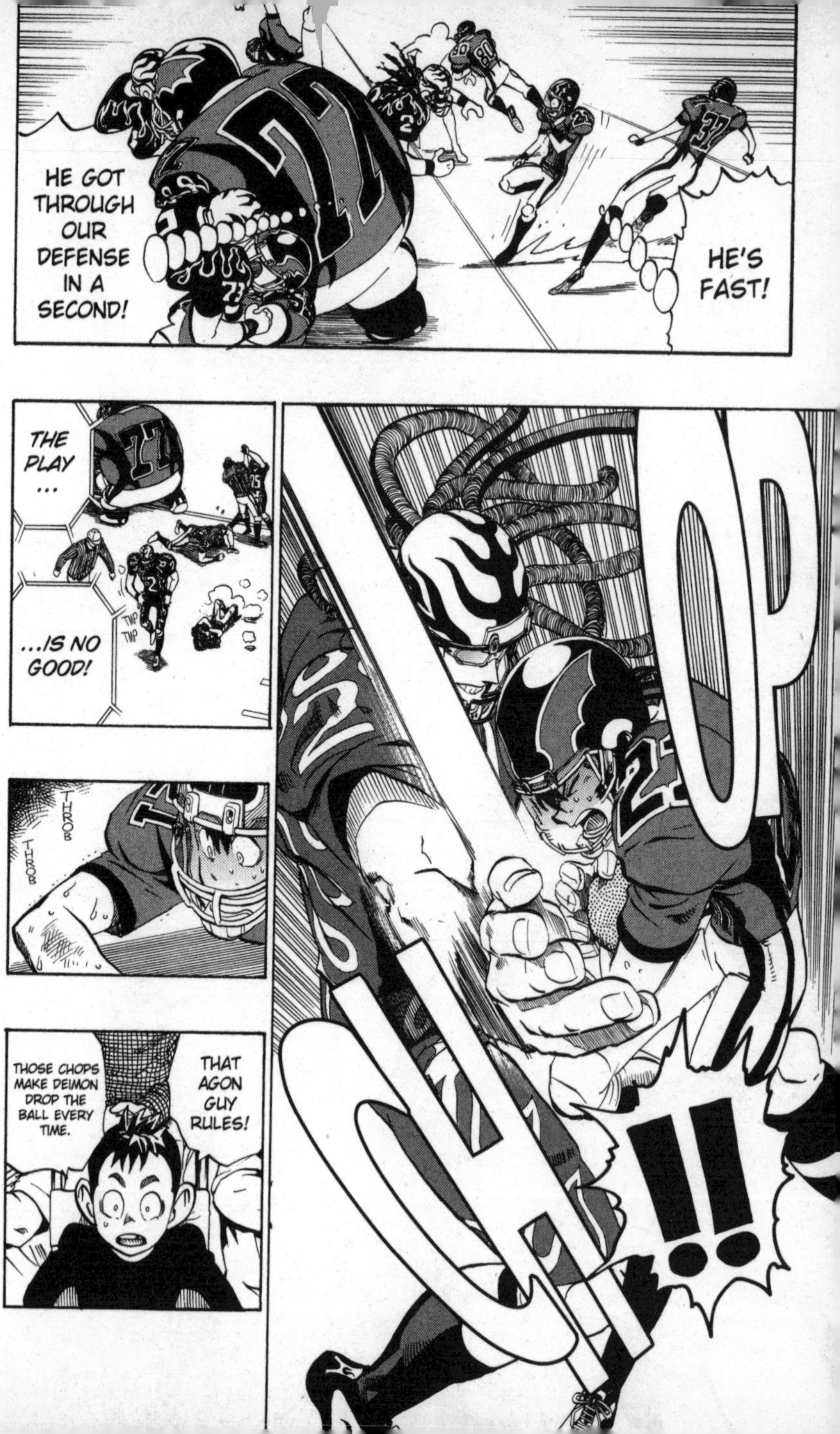
HE'S FAST!
HE GOT THROUGH OUR DEFENSE IN A SECOND!
CHOP!!
THE PLAY ...
...IS NO GOOD!
TMP TMP
THROB THROB
THAT AGON GUY RULES!
THOSE CHOPS MAKE DEIMON DROP THE BALL EVERY TIME.

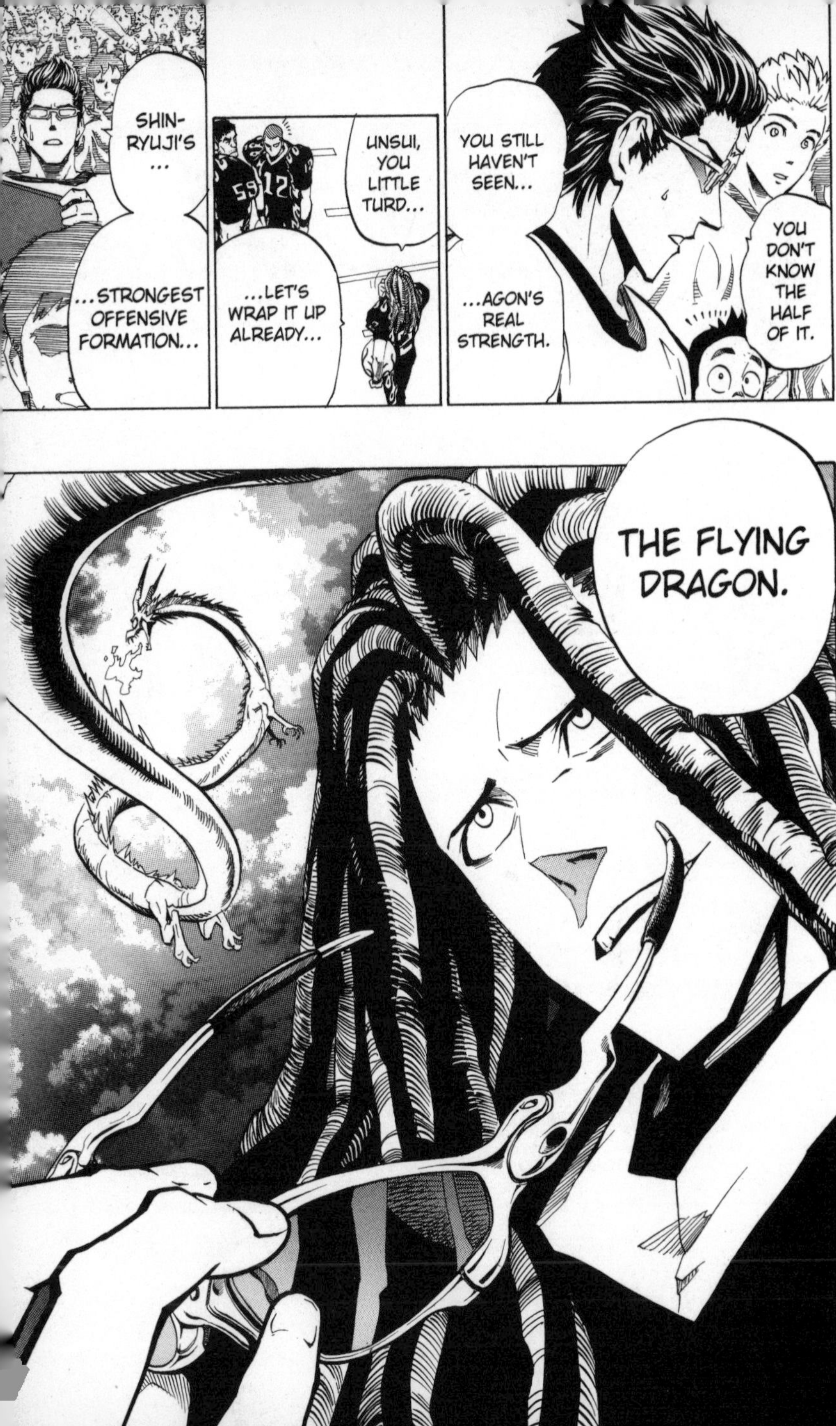
YOU STILL HAVEN'T SEEN...
...AGON'S REAL STRENGTH.
YOU DON'T KNOW THE HALF OF IT.
UNSUI, YOU LITTLE TURD...
...LET'S WRAP IT UP ALREADY...
SHIN-RYUJI'S...
...STRONGEST OFFENSIVE FORMATION...
THE FLYING DRAGON.

Investigation File #066

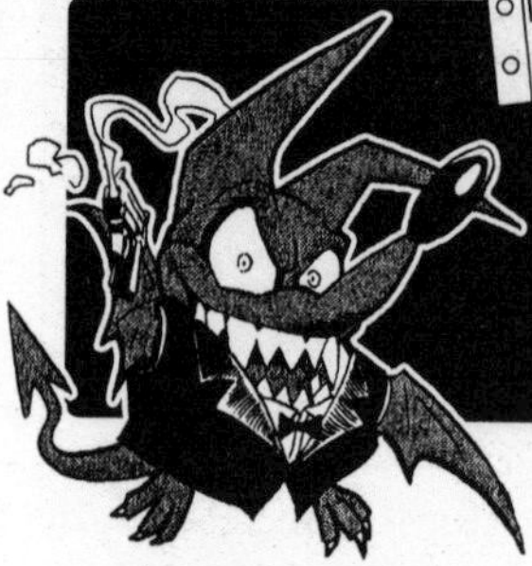

## Swipe Yukimitsu's ultimate study methods!

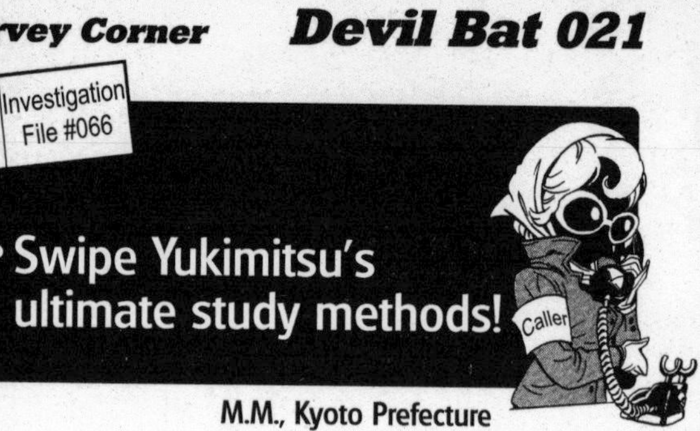
Caller

M.M., Kyoto Prefecture

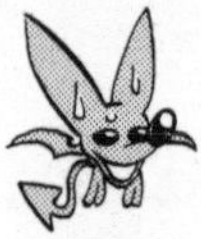

ABOUT THAT PICTURE AT THE BOTTOM...

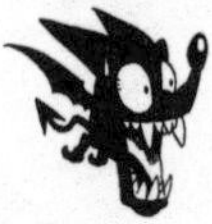

YOU SHOULD BE NICER IF YOU WANT HIM TO TEACH YOU SOMETHING!

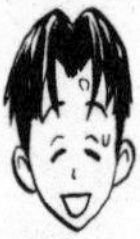

OH, IT'S ALL RIGHT. I CAN TEACH YOU A LITTLE TRICK.

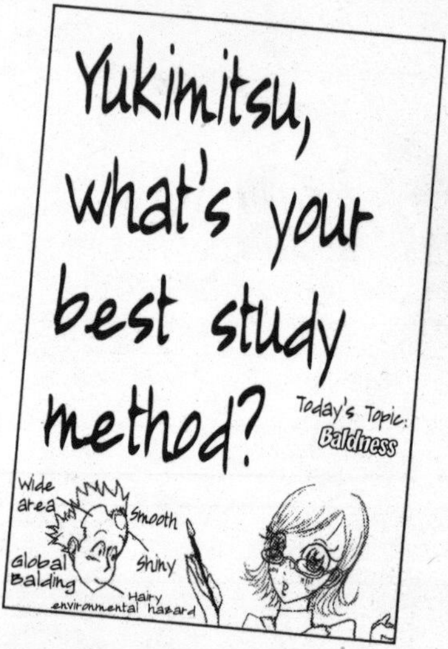
Yukimitsu, what's your best study method?
Today's Topic: Baldness
Wide area
Smooth
Global Balding
Shiny
Hairy environmental hazard

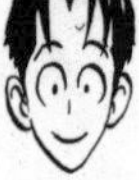

LIKE FOR WHEN YOU NEED TO REMEMBER VOCABULARY. THERE ARE SOME WORDS YOU JUST ABSOLUTELY MUST LEARN, RIGHT?

USE THIS AS A LAST RESORT.

***IMAGINE YOURSELF BEING SLAPPED SILLY AS YOU SCREAM OUT THE WORD.***

IN OTHER WORDS, MEMORIZE IT WITH YOUR BODY, YOU KNOW?

IT'S A PRETTY RIDICULOUS TIP, BUT TRY IT SOME TIME!

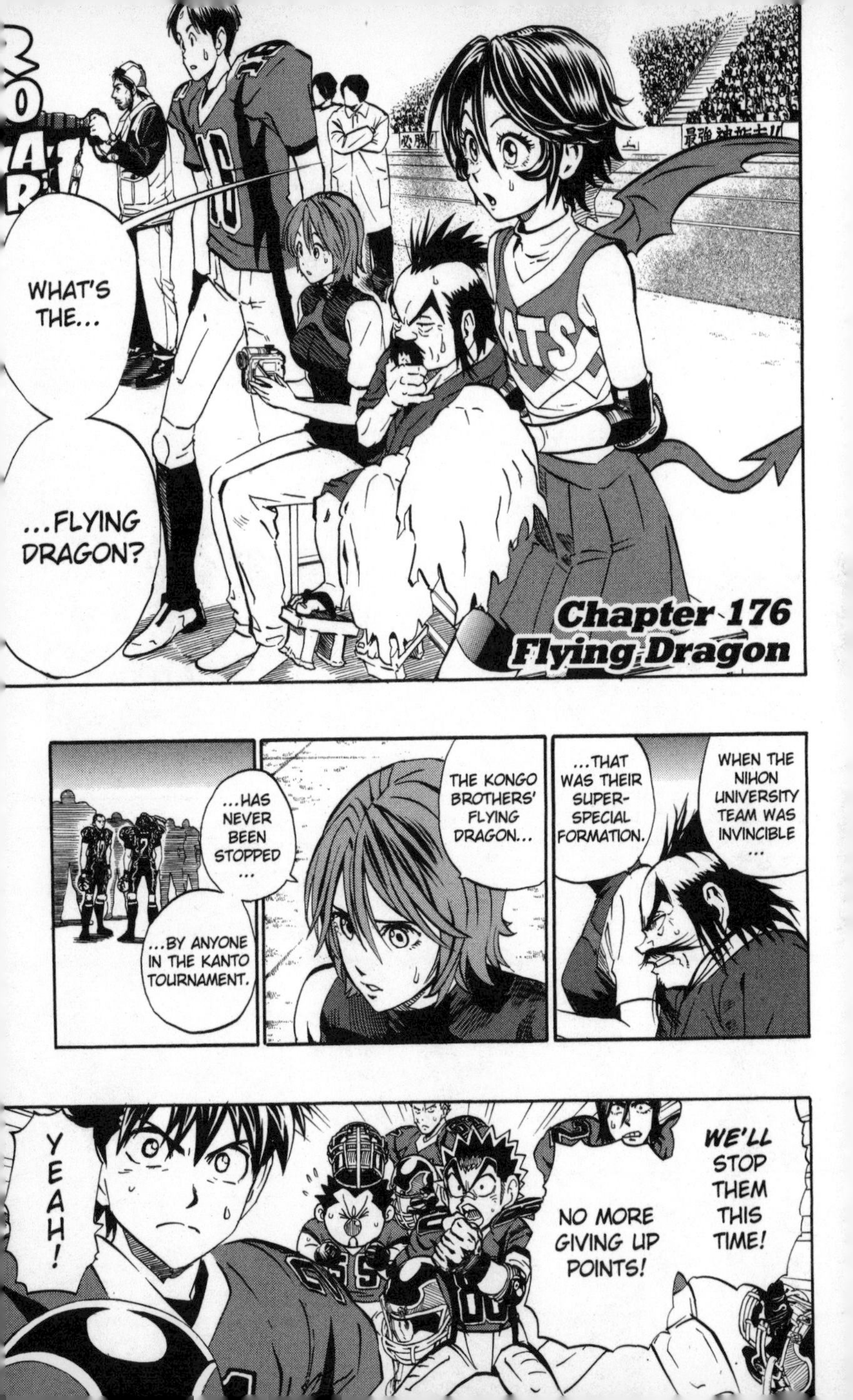
ROAR
WHAT'S THE...
...FLYING DRAGON?
Chapter 176
Flying Dragon
WHEN THE NIHON UNIVERSITY TEAM WAS INVINCIBLE ...
...THAT WAS THEIR SUPER-SPECIAL FORMATION.
THE KONGO BROTHERS' FLYING DRAGON...
...HAS NEVER BEEN STOPPED ...
...BY ANYONE IN THE KANTO TOURNAMENT.
WE'LL STOP THEM THIS TIME!
NO MORE GIVING UP POINTS!
YEAH!

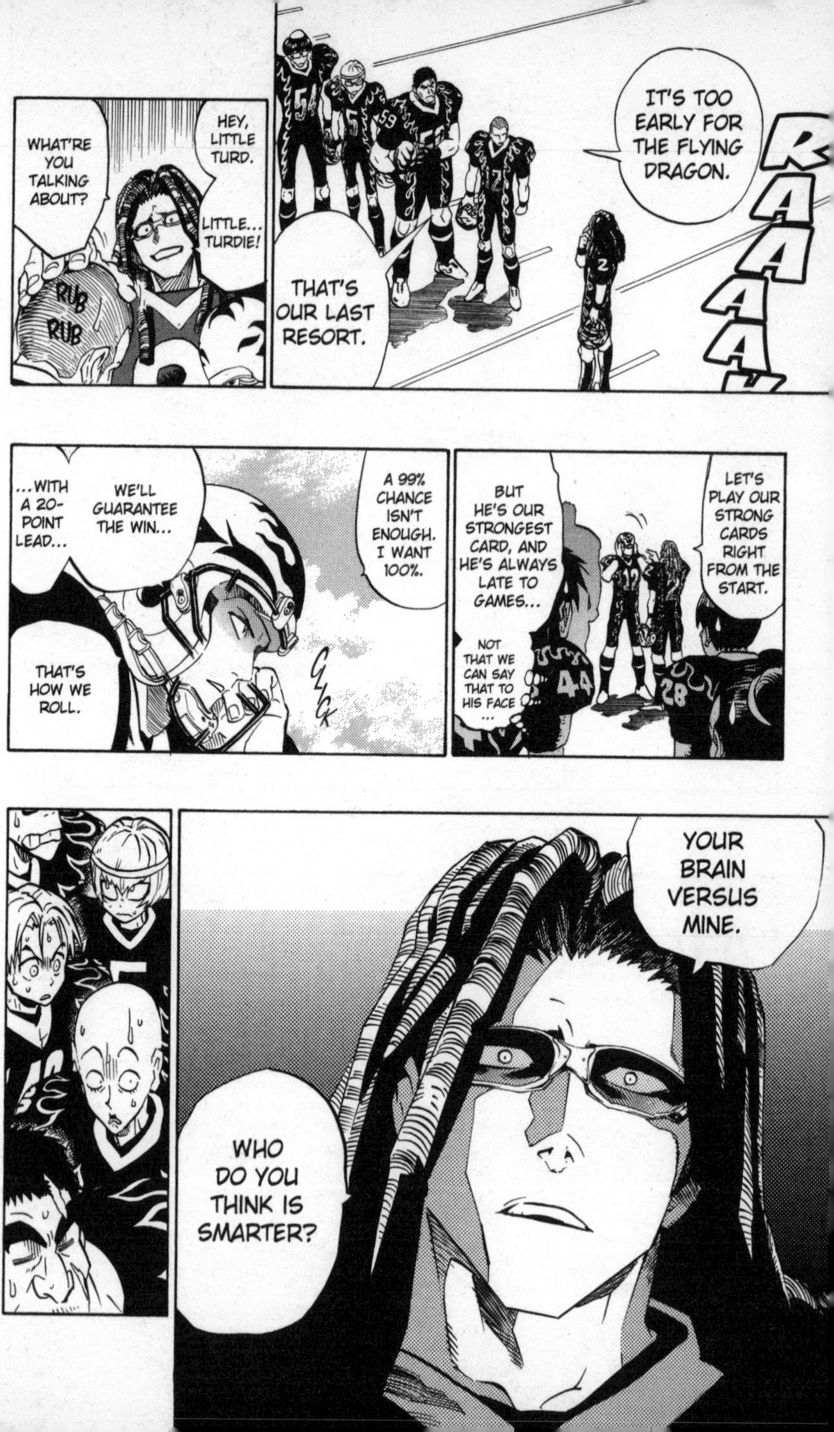
RAAAAA
IT'S TOO EARLY FOR THE FLYING DRAGON.
THAT'S OUR LAST RESORT.
HEY, LITTLE TURD.
LITTLE... TURDIE!
WHAT'RE YOU TALKING ABOUT?
RUB RUB
LET'S PLAY OUR STRONG CARDS RIGHT FROM THE START.
BUT HE'S OUR STRONGEST CARD, AND HE'S ALWAYS LATE TO GAMES...
NOT THAT WE CAN SAY THAT TO HIS FACE...
A 99% CHANCE ISN'T ENOUGH. I WANT 100%.
CLICK
WE'LL GUARANTEE THE WIN...
...WITH A 20-POINT LEAD...
THAT'S HOW WE ROLL.
YOUR BRAIN VERSUS MINE.
WHO DO YOU THINK IS SMARTER?

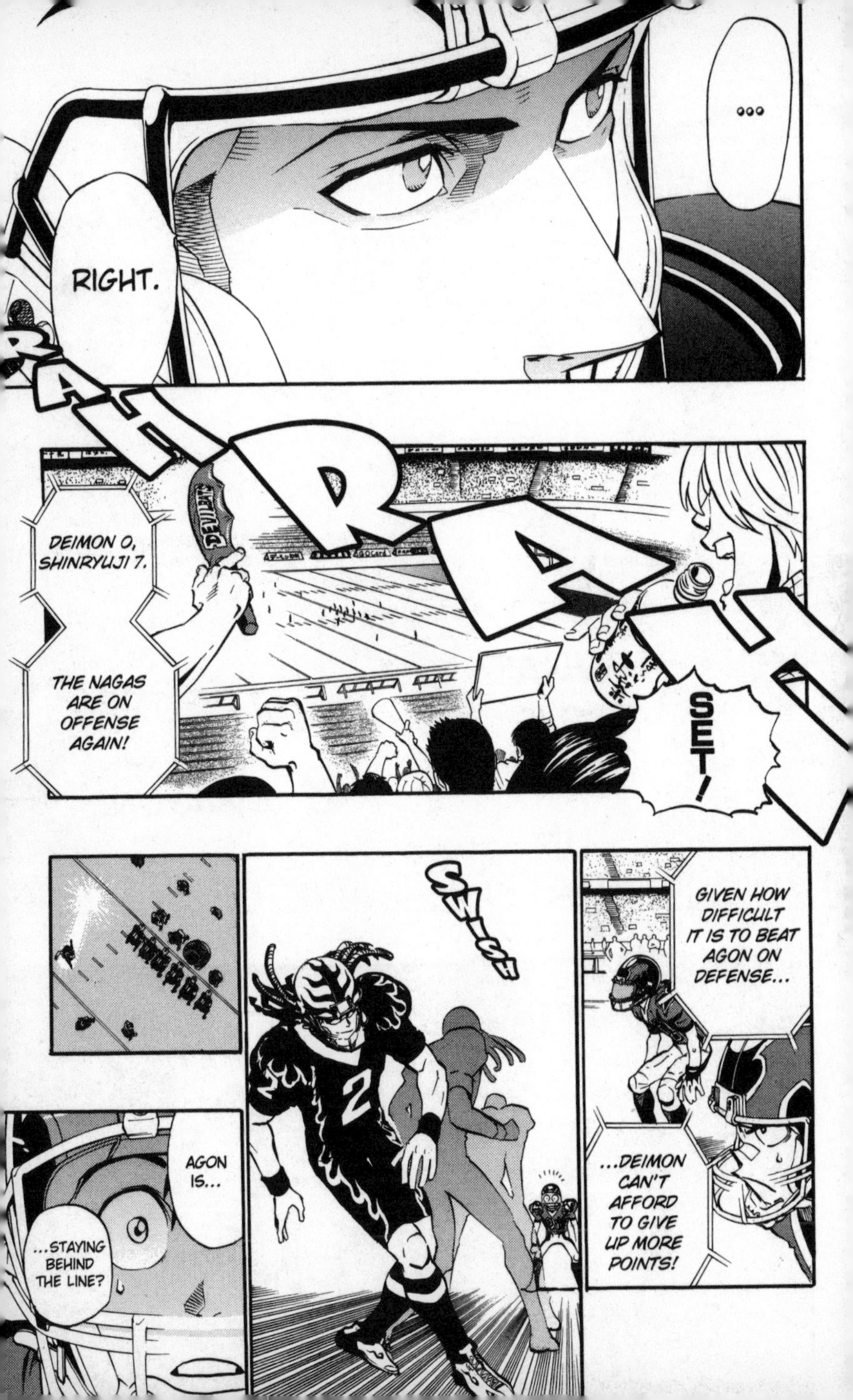
...
RIGHT.
SET!
DEVILBATS
DEIMON 0, SHINRYUJI 7.
THE NAGAS ARE ON OFFENSE AGAIN!
GIVEN HOW DIFFICULT IT IS TO BEAT AGON ON DEFENSE...
...DEIMON CAN'T AFFORD TO GIVE UP MORE POINTS!
SWISH
AGON IS...
...STAYING BEHIND THE LINE?

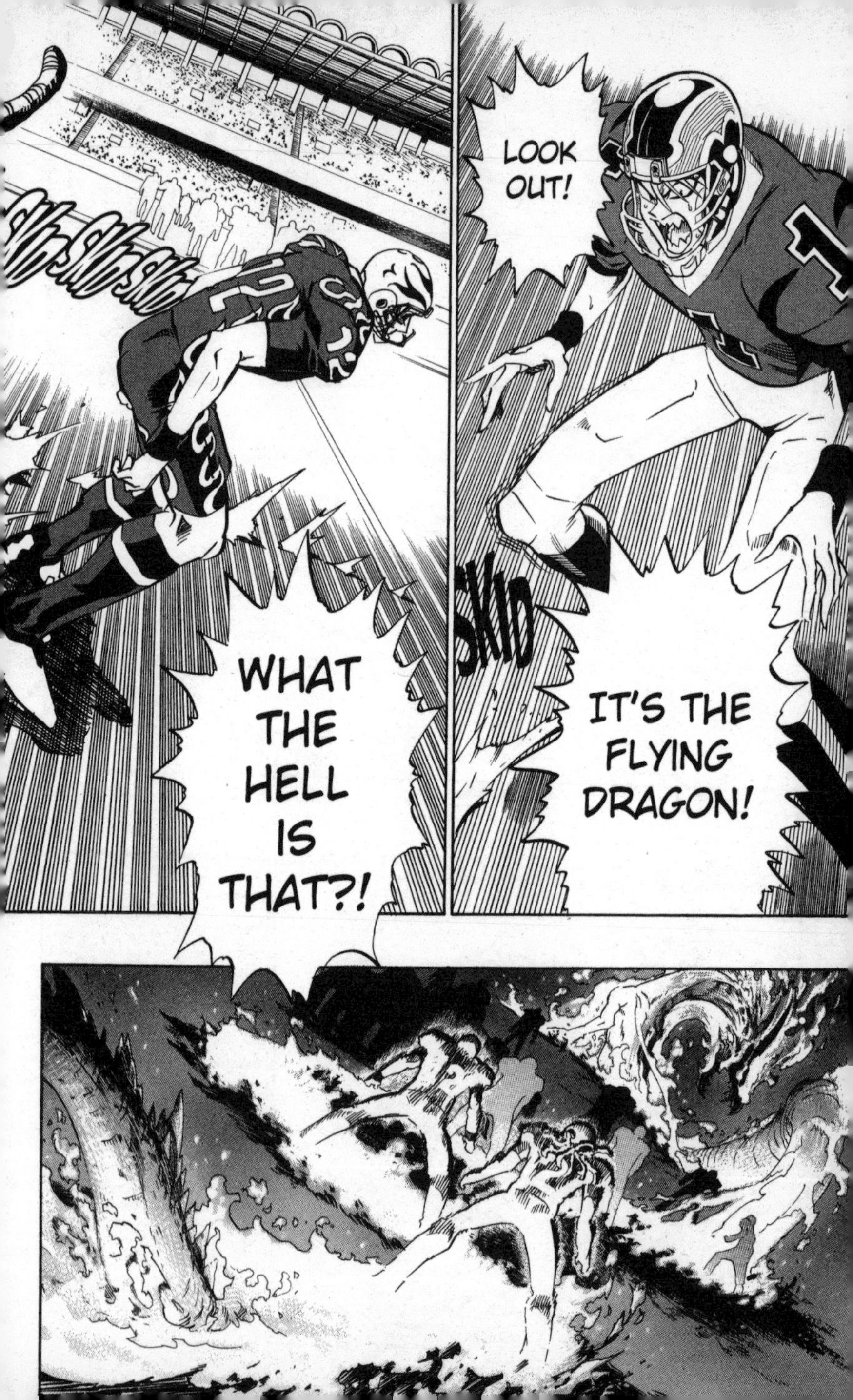
LOOK OUT!
SKID
IT'S THE FLYING DRAGON!
WHAT THE HELL IS THAT?!

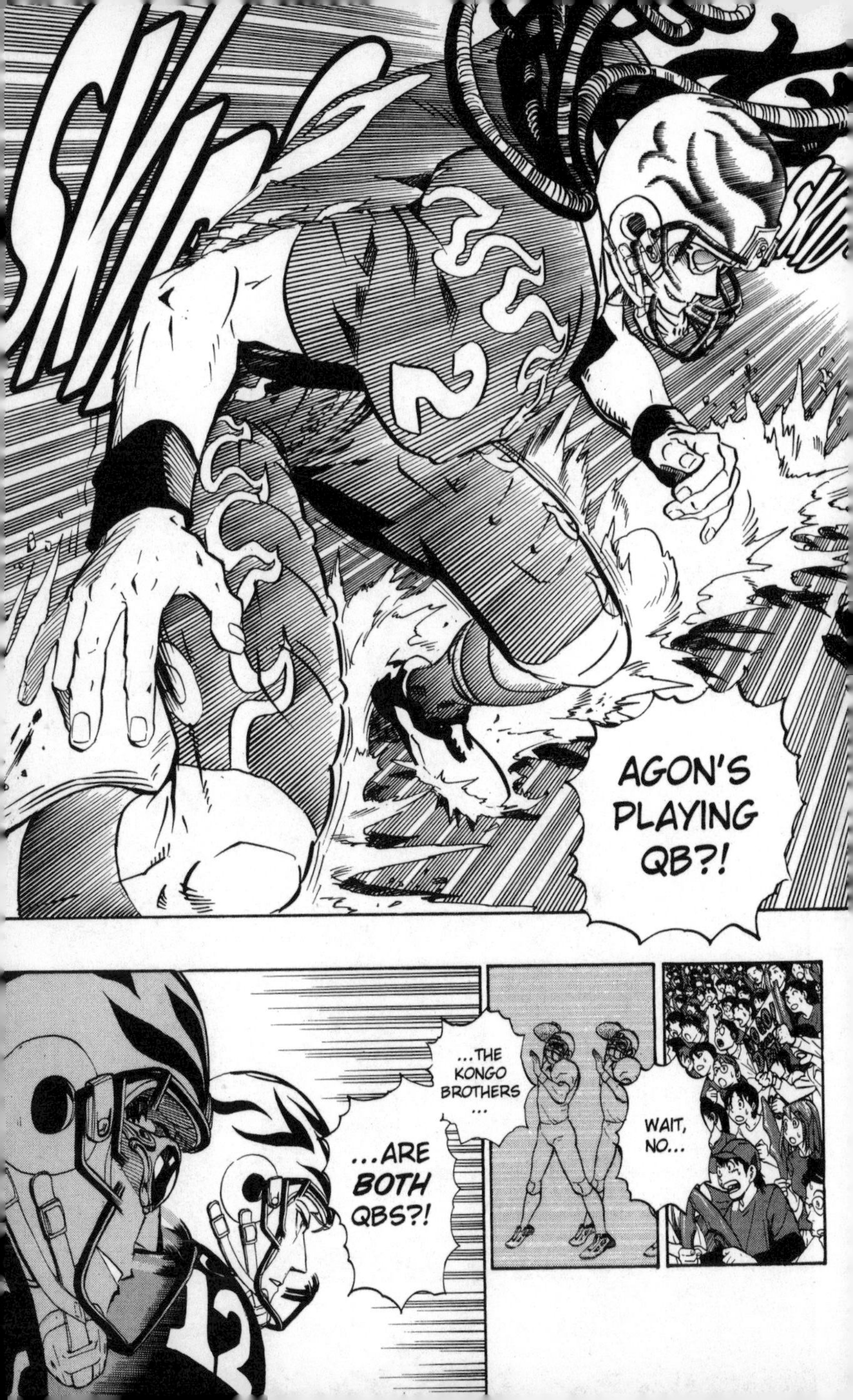
AGON'S PLAYING QB?!
WAIT, NO...
...THE KONGO BROTHERS ...
...ARE BOTH QBS?!

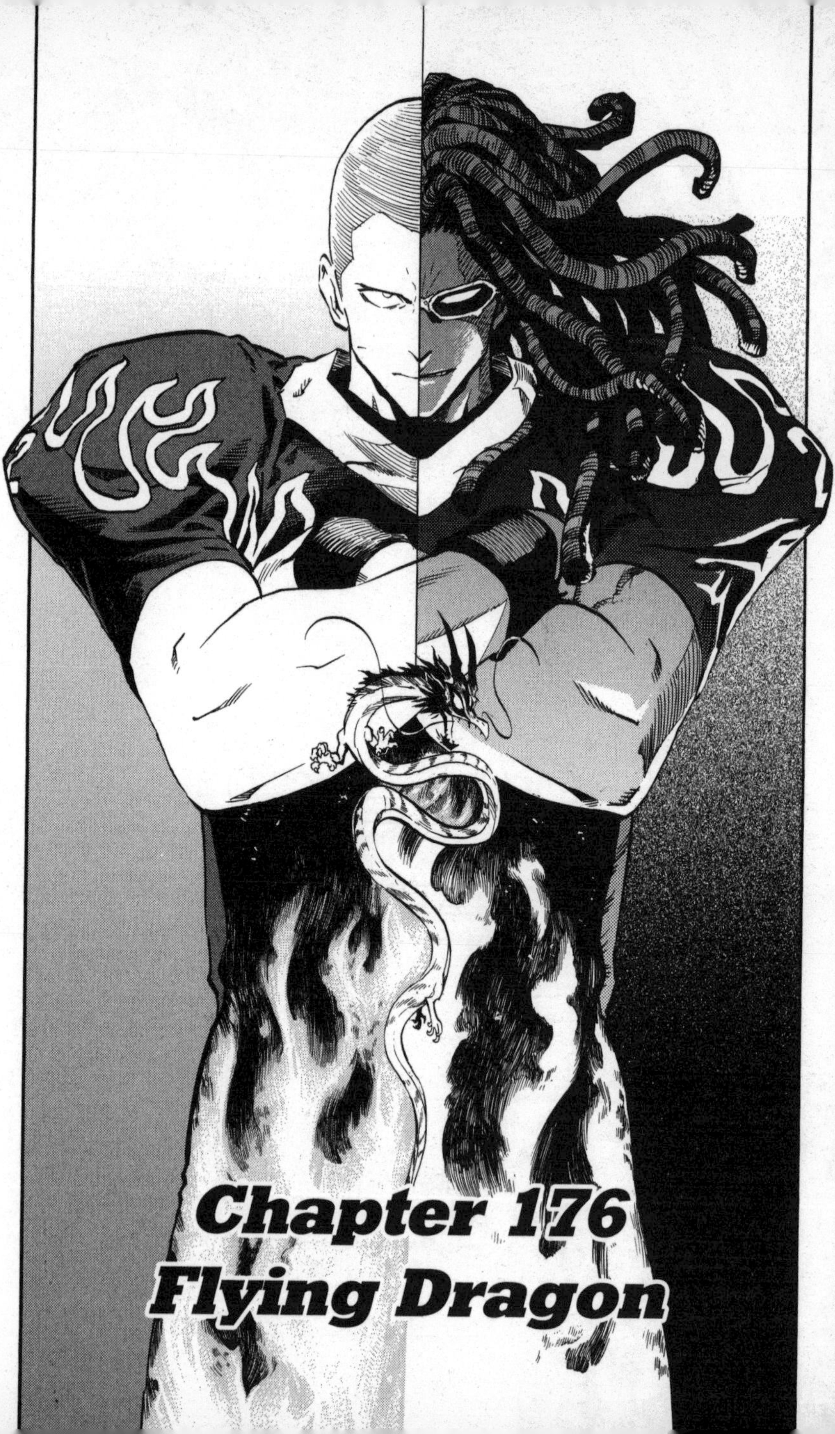
Chapter 176
Flying Dragon

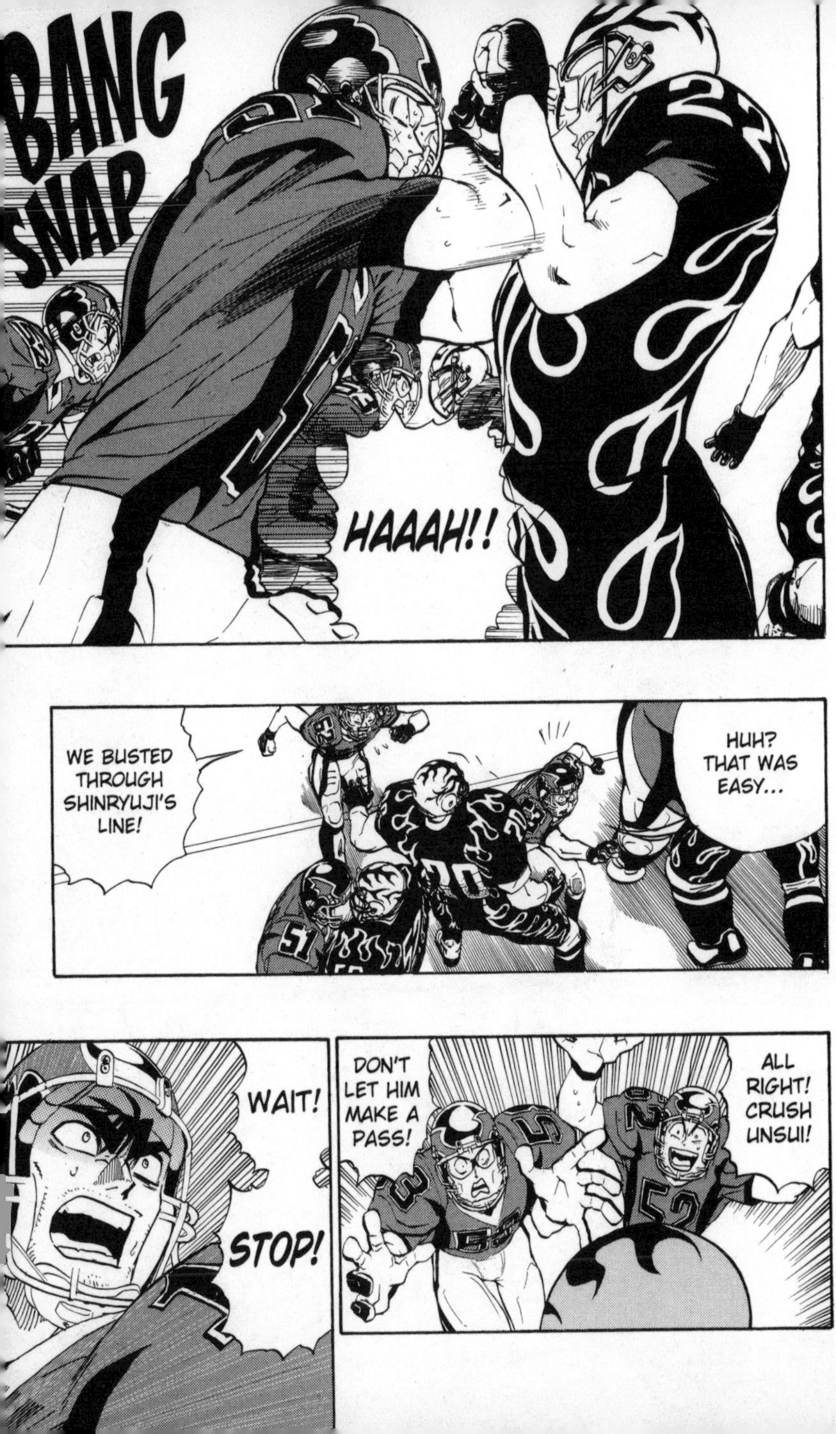
BANG
SNAP
HAAAH!!
HUH? THAT WAS EASY...
WE BUSTED THROUGH SHINRYUJI'S LINE!
ALL RIGHT! CRUSH UNSUI!
DON'T LET HIM MAKE A PASS!
WAIT!
STOP!

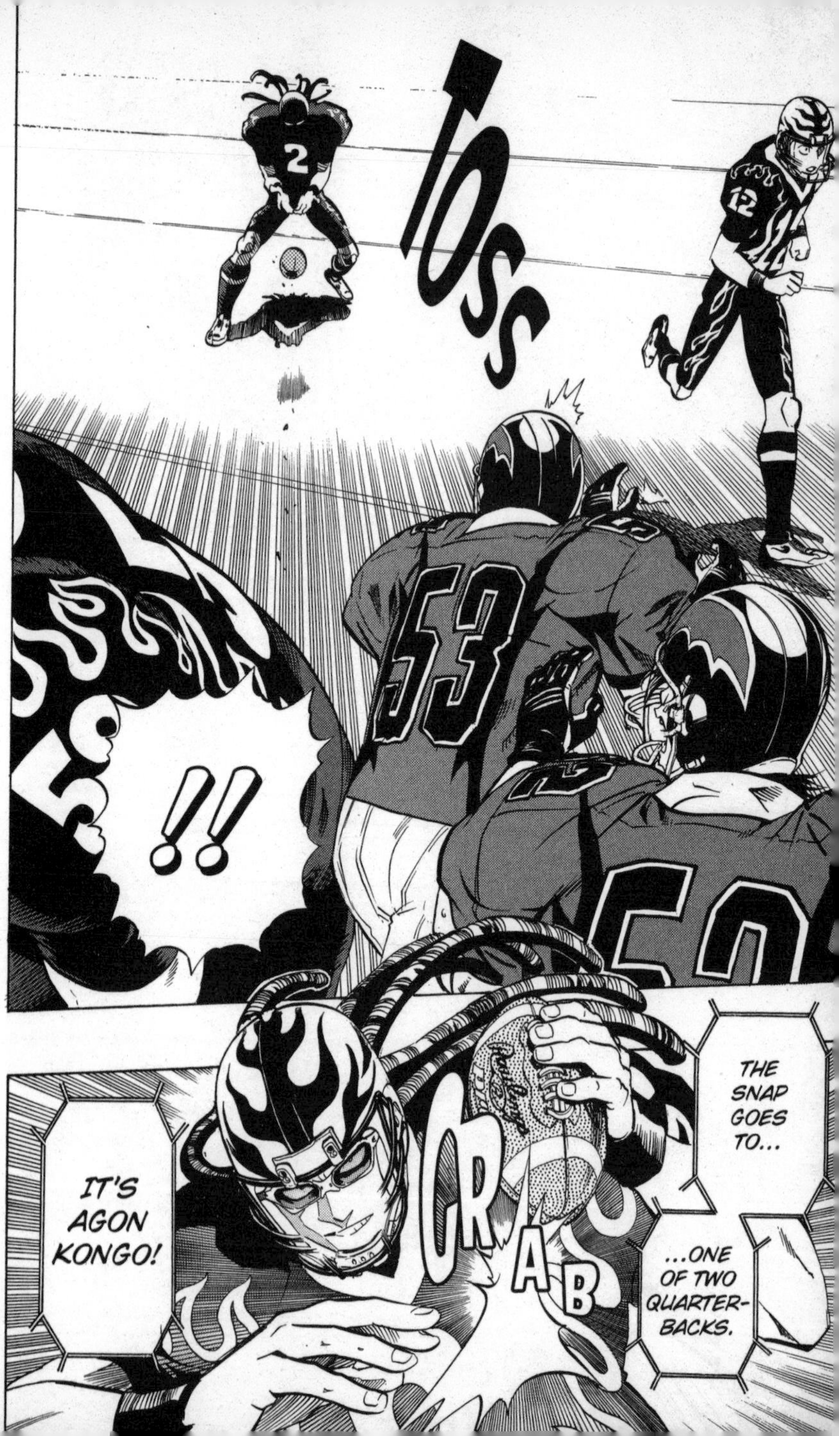
TOSS
!!
THE SNAP GOES TO...
...ONE OF TWO QUARTER-BACKS.
CRAB
IT'S AGON KONGO!

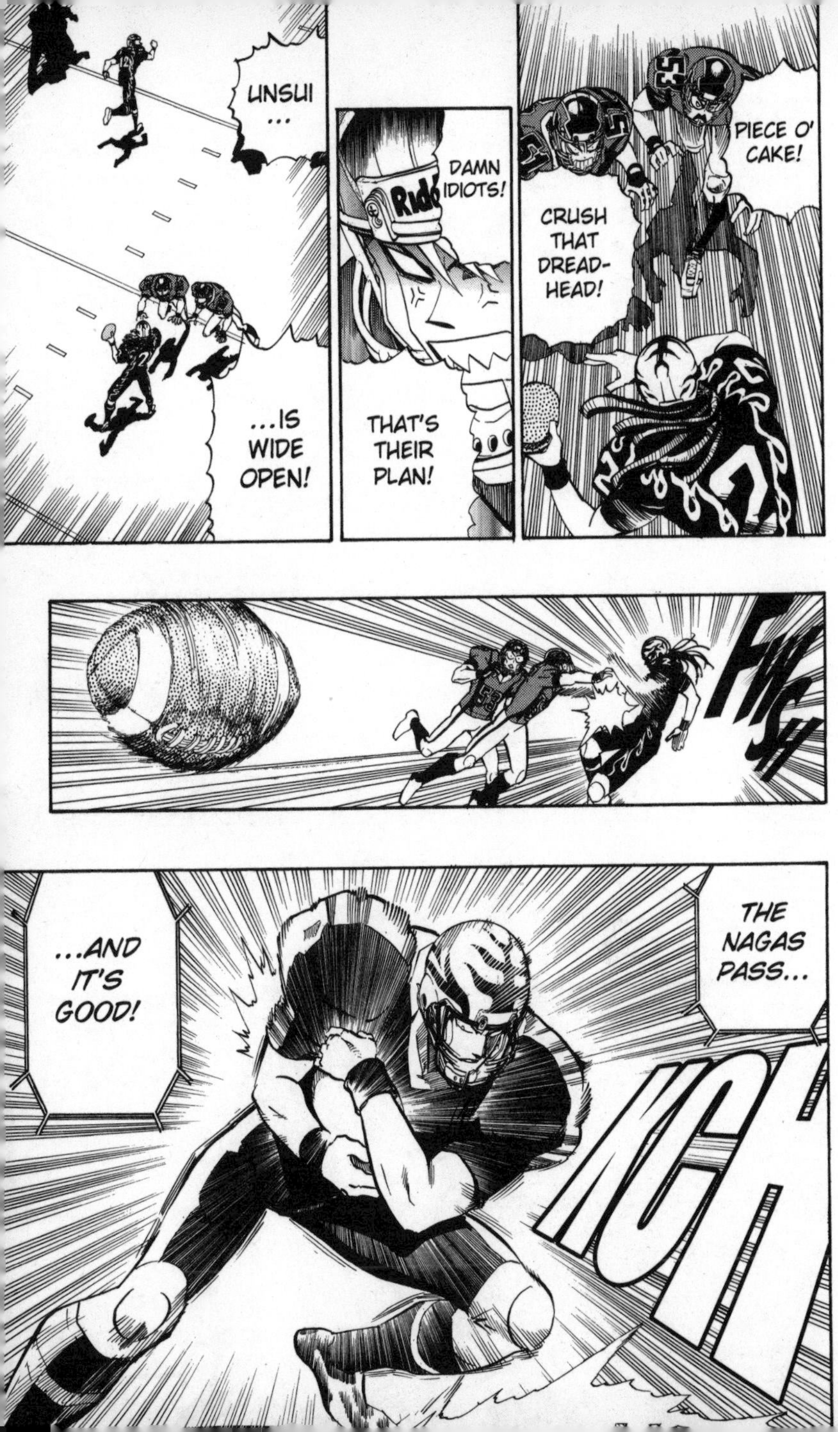
PIECE O' CAKE!
CRUSH THAT DREAD-HEAD!
DAMN IDIOTS!
THAT'S THEIR PLAN!
UNSUI ...
...IS WIDE OPEN!
FWSH
THE NAGAS PASS...
...AND IT'S GOOD!

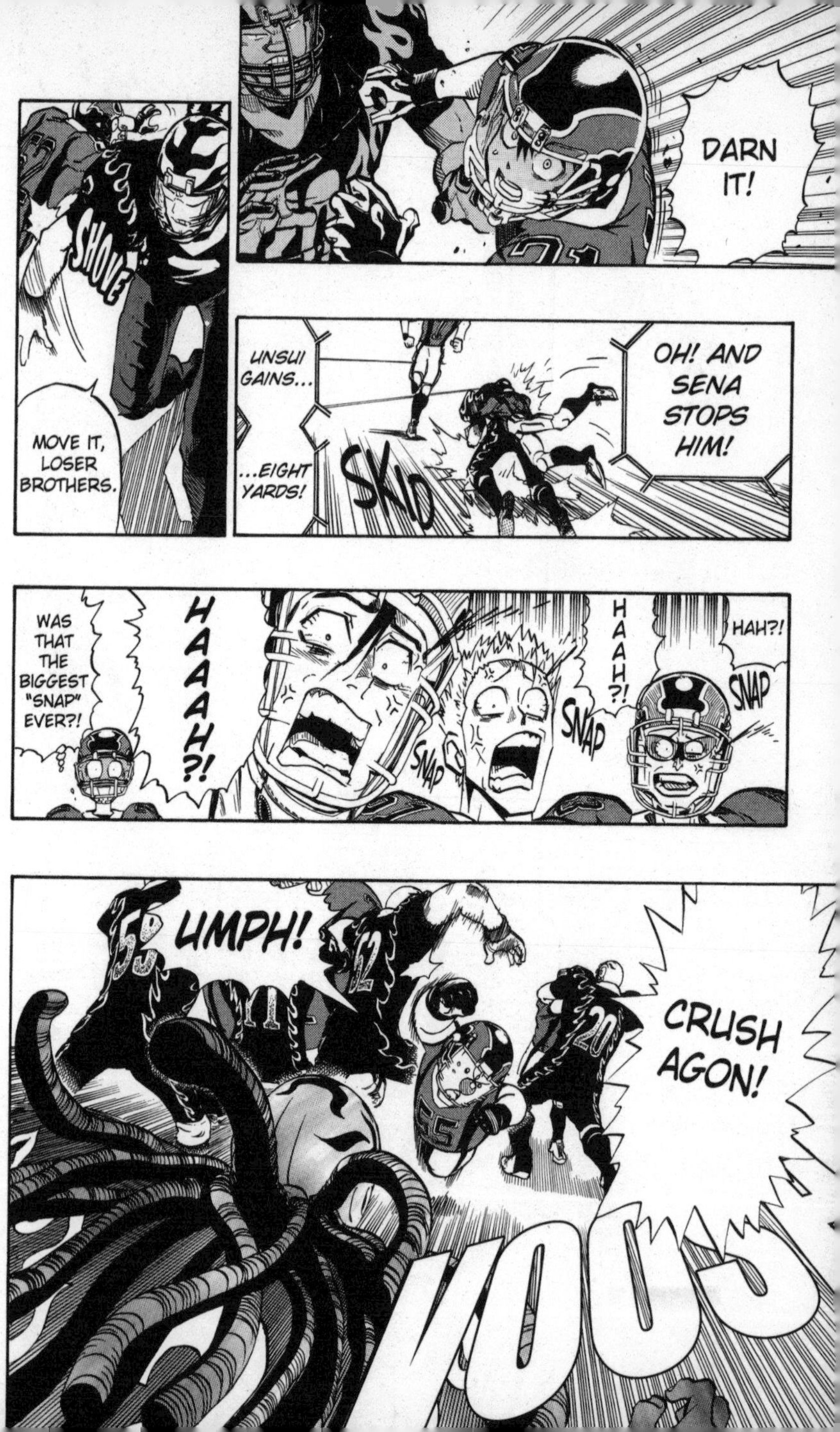
DARN IT!
OH! AND SENA STOPS HIM!
UNSUI GAINS...
...EIGHT YARDS!
SKID
SHOVE
MOVE IT, LOSER BROTHERS.
HAH?!
SNAP
HAAAH?!
SNAP
SNAP
HAAAAAH?!
WAS THAT THE BIGGEST "SNAP" EVER?!
CRUSH AGON!
UMPH!

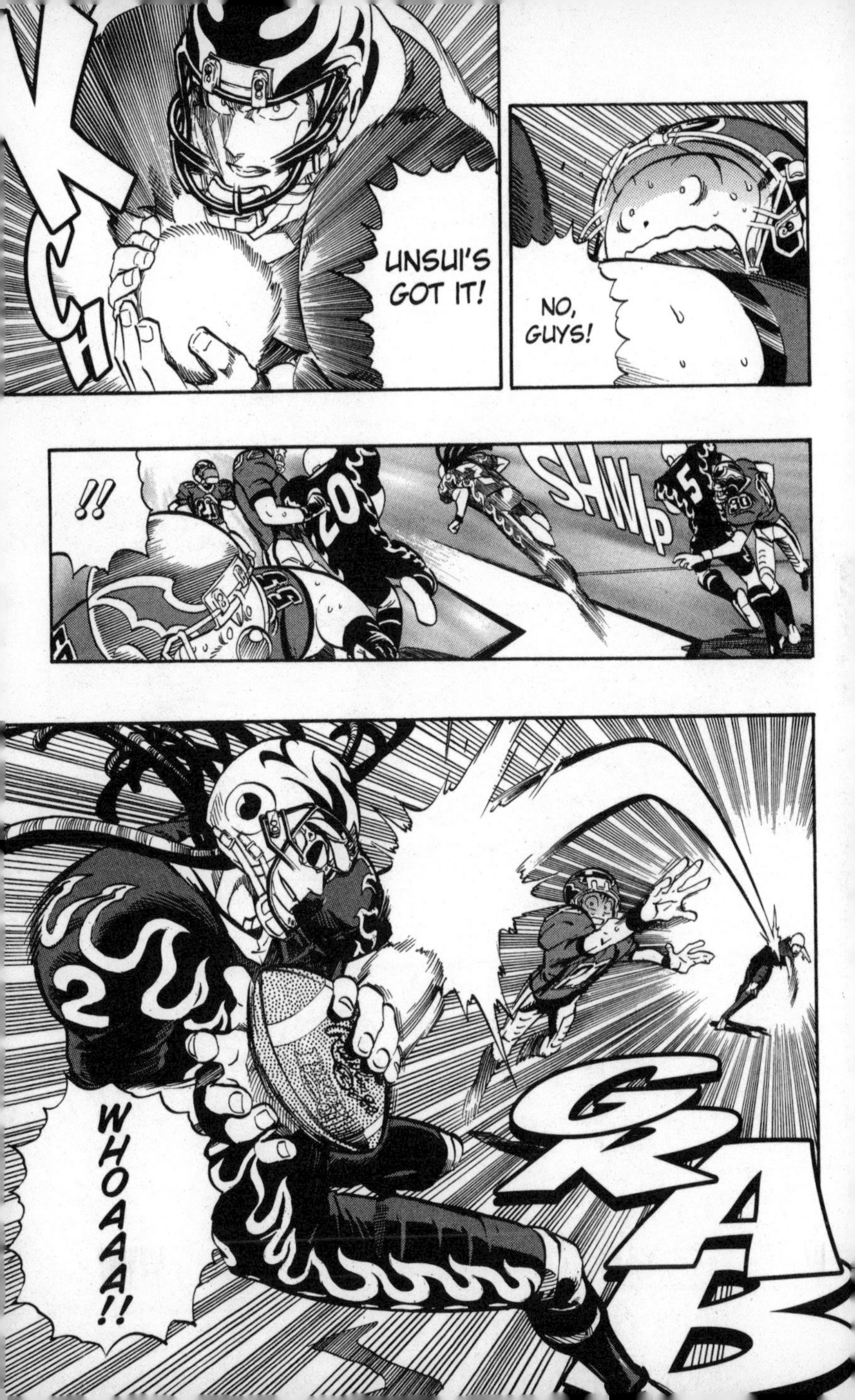
NO, GUYS!
UNSUI'S GOT IT!
SHWIP
!!
GRAB
WHOAAAA!!

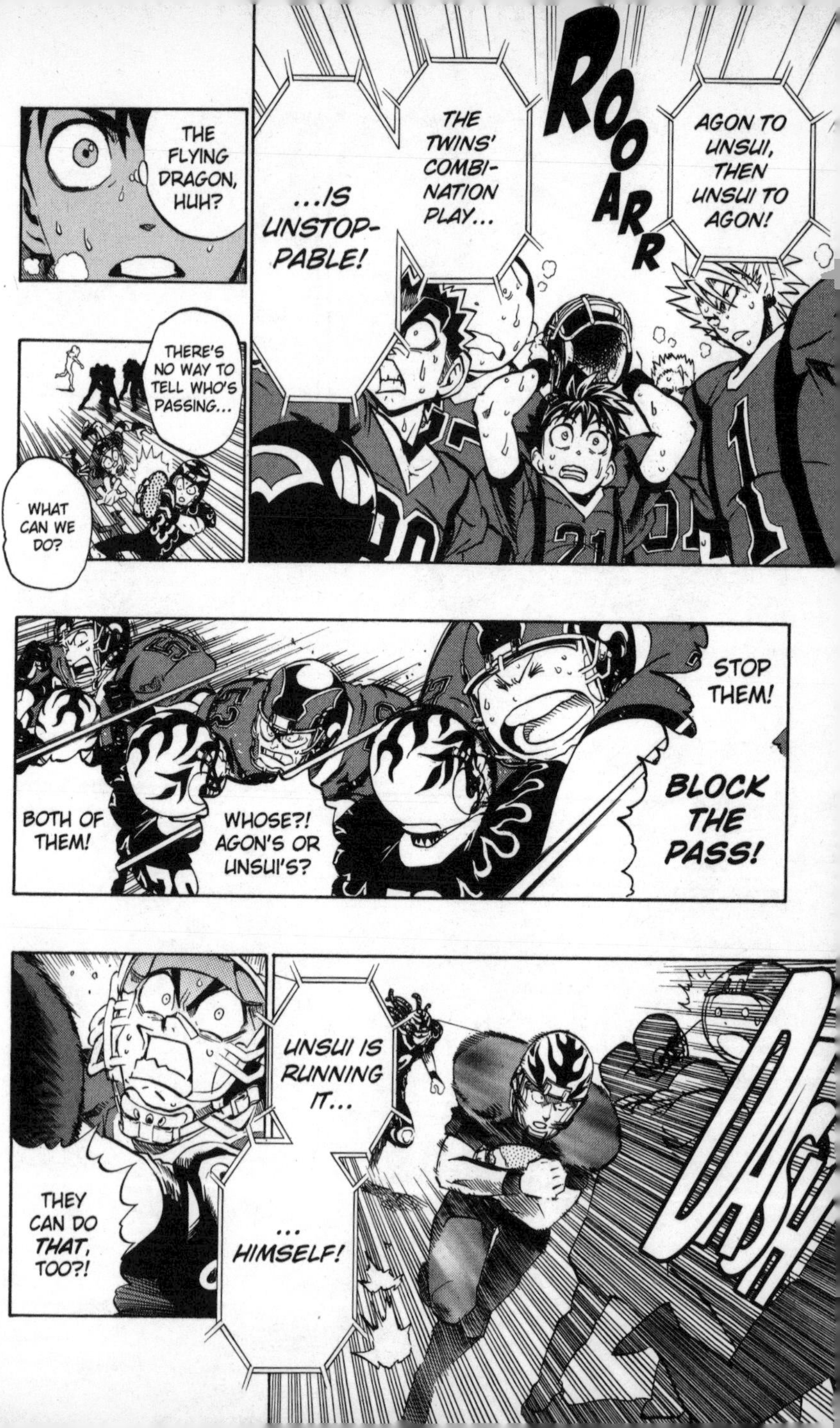
AGON TO UNSUI, THEN UNSUI TO AGON!
ROOARR
THE TWINS' COMBINATION PLAY...
...IS UNSTOPPABLE!
THE FLYING DRAGON, HUH?
THERE'S NO WAY TO TELL WHO'S PASSING...
WHAT CAN WE DO?
STOP THEM!
BLOCK THE PASS!
WHOSE?! AGON'S OR UNSUI'S?
BOTH OF THEM!
DASH
UNSUI IS RUNNING IT...
...HIMSELF!
THEY CAN DO *THAT*, TOO?!

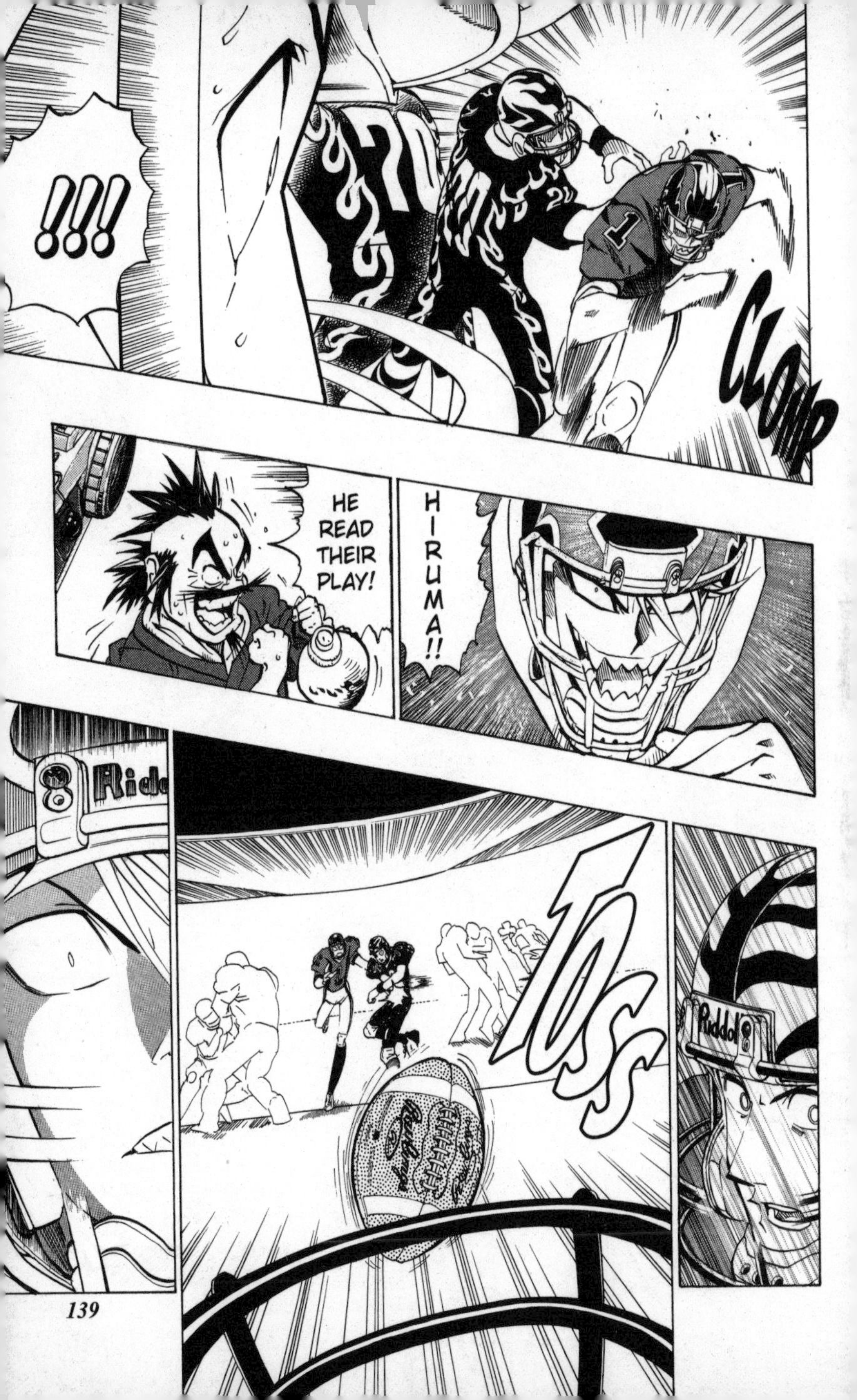
!!!!
CLOMP
HIRUMA!!
HE READ THEIR PLAY!
TOSS

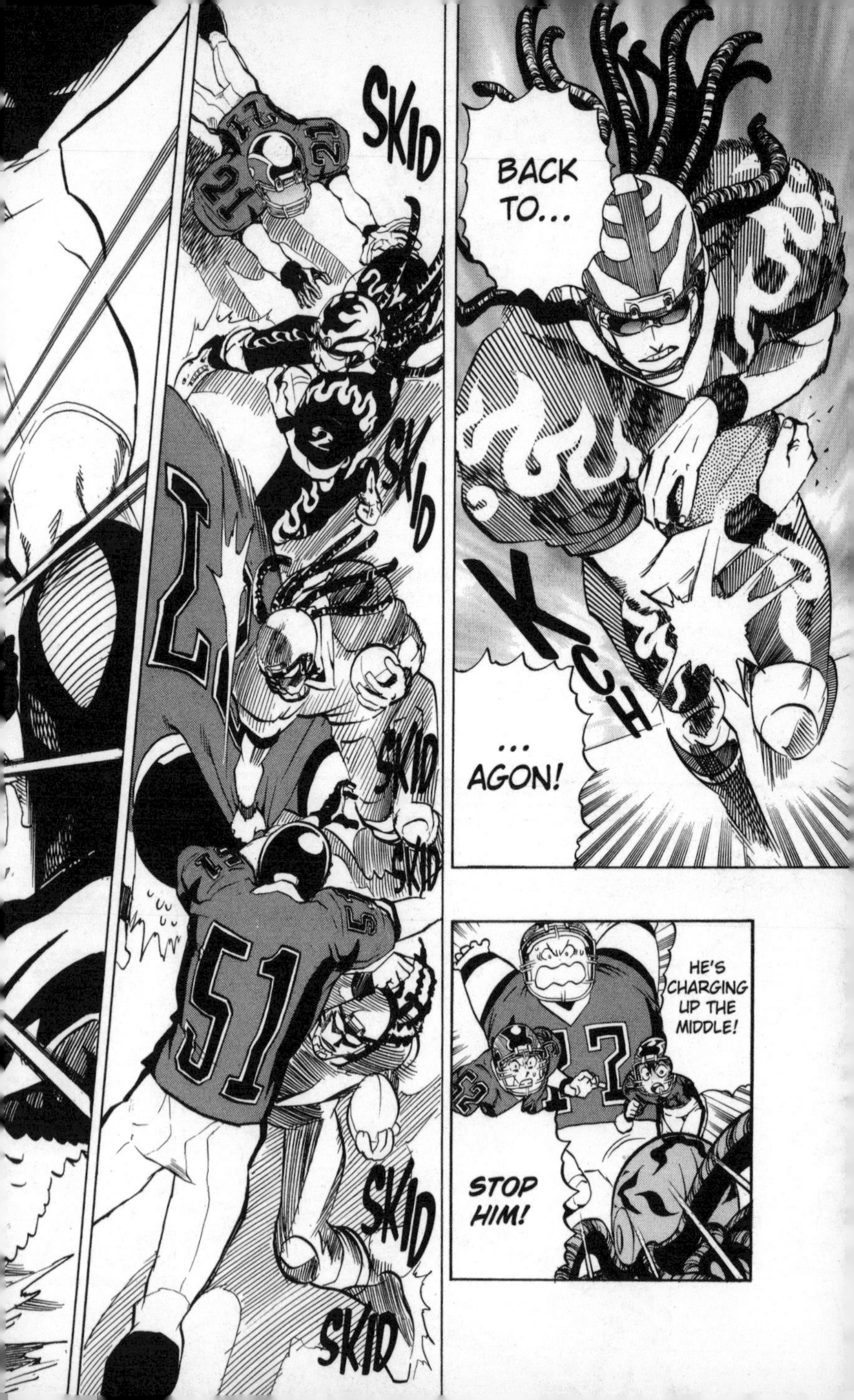
BACK TO...
KCH
... AGON!
HE'S CHARGING UP THE MIDDLE!
STOP HIM!
SKID
SKID
SKID
SKID
SKID
SKID

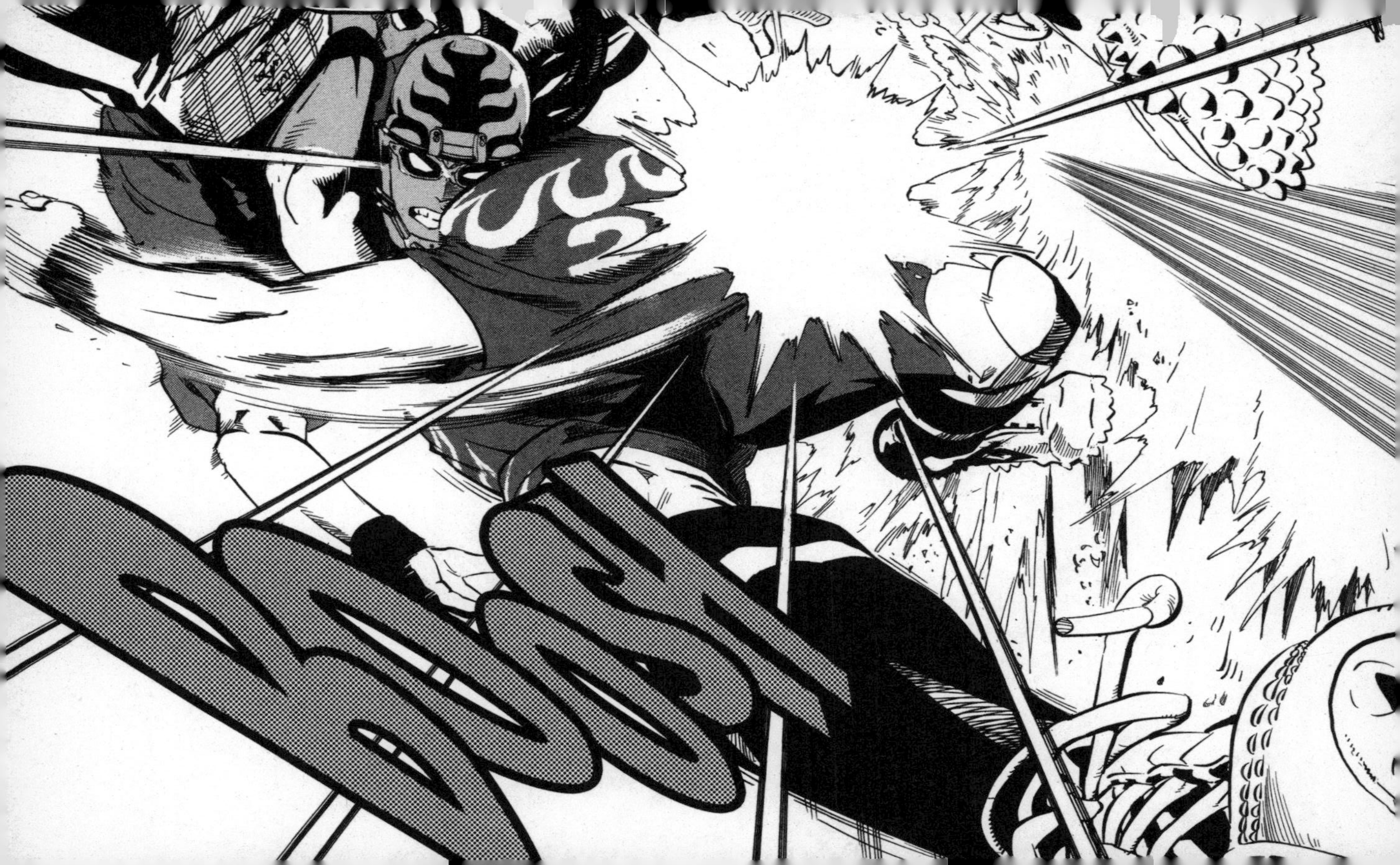

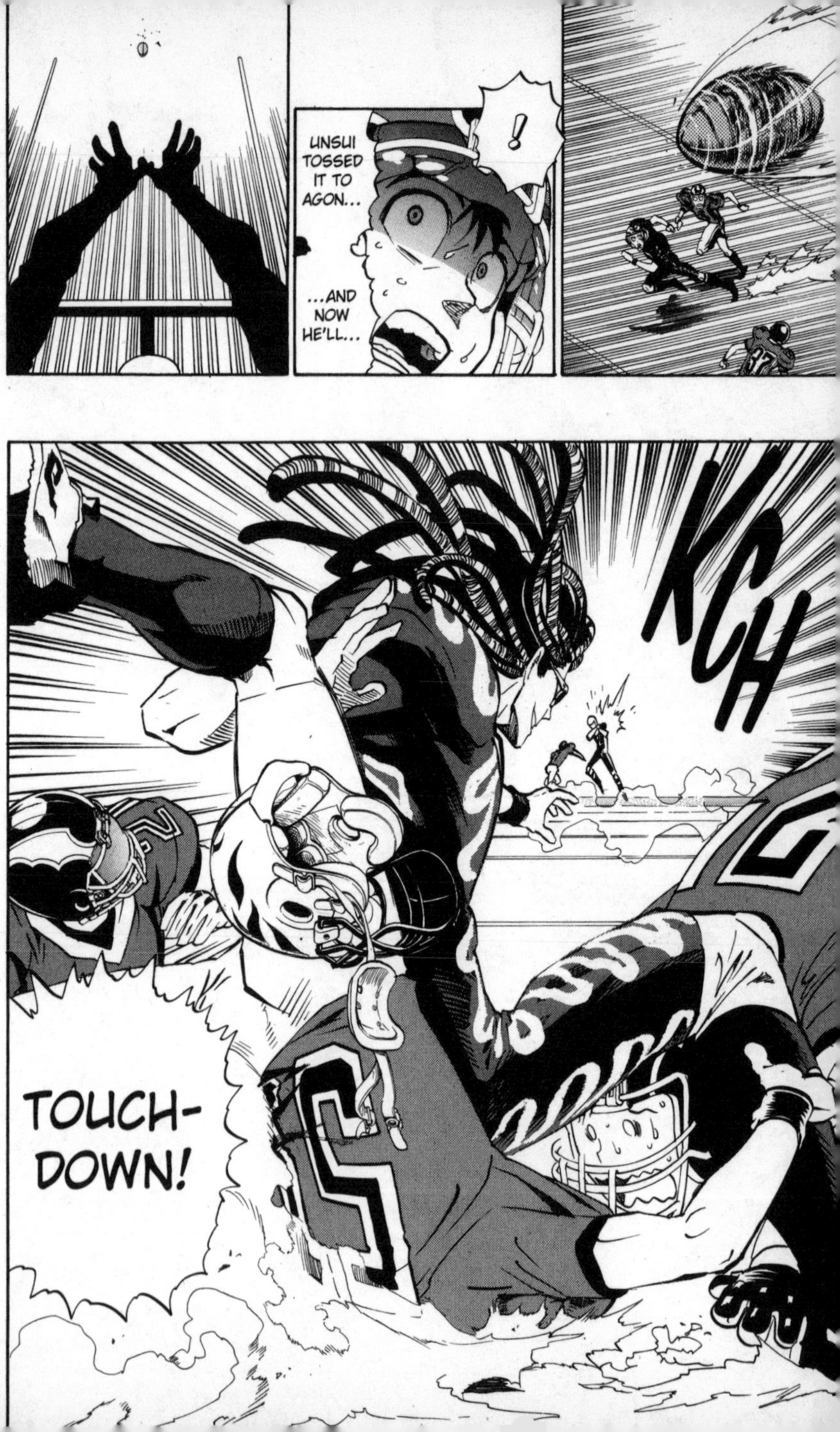
!
UNSUI TOSSED IT TO AGON...
...AND NOW HE'LL...
KCH
TOUCH-DOWN!

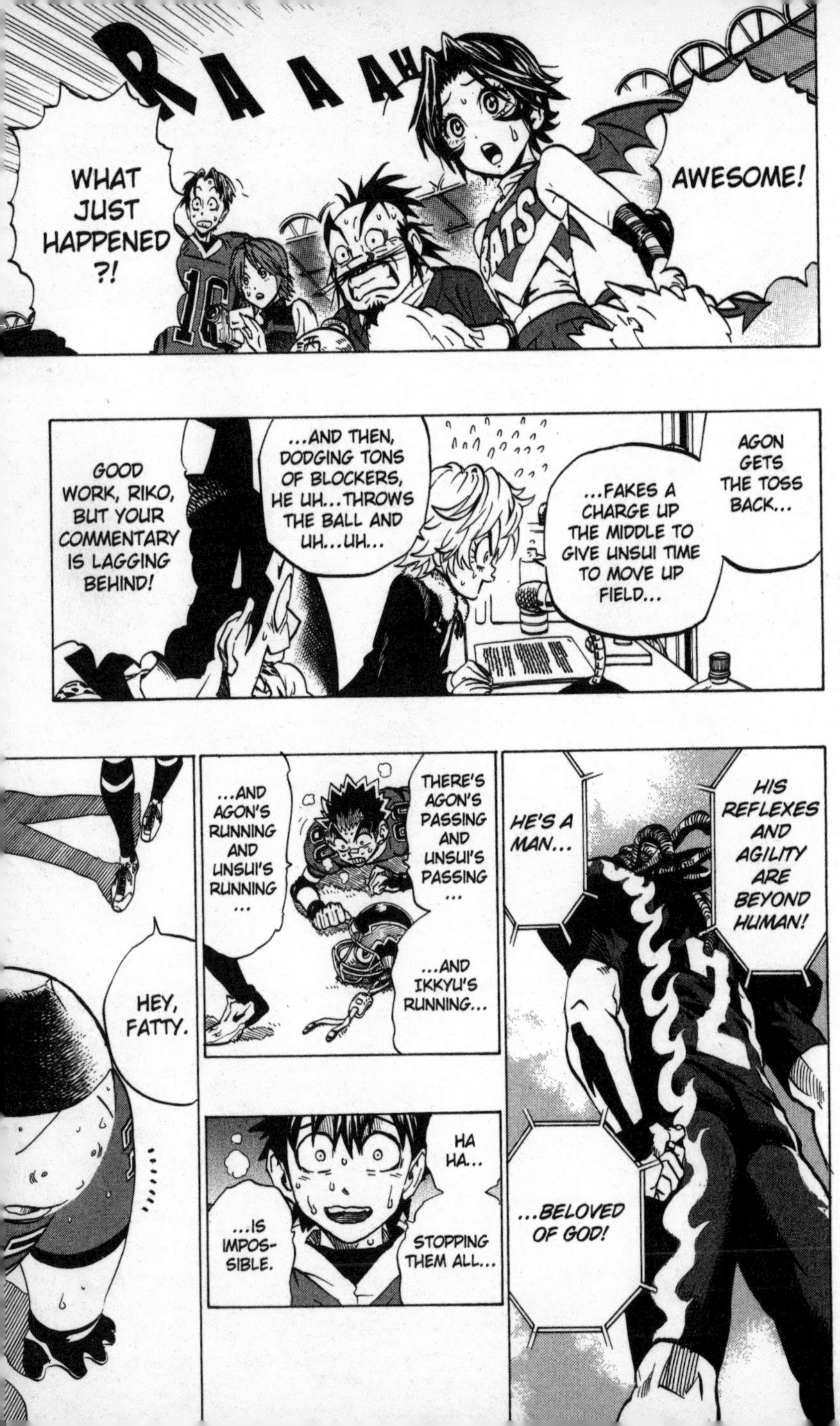
RAAAAH
AWESOME!
WHAT JUST HAPPENED?!
AGON GETS THE TOSS BACK...
...FAKES A CHARGE UP THE MIDDLE TO GIVE UNSUI TIME TO MOVE UP FIELD...
...AND THEN, DODGING TONS OF BLOCKERS, HE UH...THROWS THE BALL AND UH...UH...
GOOD WORK, RIKO, BUT YOUR COMMENTARY IS LAGGING BEHIND!
HIS REFLEXES AND AGILITY ARE BEYOND HUMAN!
HE'S A MAN...
...BELOVED OF GOD!
THERE'S AGON'S PASSING AND UNSUI'S PASSING...
...AND AGON'S RUNNING AND UNSUI'S RUNNING...
...AND IKKYU'S RUNNING...
HA HA...
STOPPING THEM ALL...
...IS IMPOSSIBLE.
HEY, FATTY.
......

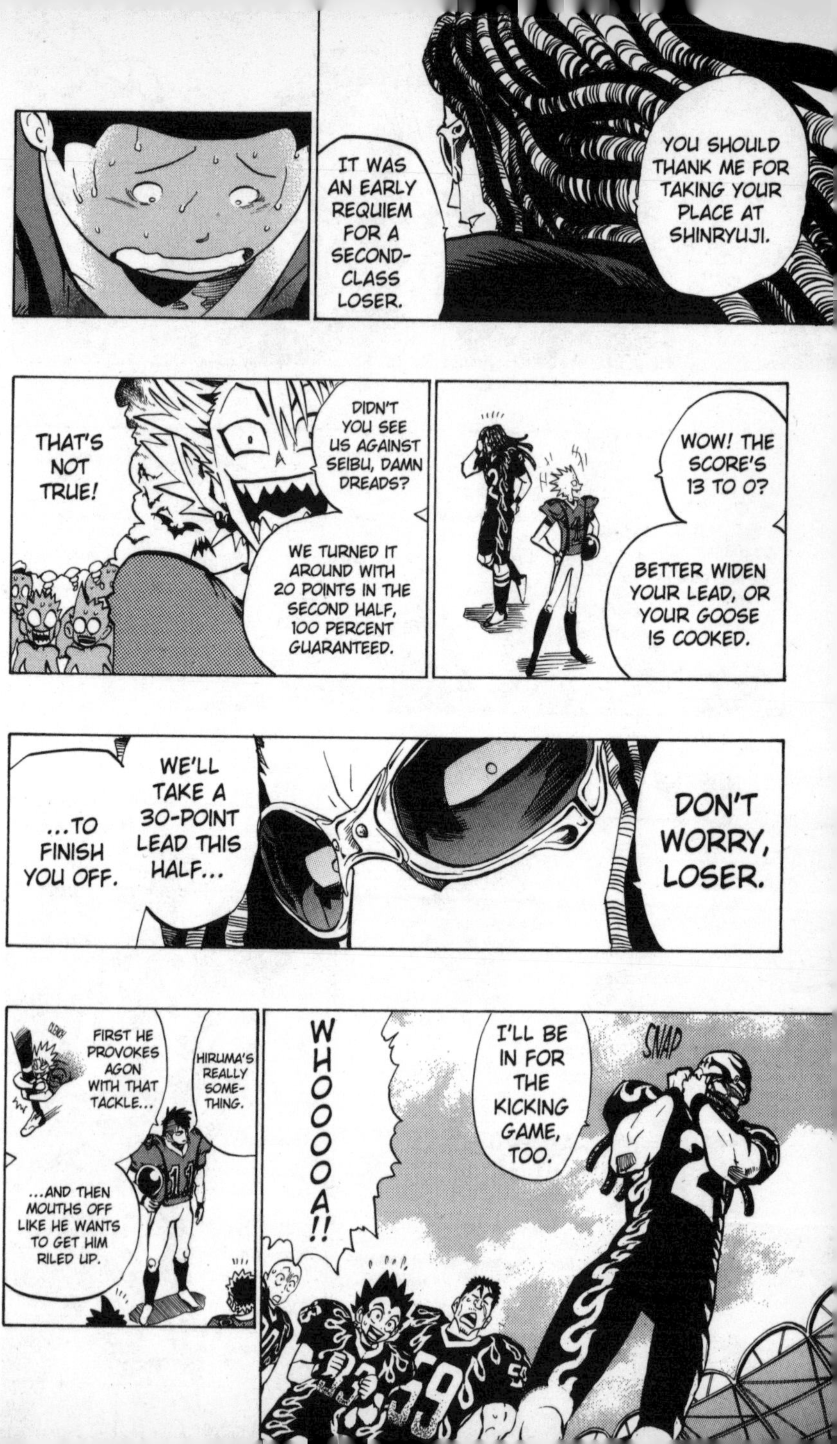
YOU SHOULD THANK ME FOR TAKING YOUR PLACE AT SHINRYUJI.
IT WAS AN EARLY REQUIEM FOR A SECOND-CLASS LOSER.
WOW! THE SCORE'S 13 TO 0?
BETTER WIDEN YOUR LEAD, OR YOUR GOOSE IS COOKED.
DIDN'T YOU SEE US AGAINST SEIBU, DAMN DREADS?
WE TURNED IT AROUND WITH 20 POINTS IN THE SECOND HALF, 100 PERCENT GUARANTEED.
THAT'S NOT TRUE!
DON'T WORRY, LOSER.
WE'LL TAKE A 30-POINT LEAD THIS HALF...
...TO FINISH YOU OFF.
SNAP
I'LL BE IN FOR THE KICKING GAME, TOO.
WHOOOOOA!!
HIRUMA'S REALLY SOME-THING.
FIRST HE PROVOKES AGON WITH THAT TACKLE...
...AND THEN MOUTHS OFF LIKE HE WANTS TO GET HIM RILED UP.

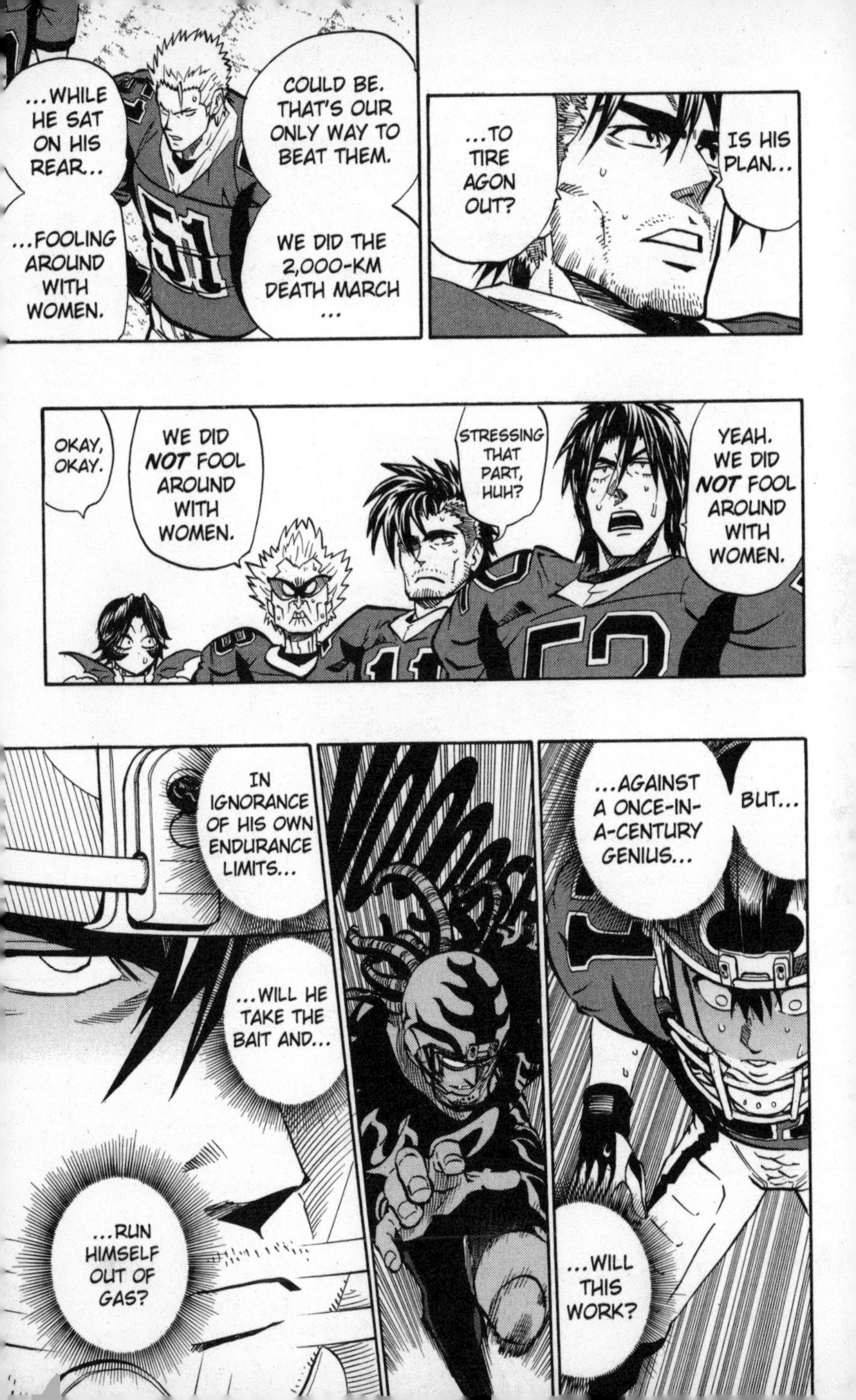
IS HIS PLAN...
...TO TIRE AGON OUT?
COULD BE. THAT'S OUR ONLY WAY TO BEAT THEM.
WE DID THE 2,000-KM DEATH MARCH ...
...WHILE HE SAT ON HIS REAR...
...FOOLING AROUND WITH WOMEN.
YEAH. WE DID *NOT* FOOL AROUND WITH WOMEN.
STRESSING THAT PART, HUH?
WE DID *NOT* FOOL AROUND WITH WOMEN.
OKAY, OKAY.
BUT...
...AGAINST A ONCE-IN-A-CENTURY GENIUS...
...WILL THIS WORK?
IN IGNORANCE OF HIS OWN ENDURANCE LIMITS...
...WILL HE TAKE THE BAIT AND...
...RUN HIMSELF OUT OF GAS?

Investigation File #067

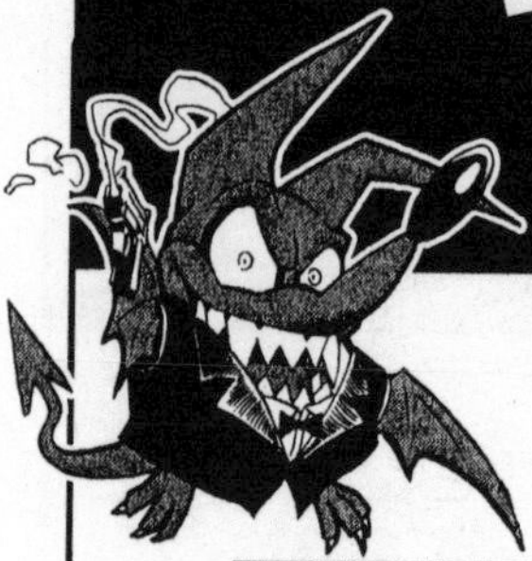

## Show us a good all-star game!

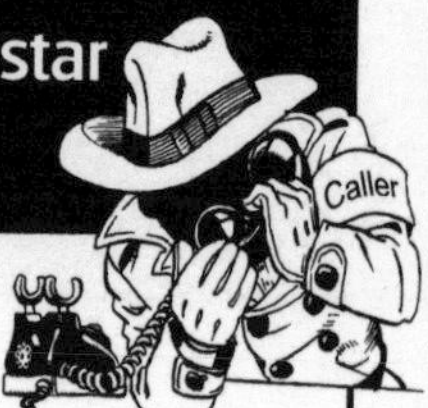
Caller

WHAT IF A TEAM LIKE THIS...

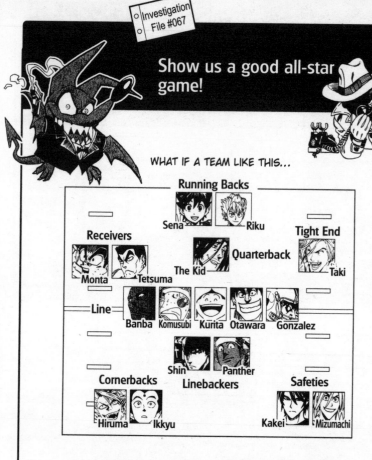

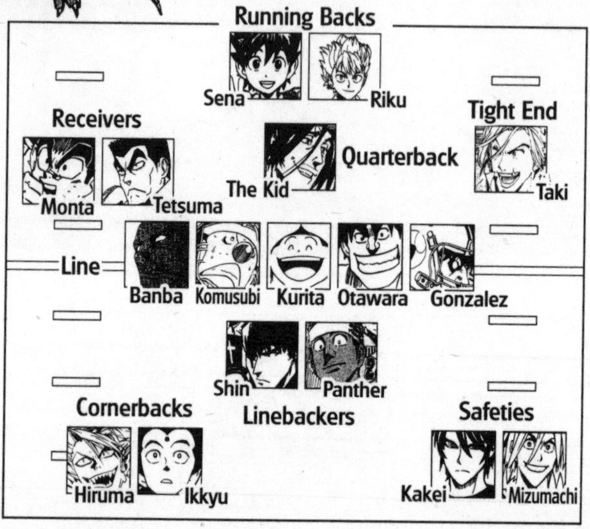
Running Backs
Sena
Riku
Receivers
Monta
Tetsuma
Quarterback
The Kid
Tight End
Taki
Line
Banba
Komusubi
Kurita
Otawara
Gonzalez
Shin
Panther
Linebackers
Cornerbacks
Hiruma
Ikkyu
Safeties
Kakei
Mizumachi

...PLAYED THE KOIGAHAMA CUPIDS? WHO WOULD WIN, AND WHAT WOULD THE SCORE BE? THINK ABOUT IT FOR YOURSELF!

Caller: Steam Engine Tootle, Tokyo Prefecture

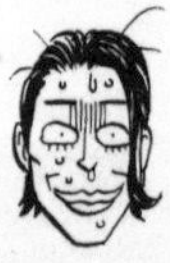

WE'D FORFEIT AT THE KICKOFF...

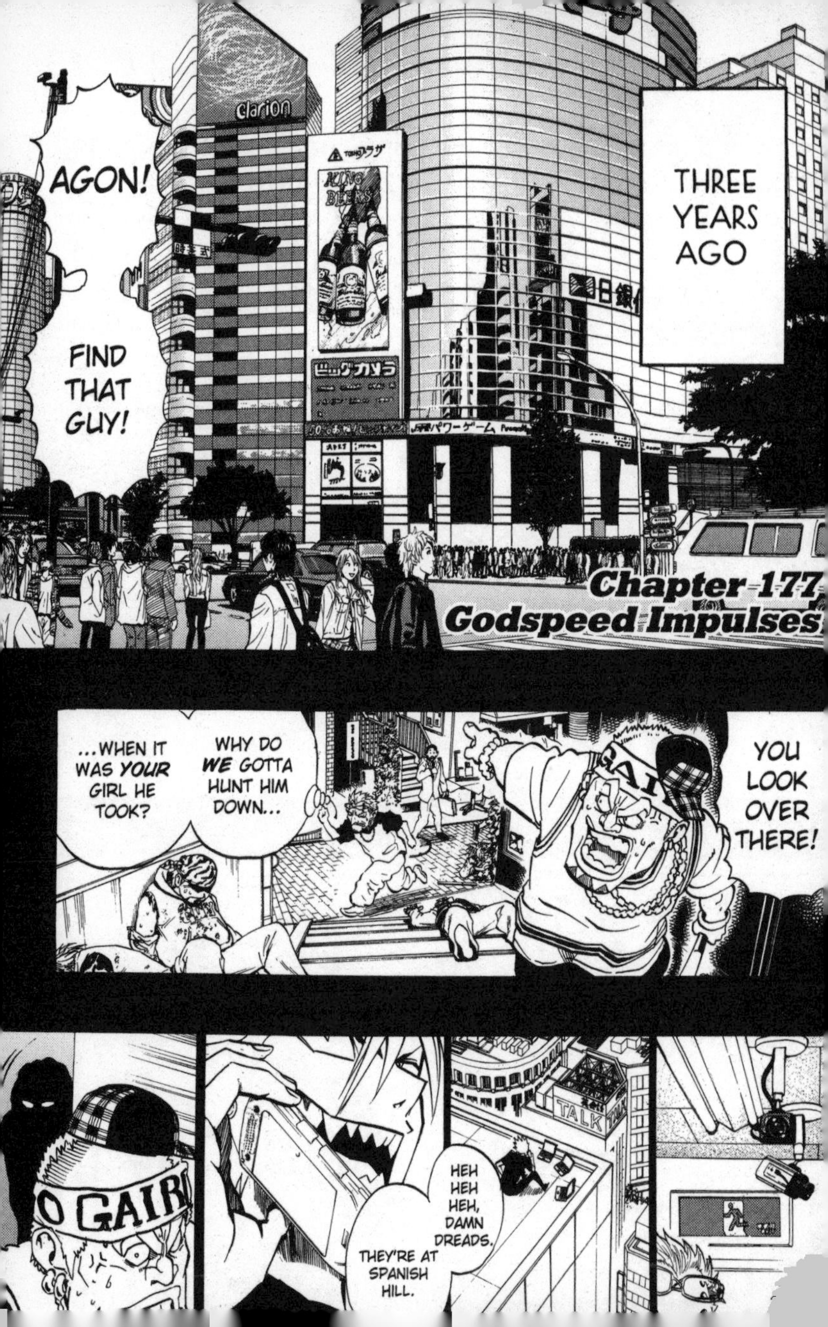
THREE YEARS AGO
Chapter 177 Godspeed Impulses!
...AGON!
FIND THAT GUY!
YOU LOOK OVER THERE!
WHY DO **WE** GOTTA HUNT HIM DOWN...
...WHEN IT WAS **YOUR** GIRL HE TOOK?
TALK
HEH HEH HEH, DAMN DREADS.
THEY'RE AT SPANISH HILL.

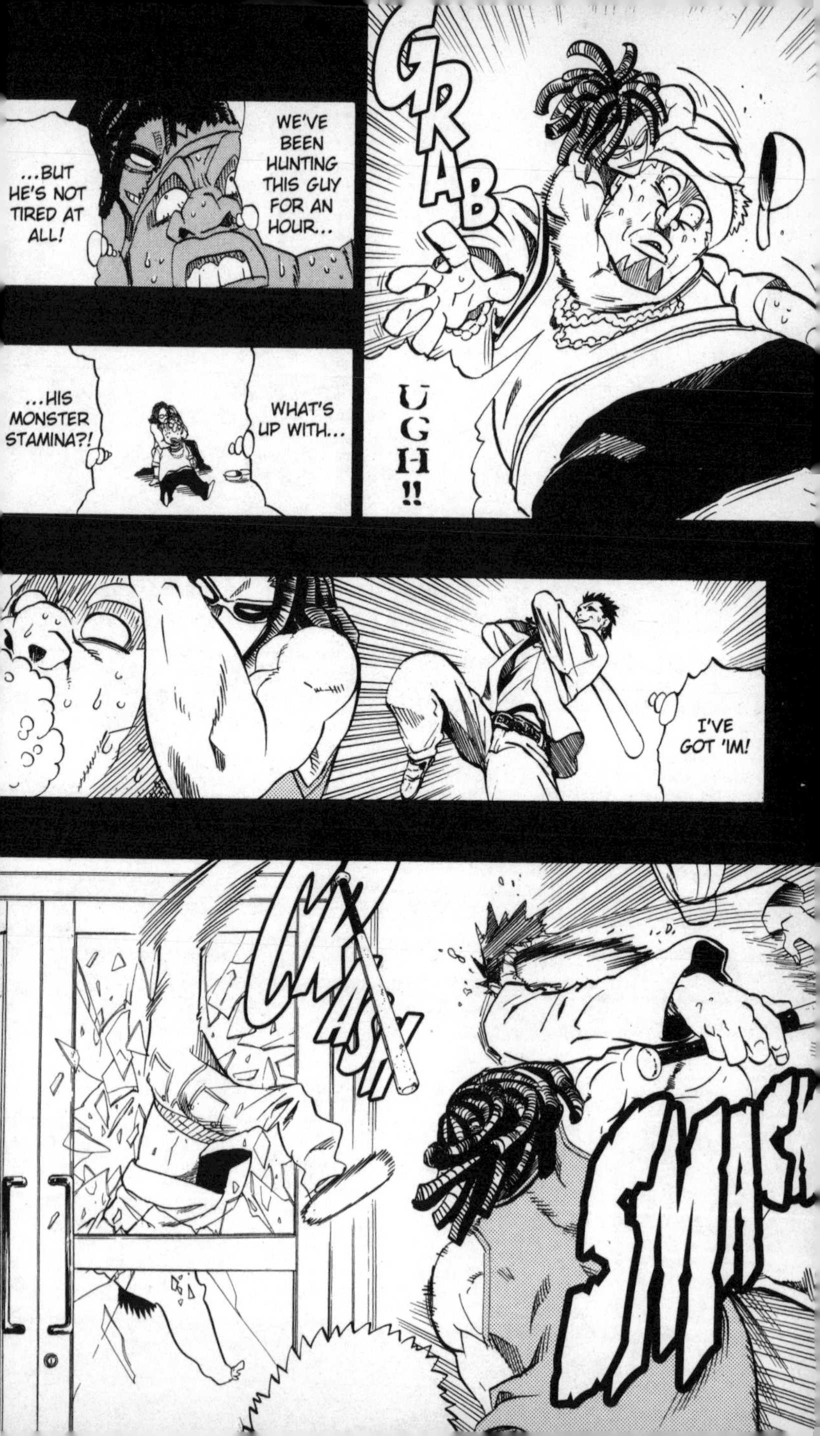
GRAB
UGH!!
WE'VE BEEN HUNTING THIS GUY FOR AN HOUR...
...BUT HE'S NOT TIRED AT ALL!
WHAT'S UP WITH...
...HIS MONSTER STAMINA?!
I'VE GOT 'IM!

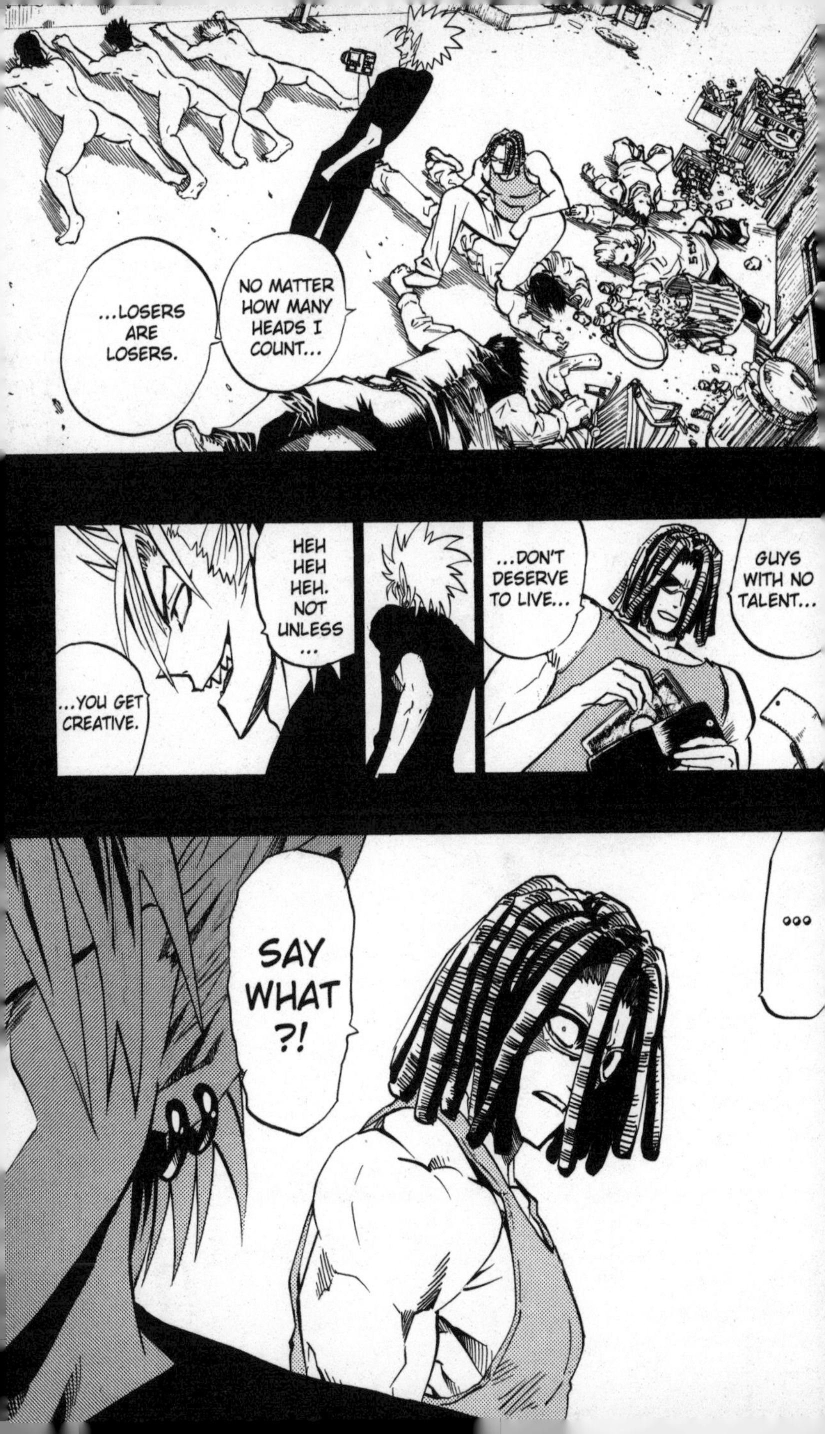
NO MATTER HOW MANY HEADS I COUNT...
...LOSERS ARE LOSERS.
GUYS WITH NO TALENT...
...DON'T DESERVE TO LIVE...
HEH HEH HEH. NOT UNLESS ...
...YOU GET CREATIVE.
...
SAY WHAT?!

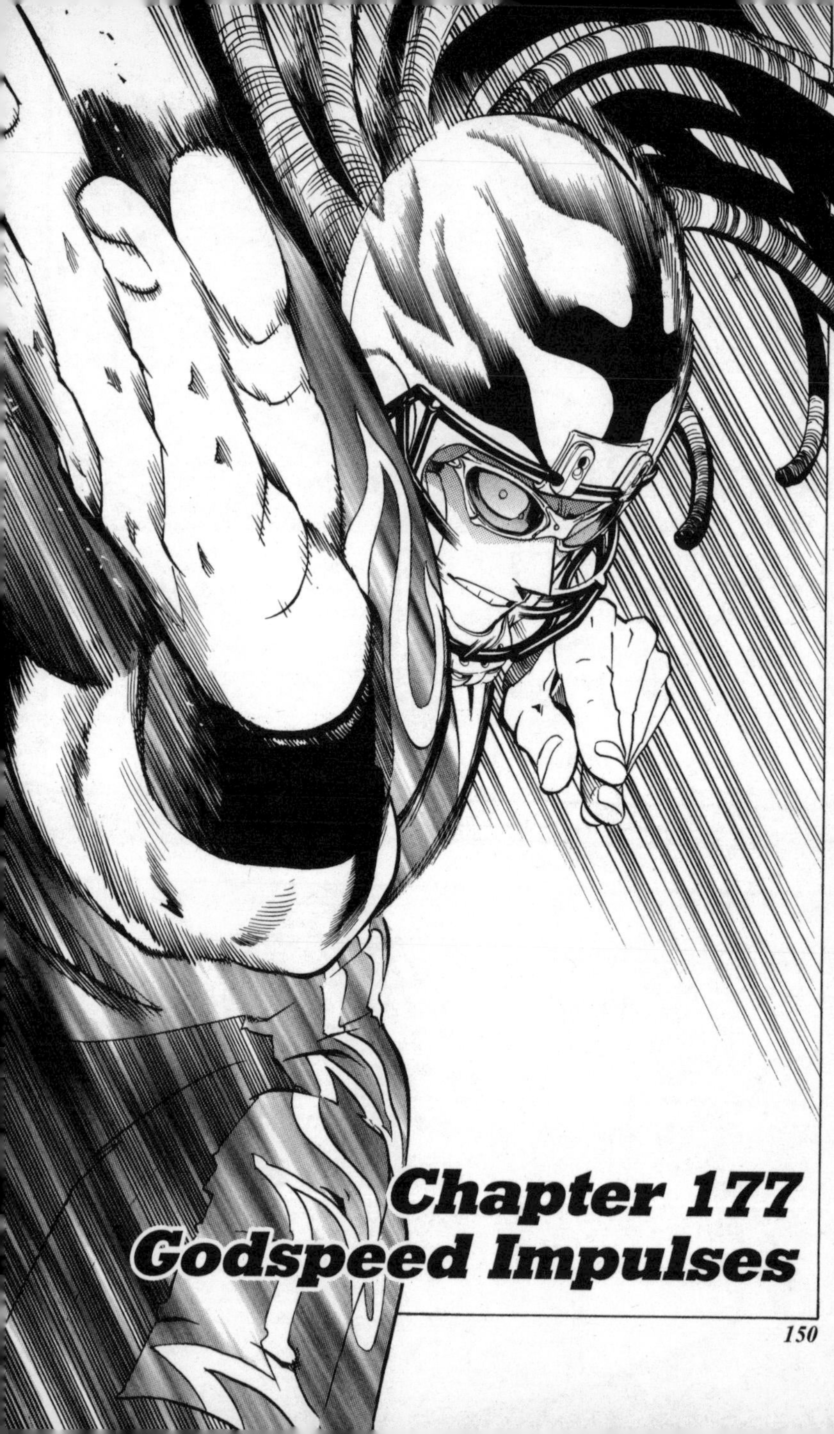
Chapter 177
Godspeed Impulses

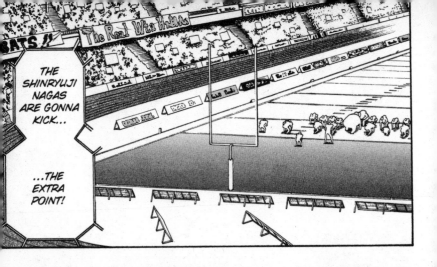

THE SHINRYUJI NAGAS ARE GONNA KICK...

...THE EXTRA POINT!

DON'T GET EXCITED.

"KICK"?!

WAP

CRUNCH

UMPH!!

WHAT PRESSURE!

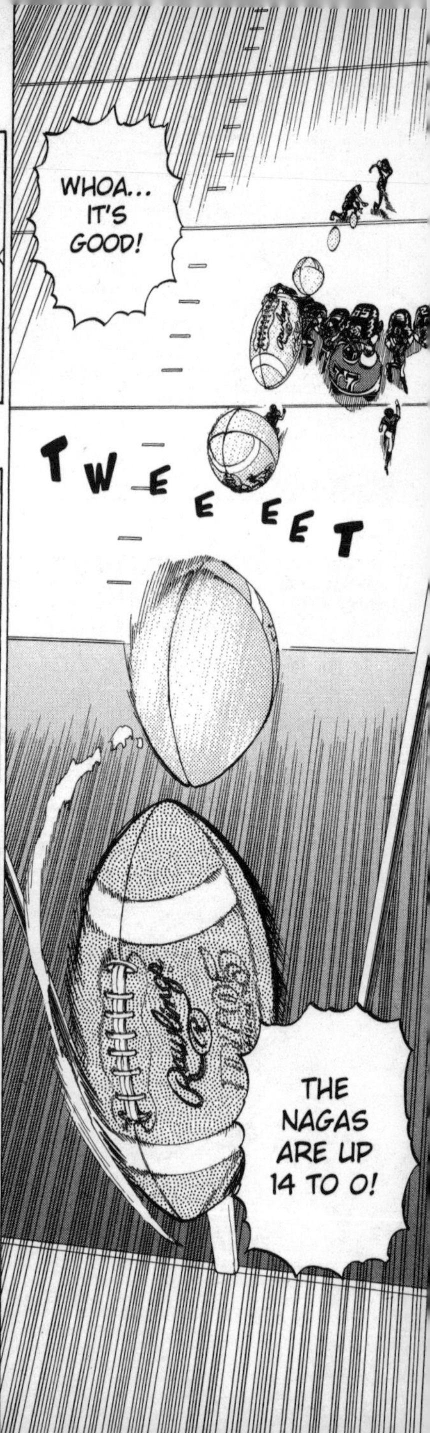
WHOA... IT'S GOOD!
TWEEEEET
THE NAGAS ARE UP 14 TO 0!

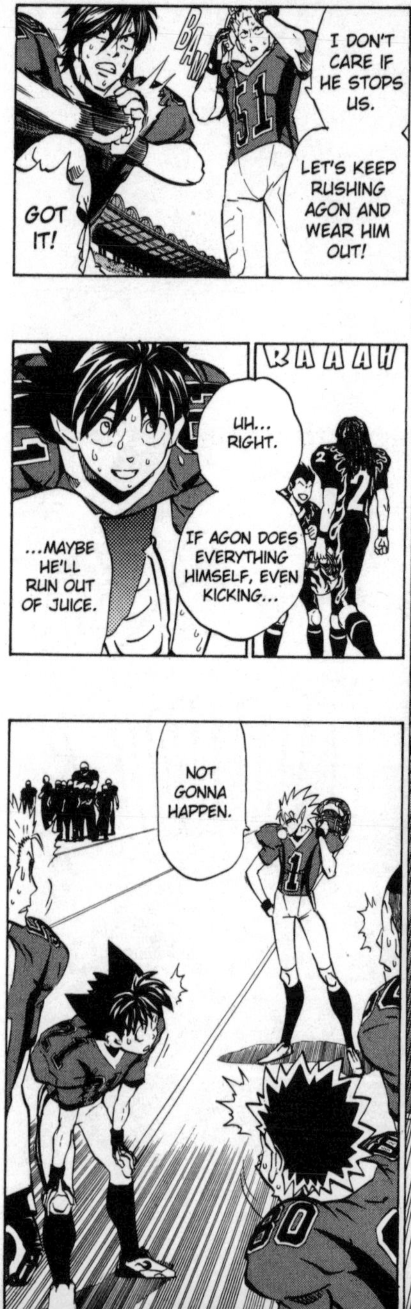
I DON'T CARE IF HE STOPS US.
LET'S KEEP RUSHING AGON AND WEAR HIM OUT!
BAM
GOT IT!
RAAAAH
UH... RIGHT.
IF AGON DOES EVERYTHING HIMSELF, EVEN KICKING...
...MAYBE HE'LL RUN OUT OF JUICE.
NOT GONNA HAPPEN.

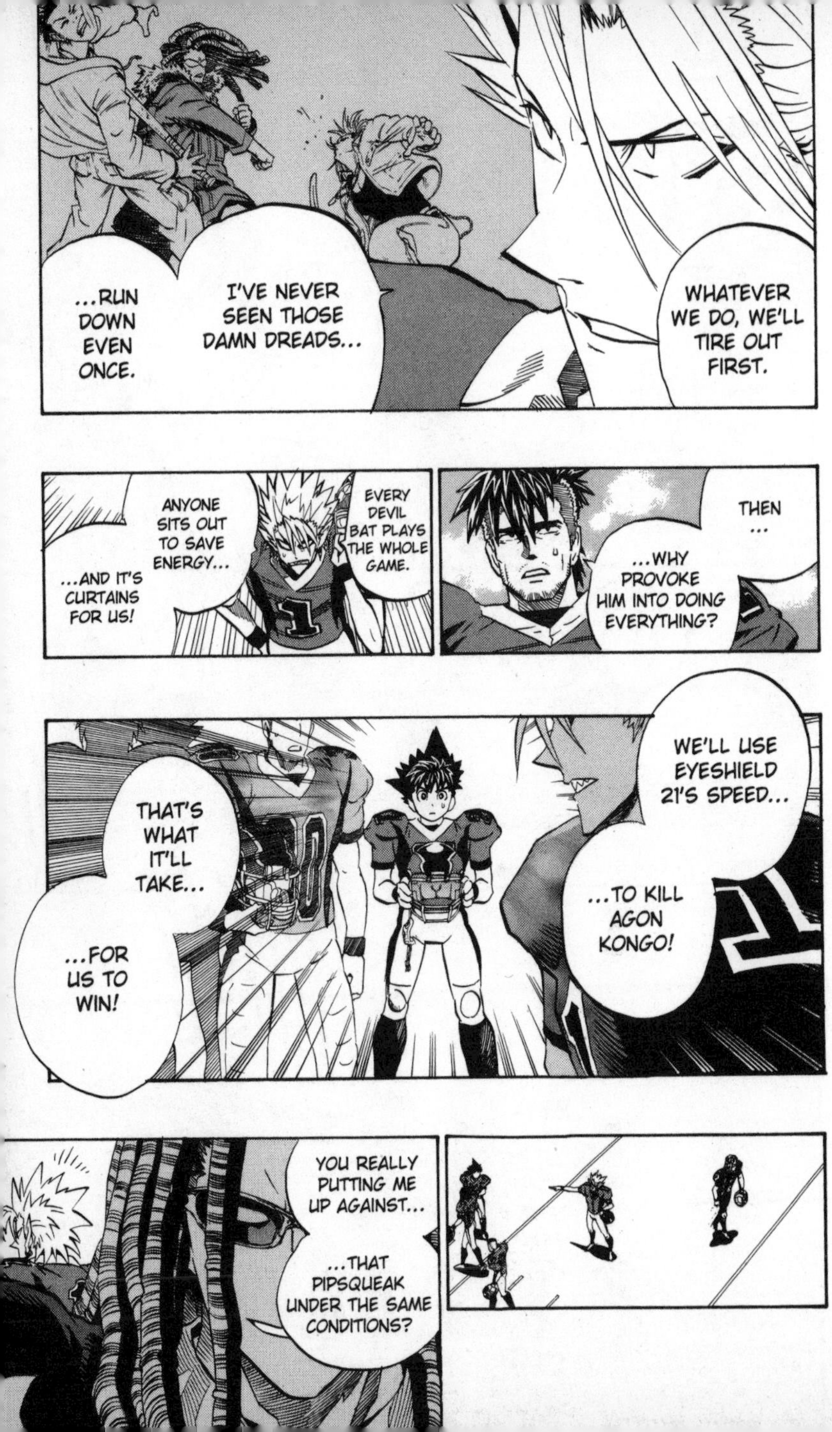
WHATEVER WE DO, WE'LL TIRE OUT FIRST.
I'VE NEVER SEEN THOSE DAMN DREADS...
...RUN DOWN EVEN ONCE.
THEN...
...WHY PROVOKE HIM INTO DOING EVERYTHING?
EVERY DEVIL BAT PLAYS THE WHOLE GAME.
ANYONE SITS OUT TO SAVE ENERGY...
...AND IT'S CURTAINS FOR US!
WE'LL USE EYESHIELD 21'S SPEED...
...TO KILL AGON KONGO!
THAT'S WHAT IT'LL TAKE...
...FOR US TO WIN!
YOU REALLY PUTTING ME UP AGAINST...
...THAT PIPSQUEAK UNDER THE SAME CONDITIONS?

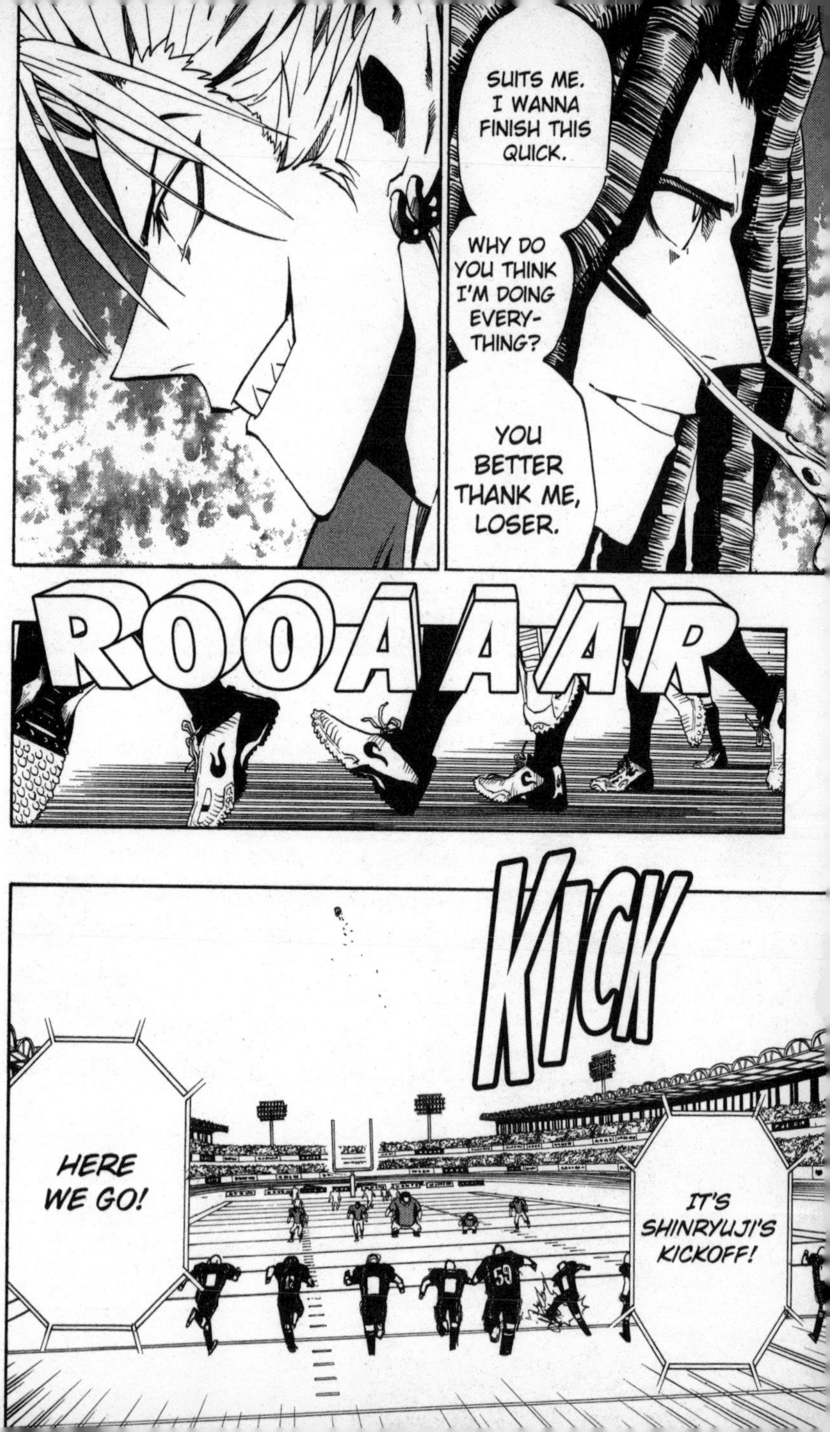
SUITS ME. I WANNA FINISH THIS QUICK.
WHY DO YOU THINK I'M DOING EVERY-THING?
YOU BETTER THANK ME, LOSER.
ROOAAAR
KICK
IT'S SHINRYUJI'S KICKOFF!
HERE WE GO!

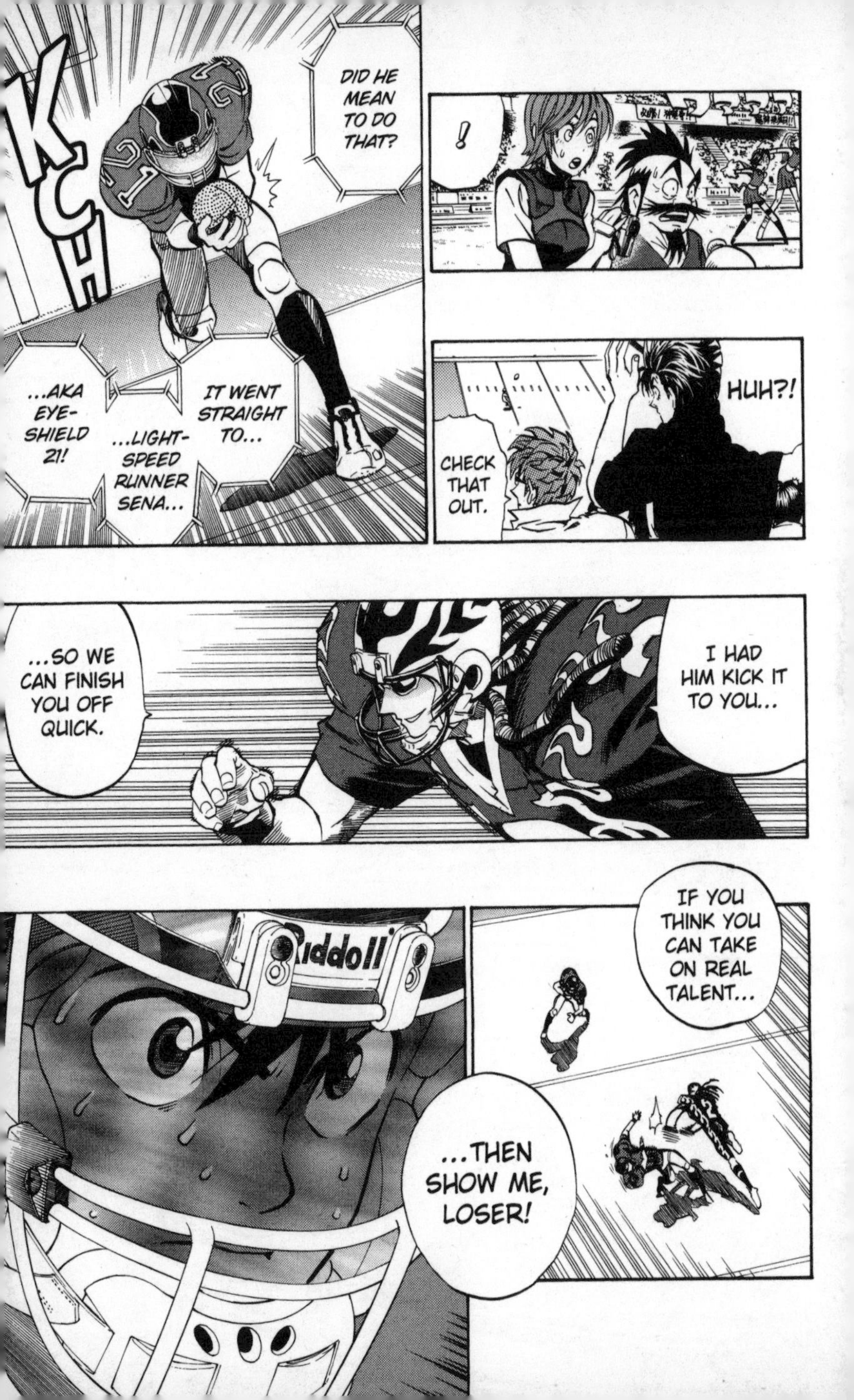
!
HUH?!
CHECK THAT OUT.
KCH
DID HE MEAN TO DO THAT?
IT WENT STRAIGHT TO...
...LIGHT-SPEED RUNNER SENA...
...AKA EYE-SHIELD 21!
I HAD HIM KICK IT TO YOU...
...SO WE CAN FINISH YOU OFF QUICK.
IF YOU THINK YOU CAN TAKE ON REAL TALENT...
...THEN SHOW ME, LOSER!

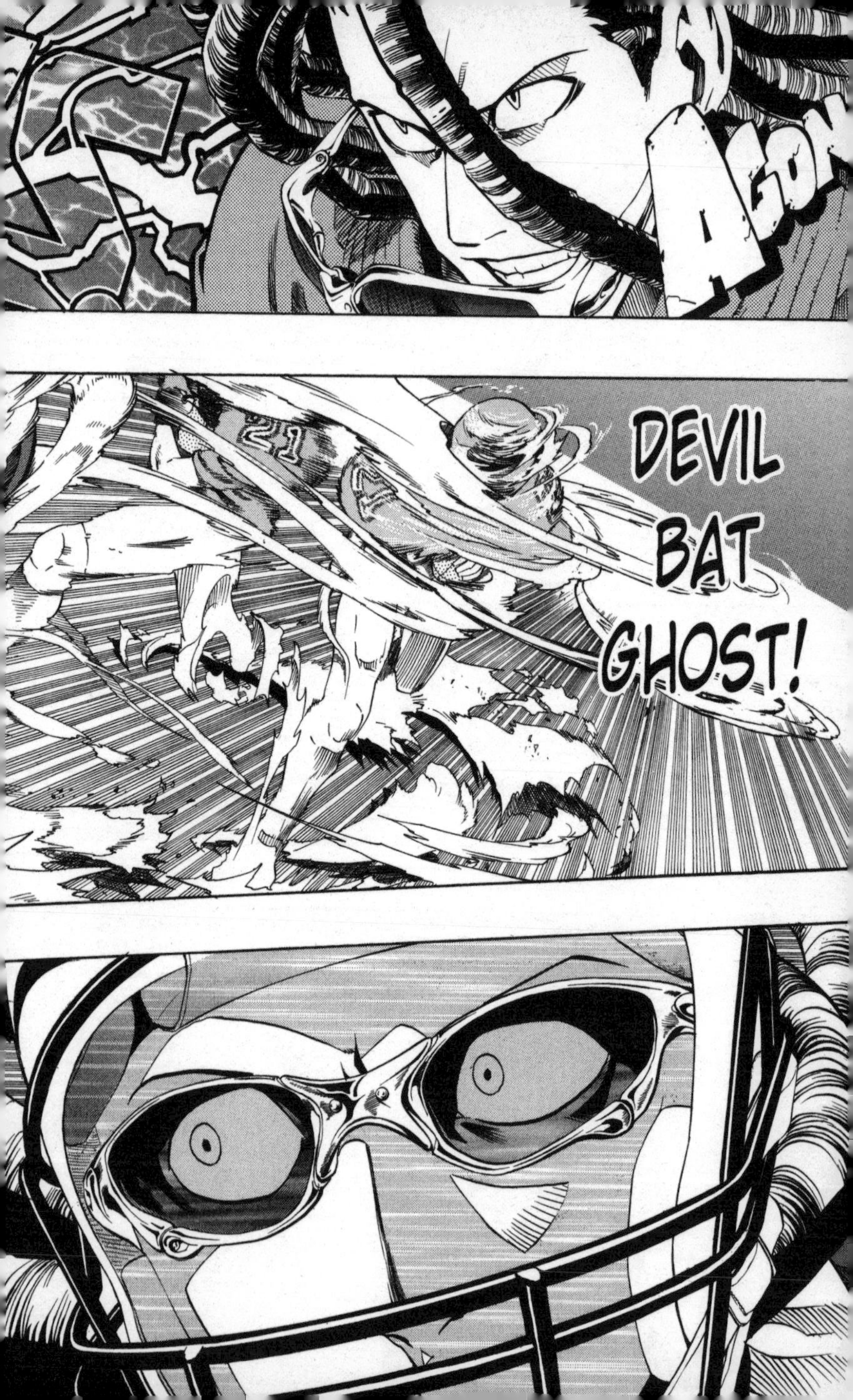
AGON
21
DEVIL
BAT
GHOST!

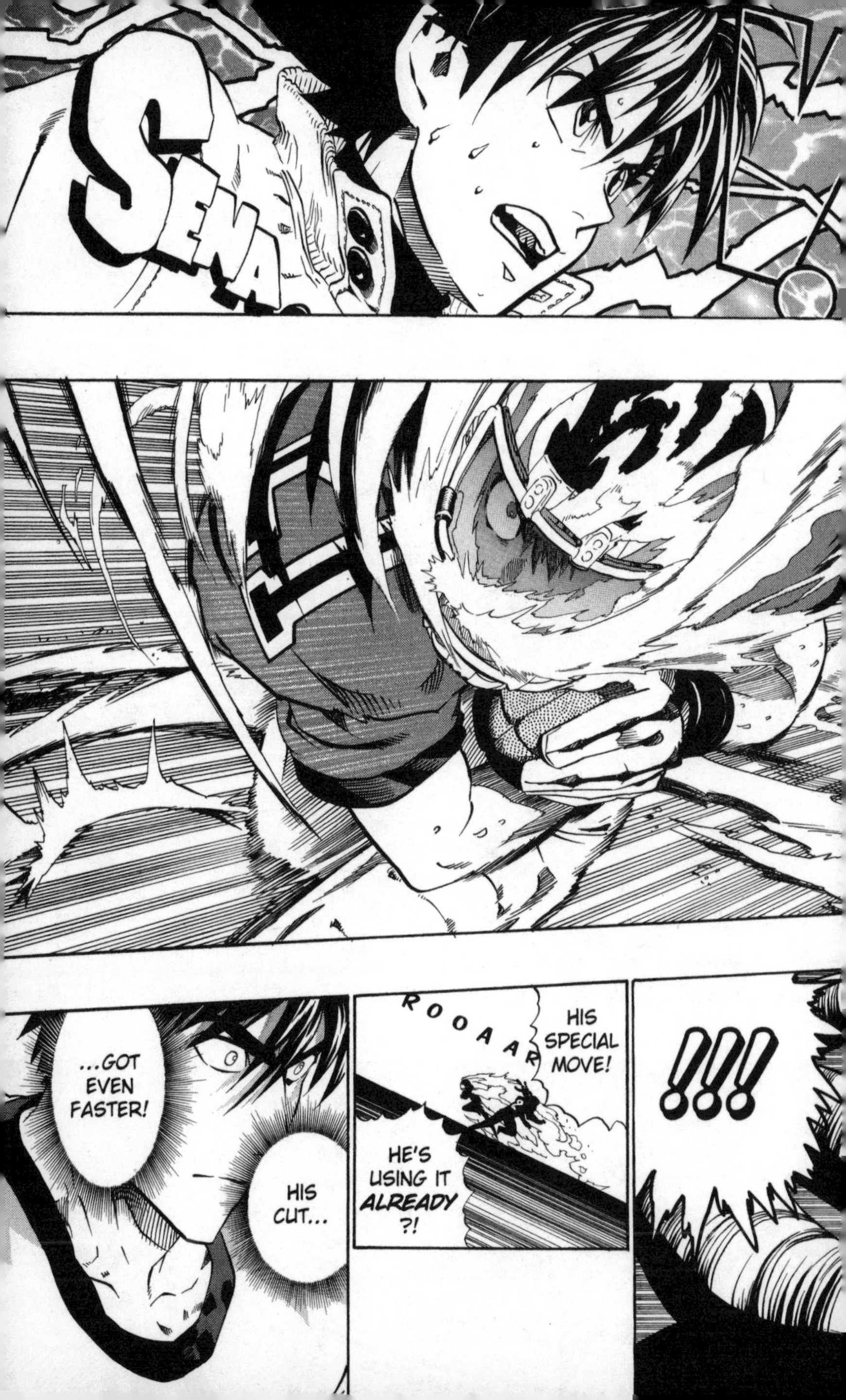
SENA
!!!
ROOOAAAR
HIS SPECIAL MOVE!
HE'S USING IT ALREADY?!
HIS CUT...
...GOT EVEN FASTER!

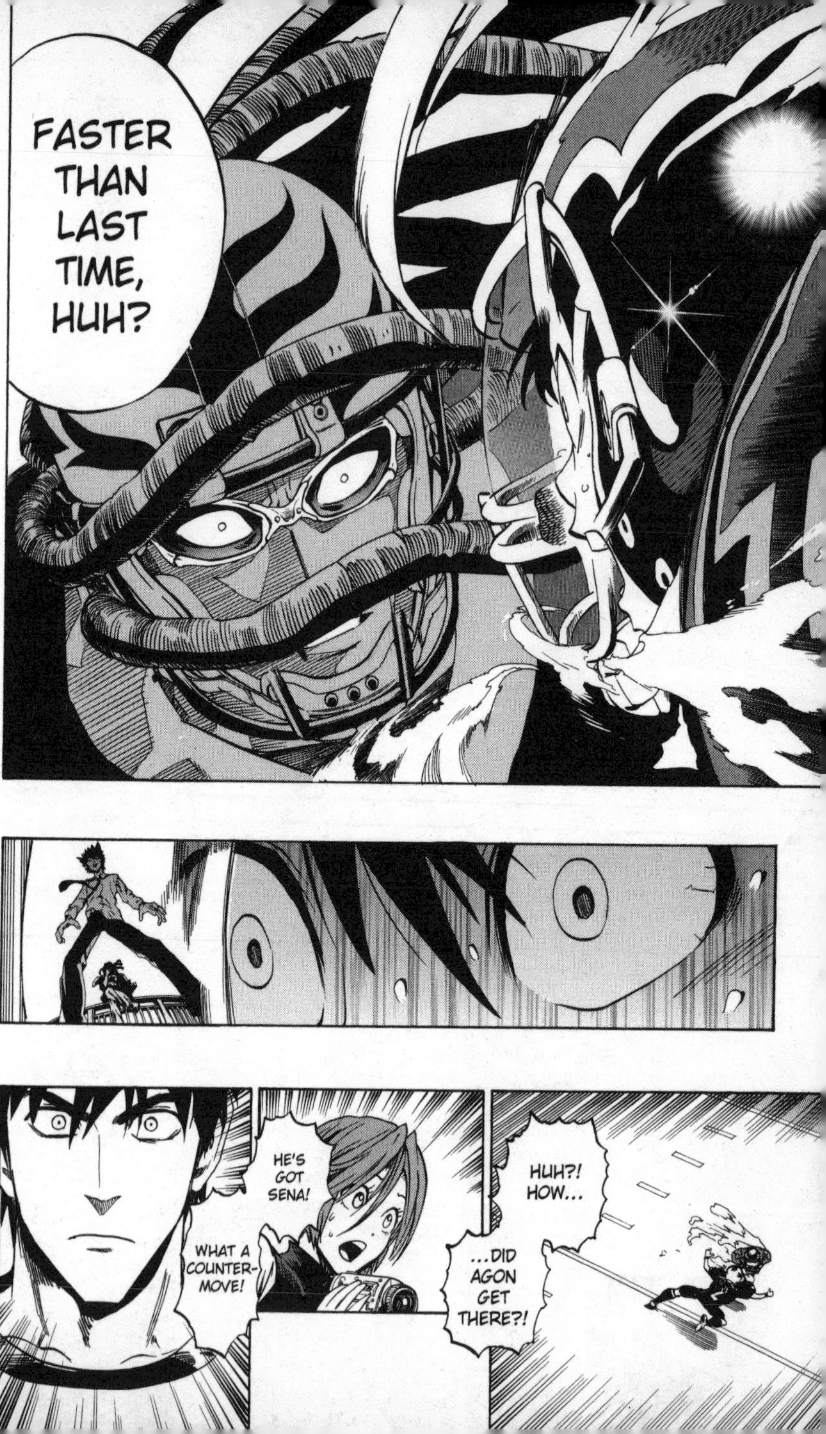
FASTER THAN LAST TIME, HUH?
HUH?! HOW...
...DID AGON GET THERE?!
HE'S GOT SENA!
WHAT A COUNTER-MOVE!

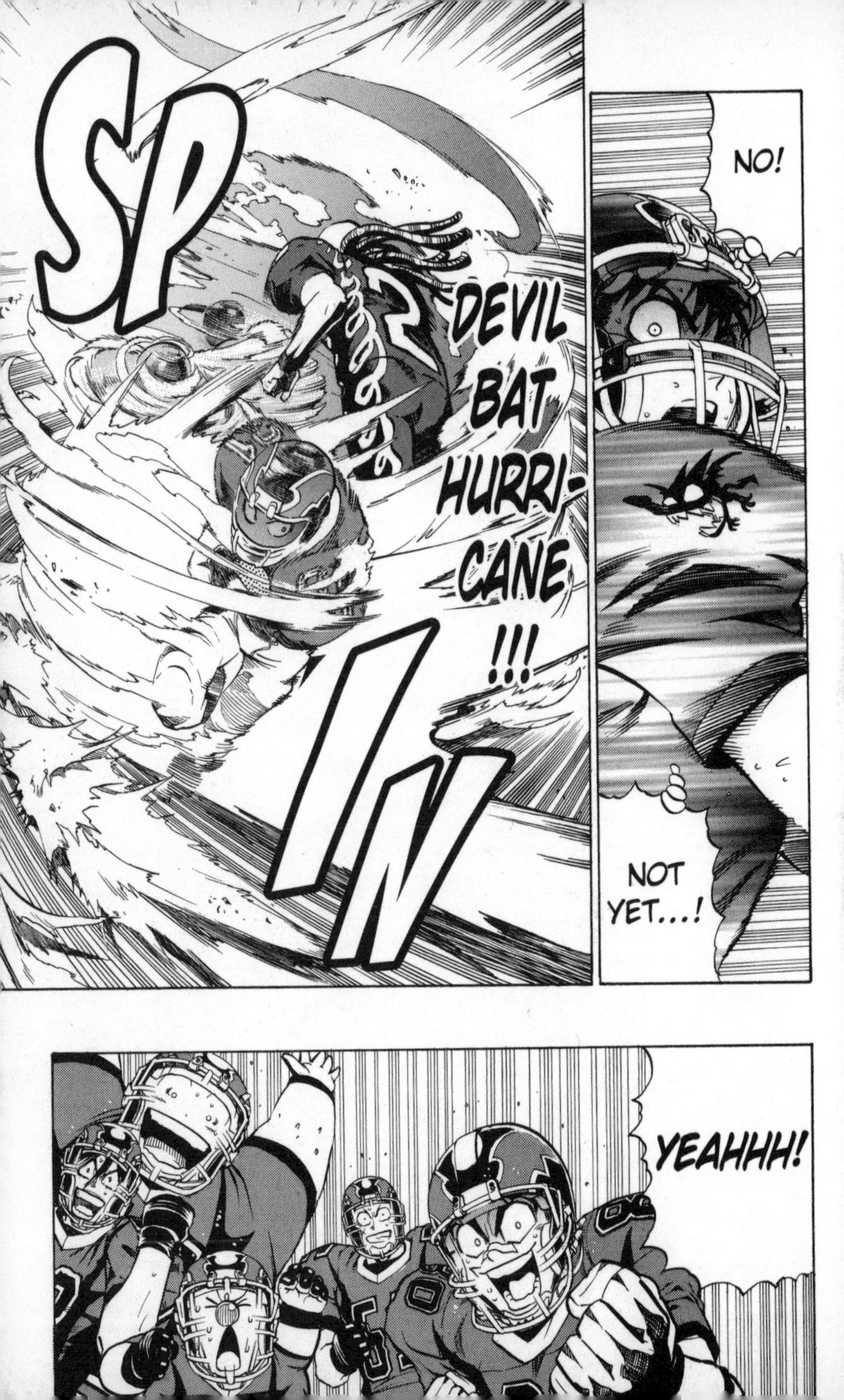
NO!
NOT YET...!
SP
DEVIL BAT HURRI-CANE!!!
IN
YEAHHH!

WELL NOW...

AGAINST A TALENT OF 100...

...YOU'VE JUMPED FROM 10 TO 15.

A NEURAL IMPULSE ...

...TRAVELS FROM EYE TO BRAIN ...

...AND FROM BRAIN TO MUSCLE.

FROM SIGHT TO ACTION...

...AGON'S REACTION TIME IS...

...0.11 SECONDS!

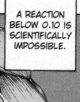

A REACTION BELOW 0.10 IS SCIENTIFICALLY IMPOSSIBLE.

HIS REACTION TIME IS RIGHT AT THE LIMIT!

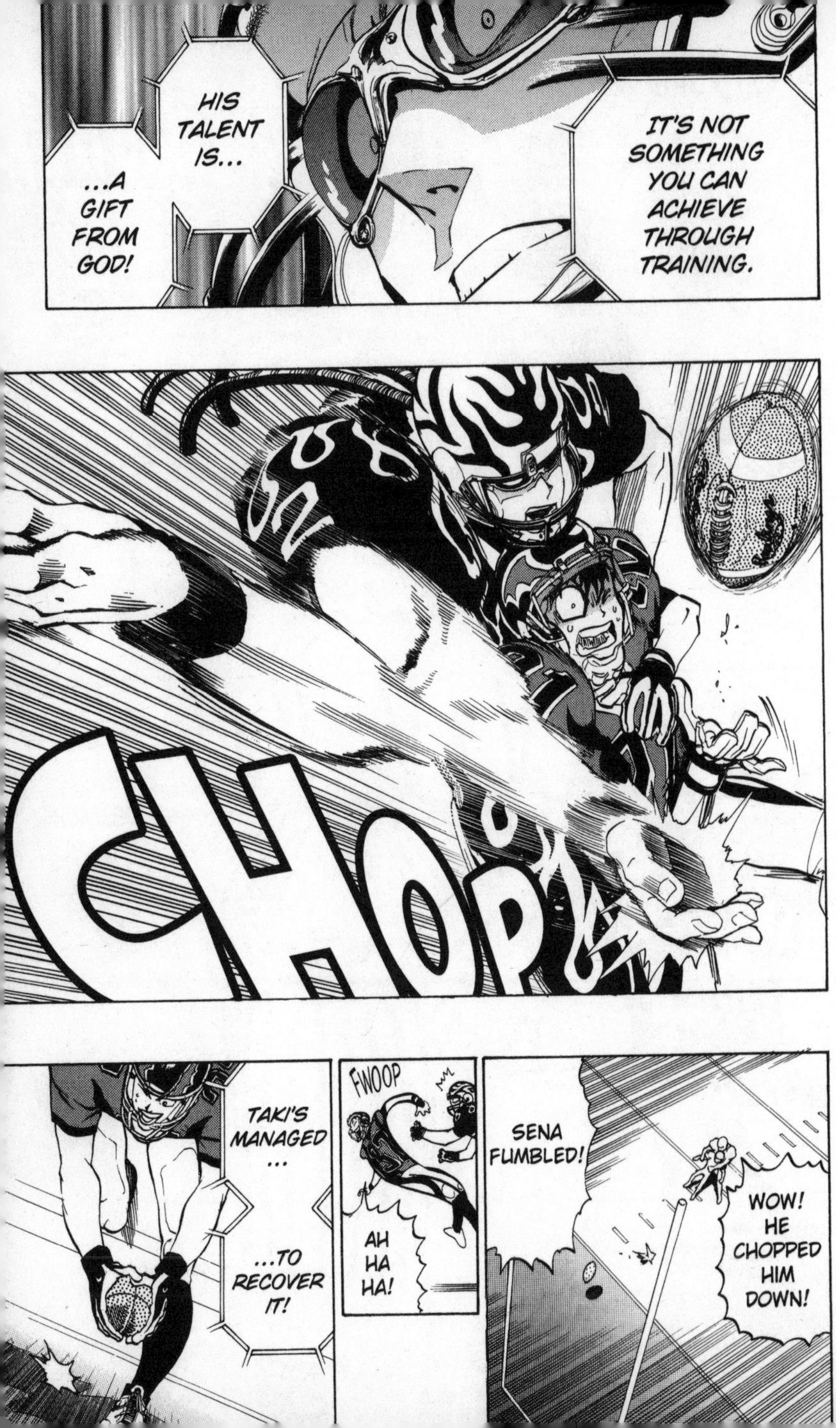
IT'S NOT SOMETHING YOU CAN ACHIEVE THROUGH TRAINING.
HIS TALENT IS...
...A GIFT FROM GOD!
CHOP
SENA FUMBLED!
WOW! HE CHOPPED HIM DOWN!
FWOOP
AH HA HA!
TAKI'S MANAGED ...
...TO RECOVER IT!

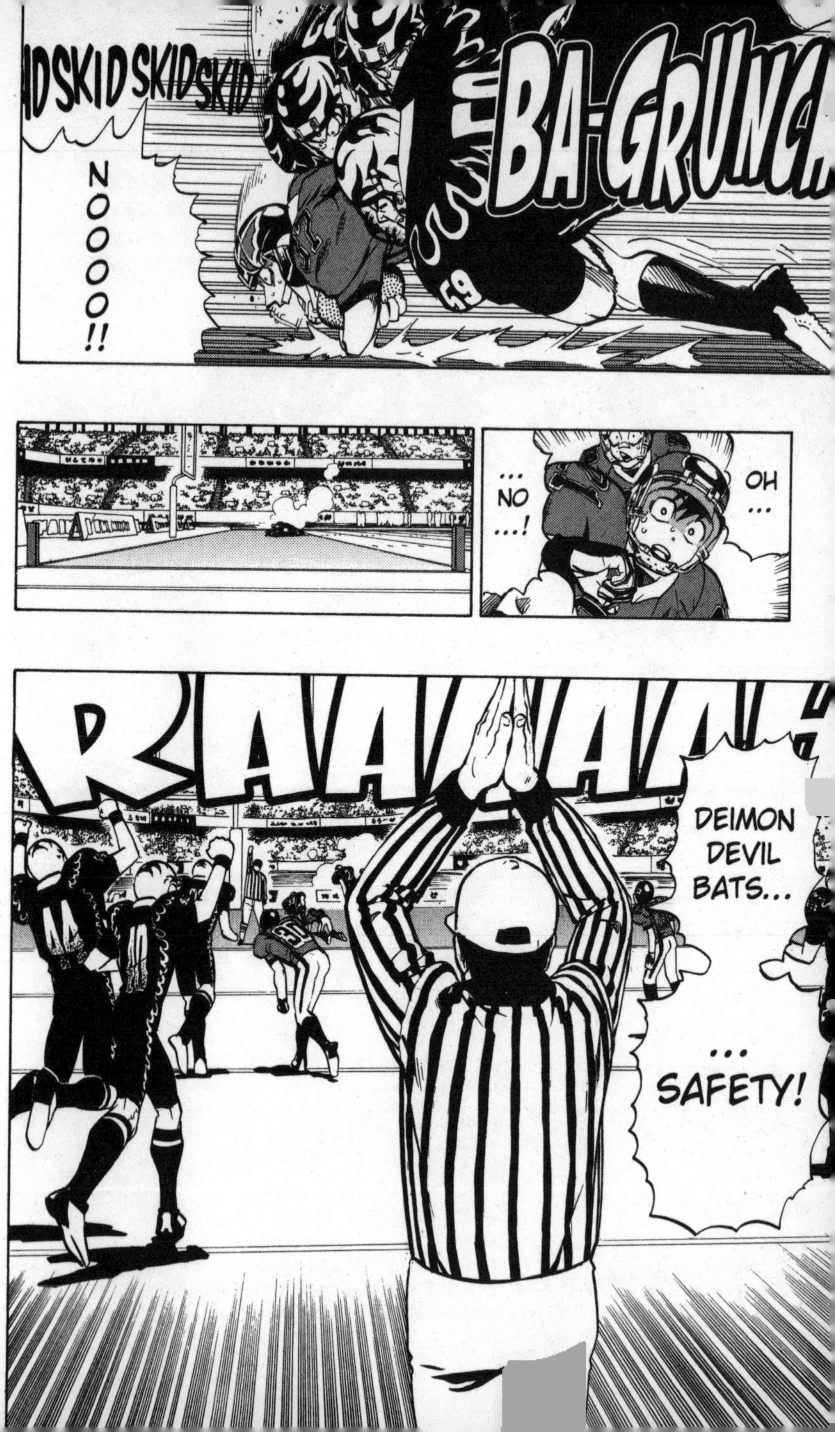
BA-GRUNCH
SKID SKID SKID SKID
NOOOOO!!
OH...
... NO ...!
RAAAAA
DEIMON DEVIL BATS...
... SAFETY!

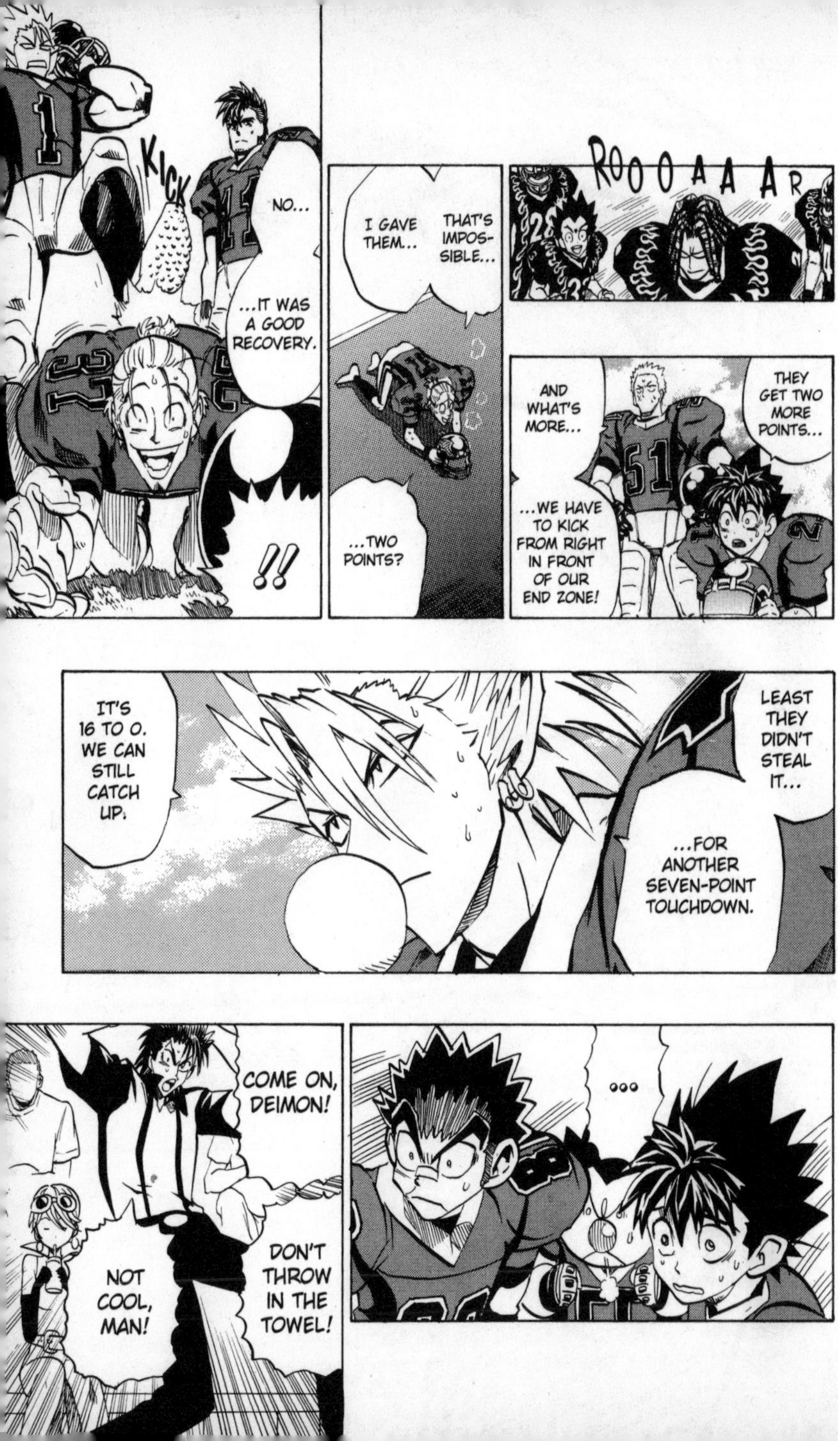
ROOOAAAR
THEY GET TWO MORE POINTS...
AND WHAT'S MORE...
...WE HAVE TO KICK FROM RIGHT IN FRONT OF OUR END ZONE!
THAT'S IMPOSSIBLE...
I GAVE THEM...
...TWO POINTS?
KICK
NO...
...IT WAS A GOOD RECOVERY.
!!
LEAST THEY DIDN'T STEAL IT...
...FOR ANOTHER SEVEN-POINT TOUCHDOWN.
IT'S 16 TO 0. WE CAN STILL CATCH UP.
...
COME ON, DEIMON!
DON'T THROW IN THE TOWEL!
NOT COOL, MAN!

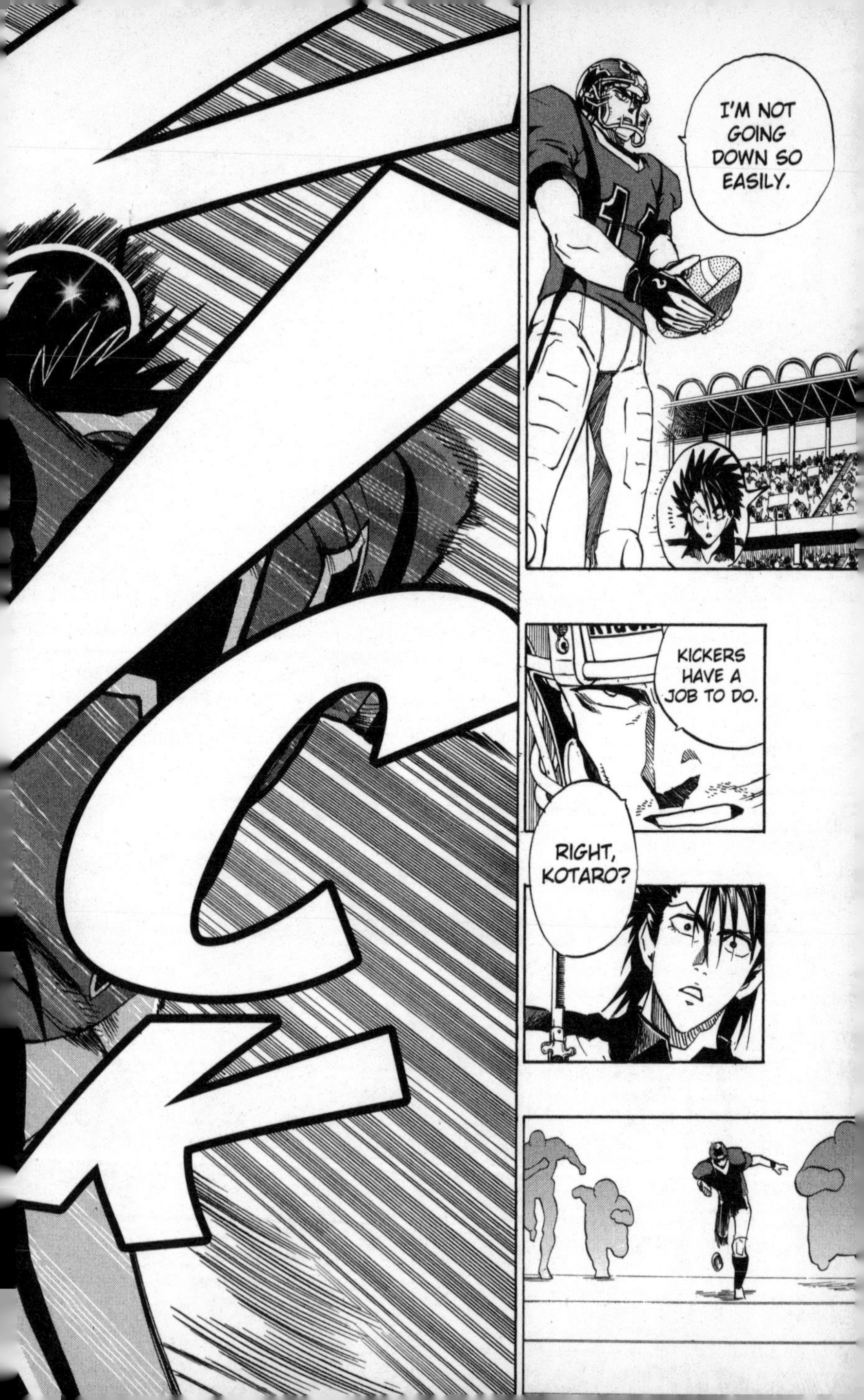
I'M NOT GOING DOWN SO EASILY.
KICKERS HAVE A JOB TO DO.
RIGHT, KOTARO?

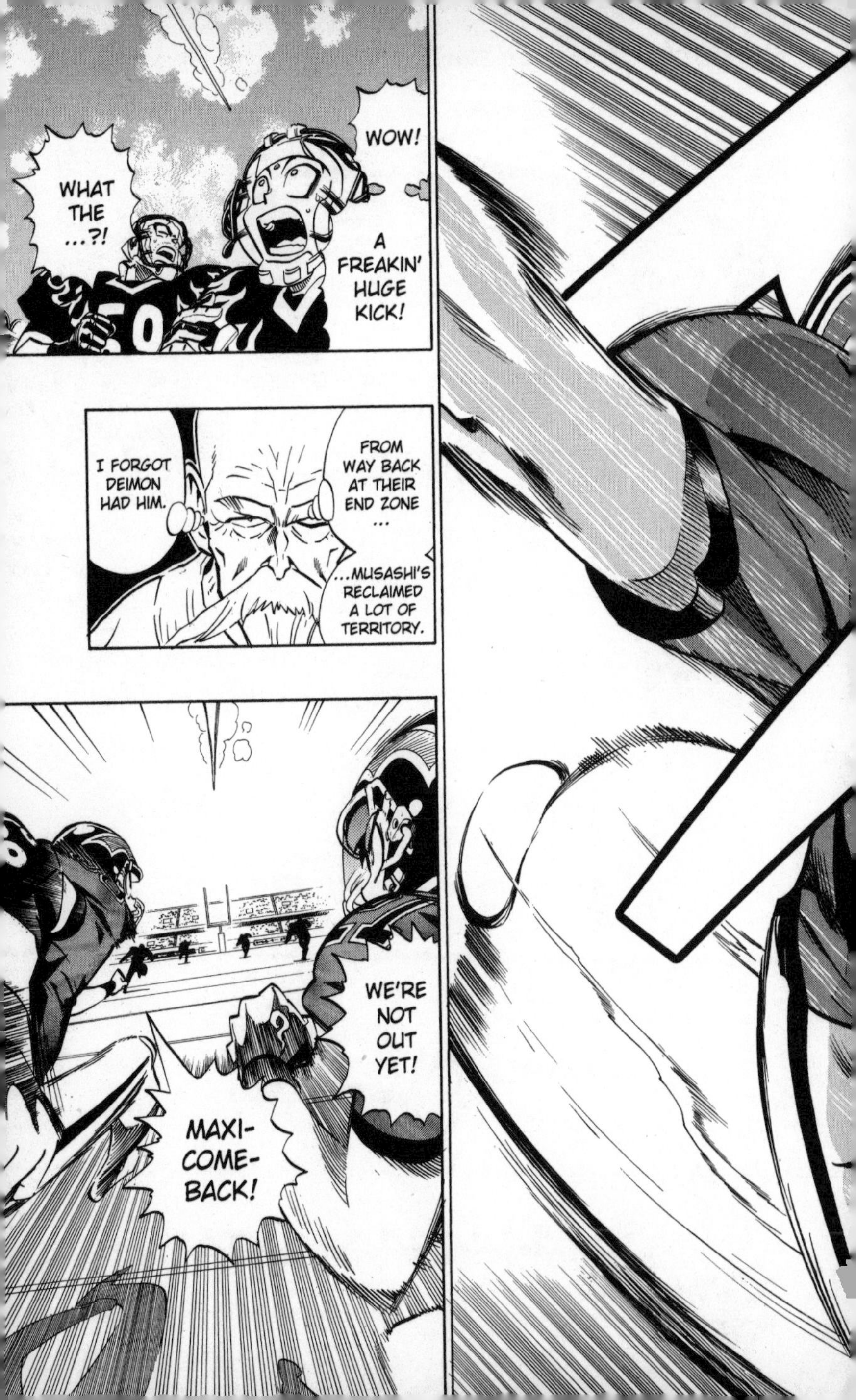
WOW!
A FREAKIN' HUGE KICK!
WHAT THE ...?!
FROM WAY BACK AT THEIR END ZONE ...
...MUSASHI'S RECLAIMED A LOT OF TERRITORY.
I FORGOT DEIMON HAD HIM.
WE'RE NOT OUT YET!
MAXI-COME-BACK!

**Eyeshield 21 Survey Corner**

# Devil Bat 021

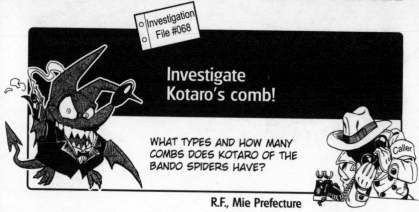

Investigation File #068

## Investigate Kotaro's comb!

Caller

WHAT TYPES AND HOW MANY COMBS DOES KOTARO OF THE BANDO SPIDERS HAVE?

R.F., Mie Prefecture

HUH? NOT THAT MANY.
I ONLY USE EACH ONE ONCE ANYWAY.

GYAAAAAAAAAAAAAH!!

## Chapter 178
## Game Over

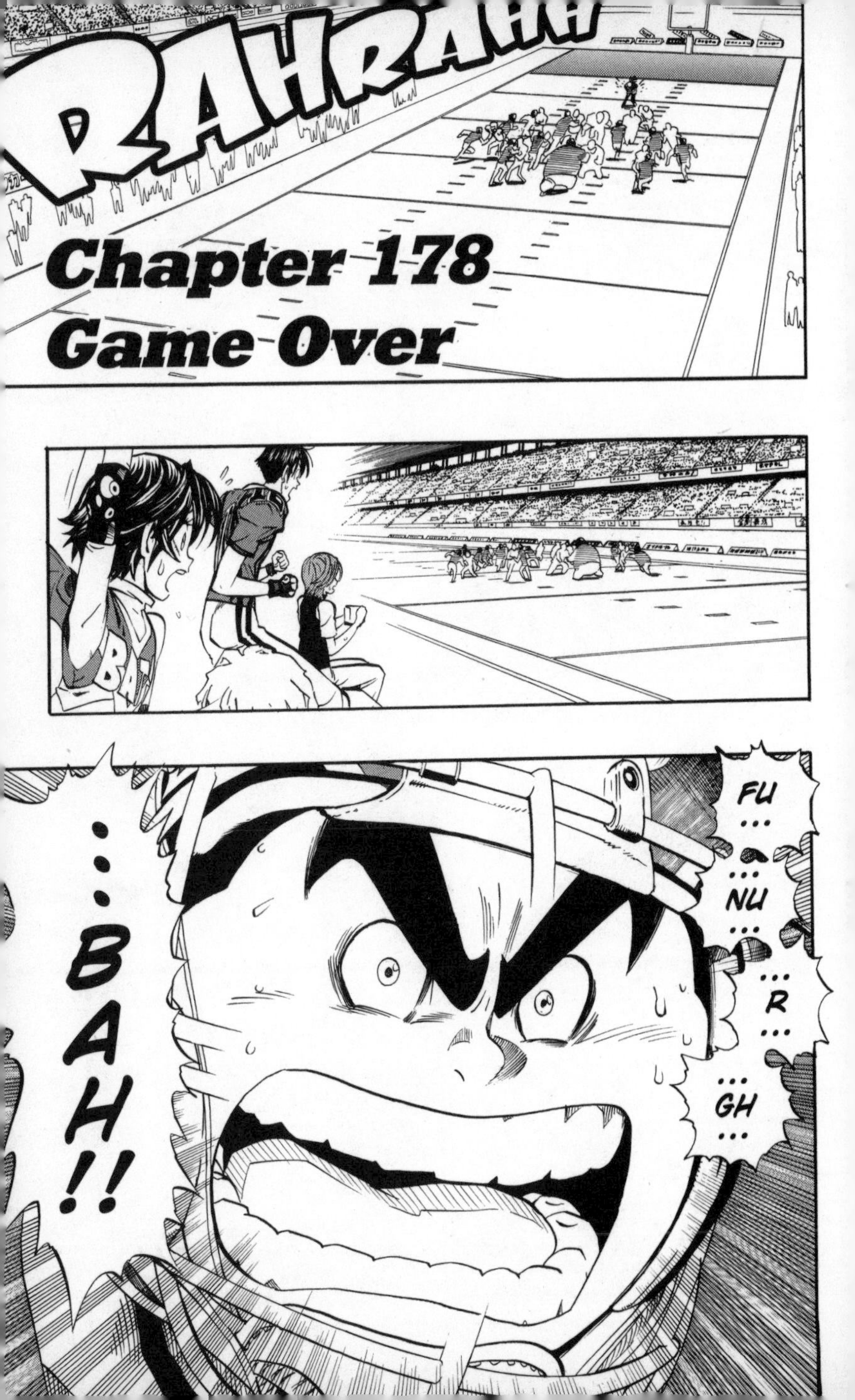
RAHRAH!!
Chapter 178
Game Over
FU... NU... R... GH...
...BAH!!

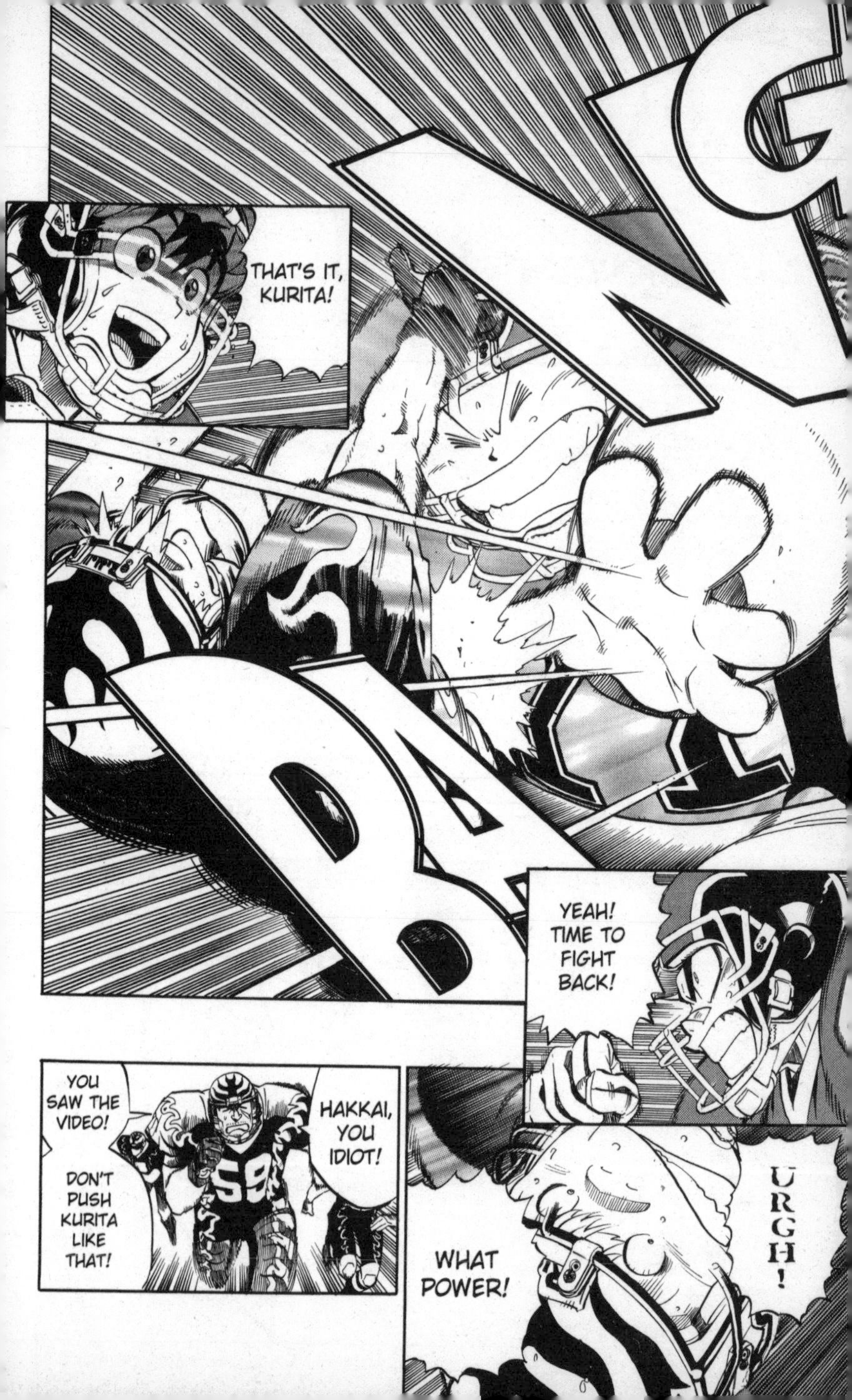
THAT'S IT, KURITA!
YEAH! TIME TO FIGHT BACK!
URGH!
WHAT POWER!
HAKKAI, YOU IDIOT!
YOU SAW THE VIDEO!
DON'T PUSH KURITA LIKE THAT!

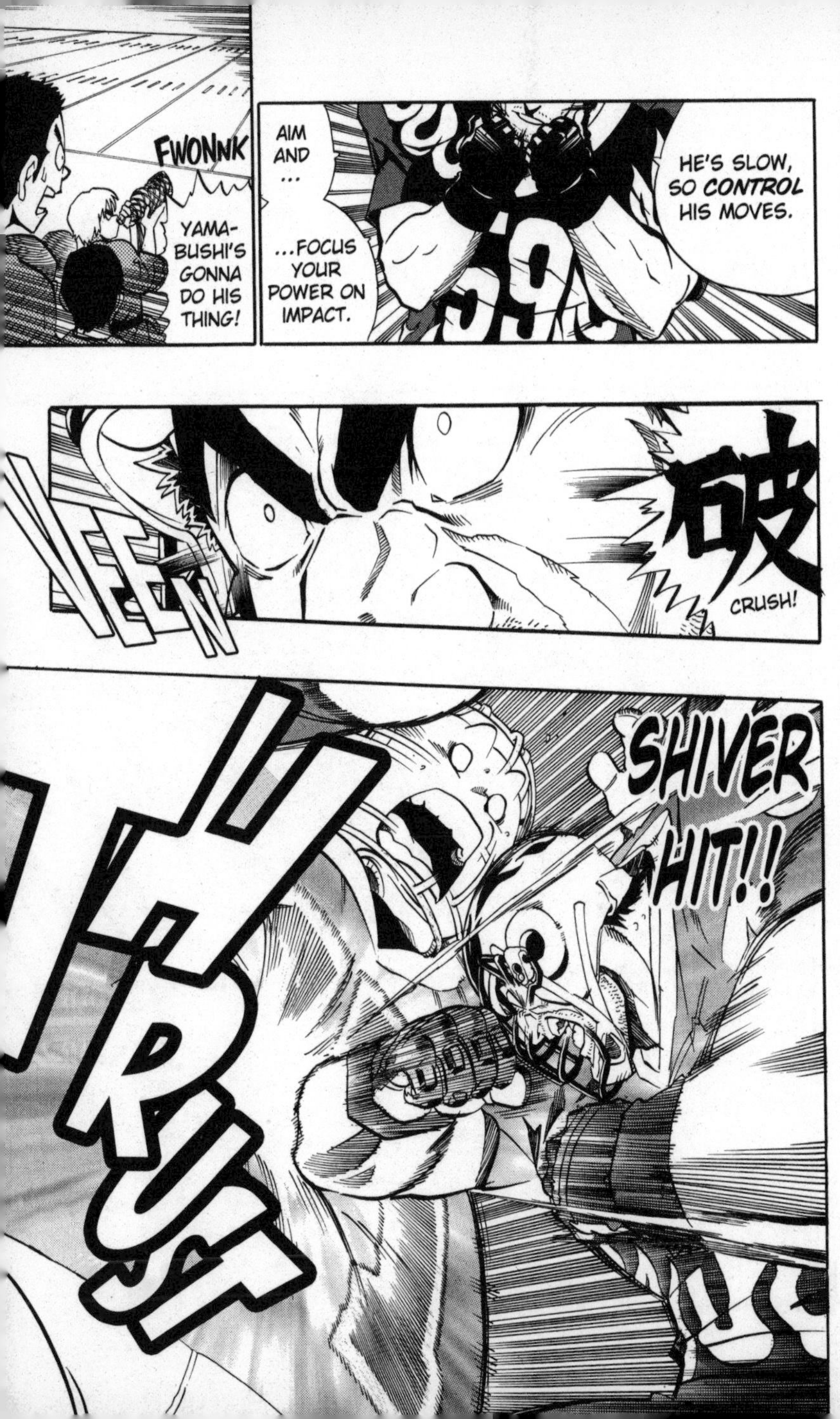
HE'S SLOW, SO CONTROL HIS MOVES.
AIM AND ...
...FOCUS YOUR POWER ON IMPACT.
FWONNK
YAMA-BUSHI'S GONNA DO HIS THING!
破
CRUSH!
VEEN
SHIVER HIT!!
THRUST

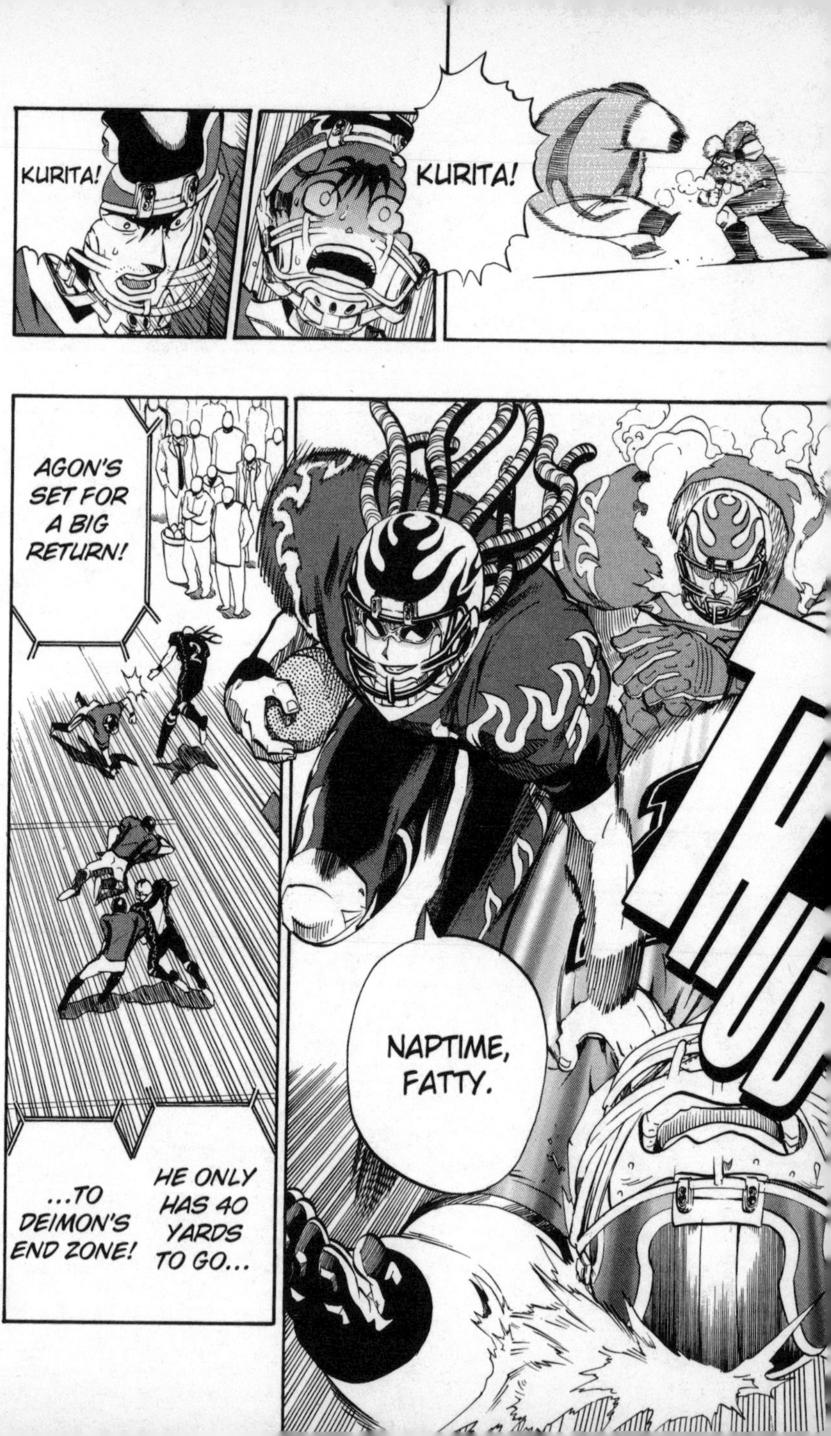
KURITA!
KURITA!
NAPTIME, FATTY.
AGON'S SET FOR A BIG RETURN!
HE ONLY HAS 40 YARDS TO GO...
...TO DEIMON'S END ZONE!

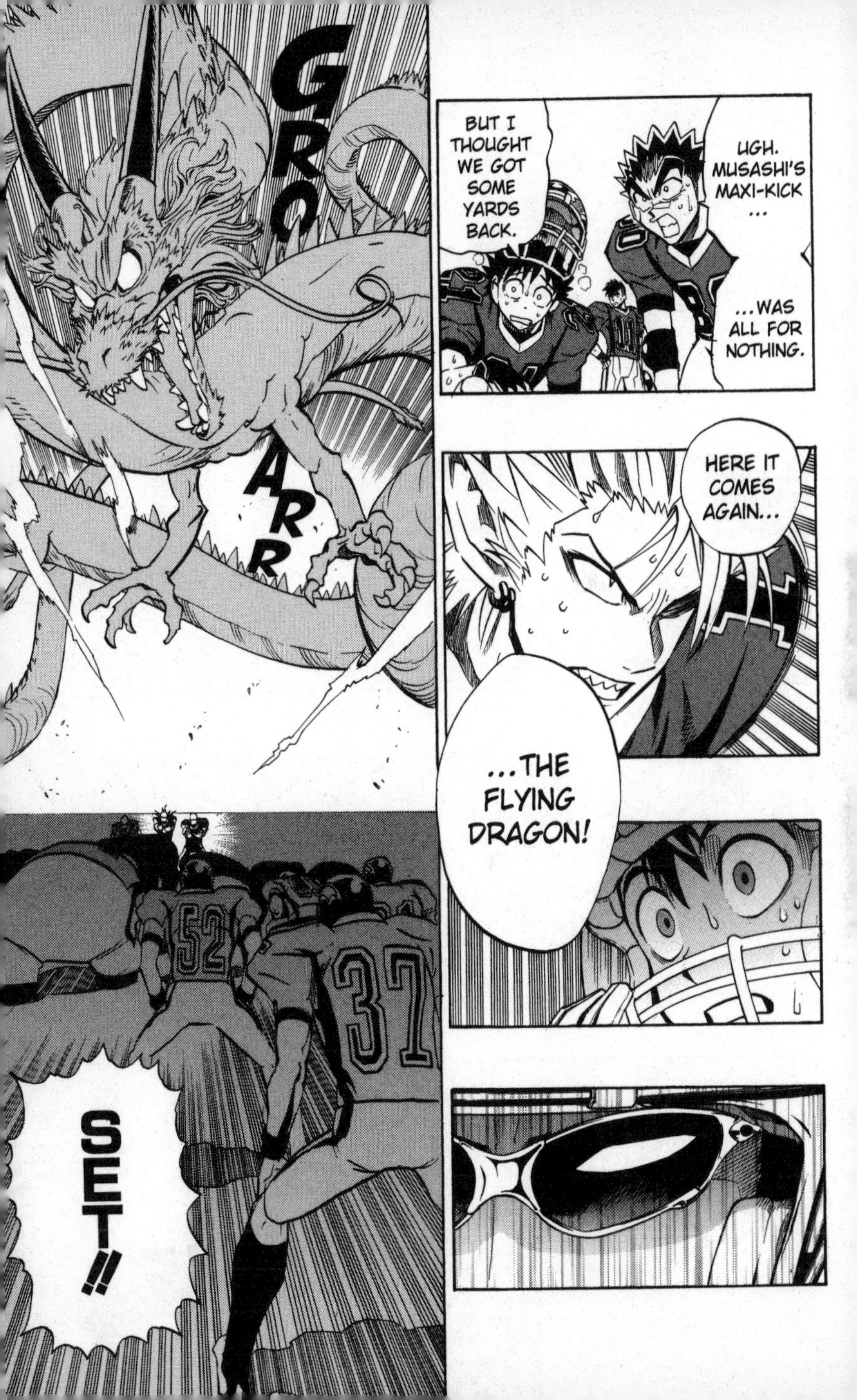
UGH. MUSASHI'S MAXI-KICK ...
...WAS ALL FOR NOTHING.
BUT I THOUGHT WE GOT SOME YARDS BACK.
HERE IT COMES AGAIN...
...THE FLYING DRAGON!
GROARRR
SET!!

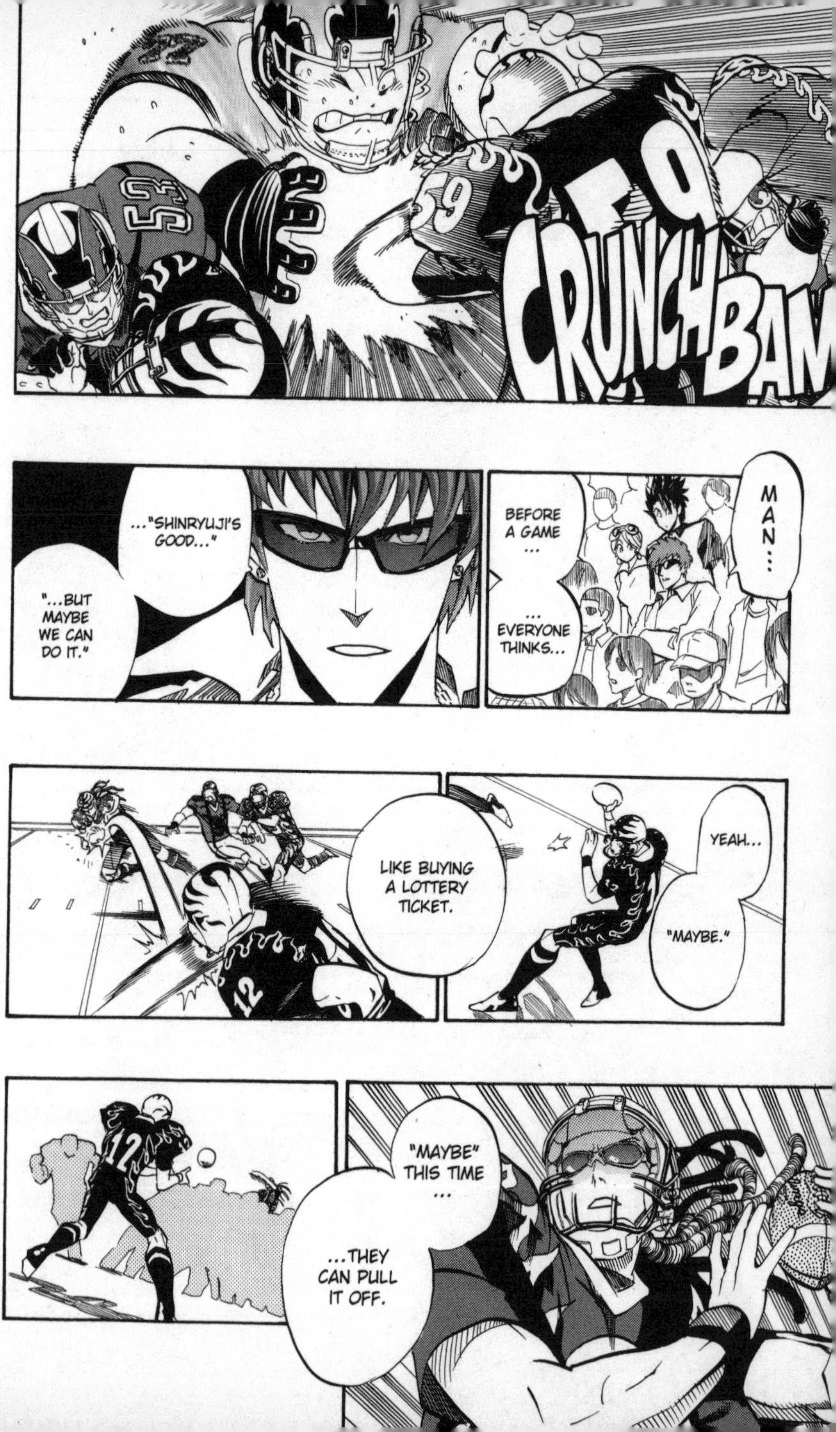
BAM
CRUNCH
MAN...
BEFORE A GAME ...
... EVERYONE THINKS...
..."SHINRYUJI'S GOOD..."
"...BUT MAYBE WE CAN DO IT."
YEAH...
"MAYBE."
LIKE BUYING A LOTTERY TICKET.
"MAYBE" THIS TIME ...
...THEY CAN PULL IT OFF.

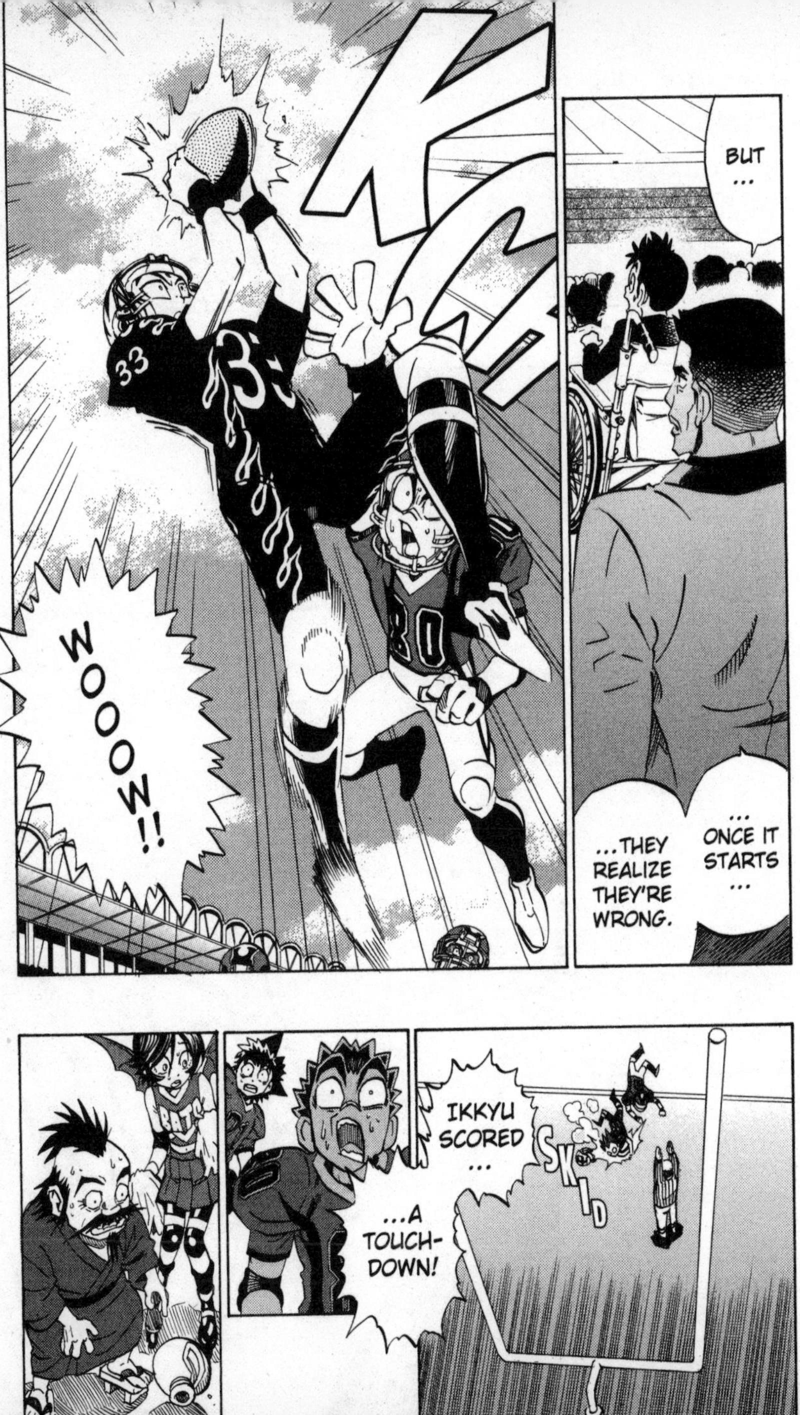
BUT ...
... ONCE IT STARTS ...
...THEY REALIZE THEY'RE WRONG.
WOOOW!!
IKKYU SCORED ...
SKID
...A TOUCH-DOWN!

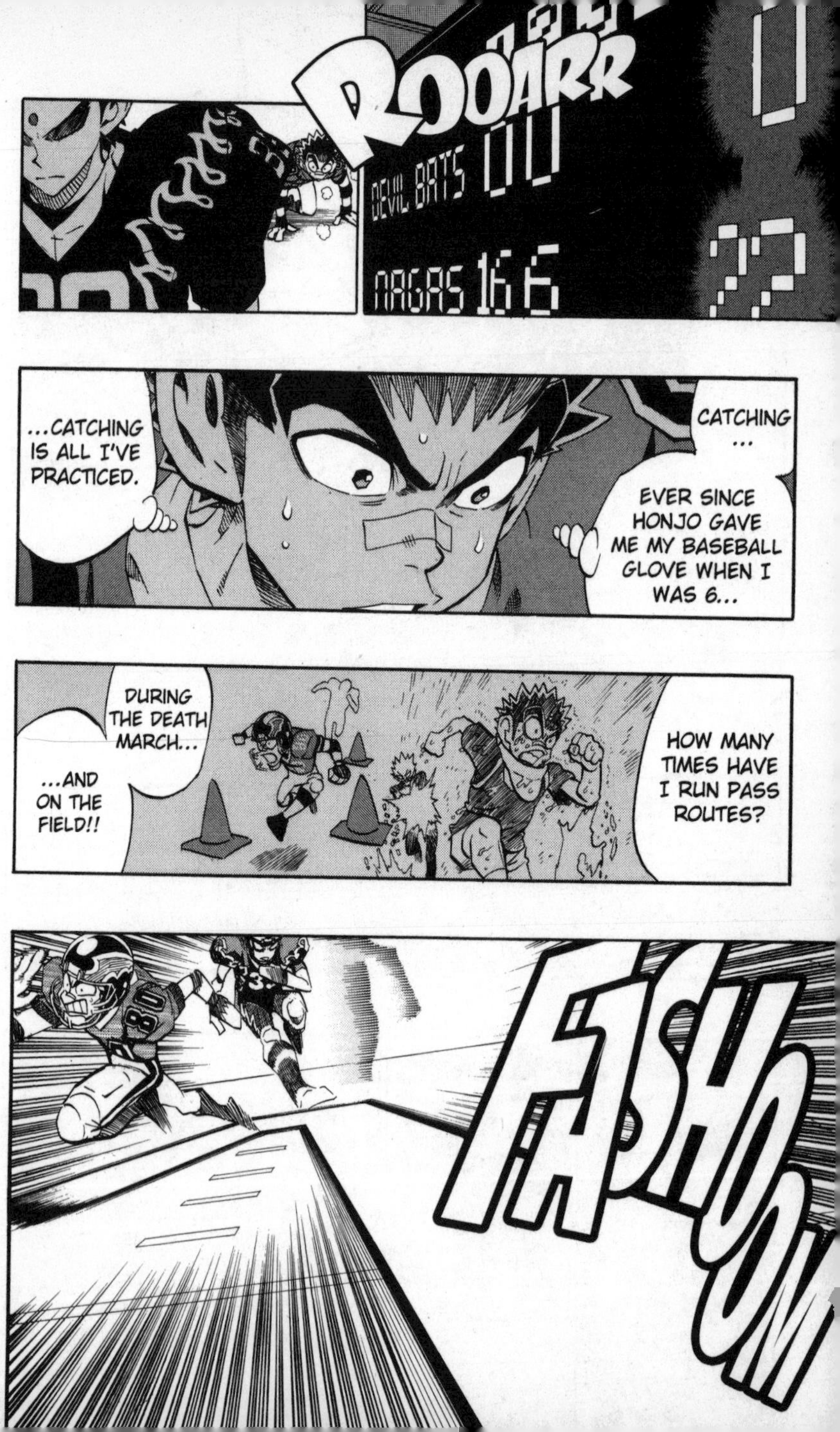
ROOARR
DEVIL BATS 00
NAGAS 16 6
22
CATCHING...
EVER SINCE HONJO GAVE ME MY BASEBALL GLOVE WHEN I WAS 6...
...CATCHING IS ALL I'VE PRACTICED.
HOW MANY TIMES HAVE I RUN PASS ROUTES?
DURING THE DEATH MARCH...
...AND ON THE FIELD!!
FASHOOM

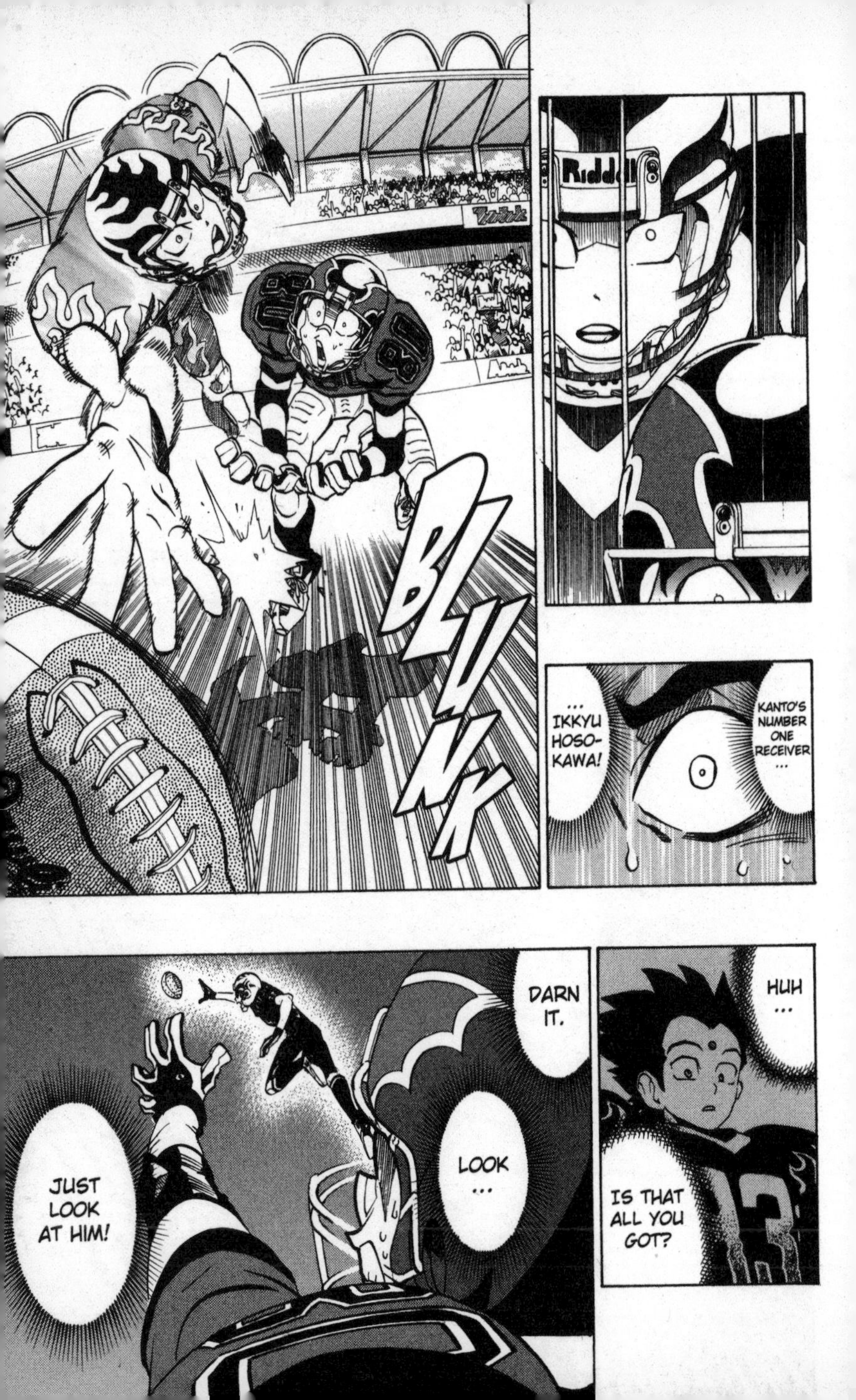
Riddell
KANTO'S NUMBER ONE RECEIVER ...
... IKKYU HOSO-KAWA!
BLUNK
HUH ...
IS THAT ALL YOU GOT?
DARN IT.
LOOK ...
JUST LOOK AT HIM!

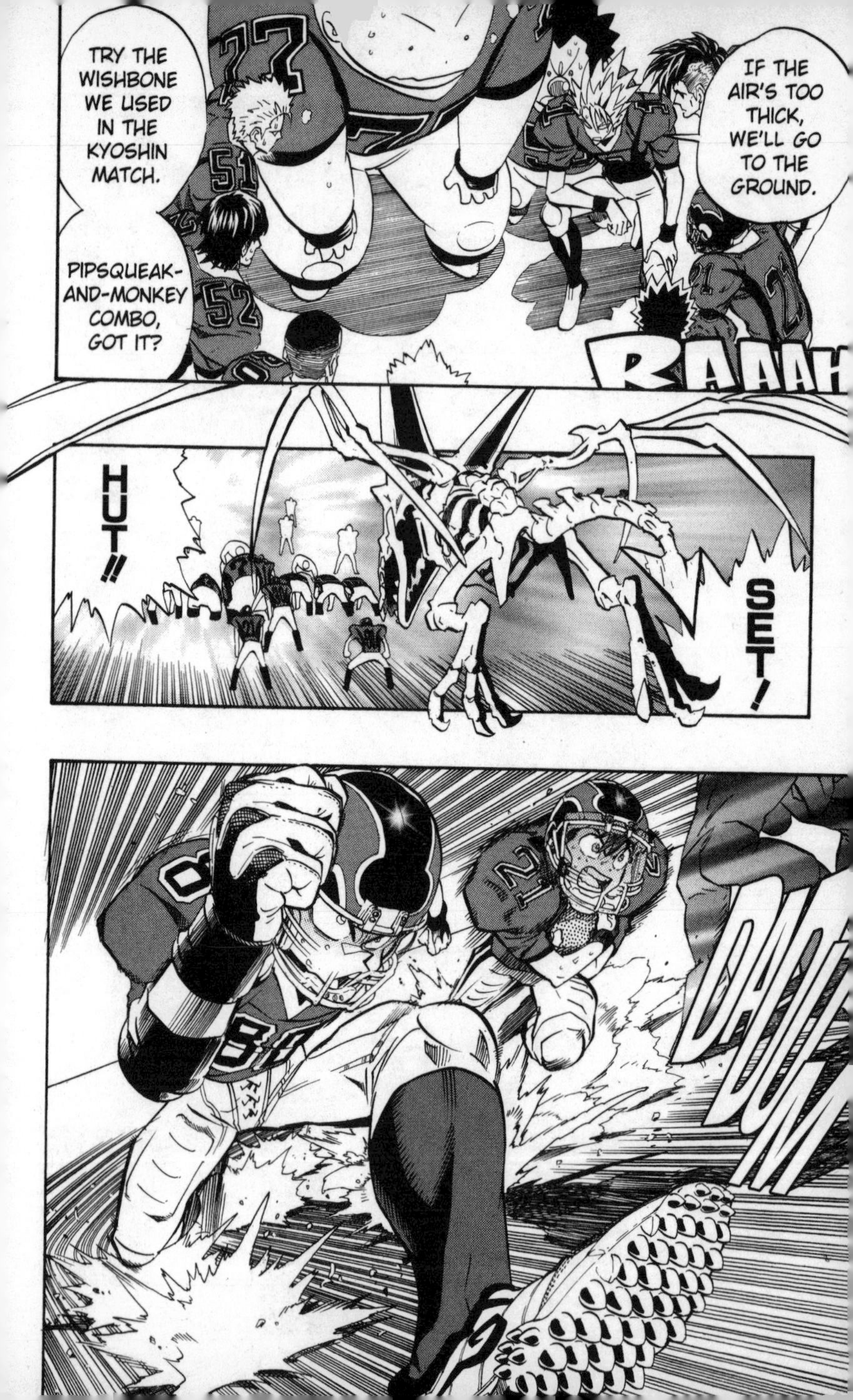

IF THE AIR'S TOO THICK, WE'LL GO TO THE GROUND.
TRY THE WISHBONE WE USED IN THE KYOSHIN MATCH.
PIPSQUEAK-AND-MONKEY COMBO, GOT IT?
SET!
HUT!!

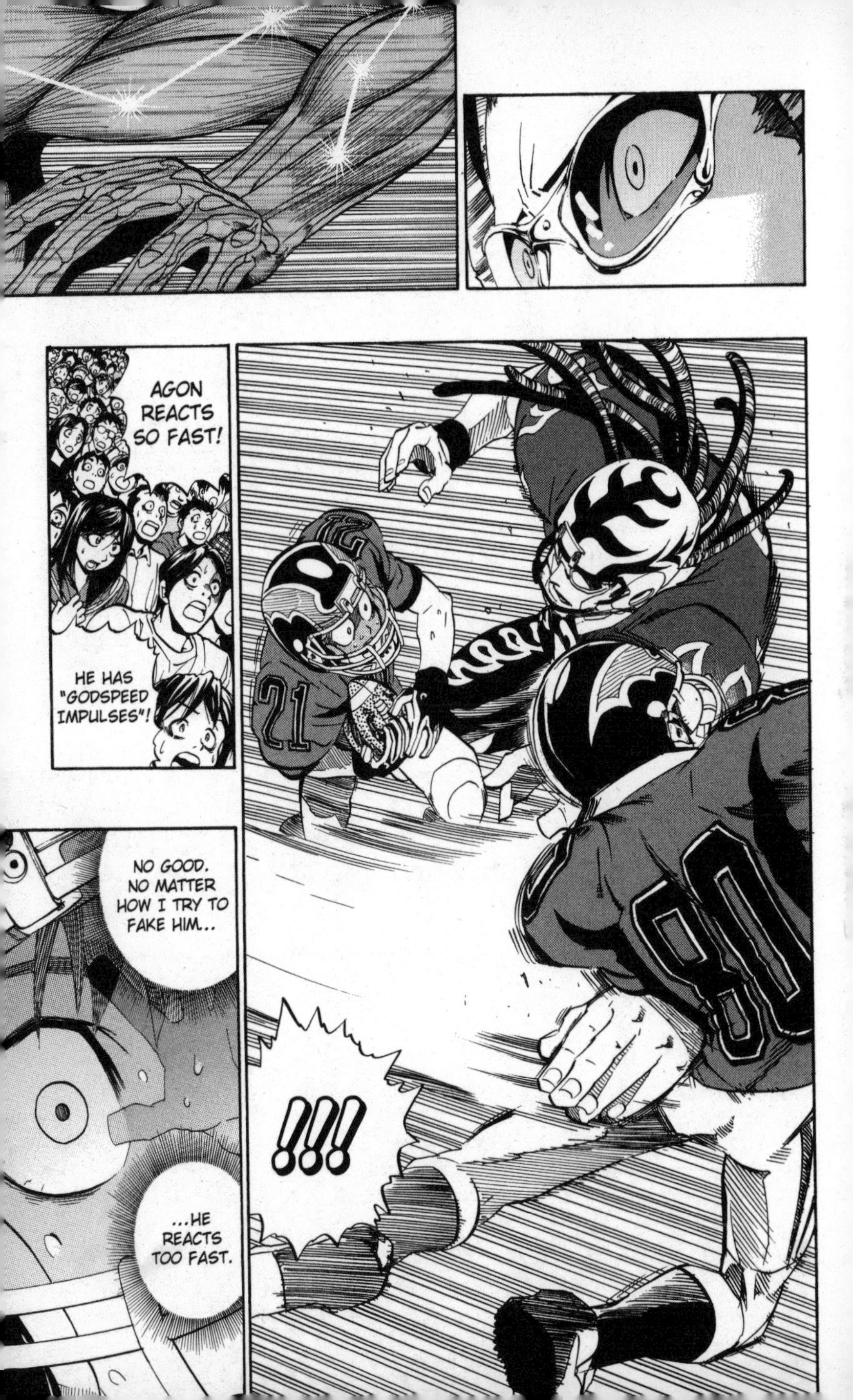
AGON REACTS SO FAST!
HE HAS "GODSPEED IMPULSES"!
NO GOOD. NO MATTER HOW I TRY TO FAKE HIM...
...HE REACTS TOO FAST.
!!!

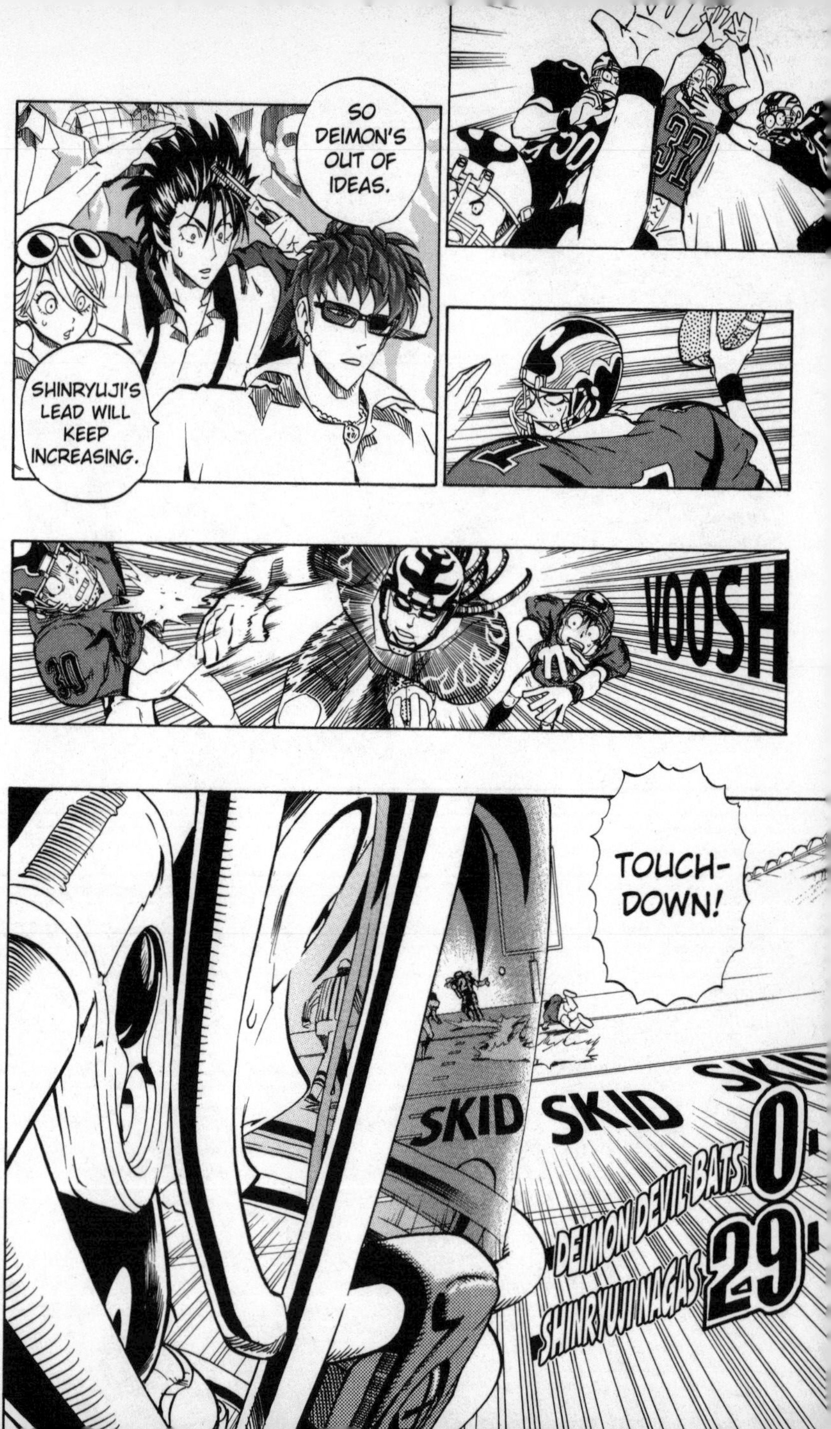
SO DEIMON'S OUT OF IDEAS.
SHINRYUJI'S LEAD WILL KEEP INCREASING.
VOOSH
TOUCH-DOWN!
SKID SKID SKID
DEIMON DEVIL BATS 0
SHINRYUJI NAGAS 29

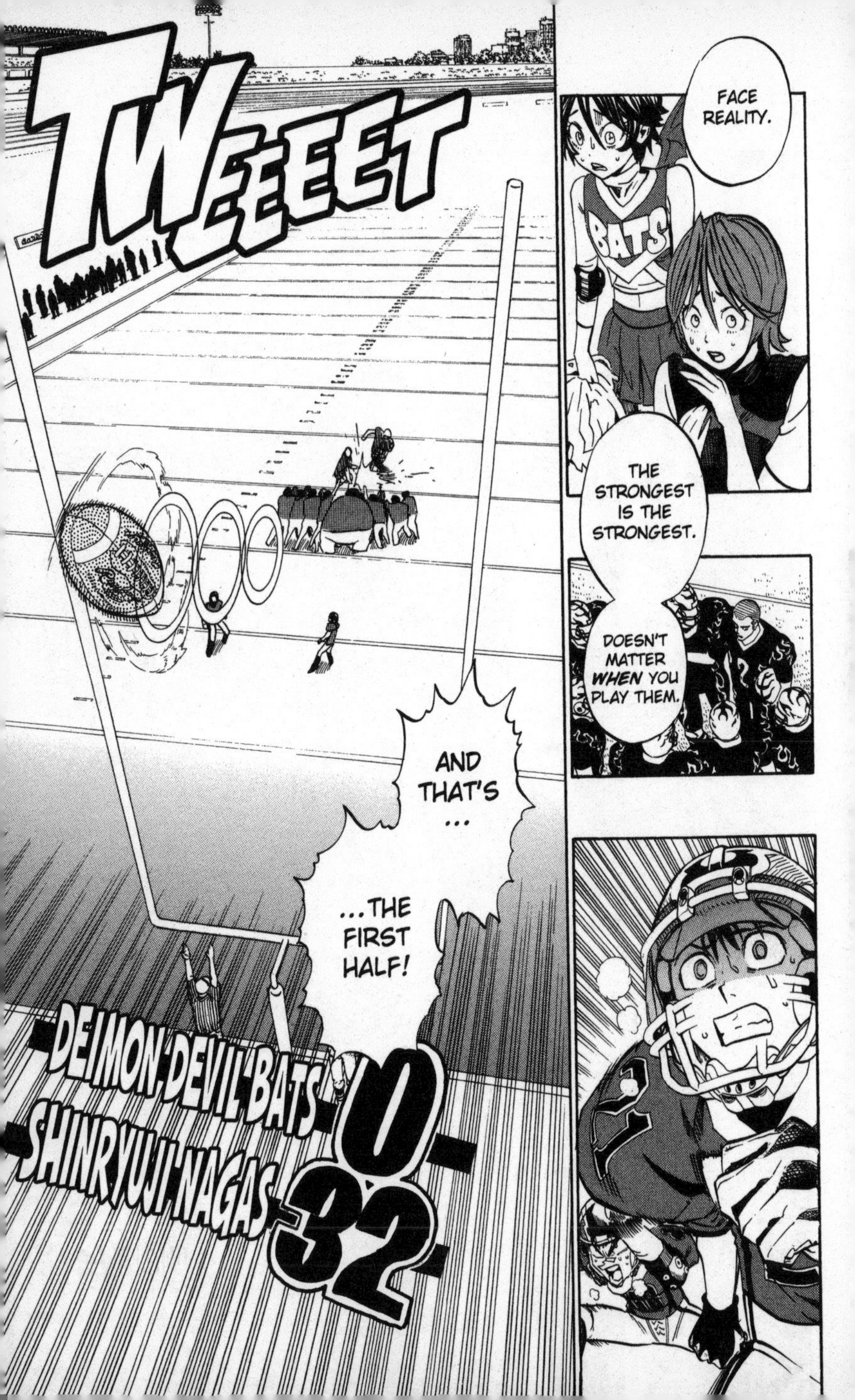
FACE REALITY.
THE STRONGEST IS THE STRONGEST.
DOESN'T MATTER *WHEN* YOU PLAY THEM.
TWEEEET
AND THAT'S...
...THE FIRST HALF!
DEIMON DEVIL BATS 0
SHINRYUJI NAGAS 32

THEY'RE LIKE DEMONS!
NO WONDER THEY WON KANTO...
...NINE TIMES RUNNING. THEY'RE AMAZING!

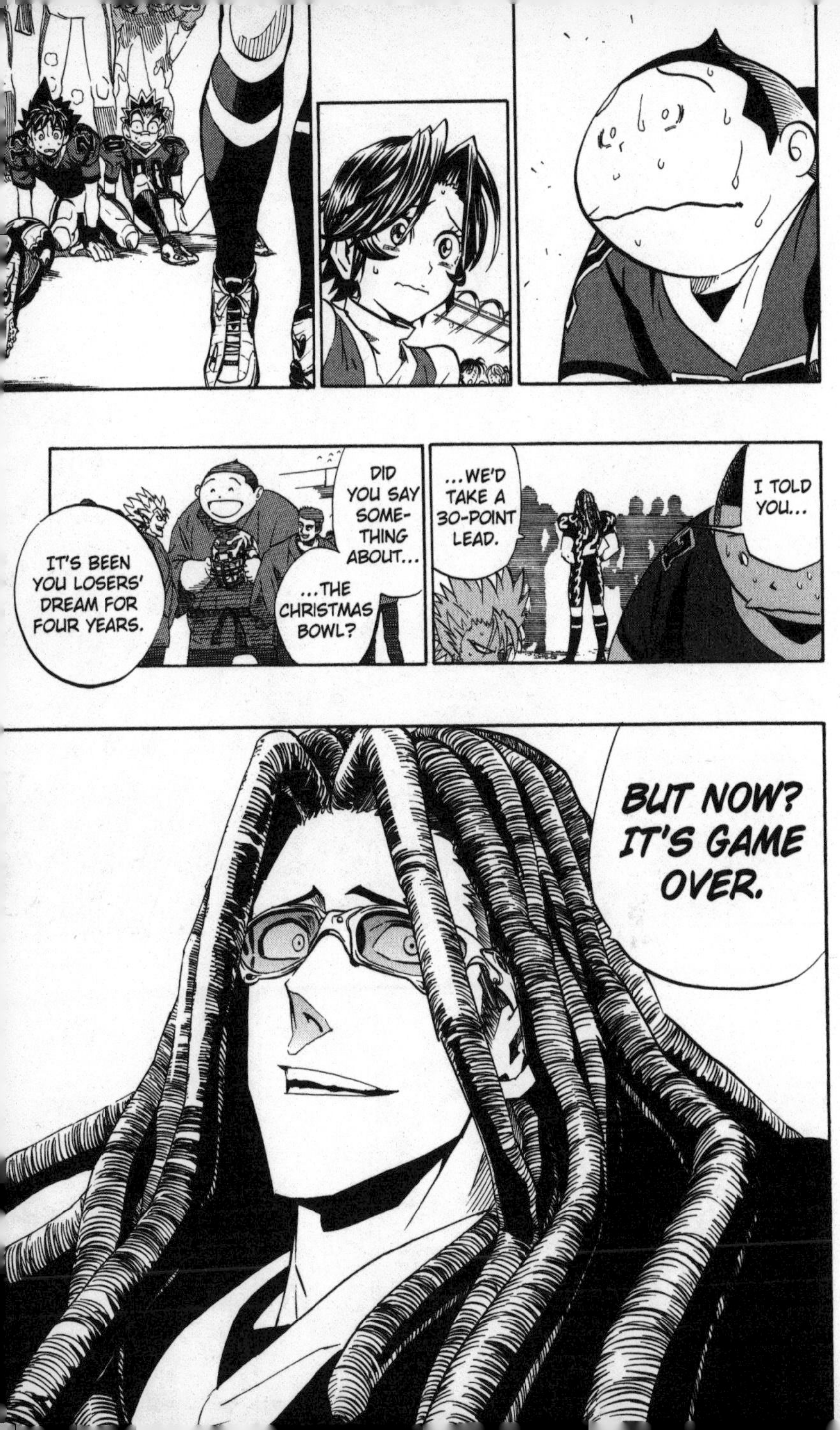
I TOLD YOU...
...WE'D TAKE A 30-POINT LEAD.
DID YOU SAY SOME-THING ABOUT...
...THE CHRISTMAS BOWL?
IT'S BEEN YOU LOSERS' DREAM FOR FOUR YEARS.
BUT NOW? IT'S GAME OVER.

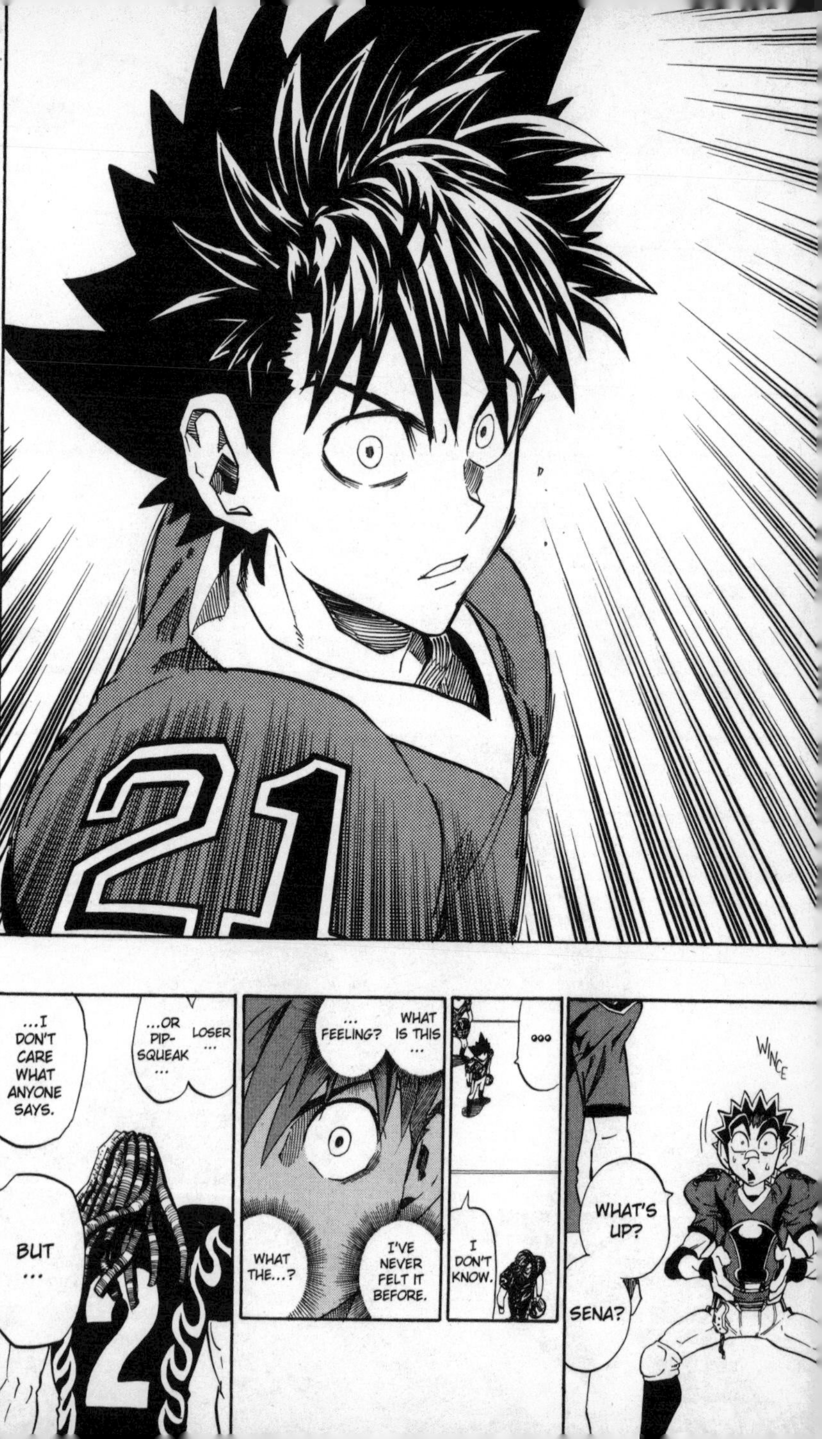
WINCE
WHAT'S UP?
SENA?
...
I DON'T KNOW.
WHAT IS THIS ...
... FEELING?
I'VE NEVER FELT IT BEFORE.
WHAT THE...?
LOSER ...
...OR PIP-SQUEAK ...
...I DON'T CARE WHAT ANYONE SAYS.
BUT ...

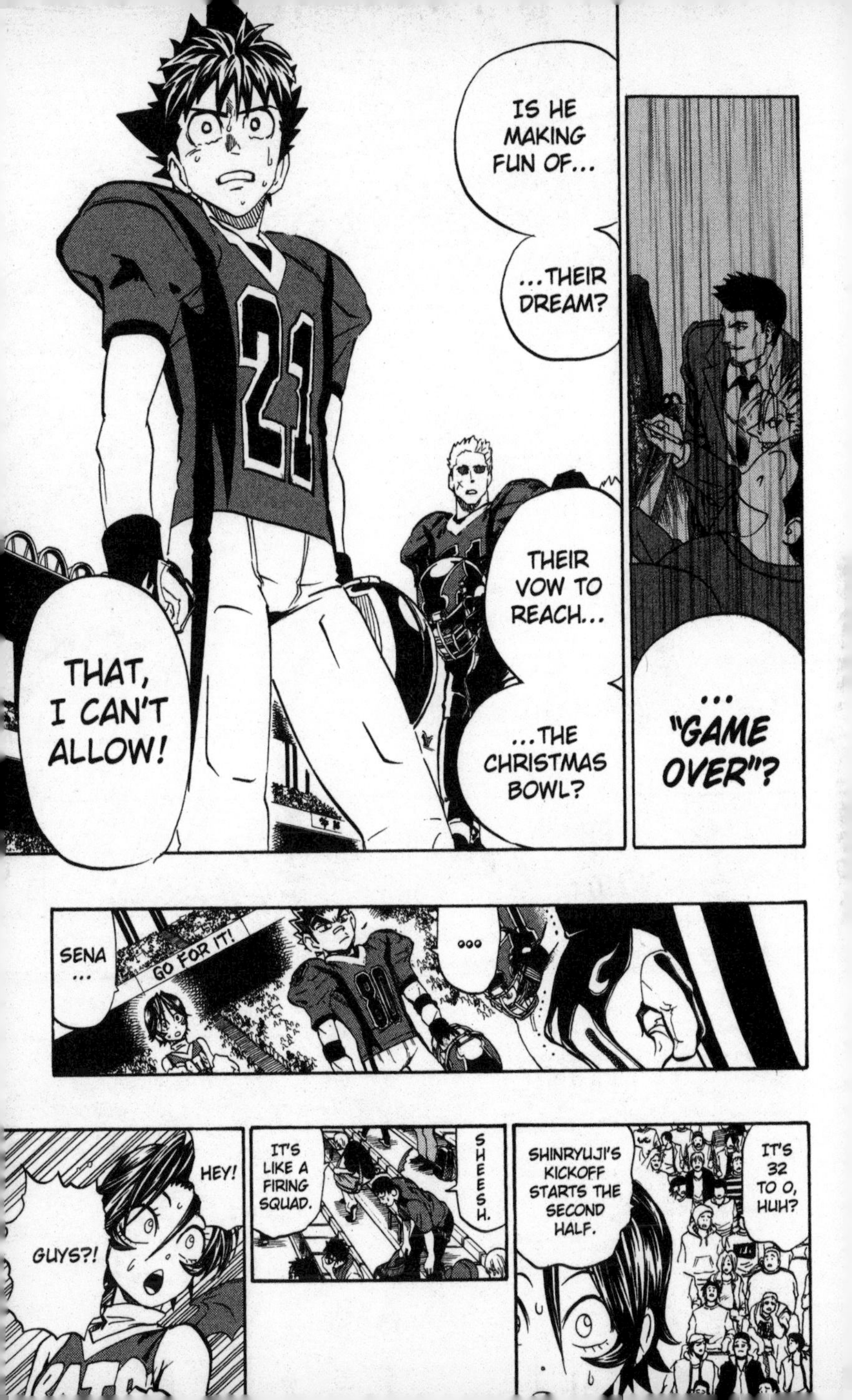
... "GAME OVER"?
IS HE MAKING FUN OF...
...THEIR DREAM?
THEIR VOW TO REACH...
...THE CHRISTMAS BOWL?
THAT, I CAN'T ALLOW!
...
GO FOR IT!
SENA ...
IT'S 32 TO 0, HUH?
SHINRYUJI'S KICKOFF STARTS THE SECOND HALF.
SHEESH.
IT'S LIKE A FIRING SQUAD.
HEY!
GUYS?!

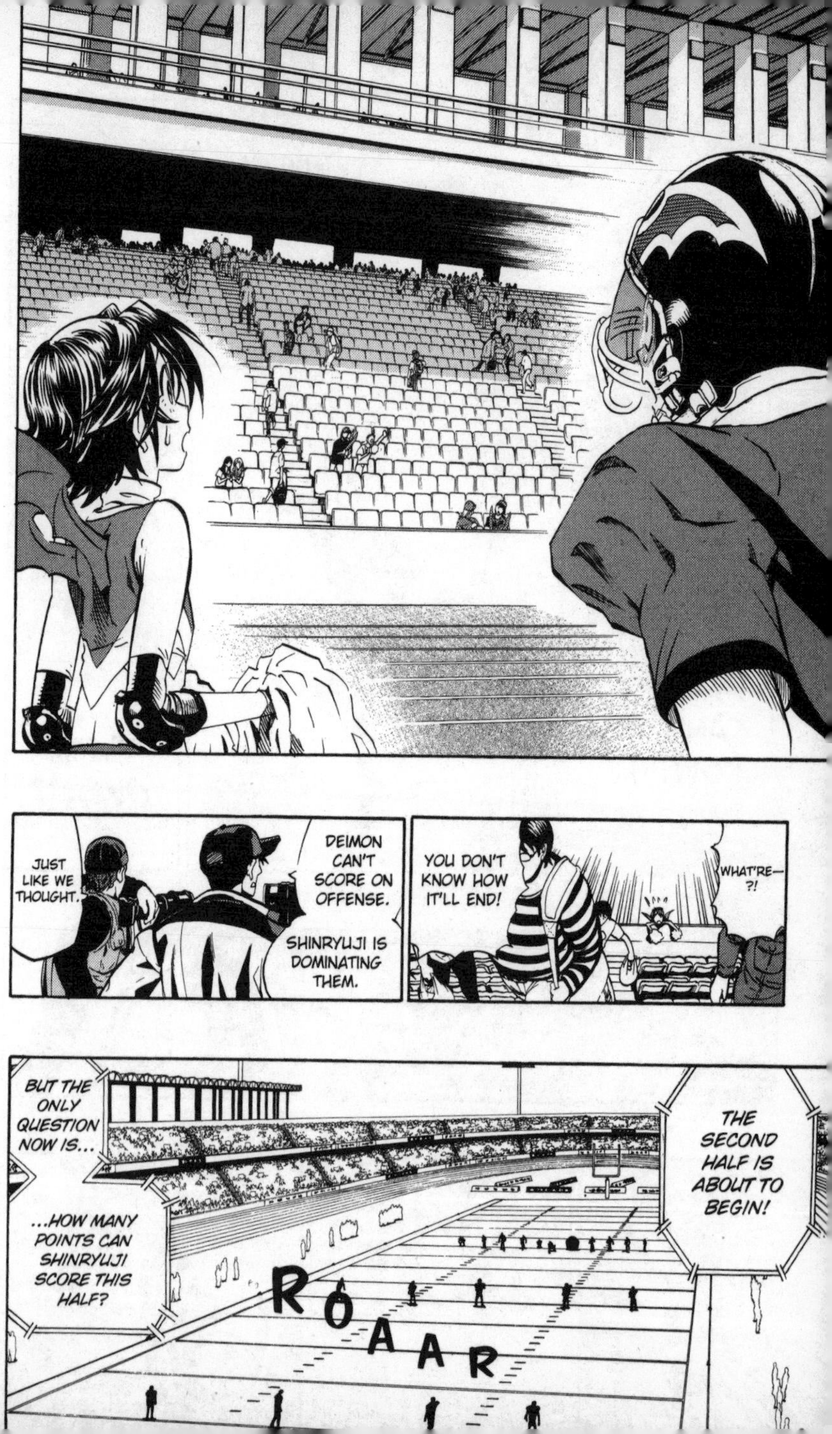
WHAT'RE— ?!
YOU DON'T KNOW HOW IT'LL END!
DEIMON CAN'T SCORE ON OFFENSE.
SHINRYUJI IS DOMINATING THEM.
JUST LIKE WE THOUGHT.
THE SECOND HALF IS ABOUT TO BEGIN!
BUT THE ONLY QUESTION NOW IS...
...HOW MANY POINTS CAN SHINRYUJI SCORE THIS HALF?
ROAAAR

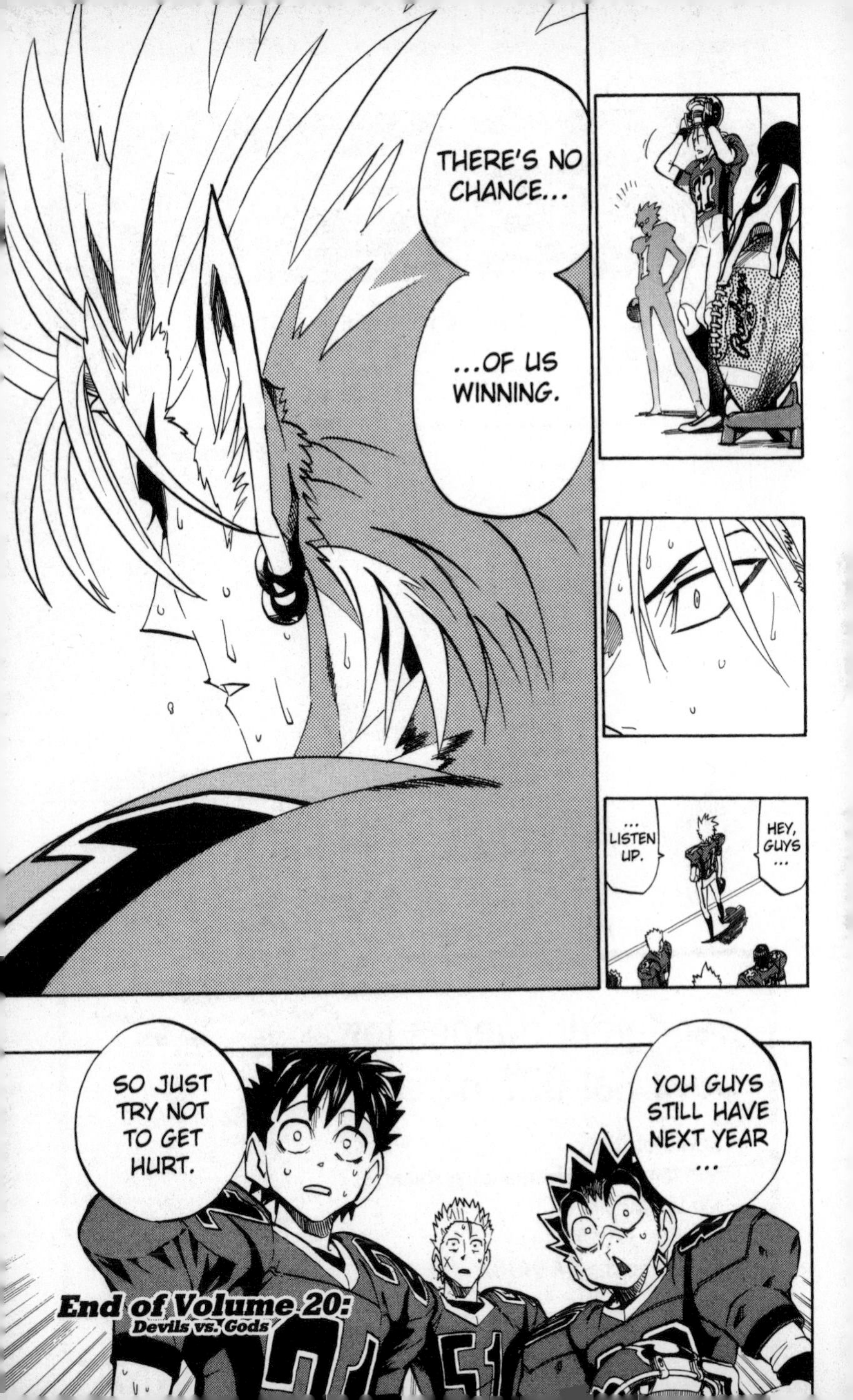
HEY, GUYS...
...LISTEN UP.
THERE'S NO CHANCE...
...OF US WINNING.
YOU GUYS STILL HAVE NEXT YEAR...
SO JUST TRY NOT TO GET HURT.
End of Volume 20:
Devils vs. Gods

Investigation File #069

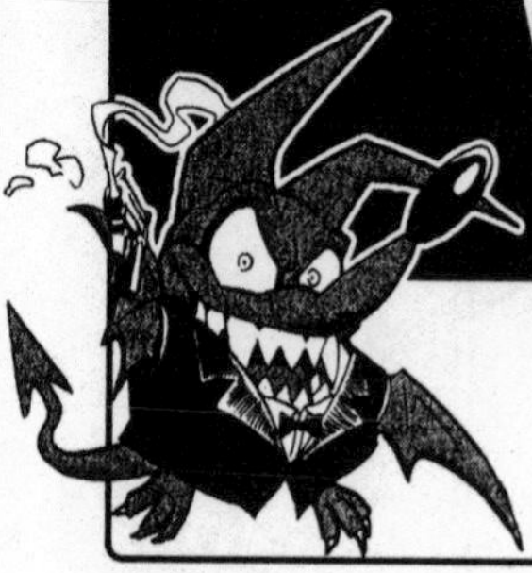

## Investigate Yukimitsu's family genes!

I HEAR YUKI HAS A SISTER.
IS SHE BALD, TOO?
PLEASE FIND OUT.

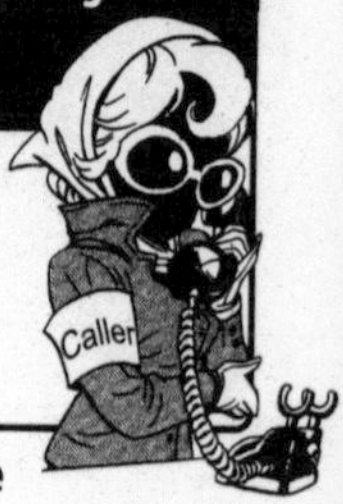
Caller

Pierrot, Nara Prefecture

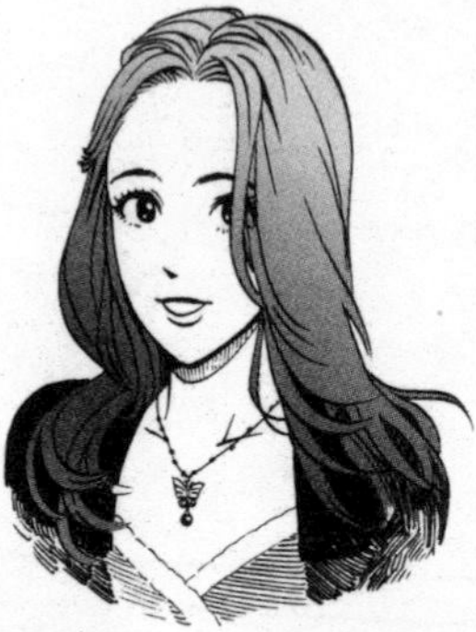

Hotaru Yukimitsu

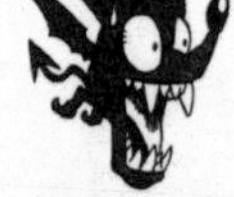

LUCKY FOR US, SHE'S NOT BALD!

## Send your queries for Devil Bat 021 here!!

Devil Bat 021
Shonen Jump Advanced/Eyeshield 21
c/o VIZ Media, LLC
P.O. Box 77010
San Francisco, CA 94107

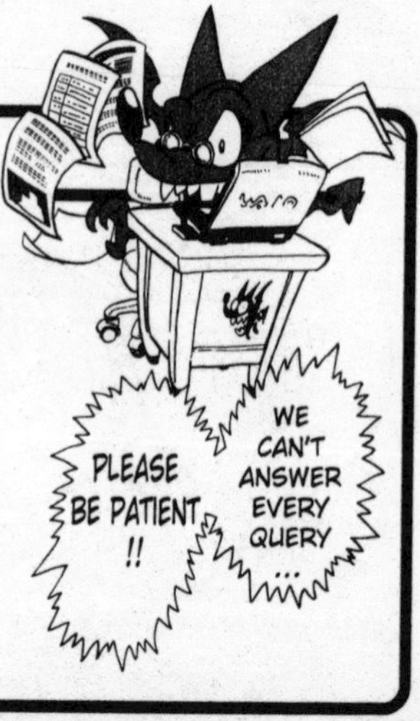
WE CAN'T ANSWER EVERY QUERY...
PLEASE BE PATIENT!!

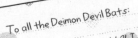

To all the Deimon Devil Bats:

Hi! I'm a big fan of Eyeshield 21. I found a perfect cake for the Devil Bats in a cookbook. It's called "devil's food cake"!! They call it that because it's very dark. (Because it's chocolate, not because it's burned.) To help root for the Deimon Devil Bats' victory, I made one. Please keep aiming for the Christmas Bowl. I'll be cheering for you guys!

Be a devil !!
(Go for it!)

P.S. I put on one strawberry for every player on the team.

S.U.

# Key Players in the

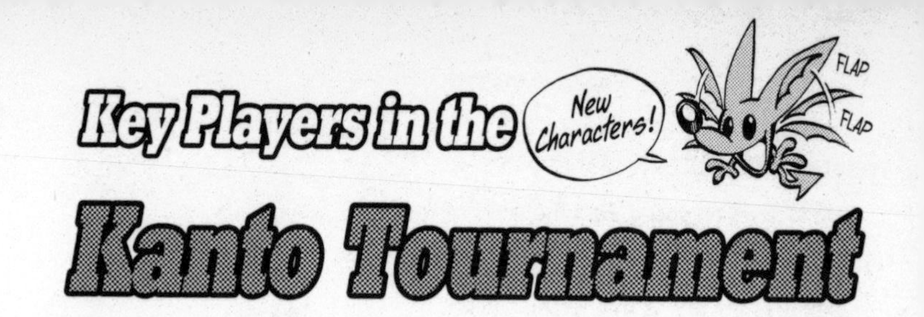
New Characters!
FLAP
FLAP

# Kanto Tournament

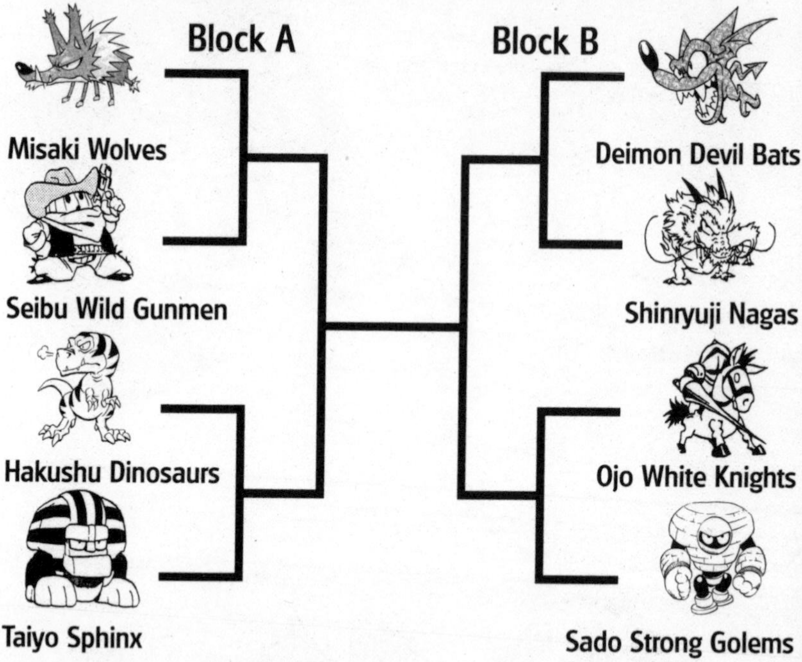
Block A
Block B
Misaki Wolves
Seibu Wild Gunmen
Hakushu Dinosaurs
Taiyo Sphinx
Deimon Devil Bats
Shinryuji Nagas
Ojo White Knights
Sado Strong Golems

### Maruko [likes to go by "Marco"] (Hakushu Dinosaurs)

He's the half-Italian son of a Sicilian mob boss, so he knows a lot about absolute power.

He lives by the concept "survival of the fittest."

He loves Italian-made suits and bottled colas.
***Toward men, rivalry. Toward women, love.***

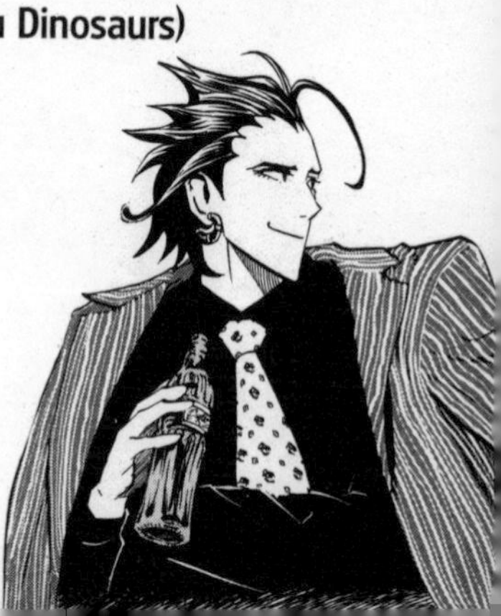

## Taiga Kamiya (Misaki Wolves)

He focuses on speed. He's the uncontested number one sprinter in Hokkaido, the northern part of Japan. "Sorry, but I don't know what setbacks are like. Is that wrong? Ha ha!" He has a very happy-go-lucky laugh.

He's very picky when it comes to shoes. ***He uses a brand-new, custom-made pair in every game.***

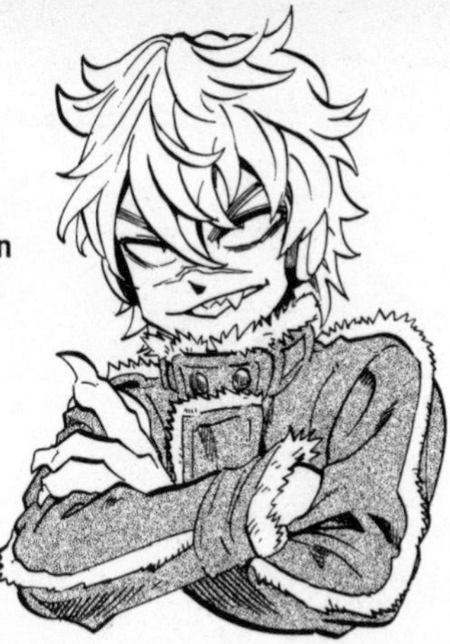

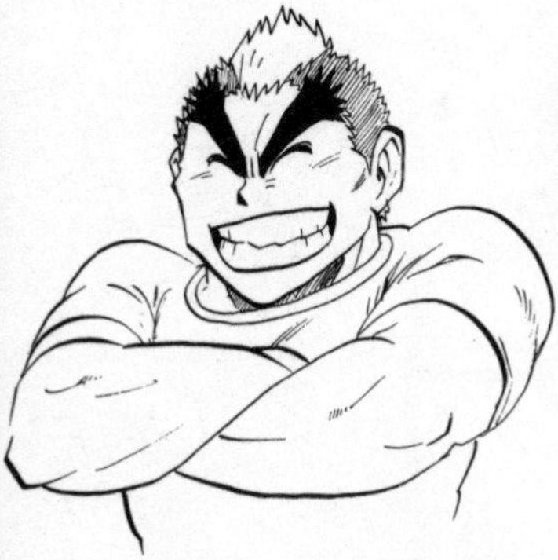

## Ganjo Iwashige (Sado Strong Golems)

***He takes protein supplements with every meal.*** He even asked his teacher if he could bring protein bars as a snack on their school trip.

He wants to make his body like iron. In *Dragon Quest*, his favorite spell is Ironize.

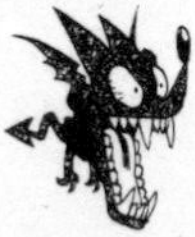

WILL ANY OF THESE GUYS STAY IN LONG ENOUGH TO PLAY DEIMON LATER? LET'S SEE, HUH? YA-HA!

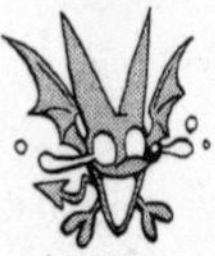

HEY, BOSS! BOSS! IT LOOKS LIKE DEIMON MAY NOT BE AROUND THAT LONG!

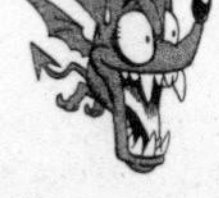

OH, RIGHT! THAT'S NO GOOD! LET'S SEE HOW IT GOES NEXT VOLUME!

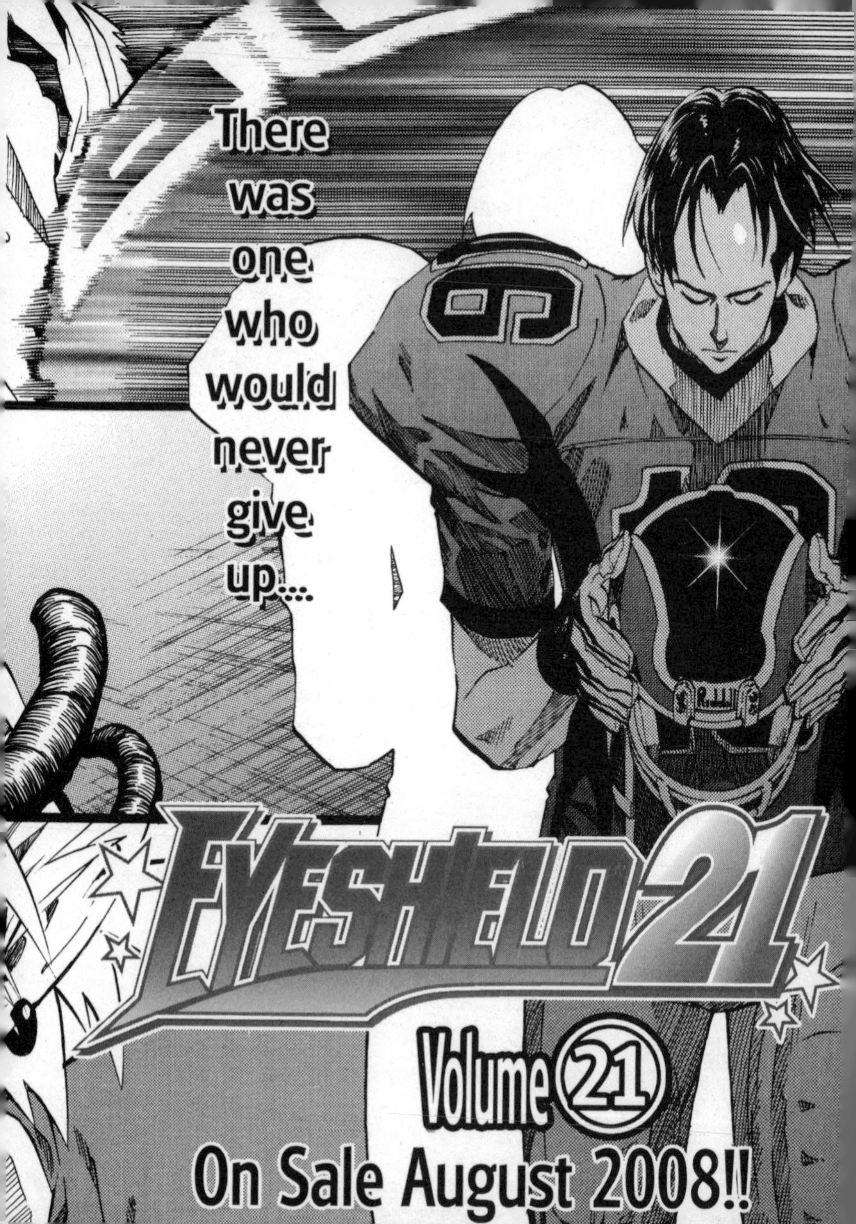
There was one who would never give up...
EYESHIELD 21
Volume 21
On Sale August 2008!!

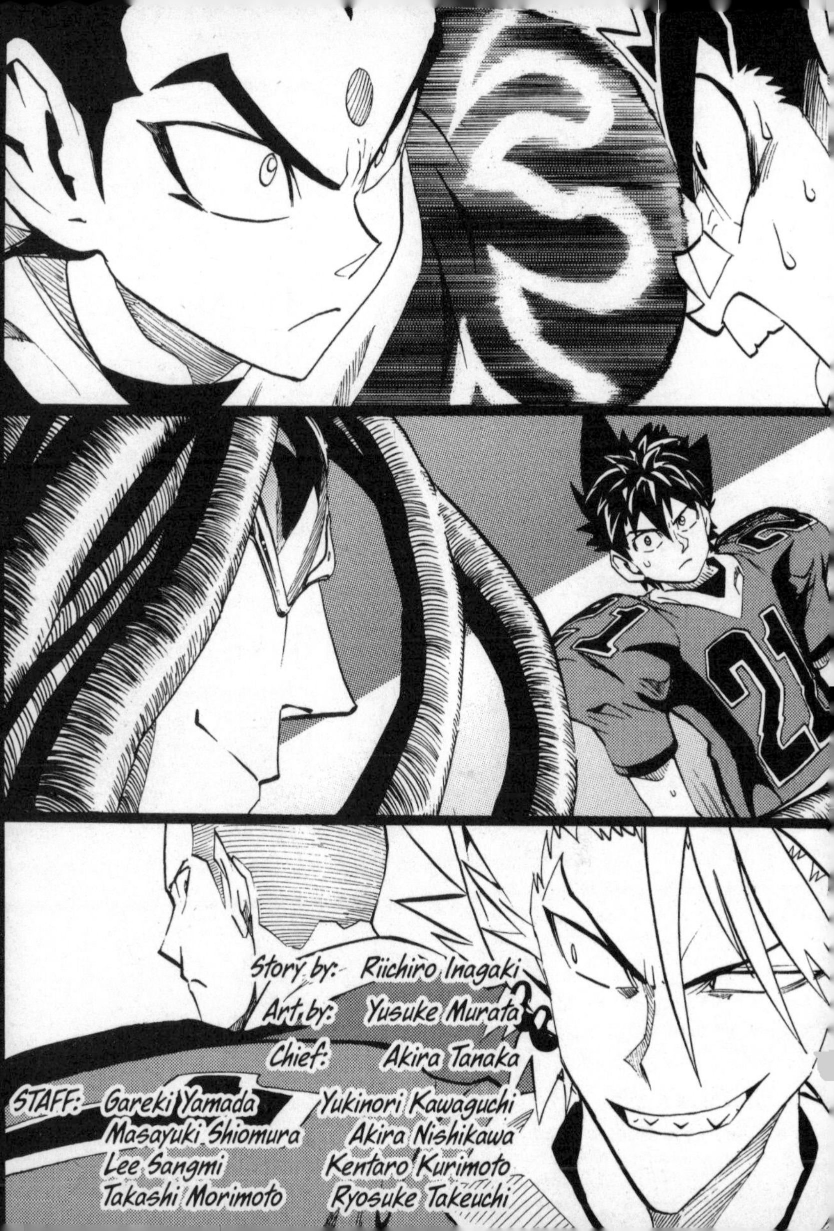
Story by: Riichiro Inagaki
Art by: Yusuke Murata
Chief: Akira Tanaka
STAFF: Gareki Yamada
Yukinori Kawaguchi
Masayuki Shiomura
Akira Nishikawa
Lee Sangmi
Kentaro Kurimoto
Takashi Morimoto
Ryosuke Takeuchi

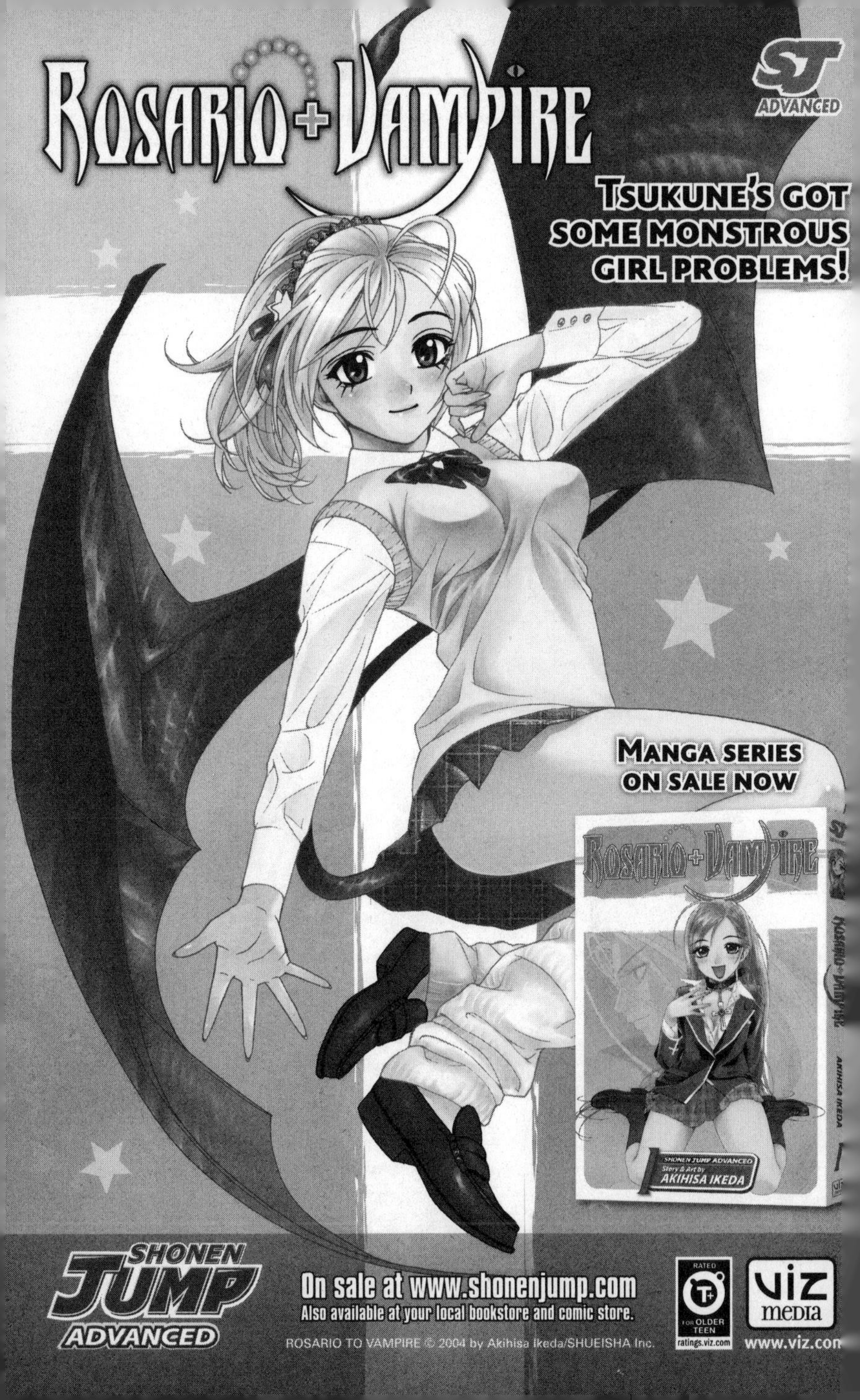

ROSARIO+VAMPIRE
SJ ADVANCED
TSUKUNE'S GOT SOME MONSTROUS GIRL PROBLEMS!
MANGA SERIES ON SALE NOW
ROSARIO+VAMPIRE
SHONEN JUMP ADVANCED
Story & Art by AKIHISA IKEDA
SHONEN JUMP ADVANCED
On sale at www.shonenjump.com
Also available at your local bookstore and comic store.
ROSARIO TO VAMPIRE © 2004 by Akihisa Ikeda/SHUEISHA Inc.
RATED T+ FOR OLDER TEEN
ratings.viz.com
VIZ media
www.viz.com

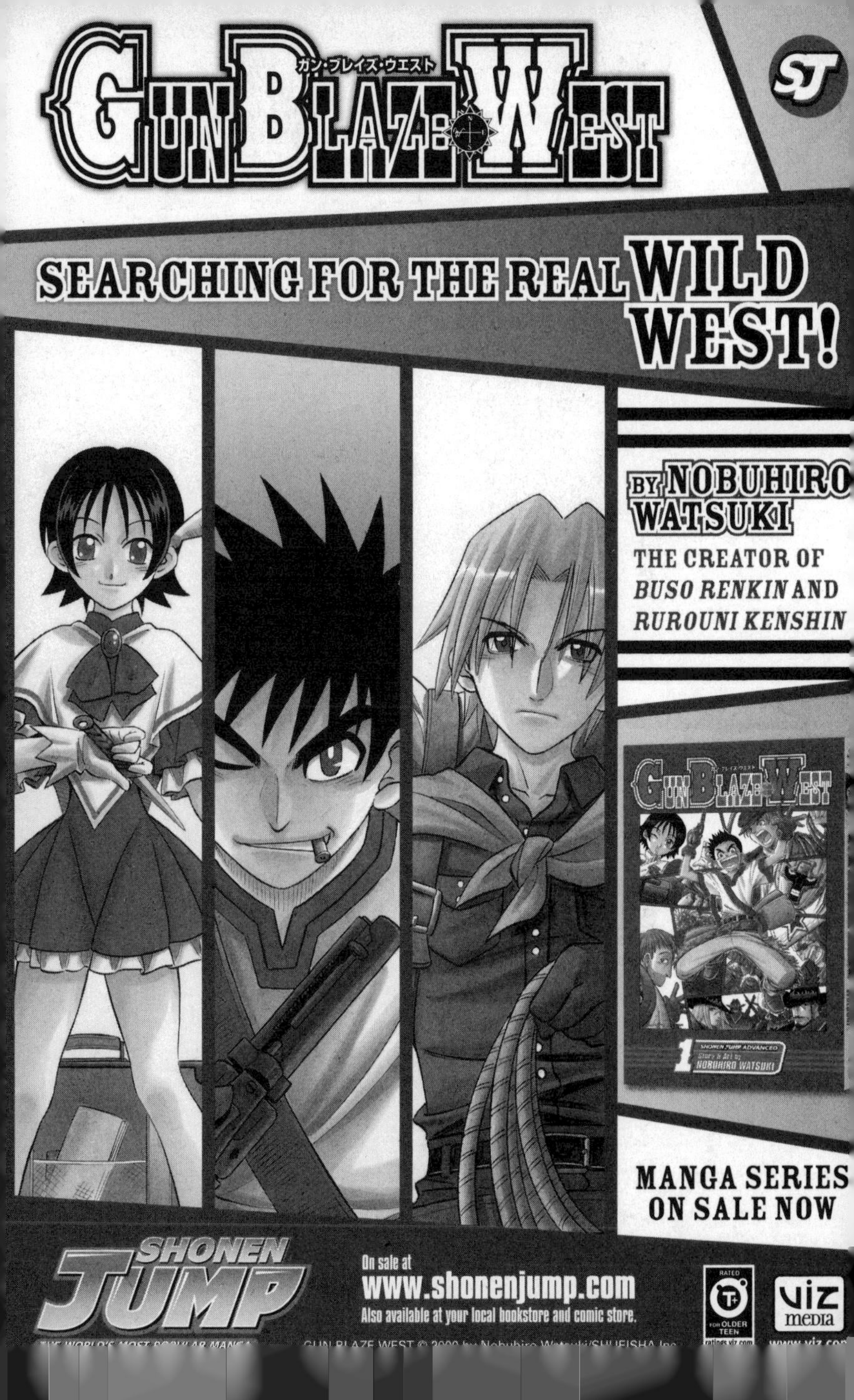

GUN BLAZE WEST
ガン・ブレイズ・ウエスト
SJ
SEARCHING FOR THE REAL WILD WEST!
BY NOBUHIRO WATSUKI
THE CREATOR OF BUSO RENKIN AND RUROUNI KENSHIN
GUN BLAZE WEST
1 SHONEN JUMP ADVANCED
Story & Art by NOBUHIRO WATSUKI
MANGA SERIES ON SALE NOW
SHONEN JUMP
On sale at
www.shonenjump.com
Also available at your local bookstore and comic store.
RATED T+ FOR OLDER TEEN
VIZ media

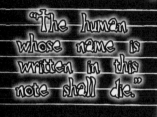

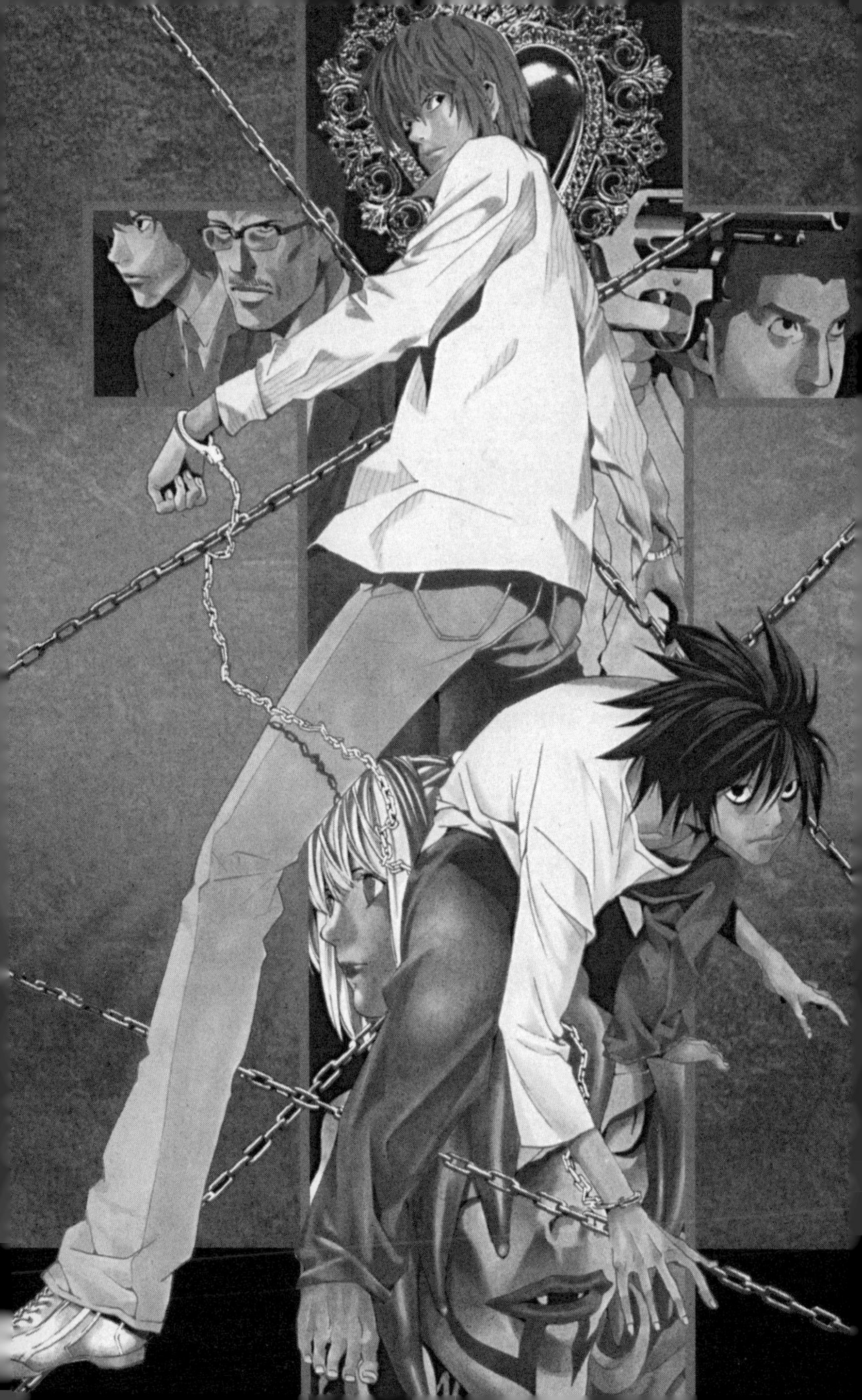

# SHONEN JUMP

### THE WORLD'S MOST POPULAR MANGA ™

**12 ISSUES FOR ONLY $29.95***

**THAT'S 50% OFF THE NEWSSTAND PRICE!**

Each issue of SHONEN JUMP contains the coolest manga available in the U.S., anime news, and info on video & card games, toys AND more!

## SUBSCRIBE TODAY and Become a Member of the ST Sub Club!

- **ENJOY** 12 HUGE action-packed issues
- **SAVE** 50% OFF the cover price
- **ACCESS** exclusive areas of www.shonenjump.com
- **RECEIVE** FREE members-only gifts

## Available ONLY to Subscribers!

RATED T FOR TEEN
ratings.viz.com

www.viz.com

## 3 EASY WAYS TO SUBSCRIBE!

1) Send in the subscription order form from this book **OR**
2) Log on to: www.shonenjump.com **OR**
3) Call 1-800-541-7919